CLAPP'S ROCK

CLAPP'S ROCK

William Rowe

McClelland and Stewart

The Canadian Publishers
McClelland and Stewart Limited
25 Hollinger Road
Toronto, M4B 3G2

Canadian Cataloguing in Publication Data

Rowe, William N. (William Neil), 1942-
  Clapp's rock

ISBN 0-7710-7750-5

I. Title.

PS8585.093C62   C813'.54   C83-098021-0
PR9199.3.R695C62

All the events, dates, and characters in this book are fictitious. Any resemblance to persons living or dead is purely coincidental.

Printed and bound in Canada by
T. H. Best Printing Company Limited.

To Penelope

If only I am keen and hard like the sheer tip of a wedge
Driven by invisible blows,
The rock will split, we shall come at the wonder, we shall
find the Hesperides.

D.H. Lawrence

1

"There comes a time," said Percy Clapp, "when a man of brain and vigour must cease to be a mere receptacle for a driblet scummed off the Sargasso Sea of Academe, and must plunge headlong into the ocean of life itself. Do you hear what I'm saying to you, Neil? *Your* time has come to make a few waves of your own! I'm counting on you, look, to come home next month and make yourself ready to run."

Neil Godwin was sitting in Percy Clapp's suite at the Savoy Hotel in London, three feet away from the cocked, vulpine face. Despite the earnest way in which these words had been spoken, Neil could not refrain from breaking into a grin. Clapp answered with the smile that many found beguiling, and waited.

"Well, again, Mr. Clapp, I'm flattered by your offer," said Neil. "But I'm already registered for the graduate degree in Law, and that would keep me at Oxford for at least another full year, I'm afraid."

"Yes, yes," said Clapp, "yes, yes. Your father told me all about your tentative plans. Nothing's writ in stone, Neil."

"Look, Mr. Clapp, I appreciate your concern on this, but I should tell you something at the outset. I'm in no hurry. I'm not very old or experienced. I have plenty of time to get into politics, perhaps in the election after the next one. I don't want to be premature about it. I'm not sure I'm ready for that yet. And there are other things I have to do first."

This response caused Clapp to levitate from his chair. "All right!" he blared, moving his small compact form to and fro so close to Neil that the younger man had to force his head back to look at Clapp's face. "Now, I want you to forget the nonsense the psephologists spout and listen to me. Because, Neil, I'm speaking as prime minister now. There is only one rule in politics. Let no opportunity, no matter how homely, slip by ungrasped, and certainly not when the circumstances are *so* propitious as they are in your case right now. I know. I know. Your native modesty prevents you from seeing what an ideal candidate you will make. Handsome. Brilliant. Energetic. Articulate."

Clapp paused to let this sink in and continued to pace. Neil darted a glance across the room at his friend, Clyde Ferritt, who for nearly a year past had been secretary to Clapp's Cabinet. Clyde stopped his eyes from sliding towards Neil's and looked out the window. He was afraid, thought Neil, that they might burst out laughing if their eyes met.

"Your dad's name is no liability, either," resumed Clapp. "Your father and I have been friends for nearly thirty years, Neil. I mean friends. Heart to heart. Brain to brain. You know that." Neil nodded solemnly. "Anyhow, I've already mentioned your possible candidacy to my lieutenants in half a dozen districts, casually of course, and they *all* want to grab you. Opportunities, Neil! My God, my son, your opportunities are legion. You are weighed down with opportunities and have but to choose the best from among the good. So. What do you say? Tell me you'll run for me if I call an election this fall."

Neil drew in a deep breath. He knew what he wanted to say but he didn't feel inclined to voice it yet again. Clyde broke the silence.

"We're due at Lord Smythe's in half an hour for lunch, sir," he said, walking to the closet for Clapp's hat and coat. "We'd better go down."

Clapp shot Clyde a look of irritation. Neil rose and said, "I'll certainly give your proposal very serious consideration, Mr. Clapp. I do have some other commitments I'd be forced to extricate myself from and I don't – "

"Of course, give it consideration," said Clapp, smiling to hide his impatience. "I would not have it otherwise. By no means do I want impetuous men around me. Now, let's go to his lordship's for that mug-up."

Outside the lobby of the Savoy Hotel waited the chauffeured, maroon Bentley, hired by Clyde for Clapp's visit to London. They got in and drove into the City. Clapp was uncharacteristically quiet, pondering and jotting down notes on an envelope.

Neil spoke a few words to Clyde, but his friend did not seem eager to disturb the silence. Neil sized him up out of the corner of his eye. During the year since Neil had last seen him, Clyde's appearance had not altered in the direction of beauty. His upper torso was hulking but looked soft and devoid of strength. Neil had noticed in the hotel that under the seat of his trousers, Clyde still seemed to have no buttocks. The term "slack arse" might have been invented especially for him, though Neil well knew that its appropriateness did not extend beyond the physical. Clyde wore no glasses, but his eyes had the sunken look of a person who has just removed a pair of thick lenses from his nose. He had no neck to speak of; and his big, angular features seemed set in a head that was too small for them. Not only did Clyde's forehead slope, but the back of his skull was almost a vertical line from top to base.

How, thought Neil, turning away, could the phrenologists have been so wrong? For Clyde Ferritt had great intelligence. Less than a year ago he had gone down from Oxford University with a brilliant first class degree in Politics, Philosophy, and Economics.

The thought of Clyde's attainment reminded Neil of his own final exams, less than a month away. He expected to get only a middling second class degree. The memory of the cause of his underachievement – a frolic of sex and love which had ended in hurt and left him no heart for jurisprudence – made him let out a sigh of remorse. Clyde turned his head towards him inquisitively, and Neil pretended to stifle a yawn while he commented on the early morning train he'd taken from Oxford. He *had* to stay and get that other law degree, he thought. And this time, he'd do the bloody thing right!

11

As important as that was to him, however, Neil knew there was a more fundamental question behind his plan to stay on in England for another year. Did he in fact want to return home for good: now or ever? He had realized during this twenty months' absence how oppressive his father's kind of local prominence had been – not to mention the expectations he frequently expressed about his son. It had been his father, no doubt, who had put Clapp up to that hardsell political pitch.

Moreover, Neil had grown to love London. During his frequent trips down from Oxford he appreciated the fullness and anonymity of the great city, especially when contrasted with the narrow watchfulness of his home, St. John's. He had already made inquiries about joining one of the Inns of Court and becoming a barrister. He was even considering the possibility of settling permanently in London and practising law here. Besides, he and his current girlfriend had a tour of Europe planned for this summer. A detailed itinerary had already been drawn up. Neil was glad he hadn't mentioned this to Clapp earlier. The statesman would have thought it foolish to weigh such a trivial factor against a glorious entry into politics.

Politics! thought Neil. Even if he did decide to go back home, now or eventually, would he want to get involved in politics with Percy Clapp? The little megalomaniac was going so far as to call himself by the grandiose title "prime minister" these days, when the established name for his job was "premier." The man was in total political control at home; and the only redeeming aspect of his tenure was the fact that the stage upon which he played out his melodramas was so small and isolated that it prevented his doing significant damage to the world.

The smallness and isolation of that political stage was another argument for staying in England, mused Neil. Suppose he did go into politics under Clapp with the idea of succeeding him at the top. He would have to work his guts out day and night at unedifying tasks, and connive and inveigle and infight as much as if he were striving to become Prime Minister of Britain or President of the United States. And if he were successful, what did it mean in the end? It meant leadership over a remote, unimportant, mist-enshrouded rock in the Atlantic.

Perhaps, to be fair, the offshore oil discoveries would make such leadership more consequential to the world in the future. But, whatever the case, Clyde Ferritt seemed to have the inside track as far as a new generation of leadership was concerned, according to the newspapers from home. Neil glanced at Clyde's face again. His mouth looked as sardonic as ever, but that warning, Neil remembered, never quite prepared a listener for the potential nastiness of his tongue. Clyde's tongue was one of his strengths. In full operation, it eclipsed his ugliness: a delight to his associates, a terror to his opponents. Clyde, Neil knew, would make a formidable antagonist.

The Bentley stopped outside the building which housed one of London's well-known merchant banks. As he and Clyde got out and followed Clapp towards the entrance, Neil visualized the last occasion on which he had seen Clapp at home. A half dozen of his Cabinet ministers had been glued in formation around their premier by some force that seemed akin to gravity. Mute and scurrying about a declaiming, striding Clapp, all the ministers were wearing long black overcoats and black Homburg hats that were too large for their heads. (The uniformed dignity of Her Majesty's Ministers was a point of insistence with Percy Clapp.) Now, hurrying along the sidewalk to keep up with the pace set by the small man in the black overcoat and Homburg ahead, Neil had a mental picture of one more minister on the outside of that tight cluster; one more minister whose ears were bent down and whose eyebrows were hidden by the black Homburg on his head: himself.

The vivid vision concluded the matter for Neil. He pushed out of his mind all the other arguments against his going home and entering politics. This alone was sufficient: he lacked all ambition to become another of Clapp's minions in a too-big Homburg hat.

Upstairs, Lord Smythe, the chairman of the bank, greeted them with great affability and led them to an anteroom where

13

the other guests were standing. "Gentlemen," he said, "I have the honour of presenting you to the Prem ... the Prime Minister of Newfoundland, the –"

"And Labrador," interjected Clapp with a mischievous grin. "Newfoundland and Labrador. You're not siding with Quebec after all these years, are you, my lord?"

"And Labrador, of course," chortled their host. "Gentlemen, the Prime Minister of Newfoundland and Labrador, the Honourable Percy D. Clapp. And with him, are two of his compatriots and *protégés*, Clyde Ferritt and Neil Godwin." The other guests were introduced and Neil was astonished at the eminence of two of them.

The party went immediately into the dining room, and Clapp was ushered to a seat at the top of the table on the right hand of his host. The long board filled up in accordance with the name cards, ending at the bottom with Neil on one side and Clyde on the other.

"Well, well," said Clyde, surveying the table, his lip curled. "They've placed me somewhat below the salt this time, to be sure. To keep my countryman company, one can only suppose. Presumably some officious twit's concept of *politesse*."

"Don't be nasty now, Clydie," said Neil, in a mother-to-naughty-child voice. "Try to be nice for a little while."

The bank officer next to Neil, perhaps the same officious twit referred to by Clyde, snorted appreciatively. Clyde's face flushed as he sat down, but he ignored Neil's injunction and started again.

"Talking about the perversion of elementary protocol," he sneered, "just look at the other end of the table. Now that's a good example for you of the British practicality that won the empire. See those two luminaries up there over whom Percy has been given precedence?"

"Yes," whispered Neil, forgiving now, and infected by his friend's derisive tone. "The one on Mr. Clapp's right with a head on him like the Piltdown skull is a former prime minister of Great Britain. The other one, on Lord Smythe's left, with the face like a tub of congealed porridge, is likewise a former prime minister of Great Britain and both are still imperial –"

Clyde, wishing he'd said that, jumped in: "And both are still imperial privy councillors, yes, of course. But our boy from the boonies takes the place of honour here today, oh yes indeed, especially since there's a possible uranium mine in Labrador involved, and perhaps a piece of the offshore oil action on the Grand Banks. Oh my, ain't free enterprise grand?"

They both chuckled. Neil enjoyed Clyde's sarcasm and cynicism when they were not directed at him. They ate their *crab en chemise* for a while and listened to the talk at the other end.

"Now there, to exaggerate wildly, is an interesting spectacle," allowed Clyde at last. "Our ragamuffin of a small-time bailiwick politician, representing in the eyes of all present, the white dregs of a lost empire, totally dominating the table talk." It was true. Clapp had taken over the conversation, not by way of exchange of views, however, but by monologue.

At first, Neil was embarrassed, but he soon realized that Clapp was so glib, so ready with the right word, so confident of his vocal powers, and so assured of his own quick and easy recall of experience and knowledge on any subject broached, that this exalted company were as dwarfed as his own ministers would have been if they had been sitting around this table now in their over-size Homburgs. Even the two leading conservative statesmen were soon reduced to elegant grunts. When one of them tried to fill a short lull with a sentence of his own, his contribution seemed ponderous and pathetically inadequate. No one looked at him.

Clapp began to tell the French de Rothschild, who was sitting three chairs away from him, all about wine, and Clyde murmured to Neil, "This should prove fascinating. Percy's study of wine consists of a cursory skim through the pictures in a Time-Life book on wines some pelt gave him last Christmas. The de Rothschild, on the other hand, owns one of the great vineyards of the world in Bordeaux."

All at the table listened to Clapp on the subject for twenty minutes, and nodded their heads. No one interrupted the flow of words, the authoritative delivery, the embellished truisms, the misconceptions and errors presented in a fashion which allowed a listener to take them as pleasantries.

After that, for another hour, Clapp gave discourses on a dozen topics. Their range was wide: a description of how Newfoundland had won the First World War (because of Lloyd George's adaptation of Newfoundland's ancient, trans-Atlantic convoy system to loosen the stranglehold of the German U-boats on Britain); an analysis of whether forcing high cadres of the Chinese Communist Party to shovel pig manure into the wind periodically was salubrious (because it forestalled hubris) or deleterious (since it made the victim vengeful); a demonstration of how Newfoundland had won the Second World War (because, in Churchill's words, "New-foundlanders are the best small boatmen in the world"). Throughout everything, Clapp bandied dialectics with him-self, recalled deft political repartees, and told funny anec-dotes, punctuating them with cuts of self-effacing wit.

Just before the table rose, he reminisced about the first time he had been invited to Buckingham Palace to be pre-sented to the Queen, shortly after he had become premier. He described his abject ignorance of protocol as he had approached the Queen in the throne room. "His Highness the Duke, by her side, regarded my antics as patiently as he was able for several minutes. Then he turned to our sovereign lady and whispered, in words that echoed throughout the chamber: 'I am well acquainted with Your Majesty's deep love for all things equestrian, but this is the very first occasion since Lord Talbot's time that a horse has been permitted to enter the throne room at all, let alone hind parts first.'" The table roared. Several of the company collapsed near their snifters in helpless mirth. "That's Phil to a tee," someone guffawed.

Amidst much blowing of noses, the host stood to end the affair. "This, I have the pleasure of saying, gentlemen," he beamed, still wiping his eyes, "is the first time since a post-war visit by Sir Winston Churchill that one of these lun-cheons has gone beyond its traditional hour and a half dura-tion. Prime Minister Clapp, on behalf of everyone, I thank you for joining us. We have had a rare privilege indeed."

Guests said, "Hear, hear," and then queued, all of them dark-suited and poised, to shake Clapp's hand before depart-ing.

Near the door, Neil and Clyde heard one of the leading British statesmen confide to his colleague, "I've never in my life come across a more remarkable public man."

"Nor I," replied the other emphatically. "He is said to have read more than forty thousand books, and I am well able to believe it."

"That," whispered Clyde to Neil, "would amount to two books a day for every day of Percy's life since he was five. Sound credible to you? A good comment on that fellow's acuity, I'd say. And people wonder why the UK is starting to lag behind the wops."

"It's probably a better comment on Percy's ability to cause a willing suspension of disbelief, Clyde," said Neil. He was looking at Clapp through new eyes as a result of this luncheon.

During the drive back to the Savoy Hotel, Clyde was effusive in his praise of Clapp's performance. "Absolutely brilliant, sir. You were a giant among pygmies."

"Is that what you think, Clyde?" asked Clapp, his face displaying scepticism for some reason. "What about you, Neil?"

"I've never seen anything like it, Mr. Clapp," said Neil. "How do you do it?"

"It's a matter of putting a high polish on one's natural brass," said Clapp. "It wouldn't surprise me if one of you two youngsters were to acquire the technique some day."

Neil had intended to catch an afternoon train back to Oxford, but at Clapp's request he returned to the suite, where Clapp at once disappeared into the bathroom. He came out drying his hands on a towel in a no-nonsense way.

"Clyde?" he said, concentrating on the towel. "Clyde. Let Neil and me have this room."

"I beg your pardon, sir?" Clyde's face showed shocked incredulity.

"Give … us … the … room."

"Leave, you mean?"

"That would seem to be the clear implication of my plain words. Yes."

Clyde heaved himself up and started to walk out in a heavy, ungraceful manner, more pronounced than usual.

"And Clyde?"

"Yes, sir?"

"Clyde. I may be old. And I may be senile. And I may be off my goddamned head. But, Clyde?"

"Yes, sir?"

"Clyde, I am not yet deaf. 'Giant among pygmies,' eh? I heard your snide remarks down at the other end of the table."

"Oh, no, sir. I was only –"

"Clyde. I heard enough from you at lunch for one day. Right now I need this room."

Neil stood there, as nonplussed by this as Clyde appeared to be during his exit. He was sure Clapp could not have heard anything.

"Your friend Ferritt has me in a bind," said Clapp. "By his intelligence and cunning he has made himself indispensable. By his arrogance and nastiness, he has made himself insufferable. You see my dilemma. Fortunately, I have hit upon an expedient that makes him just barely tolerable. If I arbitrarily give him a good boot in the rear end like that one day every month, it generally takes him two or three weeks to crawl back up to his previous level of obnoxiousness. Do you know what he calls himself? 'Chief Confidential Adviser to the Prime Minister and his Cabinet.' Pretty fancy name for bumboy, hey?"

Neil could scarcely believe he was hearing these words. Clapp and Clyde were reputed to be as close as doting father and devoted son. The scuttlebutt at home, dignified by its appearance in political commentaries in the papers from time to time, was that Clapp was grooming Clyde for leadership.

"Clyde wants to run in this election coming up, of course," resumed Clapp. "Neil! You wouldn't want the like of that to get ahead of you on this thing, would you?"

But while Clapp had been speaking, Neil had become mindful of his own failure to stand firmly behind two other friends in the past – and of his determination never to be found lacking in that respect again.

"Look, Mr. Clapp," he said hoarsely, "you were right when you said 'your friend Ferritt,' to me. Clyde *is* my friend. We've known each other for many years. Naturally, we've had our ins and our outs with one another, and our ups and our downs. Sometimes an unfortunate aspect of his personality does get the better of him. But I don't mind that and I can handle it. The point is, we *are* friends. And I'm not very interested in our being turned into arch rivals in petty provincial politics."

Once he had begun, Neil had found this much easier to say than he had expected it to be. He had also discovered that he was able to keep his eyes focussed directly on Clapp's without averting them for as long as he wished, something he was not always able to do with the eyes of even a close friend or lover.

Percy Clapp grinned at Neil. "You are absolutely right," he said. "I should not have talked to you about Clyde like that. You're his friend and, I must confess, he does seem to be a very good friend of yours as well. You know something, Neil? Of all the people to whom I've mentioned the possibility of your running in this election, Ferritt is the *only* one who has sided completely with your own argument against your doing so. I wonder why. Ah, mutual friendship! It's a beautiful thing."

Neil had to laugh along with Clapp. This old bugger was totally disarming, he thought.

The premier now brought Neil over to the window of his suite. He pointed out the sweep of the Thames and the magnificent view of the Parliament Buildings. Then, as they leaned against the casement close together like two confidants, he said softly, almost plaintively, "I have a real problem, Neil. What are you, twenty-three?"

"Yes, just last month."

"And I'm nearly sixty-three. Is there really thirty years ...? No. What is it?"

"Forty, in fact, sir," said Neil gently, ignoring the whiff of bad breath.

"My God, is there really forty years between our ages? I would never have said it, talking together here like this. I have a problem, Neil. At my age, how much longer can I last at the head of a government, even if I wanted to stay on? Two years? Five? Seven, outside. What is going to happen to our 'poor bald rock,' as Joey Smallwood used to call it, when I go? You're familiar with some of my Cabinet colleagues, the brighter ones. You have more intelligence in your little finger than the bunch of them lumped together have in their whole bodies ...."

Clapp turned towards Neil abruptly. "So does Ferritt," he said; and gazed into Neil's eyes for several seconds. "Ferritt knows that," he went on. "And Ferritt wants to take over from me when I go. And Ferritt will try to take over from me when I go. And that's my problem. Yes, he's intelligent. Yes, he's brilliant. But, it's a brilliance of a peculiar type. It's not a creative brilliance. It's an academic, analytic brilliance. It's not a positive brilliance, like: here are new policies we can implement to benefit our people. It's a negative brilliance, like: no, that program is too stupid to talk about because ... or no, that won't work and here's why. To Clyde, nothing is ever any good because it may have imperfections on the edges. He's a frustrated absolutist, Neil. If something is not absolutely perfect – and of course, nothing ever is – then Clyde believes it to be no good at all."

Clapp gripped Neil by the arm. "I know you consider him your friend. But I have to say this to you, my son. I've studied him closely during the past year, and I have seen what he is like. And no friendship means more to me than the welfare of our people. He is not a political leader. He would make a marvellous deputy minister, a wonderful chief adviser, pointing out to the man at the top any problems and defects in a plan. But ultimately there has to be a fearless, creative leader who can kick him and the rest of the civil service in the backside, Neil, and say: 'Ye have sat long enough. Ye have nattered long enough. Now, just do it!'"

Clapp had left the window and had begun pacing. "Good heavens, it's only a matter of a very few years before the billions upon billions of dollars from our offshore oil start to roll in. Can you picture Ferritt sitting there on top of that money, all alone on top of those billions? What would he do with it which would be of remote benefit to the electorate? You tell me, Neil, because I can't think of anything. More than likely he'd allow our little land to be transformed by the money-grubbers into an undistinguished, unidentifiable non-entity like, what? A suburb of Detroit-Windsor!

"That's the policy side of my problem. Now let's look at the partisan politics of the thing for a minute. Say, for the sake of argument, I were to pass the leadership of the party over to Clyde when I get out, lay on the hands and make him premier. How long would he last, do you think? He's not an attractive man, Neil. Did you know that over 60 per cent of my vote each election is women? Do you think Ferritt can hang on to that support? Then, there's the unfortunate aspect of his personality that you yourself mentioned, and which I will characterize euphemistically as loathsomeness. Wait now, Neil. I know what I'm talking about. No one can stand the fellow. He was on staff only one month before the last hold-out in the Cabinet secretariat finally had to concede that Ferritt's manner turned her guts like everyone else's, including all the ministers'.

"Oh, there's a grudging respect for his knowledge and his sharp tongue, certainly, and I'm not saying he doesn't have his uses. But political leadership? I think not. Even if I pitchforked him into the premiership, how long would he last? Until the very next election, and no longer. Our party would be defeated and that crowd in the Opposition would go into government. And no one wants that, Neil.

"Yet Ferritt will try to take over from me. And despite all I've said, Ferritt *will* take over from me. Unless. Unless. I tell you, Neil, it makes me wake up nights and sit up in my bed. But that's *my* problem. Still, it's a problem I must solve and I need help."

Clapp led Neil back to the chairs and they sat down. "By the way, Neil, I apologize for coming on so strongly before lunch about your running. When I invited you down to London, I had in mind to suggest that you run, of course. I do have to put fifty candidates into the field after all. But when I saw you again, and remembered how good you were on that political tour with us a couple of years ago, well, quite candidly, I went overboard a little. I thought I had found the solution to my ... I won't get into that again. Listen, Neil, broadly and generally now, what direction do you think Newfoundland should take in the future?"

Instead of being uneasy with the question, Neil felt himself

21

answering with authority. Not a vestige of the diffidence that was in him right after lunch remained.

"Mr. Clapp," he said. "To some, perhaps to most, this might sound hopelessly naive or romantic or idealistic. That may be your reaction, too .... But if it is, frankly, sir, I don't give – it wouldn't bother me, because it's what I profoundly believe. I believe we have an opportunity to do something noble and good with our homeland. The billions of dollars from off-shore oil, as you say, can turn our people into a replica of urban North American materialism and crassness, or it can be used to transform our land into a beautiful little Renaissance jewel.

"There was nothing mystical about the flowering of arts and intellect in the Athens of Pericles, or the Florence of Lorenzo, or the London of Elizabeth. I believe that if a large enough group of random humanity is taken (and our seven or eight hundred thousand would be enough); if the leadership is found within; if a sense of individual and community self-worth is fostered; and if the money, the cross-fertilization of ideas, the sparking, kindling, and flaming of talent are pro-vided, and so on and so on – we would see a similar blooming of our *indigenous* culture and artistry, the bud of which has already started to open. It would be just like any other cause and effect relationship that we can perceive and understand. The right internal leadership, the right laws, the right public use of the money, the right environment can achieve that, I believe. The converse is that we permit ourselves to become homogenized Americana, proud to be called 'the Dallas of the North,' *revelling* in it for God's sake!"

Clapp was all ears but the expression on his face was neutral. Then he smiled and nodded his head for a full minute. Finally, his limbs began to twitch and he leaped to his feet. "By the bowels of Christ, Neil," he said, "it's a lovely concept! I've been groping intuitively towards something like that myself, but it took you to articulate it properly. That's pre-cisely why I've had a running battle going with the federal government for the past couple of years. Precisely that ques-tion: who's going to be the master of our destiny as a people, us or them?

22

"Now there's the difference between you and Ferritt in a nutshell. Mention the Florence of Lorenzo to him and he'd say, 'Nice spot, if you didn't mind contracting the bubonic plague now and then.' Neil, to hear your espousal of so enlightened an idea for our island is music to my ears. It gives me great faith in our future. It also assures me of your return home, if not immediately, then soon. No man could possess such a vision for his people and remain long in self-imposed exile. As far as your running in this upcoming election is concerned, I'll say no more. You quite clearly know your own mind and you'll do what you think best regardless of anything I might say. Further urging of this point on my part would be presumptuous.

"Do you want to add something further, Neil? Personally, I don't want anything else to obscure the warmth and significance of this moment, myself. What do you say to our getting poor old Clyde back in here again? We wouldn't want him to burst from chagrin, and splatter the woodwork with venom, bile, and spleen."

Neil laughed and nodded his approval.

When Clyde walked in, Neil expected him to be somewhat shamefaced or, at least, to affect nonchalance, but he acted as if Clapp's reprimand had never been uttered. From Neil's subjective viewpoint, however, Clyde did appear to have undergone a diminution in stature.

Clapp now took them for a brisk long walk, ending on Charing Cross Road where he went into every secondhand bookstore and printshop he saw to look for books, maps, and pictures pertaining to Newfoundland. Clyde displayed vast knowledge on these subjects and Neil tried to hide his own comparative ignorance. Clapp seemed not to notice any disparity and asked for Neil's opinion on his finds as often as he asked for Clyde's.

That evening, Clapp had another engagement. He told the two young men to have dinner together in the Savoy Grill and to charge it to him. Clyde expressed delight at the suggestion, despite his having earlier mentioned to Neil that he was looking forward to being present at Clapp's dinner-meeting with British government officials.

When they saw Clapp to the door of the Bentley he cautioned them against hatching any conspiracies against him, and directed a wink at Neil which Clyde could not miss seeing. As the car drove off, they strolled into the Grill together.

To accompany their meal, Clyde first ordered a bottle of Chablis Grand Cru; next, a bottle of Mouton-Rothschild; and then a bottle of Chateau d'Yquem, joyfully announcing the ludicrous prices, and reacting to Neil's, "Jesus, Clyde!" with, "The slush fund in the premier's office is good for it, my boy."

Eventually, Clyde got around to what was on his mind. "You were wise to resist Percy's cajolery to come back and run. He's good at sucking people in. He already has about one hundred and fifty candidates lined up so that, when the time comes, he can pick the best fifty and jettison the rest. I've studied him closely for the past year and I know what he's like. It's best to stay clear of him, I'd say." Clyde's face suddenly simulated concern for Neil. "Unless you allowed him to talk you into it when he dragged you in there by yourself. That's his favourite ploy."

"My answer didn't change. I wanted to get your advice on it," said Neil, and watched his friend's bobbing eyebrows relax. "What about you, Clyde? Are you going to run?"

"Oh, I may and I may not. Whatever I decide to be better for the purpose of my research. This is all field work as far as I'm concerned, Neil, the amassing of raw materials for my Ph.D. thesis in Politics later on. That's why I'm able to put up with Percy's shit. I treat his bluster and his insults just as I would the ritualistic bravado and posturing of a tribal chief in the highlands of New Guinea – something to be observed and noted without personal involvement. That detachment, plus the fact that my old man is loaded with dough, means I can get out from under Percy whenever I want to. Christ, I'd hate to be stuck under Percy and not be able to feel that I could just pack up and pull out whenever the desire hit me, which is precisely the galling situation you'd be in, Neil, if you were to come back and run now. I'm saying that as a friend."

"What about the offshore oil billions, Clyde?" asked Neil,

unable to resist playing with him a little. "Don't you find that prospect attractive? You're going to need all the oil money, in addition to your old man's dough, if you keep ordering three plates of smoked salmon at the Savoy Grill and tucking into the saddle of lamb like that."

"Offshore oil billions!" scoffed Clyde, after he'd permitted himself a smile of pleasure at the notice taken of his gourmet tastes. "You and I will be enjoying our retirement when that comes through, and even then, the Government of Canada will rip off the lion's share. Look, Neil, we have to face one small fact as Newfoundlanders, you and I. As you yourself mentioned to me in Oxford last year, we belong to a flyspeck on the map, without importance to itself or the world. What is the future for anyone in politics there? It's quite simply too minute a political forum for anyone of ability to waste a lot of time on."

"I never believed that at all," Neil lied, enjoying this enormously. "I was just mouthing the words at the time. You're the political scientist, not I. But I can't see why a politician of great talent should be limited by obscure place of origin. If such a politician were to thrust himself to the top of our own poopy-assed little place, why must he then stop there? It seems to me that the possibilities are boundless. Take the analogy of the three great rampaging psychopaths of Europe: Alexander, Napoleon, and Hitler. Didn't they all rise out of peripheral territories, barely or not at all politically part of the vast areas they ultimately gained control over? Far from being a hindrance, birth on the geographical fringe may be a prerequisite. I've come more and more to the view that obscure birth in a remote region allows me – I mean, allows one – to see the main chance more clearly and to recognize whether, ah, one has the stuff to seize it."

Clyde grinned wanly. "Well, that's one theory of transcendent leadership," he said, trying to import a trace of scorn into his words. "But for every Napoleon, there are a thousand strutting Jivaro tribesmen, each dreaming about taking over all South America one day."

Neil smiled and said, "Of course, Clyde, of course. I was

just being ridiculous." He focussed his eyes on the distance and pretended to be trancing on a vision of transcendent leadership.

During the next hour, while they chatted and joked amiably on other topics, Neil noted that Clyde lost no opportunity to study him surreptitiously whenever he looked away and went into one of his artfully beatific trances.

Clyde signed with a flourish a bill approximately equal to a term's stipend of Neil's scholarship, and reminded Neil of Clapp's invitation to take the extra bed in his room. Neil declined, saying he would catch the last train back to Oxford in order to get an early start on his books in the morning. He wrote a note to Clapp thanking him "for everything," underlining "everything" twice. Then he loosely folded the note and asked Clyde to deliver it, visualizing the consternation on his friend's face when he tried to impart meaning to the emphasized word.

In the lobby, they lingered and chatted. They shook hands, said warm goodbyes three times, and looked forward to seeing each other again soon. When Neil's taxi arrived, Clyde walked him to it, and waved as it pulled out into the traffic.

Instead of telling the driver to take him to Paddington Station, Neil gave him the name of a street off Russell Square in Bloomsbury. There, under the familiar sign heralding the Bloomsbury Group Bed and Breakfast, he got out and entered the building. The driver had not been able to keep back a comment on the contrast he saw between the elegance of the journey's start and the seediness of its end. And Neil himself, as he took his key from a landlord lacking all lubricating courtesy, and made his way up the staircases to his roachy room next to the roof, was struck more forcefully than ever before by the rattiness of everything and the pervasive stench of ammonia which, strong as it was, could not mask the fetor of decay.

To take the damp nip out of the air in his room, he stuck a couple of ten pence pieces into the small gas heater and lit it, envisioning, as he did so, the towel warmer in the bathroom off Clapp's suite. He positioned his body on the bed, avoiding, in a practised way, the three worst springs, and gazed at his old friend, the puce stain on the wall opposite.

He had been wise to come here to think a while alone before going back for another three weeks, or another twelve months, to the "Sargasso Sea of Academe." Neil smiled at the thought of Percy Clapp and then, before he was able to control it, a surge of sudden anticipation stood him up on the linoleum floor. "'We must take the current when it serves,'" he quoted to the garret at large. "'Or lose our ventures.'"

2

Neil Godwin was twelve years old when Percy Clapp and Clyde Ferritt, independent of one another, impinged upon his life. He had known both of them before, but vaguely. His own father and Ferritt's sat on a schoolboard together. And to Neil, Clapp had been merely another one of scores of frequent visitors to his father's house.

One afternoon, Neil was watching a junior high school soccer game, frequently glancing at the cheerleader from the other school whose blonde pre-pubescent beauty was causing flutterings in his midriff, when he heard a boy's loud voice: "Did you ever see a Gawker up close?"

Neil turned and saw Clyde Ferritt pointing at him and proclaiming to the group of nearby cheerleaders. "That's a Gawker over there right now. See him? The Head Gawker's son. I *told* you they all looked like basket cases with brain damage."

Neil had been taunted by boys before. Fiercely defensive of his father's cause, he would always demand a retraction, and at home afterwards his father would deplore violence while examining with pity and pride Neil's new scratches and bruises.

Clyde's jeer and the girls' laughter, however, made Neil behave in an unusual way. He pretended he had heard nothing. During the next spate of cheering for a play on the field he left the crowd and went home, attempting to walk with dignity, but feeling as if he were skulking away in mortification.

Ernest Godwin, Neil's father, was Chief Elder of a flourishing sect which called itself "The Gazers on the Goodlike Glory of God's Full Fair and Fearful Face." In the parlance of non-adherents, its members were "Gawkers" and Ernest was "Head Gawker." The Gawkers formed an institution of heroic stature for many Protestants in the lower social strata of the city among whom the Godwins lived. All his life, as his father's son, Neil had shared and upheld that view without question.

After the soccer game, he began to wonder for the first time what exactly this group he belonged to was, and why it provoked the mocking contempt of outsiders, including some outsiders to whom he himself was attracted. For several sabbaths he actually listened to the familiar words of a passage in his father's sermons which comprised a kind of Gawkers' credo. The ritual would begin with participatory theology by the congregation. A man would stand and interrupt Ernest Godwin in the middle of a sentence.

"Chief Elder Godwin!" he would bark. When he got full attention, the man would begin to rub his hands like Uriah Heep. "I just wants to inquire," he would say, "by way of no harm, how we *knows* we are God's chosen ones. Seeing as how I finds it *awful* hard to get anyone else to believe it."

Ernest Godwin's face would take on an appearance of panic for a moment. During the stunned silence, someone in the congregation would yell, "Fire that blasphemer out!" and another would shout back, "No, answer his question!" The argument would rage among factions of the congregation for a few minutes while Elder Godwin mused alone on the stage.

"You ask," he would begin again, as if uncertainly, "how you know you are the chosen ones. It is a hard question. Because it is not altogether obvious, I am thinking, why the creator of the universe would see fit to choose *us,* out of the many *excellent* possibilities open to him. Have we deceived ourselves? Have we been driven together here by a purely selfish longing to save our wretched, unexceptional identities, to preserve these tattered and mangy wisps of self-awareness? And while we are persuading ourselves that our feeble and miserable spirits are chosen for eternal preservation, does the all-powerful Preserver himself look down at us and laugh? Is that the situation here?"

The congregation would look at each other and let their eyes reflect fear of that dreadful possibility. The Chief Elder would then close his own eyes and say in a quiet voice: "There is a sunny meadow of fluffy, soft, and cuddly lambs bouncing on the glistening grass. A shepherd watches over them. One lamb alone is different. He is stunted, scrawny, runty, and lame, and his coat is scraggy, smelly, and sparse. He knows he is somehow different from the rest. The cute and cuddly, woolly and plump lambs can also see that the runty lamb is different from them. And the shepherd himself pays no attention to the scraggy runt, ignoring him in his far corner of the field near the founderous bog, while he cleans and cares for the beautiful lambs.

"You, my brothers and sisters," Ernest would suddenly blare, "are that runty, scrawny lamb!"

The congregation would now look as if they had been crowbarred between the eyes. Many had a natural talent for assuming the look. "No!" one would bawl. "Yes!" Ernest would bawl back. "I wants to be one of the cuddly lambs," a woman would scream. "Well, you're not one, and you're not going to be one," Ernest would yell at her. Men would rise and form their hands into fists, but the Chief Elder had begun again.

"In a few short weeks, the shepherd leads the woolly little lambs out of the sunny, flowery meadow – they all the while baaing their love to him – and down a hard path to a dark satanic pen. There, the plump lambs are held under the butcher's knife, and their throats are ripped open, and their warm blood gushes out, and they bleat piteously now, their pretty almond eyes flickering about for the sight of the loving shepherd's face. But all in vain. There is no salvation. For the shepherd is already gone back to the sunny meadow, to the new flock of lambs bouncing joyfully on the grass.

"And generation after generation of fat and fleecy lambs come under the shepherd's caring eye, and then under the relentless savagery of the butcher's blade. But the skinny, lame, and runty lamb lives on, keeping to his remote corner of the field, and gazing from afar on the goodlike glory of the shepherd's full fair and fearful face, spared the murderous butcher's knife ....

"You, my brothers and sisters, I say to you again, are that runty, scrawny lamb. And if that's not the truth, let the left hand of the Almighty grab me by the scruff of the neck, and let His right hand seize the slack of my trousers – like this, look – and let Him pitch me headlong into the gaping maw of the ocean!"

Neil's father would pause dramatically, and the congregation, despite their familiarity with the story (many had been mumbling the words in unison with him), would lean forward in their seats in suspense. Then, after another minute of daring silence, he would say quietly, "It was twelve years ago, my friends, that I first offered to sacrifice my hide on the altar of truth, just after I started my preaching, way out there in Maggotty Cove Motion where my blessed son, Neil here, was born. And I have yet to suffer that divine dip in the sea."

The congregation would laugh ritualistically, and settle back to bathe in Ernest's depiction of wonderful things to come.

"Yes!" the Head Gawker would resume with a roar. "Yes! You *are* the skinny, lame, and runty lambs on earth! But the infinite intelligence of the universe has shown me a picture in perfect clarity of each of you in your completed states, a heaven-sent snap of your fleecy souls inside the rotting flesh and the slimy entrails and the halting limbs that bind you to this rock."

Ernest Godwin would then explore for an hour the details of this celestial snapshot, first in negative: ("... no drudgery, no debts, no demoralizing doubts, no sinking down in desperation, no slavery for simple survival, no unloved work for daily needs ...); and then in positive: ("... striving to create, yes, but within your talents ... struggling to produce, yes, but within your desires ... giving love and getting love, consummate love to sate your mutual emotional hunger ...).

Neil saw and heard the great heaved-up moans of contentment from the listeners, the occasional one sliding fluidly to the floor and babbling in glossalalia. He noticed that every week the congregation increased in size from an inflow of new people who, like the old hands, had their hard lives stamped on their faces, dress, and manners. He contrasted the children around him with the well-nourished, fashionably dressed, vivacious kids at the school of his favourite cheerleader. He studied the words on the sign above his father's head: "Gazers on the Goodlike Glory of God's Full Fair and Fearful Face" – the only embellishment to the simple letters being that the two O's in Goodlike had been painted to look like two eyes in a state of bliss.

And within a month of Clyde Ferritt's gibe, Neil was possessed of a terrible knowledge. He *understood* why others regarded his father and his father's vocation and his father's disciples as a contemptible joke, and he felt ashamed to be a Gawker and he felt great guilt for his shame. He prayed that his new understanding would evaporate and leave behind only the urge to protect his father's church, the old fellow-feeling and pride, and especially the old undoubting faith. But he could not make it happen. Indeed, the more he reflected on these matters and compared his father's form of religion with other forms, the more sceptical of all religious conviction he became. Neil's sense of loss as his religious belief withered, his embarrassment at being taken for a Gawker, and his guilt at his secret abandonment of his father's church were profound and, for a long time, grievous to him.

One day during this period, Neil and his nine-year-old sister, Jane, were strolling home along the sidewalk together when they saw a horde of children milling around a nucleus which moved at a slow but constant speed down the middle of Military Road. The centre of the throng was a man who, when he wasn't making gross, toothless, chewing motions with his mouth, had a slack and foolish grin on his face.

Strung from his neck like a drum was a large apple juice can upon which he beat with a small kindling stick. Kids would take turns to sneak up and touch his frayed overcoat, and then scurry away screeching, the same mixture of ecstasy and terror on each pink face. The man never stopped looking all around in moronic delight at his following.

Tight to his side was a stooped and twisted woman. No taller than most of the children, she would have achieved the

32

inconspicuousness which her demeanour indicated she desired, if her regular marching stride in step with her companion, and the big protuberance on her back, did not so clearly distinguish her from the tangle of straight and bounding young.

These two were the Goofy Newfy and the Hump, a familiar sight. Their names had been bestowed on them, so conventional knowledge had it, by American Servicemen from the former Airforce Base at Pepperell and the Naval Base at Argentia. "Go, Goofy, go! Go, Goofy, go!" was the chant which underlay the general clamour of the crowd around the pair. But soon it was disturbed by a sing-song bawl from a teenage boy on the sidewalk: "Let's go jump the Hump oh, babee! Let's go jump the Hump!" He was quickly joined by the raucous, breaking voices of his pustule-faced friends.

At this new refrain, the woman's head and hump began to shake. Neil looked down at his sister. Her eyes were wide and the concentration on her little face made his heart ache. He took her arm and walked on, wishing she'd been spared that sight.

"Did you see the woman shaking, Neil?" asked Jane. "She must be crying." He squeezed her shoulders and nodded grimly.

"Why was she there with him, Neil?"

"I don't know, Janie."

"I mean, why would she walk along with him like that if it was going to make her cry?"

"Janie, I don't know," he said, with an unintended edge to his voice. Then he added gently, "Maybe she's looking after him or something. Maybe she's as cracked as he is. Maybe she's his wife or something."

Jane assumed her look of concentration again. She walked along in silence for a few minutes and said, "Gaw, Neil, she must be even crackter than him to go with him like that in the first place."

Neil didn't answer. He was preoccupied with the Goofy Newfy rather than the Hump. His first reaction had been pity. Then "There but for the Grace of God go I," and "Count your own blessings" went through his head in his father's voice.

Neil now rejected the pity as useless and the saws as false comfort. There was no difference between himself and the loony, he thought. There only appeared to be a difference, from a self-centred point of view. If all life was meaningless, as he had recently concluded, how could one life have more meaning than another or be of more value or have greater quality, in the end? Viewed rightly, in the context of a universe in which all was meaningless and futile, he and the Goofy Newfy were precisely the same – equally unimportant and inconsequential, and equally exposed, without hope, to the random hurts of an indifferent cosmos.

At first, Neil felt his usual thrill of pleasure in using his own intelligence to arrive at his own conclusions, but then the full implications of his dismal verity struck him and caused him to shudder. He stopped on the sidewalk and dwelt in morbid fascination on the thought. He was able only to shake his head in response to Jane's challenge to race her to the door of their house.

"Neil," she said in irritation, "what is *wrong* with you these days, anyway? You're always in a daze."

That evening, Ernest Godwin brought Percy Clapp home to dinner again. Neil was more conscious of his father's friend now, as Clapp was in the middle of his first campaign for premier and his calumniations of opponents made him a frequent spectacle on the television news. But to Neil, Clapp was still just part of the world of his father from which he felt himself to be totally divorced.

He responded in monosyllables to Clapp's attempts to engage him in conversation. Ernest's glower and fierce whisper, "Be more polite!" accomplished nothing, and at length Clapp turned to sister Jane, whose saucy rejoinders delighted him.

"You going to vote for me, Jane?" he asked at last.

"No," said Jane.

"No!" growled Clapp in mock dismay. "Why not?"

"I saw you on television again before supper." Jane was squirming in anticipation.

"You saw me on television and you're not going to vote for me? Explain yourself, young lady."

34

"Because," said Jane, her face aglow, "to get people to notice you, you're always doing something *weird*! You're just like that Goofy Newfy."

Ernest and his wife glanced at each other and then at Clapp. They turned to Jane and all four of them broke into laughter simultaneously. They looked at Neil. He started to chuckle and, feeling as if a vise had relaxed its grip on his heart, he was soon guffawing with pure enjoyment for the first time in weeks.

An image of Percy Clapp as the Goofy Newfy became fixed in his mind.

3

"'We've sent young Clyde to Lakefield for his last couple of years of high school,' old man Ferritt shouts to me at the schoolboard meeting," Neil overheard his father telling his mother. "'You may have read about that school in the newspapers, Ernest,' he yells. 'It's the same one the Queen is sending Prince Andrew to.'"

This information did arrest Neil for a moment on the lower landing of the staircase, but then he continued his progress up, three steps to a bound. It was not a sense of the meaninglessness and futility of life however, which dismissed his pang of covetousness. It was a sense of urgency. Several months ago, all Neil's religious and philosophical doubts had been swamped by a great tide of certainty: a comprehensive horniness. And he was on his way to the bathroom now to act yet again on the promise of final relief if only the turgor were fondled away this one more time.

Neil's erotic plans for himself were not restricted to masturbating his urges into a fistful of toilet paper. Indeed, he had hoped to be far gone by now into intrigues of hardcore sex, unredeemed by social content. But despite much plotting, his sole sexual experience in the presence of a female had occurred when his sister, Jane, to the shock of both, had opened the bathroom door on him at the peak of one of his monotonously regular pulls.

Nightly, for another year, he wondered where all the rampant teenage sex that everyone said was going on everywhere, all the time, actually was. For guidance, he turned to Muck Barrows.

David "Muck" Barrows was in Neil's class at school and the hero of the male students. According to his own etymology, his nickname was an early recognition of his sexual prowess. No one disputed this to his face, but all knew the name derived from his father's occupation of unclogging sewers for the city.

Muck was athletic, nimble-minded, and unruly; and, what was germane to Neil's needs, forward with the girls. Neil initiated a long and detailed conversation with him on fornication, putting forward much intricate theory and clinical book knowledge. Muck responded by drawing upon his apparently limitless store of first-person sexual vignettes. They were elated at how superbly they complemented each other.

The next Saturday, they hitchhiked together to a community thirty miles from St. John's. On the roadmap, it was identified as King Henry's Harbour but everyone called it Hank's Hole. Muck knew the place well. Between rides he described the proclivity of its pubescent girls to yield their favours without fuss or pomp. "Neil, they're just like the minks, b'y," he summed up.

In Hank's Hole they went into the Keenteen and played pinball. Fortunately, the male *habitués* of the snackbar were already aware of Muck's scrapping abilities and controlled their resentment at the notice which one dozen gum-chewing, smoking, and giggling girls, all of them crammed into a booth designed for four, were taking of the two boys.

After dark, Muck led Neil out to the parking lot where they leaned against a pickup truck and waited. When the girls came out, expressing their love of fresh air, Muck gave Neil a running commentary on each and decided on the two prettiest ones. The four of them then strolled across the road to the field and separated into couples.

Amidst the swarms of blackflies and mosquitoes that descended on them, Neil and his partner sat on the damp spring grass. Without preliminaries, she put her arms around his neck and glued her lips to his. After fifteen minutes of that, Neil felt familiar enough with her to escalate to foreplay. He attempted to inch his hand under jeans that were already too tight about hip and waist to admit a fingernail, and then fumbled with buttons and zippers. She displayed skill in keeping these done up.

At length, Neil spoke his first words to her: "Muck said you let *him* screw you."

"That Muck!" she snorted, re-fastened her lips for another half hour, and brushed away Neil's gropes at her nether regions as perfunctorily and uncomplainingly as she brushed the blackflies and mosquitoes off her neck and face. When they heard Muck approaching, she turned her body enough to allow her breast to linger in Neil's hand for a few seconds before she stood up. Neil nearly passed out.

"This one has got to go jeesly home," said Muck of his companion.

While they were walking back to the Keenteen, Neil's girl took his hand and stopped in front of him. She stood on her toes and kissed him. "Tomorrow night again, okay?" she said, bringing her clasped hands between their bodies. "At my house, okay? Mom and dad'll be in St. John's. We'll meet at the Keenteen, okay?" Feeling his knuckles against her pelvis and the back of her hand against his crotch, Neil nodded mutely.

On the highway, Muck asked, "Did you get in?"

"Nearly. Not quite," said Neil.

"Never got in!" exclaimed Muck. "I can't understand that. She must have been on the rag. That's the only answer. Tomorrow night she'll let you for sure at her house. I'm tired of screwing her there."

They had to walk a long distance before they were picked up and Neil was unusually late getting home. But Ernest Godwin asked no questions. In fact, he seemed pleased to have an opportunity to make this speech: "You have arrived at an age now, Neil, where you are entitled to a large degree of privacy and responsibility and to your parents' trust in you to use that privilege and carry that burden in a mature and creditable fashion."

Neil went to bed and wrestled all night with an erection

peculiarly adolescent in its rigidity and duration. A phantasmagoria of the girl's and his own bodily parts in intimate conjunction with each other never left his mind. He kept reckoning the hours that had to pass before he would bring about the delicious reality of each fragment of fantasy.

In the morning he heard from bed his father on the telephone. The occasional word like "Barrows" and "King Henry's Harbour" reached him. Ernest's shout to him to come down brought about the detumescence which Neil had striven vainly to attain for the past hour. He remembered that his father had a church in Hank's Hole.

"Didn't I tell you to be home by eleven o'clock on the weekends?" his father demanded.

"No," said Neil.

"I'm sure I did," said Ernest. "But even if I didn't, it makes no difference. For your disobedience last night or your irresponsibility, whichever it was – and they are equally reprehensible – you will stay in the house today and tonight and all next weekend, apart from going to church."

Neil was flabbergasted by the severity of this punishment for a non-existent offense from his previously indulgent father. At first, he could not say a word. And when he did argue against it, Ernest remained firm.

Two weekends later, he returned to Hank's Hole with Muck. They arrived in time to see the girl of Neil's fortnight of dreams getting aboard a powder-blue Cadillac driven by the son of the local lounge owner.

That night, in a liaison arranged by Muck, Neil's sexual initiation took place with a pitiably slow-witted teenage girl not far from the Gawker's lodge in Hank's Hole. It was an episode that became so distasteful in Neil's mind afterwards that even Muck's unexalted sense of personal dignity did not prompt him to suggest its repetition during their summer on the prowl together. "Jesus, Neil," he would say, whenever the subject came up. "I had to get you started somewhere, with your old man shagging everything up."

Back at school for their final year, their close association soon became a frequent topic among the distressed teachers: "Smoking like two tilts ... Booze in cough medicine bottles ...

I'm sure they were drunk in my Trig class ... Pipping off from school to play poker and pool ... Heavy petting behind the curtain in the auditorium ... That Barrows will have Neil on the dope next!"

The principal paid a special visit to Ernest at home. Neil was called in towards the end of the conversation.

"And so, Mr. Godwin, I tell you truthfully that just one of those acts of folly would have warranted the expulsion of a student who didn't possess Neil's past academic record and future potential."

"I appreciate your discretion," said Ernest. "It is quite obviously part of the low cunning of young Barrows to join up with Neil for protection from the consequences of his own idiocies."

"Exactly, sir, exactly. And I'm very much afraid that if Neil does not immediately resist being manipulated by Barrows, he will be giving up his excellent prospects of winning the gold medal and scholarship for highest marks in the whole school system."

This caused Ernest to become quiet and reflective, and the principal, satisfied with the effect of his words, left. Then Neil's father emitted imagery regarding Barrows which became muddier the more his anger increased, though its drift remained clear enough: "That strait-jacket case in training, that local pilot project for the mainland Mafia, that embryonic Beelzebubic breakthrough!"

Neil, without meaning to, roared, "You might know lots of big words but you're still a stupid idiot!" He closed his eyes tightly for an instant and when he opened them again he could barely see his father coming towards him through his blurred vision. He raised his arms to protect himself and quickly blinked the tears away. There was a smile of compassionate love on his father's face. Neil angrily twisted away from the arm around his shoulders and turned his back.

"Don't be led astray by Barrows, Neil," Ernest murmured, after a silence. "That's all I'm saying. People care about you, you know. Don't throw away that scholarship. You're only sixteen, my son. Your whole life is ahead. University. A good profession. The sky's the limit for you. Someone with your ability could become premier for heaven's sake. Don't let yourself be led by the likes of Barrows."

Led by Barrows. How it grated on Neil's nerves to hear all the time that he was being led by Barrows! He was not led by Barrows. Their shenanigans were jointly inspired, with the edge in initiative going, if anywhere, to Neil himself. It was true, though, that Muck was a natural leader of adolescent scruffs. It privately pained Neil whenever they met up with a mutual acquaintance, to see Muck greeted effusively while Neil's own presence would be barely acknowledged. When their friends were around, Neil felt himself to be a mere adjunct and sidekick, a foil of Muck's. The fact that the value adults placed on the two of them was precisely the opposite was no comfort to Neil. He wished his teachers would stop singling him out as the class paragon of knowledge and comprehension, and making comments like, "Neil, this shows great appreciation of the complexity of the period," or "You demonstrate deep sensitivity to the dilemma of Sally, the heroine," as they passed back History and Literature tests. And he framed his answers in order to make them stop.

Following further pep talks from his principal, augmented by exhortations from Ernest, Neil stepped up his night-time peregrinations with Muck. They alternated between hanging out in teenage joints looking for girls, and going aboard foreign vessels in the harbour to dicker with Spanish, Japanese, or Greek sailors over the price of an execrable litre of brandy, sake, or ouzo.

One night near the end of their final year of school, they swallowed a bottle of port each in two gulps and meandered along the waterfront. The rumours that Portugese sailors cut their wine with iodine or spirit varnish lent a heady sense of risk-taking to the adventure. Three uniformed seamen came towards them on the sidewalk and politely moved to one side to let Neil and Muck pass. Without warning, Muck seized one of the sailors around the waist, hoisted him into the air, and threw him halfway across Water Street. Trouser legs flapping, the other two ran over, picked up their fallen comrade, and hurried away.

"Goddamned Yanks, always trying to take over," muttered

Muck, while Neil bent over, swaying and laughing. They continued to stagger foolishly along singing, to the tune of a Mozart divertimento, an air popular during the years of the US base in St. John's, and for some reason considered by their age group to be the definitive anti-American putdown:

There once was a Newfy maid
Who said she wasn't afraid
To lie on her back
In the middle of the shack
And let the Yankees fiddle with her crack.
Her mother was surprised
To see her belly rise
And out popped a nigger
With his hand on his jigger
And his balls between his eyes.

On they stumbled, the incident a high point of adventure in their clouded brains. It provoked frequent bursts of laughter as one of them would recall and vainly try between gasps to articulate another humorous aspect of what had happened. And then they both became aware at the same time that behind them on either side of the road, quickly gaining on them, was a score of uniformed men. Many of them were carrying something in their hands. The boys took off down the street.

"Up this alley!" Neil shouted, knowing that at the end of it were the steps which led to the street on the higher level, not far from the police station. He was glorying in taking charge like this, wishing, in the mist of his brain, that someone else was there to see him handle it. Muck was dubious, wanting to outrun the sailors, but he followed when Neil turned. They sprinted to the wall at the end. The alley was a loading berth for trucks and had high concrete walls and closed steel doors on all sides – except the entrance through which they had come and into which white faces were already cautiously peering.

They felt around frantically in the dark but could find no opening. When a flashlight came on ahead, Neil crouched down by a side wall and fell forward: his heels had met with emptiness instead of the bottom of the wall as expected. He thrust his hand into the narrow gap but felt nothing. The opening was a couple of feet long and several inches high and, under different circumstances, he would have concluded that no adult human body could fit through it. By turning his head sideways, however, and with the slime on the ground acting as a lubricant, he found that his head could just slip under and that the rest of his body could painfully drag itself in. At Neil's fierce whisper, Muck came through the gap with great speed, tearing his ear in the process.

They huddled together in the darkness. "This is great, Neil," said Muck. "I thought we were done for there for a minute." He laughed half-audibly at their new security, nearly spoiling it. Outside, voices blustered and an occasional flicker of light hit the opening.

One sailor spotted the gap with his flashlight, but he was discouraged from looking in by the others because the opening was obviously too small and because "even a filthy, fucking Newf wouldn't have the stomach to crawl in that crap." Besides, another had already found the means of escape in a corner where there were protruding nails and chunks of broken concrete.

"It's too goddamned bad those fucking Newfs got away," said a voice. "It really is. It would have been a good thing to kill one of those Newfy punks and let the other one bring back the news who did it from his wheelchair. Aw yeah, there would have been a fuss, sure. But who'd give a fuck on the mainland about a couple of Newfs. It would have all blown over and this fucking hole would get the message not to fuck with the Canadian navy."

There was a chorus of agreement and another voice said, "I'm sick and cocksucking tired of always being the good goddamned guys for the cocksucking world."

"Stupid goddamned Newfy fuckers! Probably took us for Americans. We always get the shaft right up the hole from people who think we're Americans."

"Listen, buddy. If they thought we were Americans, no punks would have pulled that stunt – not even stupid Newfies who are so fucking stupid, they don't know the war is over.

Fucking Yanks got the right idea. Don't put up with no shit. Send in the fucking Marines if anyone farts and stinks up their breathing space." The voices were moving off now.

"Fucking right. That's what got the Yanks where they are today. Trudeau is as useless as a prick on a priest."

"Why is it that you bring religion into this matter?" asked a voice with a French accent. The subsequent accusations and disclaimers of anti-French Canadian prejudice finally faded out of the alley.

"Did you hear what those bastards were going to do with us?" asked Muck. "And here we are, part of Canada! I thought Canadians were supposed to be nice guys." They had another half-hysterical bout of survivors' laughter.

"So did I," said Neil. "They sounded just like Americans to me. Except for the French guy. That's the first time I've seen a big bunch of Canadians all together like that. No wonder old Percy is crapping on them all the time!"

They managed to scrape through the gap again. At the entrance to the alley, they were surrounded by two dozen sailors who had been hiding in wait. Muck yelled to Neil to come, and with jack-rabbit suddenness, evaded ten pairs of hands and was gone.

"We've got one goofy Newfy, anyway," said a seaman. "Let's put the boots to him."

Neil stood motionless and stolid while they closed around him. His mind had become clear and devoid of fear without conscious effort. Nothing happened. He looked straight at the men before him, and gradually the taunts and insults died. After a silence, one of the sailors said, "If this wasn't part of Canada, we'd kick the shit out of you. But we're all Canadians here tonight and we've got to stick together or the whole country will go to ratshit."

Neil felt so in control now that he sneered and walked at the men in front of him, who stepped aside. "He *is* only a kid, boys," apologized one of the sailors to his companions.

A few hundred yards along, a police car stopped, and Muck, ashen-faced and drenched with sweat from running, got out. The two policemen were delighted at not having to rescue anyone from rioting sailors. When Neil described how he had

44

faced down his would-be killers, one of the policemen said, "You're only lucky that wasn't an American boat in port. That's the difference between Americans and Canadians. If that was Americans, my sonny boy, you'd be holding your guts in now with two broken arms."

No amount of entreaty would keep the policemen from getting their names and addresses and driving the boys home. "Two young punks wandering around the waterfront at all hours. You're lucky you never ended up getting it dogstyle in one of those alleys, a cute little fellow like you, Godwin. You know what those foreign fairies are like, don't you, for Chrissake? And the whiff off of the two of ye! I hope that booze wasn't bootleg. Of course, now, I knows it was. Get that down Constable Primmer. Something else to go on their records. Boys, ye're finished!"

After the police had given Ernest Godwin an embellished account of their reasons for taking Neil into protective custody and had left, his father said, "Neil, Neil, my son, my son, what next, what next? Fourteen or fifteen years old. Brought home in the paddy wagon dead drunk and covered with filth, after causing a riot in the middle of the night down in the Sodom of this city. My good God in His Heaven above, Neil, my son, do you have any idea of the embarrassment to the members of my church if the Chief Elder's son got himself into serious trouble?"

"Sixteen. And how can anyone embarrass that tribe, Head Gawker," Neil spat out, "if being members of the Gawker church doesn't embarrass them already?"

The earlier plaintive querulousness of his father's voice changed. "Don't you ever call me that again, you traitorous whelp!" he bellowed. "I'm not even going to ask you if it was you and your pal, Barrows, who broke into my lodge in Hank's – King Henry's Harbour that night last week when you never came home at all, because I will commit an ungodly act on you whether you lie to me about it or whether you admit the truth. You bloody young … "

Neil readied himself for a clubbing death from the book his father was holding in one hand and banging into the palm of the other. His mother got up from her chair behind Ernest and approached her husband, her hands assuming position to haul him off her son by the neck. His father turned abruptly, and not noticing that he nearly knocked down his wife, strode out of the kitchen.

The brusque, grim-faced exit was to remain Ernest Godwin's major stratagem, during many future temptations, for avoiding the sin of filicide.

4

Neil and Muck Barrows entered university in St. John's together. Neil, to his father's disappointment, had barely missed winning a scholarship and Muck had picked up just enough through his haze in the classroom to qualify for admittance. Clyde Ferritt was a conspicuous presence at the university. He had been there a year already, and seemed to Neil to be well on his way to becoming the big man on campus.

Seeing Clyde directing with relish the debasing Orientation Week exercises for freshmen, Neil recalled a recent report by his father to his mother on the senior Ferritt's remarks at a schoolboard meeting: "We had an agonizing decision to make, Ernie. Clyde was accepted at both Harvard and Yale, of course, but surprisingly enough, making a choice between those two was not our problem. You see, when he finally finishes university the boy wants to get into politics. He has his heart set on becoming premier here first, heh, heh, heh, and after that, well, heh, heh, heh. So. We decided there were some compensating factors to his coming back here for his first degree. Let him get to know, so to speak, some of the brighter young fellows he'll have to work with later."

Apparently realizing that Neil was within earshot, Ernest Godwin had left off his disdainful mimicking and had finished gloomily with, "Well, at least old Ferritt has something to be proud about."

The main fatherly emotion incited in Ernest by his own son continued to be worry. After the first week of term, Neil and

Muck gave up going to most classes and spent the time at the neighbouring tavern where it was the custom of the proprietorship to wink at the shortfall between a student's years and the age of majority. There, by dint of practice, Neil learned to down, and to keep down some of the time, a couple of gallons of beer of an afternoon and evening.

This pastime caused ordeals at home, especially on those nights when Neil woke up vomiting and rushed to the bathroom. Invariably, Ernest would come in and hover over him and augment his heaving anguish with questions on the state of his health. Then he would help Neil back to bed, feeling his forehead, and sit there in the dark until Neil fell asleep or another eruption took place. He would ignore Neil's snarled demands to be allowed to puke in peace but frequently wished aloud that the bother of fatherhood were more spiritually rewarding.

In the student commonroom and at the tavern, eight or ten other students, with nothing in common except the haphazard fact that they were frequently in each other's company for want of the wit to find something more edifying to do, joined Muck and Neil in developing a sense of group elitism. Two years later, Neil would sardonically explain it to Clyde Ferritt: "Priding ourselves on always having marvellous times together, we decided, on Barrows' suggestion, to institutionalize that banal togetherness into a 'fraternity.' We invented a name shrouded in mawkishly facile mysticism of the us-against-them variety, and an identifying lapel pin of meaningless, but aesthetically repellent symbolism. I knew then that a disinterested appraisal of the track records of the members would rank our quality from mediocre to low, but I also noticed, as you will remember as well, Clyde, that the group became, after a few weeks of strutting self-puffery and display of ugly lapel pins, the single most sought after organization on campus among the great majority of students who had not demonstrated personal prominence in anything and would have no difficulty in accommodating themselves to the fraternity's basic tenet of scoffing at anyone who had."

Clyde Ferritt, of course, was a natural target. Yet, throughout that year, he always greeted Neil by name in a genial way whenever they met. But neither he nor Neil ever stopped for a chat in those days.

Ernest Godwin arranged a job for Neil with the Better Roads Corporation that summer. Percy Clapp's friend and financial supporter, Wolfe Tone McGrath, owned the company. Neil had expected to work on one of the company's projects in or near the city, but when he showed himself at head office, he discovered that he would be passing the summer at a construction camp in Tom the Bay, four hundred miles away. No change in job site was possible, said the personnel manager, as if he had anticipated the question. And upon arriving at the camp in Tom the Bay, Neil learned that the nearest settlement was thirty miles distant over a tote road, three hours of discomfort one way in a four wheel drive vehicle. Neil suspected in his father a motive ulterior to his son's gainful employment and he resented it.

By way of reply to Muck who, not having been able to find a job himself, described in his letters stimulating examples of his vagrancy in the city, Neil could only lament that the absence of any women in or near the construction camp guaranteed his finishing up the summer in Tom the Bay with a right palm on him like the pelt of a persian cat.

One night he sat down at the office typewriter to compose for Muck some raunchy slander against those who were responsible for the frustration, loneliness, and dudgeon he felt at being stuck in Tom the Bay all summer: Ernest Godwin, Percy Clapp, and Wolfe Tone McGrath. By the time he had finished typing a half dozen pages, however, the work had become a filthy allegory of the means used by Clapp and his henchmen to maintain themselves in power. He sent the sheets off to Muck.

When university began again in the fall, Neil and Muck laughed so much together at the piece that Neil suggested it be shown to their fraternity brothers. Muck agreed to let them see it.

The next day in the student commonroom, Neil heard the readers of his work attributing authorship to Muck Barrows between guffaws.

"Didn't you tell the boys I wrote it, Muck?" asked Neil.

"No way!" said Muck. "You'd get in the shit if someone in the president's office gets wind of that, or if fantastic Ferritt found out about it, so I'm not telling anyone who wrote it."

Neil thought Muck's attitude was somewhat extreme. The whole thing was only a bit of fun, sure, he said. Hearing their buddies laughing in the commonroom, Neil regretted that he was missing this chance to be regarded as the literary lion of the student body. Preserving the fingered and ragged pages became important to him now. He got them back from Muck and went to the Student Council office to copy them. Over the next few days, he thought, he would somehow modestly get it across to everyone that he was the author. Then he would see the looks of admiration, hear the congratulations.

The secretary at the council office insisted that she was the only one permitted to use the copier. Neil gave her the document, stressing its absolute privacy. Ten minutes passed before she returned to say the copier was not working. Looking away from him, she handed the sheets back without smiling.

The note two days later from University President Gorman requesting Neil's presence at his office contained no reason for the audience. Neil went there at the time indicated and saw President Gorman, three faculty members, Clyde Ferritt, and a man he did not know, huddled around the desk. They looked up at him from the papers in front of them.

"Be seated, Mr. Godwin," said President Gorman. "We are just concluding an irregular meeting of the University Discipline Committee. Let's see. You are acquainted with everyone? Mr. Ferritt is here as President of the Student Council and Mr. Randolph Rute is the representative from the Board of Regents." Neil recognized the latter name as belonging to a leading labour organizer. "Are you familiar with this, Mr. Godwin?" The president tossed over a copy of Neil's typewritten sheets and rubbed his fingertips on his lapel.

Neil picked up the papers and leafed through them as if genuinely curious about their contents. The obscenities leaped up at him and he tried to keep his face from reddening. To steady himself he stopped his eyes and read therein the description of Clapp's manner of dealing with his opponents:

> Clapp and his minions, Albert Toope, the Minister of Justice, Wolfe Tone McGrath, his financial supporter, and Clyde Ferritt, the Leader of his Party at the university, form a closed circle around each Opponent they encounter and perform a grotesque dance involving hard, synchronized kick-steps towards the centre of the circle. Clapp smiles and speechifies at Curious Observers, distracting their attention, until the Opponent is allowed to crawl away, trailing behind him a mess of puke, piss, snot, and shit. Head Gawker Godwin then comes on the scene and directs a group of willing Ordinary Citizens to pick up these substances and dump them in an urn labelled "The Blood, Sweat and Tears of our Great Leader," over which sacred receptacle the Head Gawker then declaims a moving benediction.

"Well, Mr. Godwin?" said President Gorman. Neil raised his hand slightly and skimmed on down through the sheets as if not yet quite certain whether he was familiar with this particular piece of work or not. His eye caught a portrayal of Clapp's relationship with the governed:

> There is a long queue of Ordinary People leading into Premier Clapp's office. All are naked, the shirts and drawers having been long ago stripped off them by successive governments. Despite that, the sole object of their visit to Clapp's office now is to entice him to screw them silly again. Inside his office, Clapp is obligingly banging away at them each in turn, male and female alike, while his official legal adviser, Albert Toope, holds open the appropriate orifice for him in each case, and Wolfe Tone McGrath guides Clapp's gargantuan gapstopper in. Clyde Ferritt is so smart, he has two jobs. First, he must hold one of Clapp's galloping gonads in each hand to keep his leader from rupturing himself in his zeal. And then, after Clapp is finished with each Ordinary Person, Clyde must brand across the cheeks of his or her arse, as a memento of the visit, words of the recipient's choice, such as: "Quaint Newfy

Accent," or "Newfy Hospitality," or "Salt-of-the-Earth Newf," or "Charming Newfy Way of Life." In the meantime, Clapp is regaling everyone with non-stop sweet talk and bombast, made impressive to Mainland Journalists by the intermingled exhortations to his own phallus paraphrased from Shakespeare. For instance: "And thou, all-quivering cunt-cleaver, smite wide the tight rotundity of this twat!" Throughout all this, Head Gawker Godwin intones a fervent appeal to God to sustain Clapp's hard-on to the benefit of us all, forever and ever amen.

Gentle Jesus! thought Neil, in the sober ambience of the president's office, *I must have been an out-and-out pervert when I wrote that stuff this summer.* He put the sheets down and nodded in the direction of the president, hoping he didn't look as shame-faced as he felt.

"I take it then, finally, that you *are* familiar with it," said President Gorman. "Now, gentlemen, let me repeat for Mr. Godwin's benefit what I said earlier, so that he may be fully seized of the seriousness of this matter. I received a phone call last night at home from the Honourable Albert Toope, the Minister of Justice. He was calling on Premier Clapp's behalf, he said. Somehow a copy of this document has come into the hands of Mr. Clapp. The premier, Mr. Toope said, believes that his first duty to this university is to protect its good name in the minds of the people. Therefore, Mr. Toope said, Mr. Clapp strongly suggests for the future good of the university that the creator and disseminator of this dirt, blasphemy, and slander must be expelled from this institution of higher learning. I agreed with Mr. Toope that extreme disciplinary measures are warranted for bringing the university into disrepute, and I told him to assure the premier that I would find and expel the student responsible." Everyone nodded thoughtfully, except Randolph Rute the labour leader who was rubbing his eyes and yawning, clearly out of his depth.

"Now, Mr. Godwin," Gorman began again. "Do you know who wrote this thing?" He stared at Neil over his glasses, waiting for him to say something. Neil remained silent. He dearly did not want to be thrown out of university in public ignominy. He saw his father's face. His heart and stomach felt fused into one heavy, sickly lump in his gorge. Then, a sense of outrage at being subjected to this rose in him and he was taken by a passion to grab the convincing, controlled president by his sapient white head and beat it against Clyde's simian brow until both dead and slippery weights fell from his grasp. He waited too long before acting, however, and the urge left him.

"It is bruited about the campus that a student probationer wrote it," resumed Gorman. "One David Barrows." Neil remained silent. "Come, come, Mr Godwin. I am told you are an acquaintance of Mr. Barrows, but any display of loyalty to him in these circumstances would be totally misguided. Surely you saw the blasphemous insult to your own father there, not to mention the libel of your father's friends, Premier Clapp and Wolfe Tone McGrath. So please confirm this detail of what we already know: Barrows is responsible for this?"

Neil longed for confidence to flow through him as it had done on the night in the alley with the sailors. He would take on this whole bloody lot as well. But confidence did not come. "No ... well, I don't think so," he mumbled.

"Your answer sounded *very* lacking in conviction, Mr. Godwin," said the president. "You don't think so? I hope I don't have to remind you of the consequences to yourself of deliberately misleading – "

"Hang on, hang on!" interrupted Rute, the labour leader. "I don't believe this!"

Neil readied himself for harassment from the new source, while Rute rubbed his eyes and shook his head sharply as if to clear his brain of the past hour of learned logorrhea.

"This is the first time," said Rute, "that I've been at one of these meetings, and I didn't say anything before because I was interested in learning the proper procedures first. Ha, ha, ha, ha. I've got to tell you the honest to God truth, now. I found your yarn here a little bit tame. Especially reading it right after coming from an organizing meeting with a shift of student nurses down at the children's hospital. I say, forget it. Forget the whole thing."

President Gorman forced himself not to return the condescending smiles regarding Rute aimed at him by the faculty members, and spoke as to a child. "Did you read it all, Mr. Rute? Did you see all the bad words in it? Premier Clapp is your friend, isn't he? And you're his friend too, aren't –"

"My opinion, representing the Board of Regents, is forget this tomfoolery," said Rute, standing. "This meeting's over, I hope?"

President Gorman was on his feet, too. "Of course, I value your opinion greatly, Mr. Rute, as I do the majority opinion that we must deal effectually with this folio of filth which is what our premier, Mr. Clapp, aptly called it. I shall study the matter further and call another meeting on it later before any action is taken, of course."

On the way out, Randolph Rute gave Neil a broad, grinning wink.

Passing off his visit to the president as complaints about class-cutting, Neil did not tell Muck he daily expected him to be summoned before the discipline committee. But when, after weeks had gone by, Muck was not summoned, Neil concluded that Rute's attitude must have prevailed and his anxiety over the possibility of having to sacrifice himself to save his buddy diminished.

Neil and Muck settled down a little during this term and their interests diverged somewhat. Muck joined the university Army Officers' Training Corps and begged Neil to do likewise. But Neil, after attending one familiarization session, declined. He found he shared none of Muck's growing fascination with rigidly ordered hierarchies and with analyzing the lines of interaction and control among the various agencies of Nazi Germany and of Communist Russia.

After the Christmas exam results for that year came out both friends were happy. Neil had done well, if not outstandingly, in all his courses, and Muck had passed four out of five, a marked improvement over the two out of five he'd passed at the end of his first year. Bent now on becoming an officer in the army upon graduation, Muck showed his new determination to work towards a good degree by studying constantly through the last week of the Christmas vacation.

The day before the new term started, Muck came to see Neil in dismay. He had just received a registered letter from the registrar's office stating that he had been refused re-admission for the new term, under a rule in the university calendar which required a student on probation to pass every subject in the examinations next following his being placed on probation. Neil was stunned. This was an unheard of application of that rule. Invariably, the passing of three out of five exams in the finals had been sufficient to allow re-admission, let alone the passing of four out of five at Christmas.

When Muck wondered whether he should go personally to see the president, Neil, with ambivalent feelings, encouraged him to do so. He came back from his visit in a baffled rage. "The rotten prick wouldn't even talk to me! He picks up a book and reads that goddamned rule out loud and says, 'You've desecrated the English language enough for fifty undergraduate careers.' Get out, he says. Jesus Christ, Neil! He was the one who was all frigged up. I passed my measly jeesly English course this year for fuck's sake. Got fifty-three this term in the lousy goddamned thing!"

Muck's letter to President Gorman to point out that there were other probationary students who had not passed all their exams but who had been re-admitted, received a terse reply: "In all of those cases, there are extenuating circumstances. In your case there are none."

Neither Clyde Ferritt nor anyone else on the Student's Council could see any way around the rule when Muck approached them. The personal intervention of his commanding officer in the Officers' Training Corps to state that Muck was first-rate officer material, was unavailing. Neil himself had been short on suggestions. He had thought about getting in touch with Randolph Rute of the Board of Regents regarding the injustice, but never acted on the thought.

Muck gave up and looked desultorily for a job. During the first weeks of the new semester, he hung around the commonroom waiting for Neil to finish his classes and go to the tavern with him. Neil began to avoid the commonroom and hid in the library. He stopped going to the tavern altogether. Muck was sure to be there, surrounded by a permanent court of other unemployed young men. Neil felt uncomfortable with Muck now. It was true that you began to despise the one you hurt, or allowed to be hurt, he thought, especially when there was no remedy. What could he do? Tell President Gorman he himself had written that piece of foolishness? That would only get himself in trouble and not help Muck. Gorman could not use it to go back on his official reason for turfing Muck out. There was nothing he could do, he reasoned, and he did nothing.

When Muck phoned to say he was leaving for the mainland in the morning as a private in the regular army, Neil detected the first note of sadness he'd ever heard in his voice. Instead of the relief at Muck's departure that he had expected to feel, Neil felt remorse and shame for his betrayal of his friend, and bitterness towards Clyde Ferritt and Gorman for putting him in a dilemma which revealed to him his own moral cowardice.

As for Percy Clapp, Neil no longer conceived of him as the Goofy Newfy. That mental representation had evanesced during the weeks following the meeting of the discipline committee. It was later, during a visit to the Marine Biology lab to see the monstrosity on exhibit there, that a new image of Clapp formed in Neil's mind. "Oh yes, oh yes," said the Biology Professor proudly, answering a question, as he fondled the head of the seventy foot long giant squid which had recently washed up dead on a beach. "Oh yes, indeed! This specimen, when it was alive in the ocean, was certainly capable of reaching up out of the murk with those tentacles and pulling a small, unsuspecting craft down below the surface...."

5

Neil spent his remaining time at the university on his studies, student activities, and sports. His grades were now among the best there. He filled top executive positions in a number of campus societies. His prowess in two carefully chosen non-team sports provoked praise in the student newspaper. He had many friends, but no best friend. He enjoyed being a loner – gregarious and outgoing in the eyes of others, but within himself, he knew, a loner. He would keep it that way henceforth, he told himself. It was his natural bent, from which his interlude with Muck was, and would remain, his only aberration. For, vaguely linked in his mind with being a loner was a growing sense of his own destiny. It was an abstract sense of destiny at present, though sometimes, different concrete delineations of it would throb ephemerally across his thoughts. It had only to settle into stable shape, he felt, and there was plenty of time for that.

Neil had some pleasant conversations with Clyde Ferritt during Clyde's last year at the university. He had tried for several months after Muck's expulsion to maintain an open contempt for Clyde, but gradually he faltered. Clyde initiated chats whenever they found themselves near each other. Soon, every time they encountered one another, they lingered together a little longer than necessary and talked. But right up to Clyde's departure they never deliberately sought out each other's company. Neil thought he could sometimes detect a flavour of condescension in Clyde's dealings with him.

After Clyde was selected Rhodes Scholar and left for

Oxford, Neil had to admit that he missed him. He found that he had enjoyed Clyde's cynical first reaction to everything he heard or saw, a reaction expressed in sardonic one-liners. In content, they were similar to Neil's own attitude, though he knew he could not yet match Clyde in form.

During his last year at university, Neil decided that he, too, would apply for the Rhodes Scholarship. He discussed it with his father. Ernest and he were friendly and close now. Ernest had been tactful enough not to display too much joy at Muck Barrows' disappearance from his son's life. Only once in that respect had Neil overheard him extolling to his mother the potency of persistent prayer. In their conversations, Ernest proceeded on the premise that Neil's talents and potential were limitless. Neil often felt pregnant with glorious expectations afterwards, accepting as a normal concomitant the occasional lurch of anxiety in his gut. He was surprised, therefore, when Ernest advised him not to apply for the Rhodes this year. He asked why not and his father told him.

One hundred years before, Newfoundland had gone through a period of Northern Ireland-like sectarian violence. The little colony's leaders had been wise enough to devise an expedient to extend what could have been merely another short truce into everlasting peace. They had put in place a system to ensure equitable representation based on religion in all public institutions. The religious representation was along the lines of Anglican, Roman Catholic, and Dissenters (all the others). Thus, the Supreme Court Bench would always consist of an Anglican, a Catholic, and a member of another denomination. Prime ministers would strive to build their Cabinets in a similar fashion. The leadership and membership of government boards and agencies would be distributed among the three religious divisions with jealously watched scrupulousness. Schools would operate on a denominational basis, funded fairly by the government. Jobs in the public service would be obtained by merit tests within a scheme of tacitly agreed quotas.

The whole was a system for the general good, designed to make sectarian peace prevail. And sectarian peace did prevail. Violence based on dogma disappeared. Everyone knew where he stood. No one could complain that one division was shown more favour than another. Everyone could expect fair treatment within the system. One simply had to play by the rules, and all were expected to do so.

"Therefore, Neil," said Ernest, "I would strongly advise you to apply for the Rhodes next year. Last year, an Anglican, Clyde Ferritt, won it. This year is the turn of a Catholic. Next year come the others, of which you as my son are one."

Neil was well aware of the general system, of course; but he argued against the possibility of its applying to a scholarship so entirely based on an individual's scholastic, leadership, and athletic qualities, and he knew there was no one else graduating this year whose combination of these qualities approached his own. Even if the formula described by Ernest had applied to the scholarship in close cases, it would not be applied flagrantly against an unmistakably better qualified person. Despite Ernest's head shaking and admonitions to be reasonable, Neil submitted his application with confidence.

Following the interviews and the selection, Neil congratulated the winner, a nephew of a monsignor, warmly. He was not boorish enough to point out to anyone the substantial disparity in his favour between his own exam results, sports achievements, and student activities, and those of the new Rhodes Scholar. Except to his father at home.

"I get the picture," he announced sarcastically. "Destroy the chances of a deserving individual to feed the egos of competing witch doctors!" He had more to say, but he stopped, suddenly remembering his father's vocation. "I'll try again next year."

"It's worse than you think," Ernest informed him. "There has never been a case here, I understand, where a person who unsuccessfully applied for the Rhodes one year has won it the next."

"What?" Neil was amazed. "What a paltry little shit heap this place is, to be sure! You're telling me I am completely screwed because of the incantation that was muttered over me at birth?" Again he stopped, puzzled at the ambiguous expression on his father's face. It looked like a smile but it must have been a frown at his use of too vigorous language.

"I won't say I told you so," said Ernest. "But I do say: learn the moral. Play by the rules. And beat them all at their petty little game."

"Shag their games," snapped Neil. "As soon as I get my degree here, I'm off to somewhere civilized where they've at least heard of the concept of meritocracy."

"We'll see what happens," his father replied. "Keep working for a good honours degree."

Within a month, Wolfe Tone McGrath announced that his company was establishing a foundation to award an annual scholarship to graduates of the local university. It was something he had been contemplating doing for years past, he said. The scholarship was equal in financial value to the Rhodes, but superior in that it was tenable at any university of the recipient's choice in the world. The foundation would see to the scholarship winner's admittance.

Wolfe Tone McGrath was the scion of one of the few continuously successful fish merchant families. His father's wealth had paid his fees and his own intelligence had earned him degrees from Harvard and the Sorbonne. Later, he had spent a year directing a nearly successful fight against Percy Clapp's ascendancy to the premiership. Having won the election, Clapp had courted the young McGrath publicly, explaining that, "Our population is so small while our problems are so enormous that I cannot afford to waste the brains of this brilliant man on fruitless conflict." McGrath had succumbed to the ardour of his suitor.

Striking out on his own, McGrath established a road construction company which, by local standards, became a gigantic empire. Wagging tongues attributed his business successes to his new friendship – malicious tongues said, partnership – with Percy Clapp. It was now Clapp himself who introduced the legislation in the House to establish the Better Roads Scholarship Trust, with a selection committee consisting of Wolfe Tone McGrath and his nominees.

"A lovely game," muttered Neil, when his father encouraged him to put his application in at once. "I'll go along with it this time, just to get out of this place for good."

A week before the interviews, however, Neil learned that

the rules were subject to change without notice while the game was in progress. McGrath and Clapp had just had a public and acrimonious falling out. No reason for the rupture was stated by either party. In the St. John's taverns, polemics on the issue raged between those who argued that the breach was McGrath's fault because he had not contributed enough to what was loosely described as Clapp's election fund, and those who argued that Clapp was to blame because he had not handed McGrath a satisfactory number of government road construction contracts without public tender. Whatever the real reason for it, this abrupt termination of a fast friendship of nearly ten years standing provoked a highly audible and entertaining debate between the two men, each developing, with respect to the other, specifics on the theme of whose hind legs – not to mention front legs – were deeper in the public trough.

When Neil was called to go in for his interview, he entered with the awareness that his father's well known support for Percy Clapp had suddenly become a decided liability. Ernest himself had protested his continued confidence too much all week. Sitting down at the table, Neil spotted the familiar bearded face of Wolfe Tone McGrath. He looked extremely grouchy, no doubt because of the labour unrest that had plagued his company all year, and the fact that, latterly, Percy Clapp had been the reverse of helpful to him in these difficulties. Where formerly, Clapp used to refer to McGrath as "this epitome of humanity in private enterprise and public weal," he had, during the past week, and in one television interview alone, adverted to McGrath as Simon Legree's lash, Atilla the Hun's hit man, Torquemada's moral disciple, Captain Bligh's boots, and the Pharisees' factotum. He had also made mention of, "this fellow McGrath's fat purse, over-gorged and bloated with his downtrodden workers' rightful earnings."

Before Neil had quite settled into his chair, he heard the thick, neckless man next to McGrath mutter, "Jeez, that's Ern Godwin's young fella, en't it? En't they Clappers to the backbone?" McGrath put his finger to his lips.

The chairman, McGrath's lawyer, coughed and immediately asked Neil what he considered to be "the single greatest problem facing mankind at this particular point in time." Neil saw the faces of starving children, thought about the atomic weapons that were becoming as common as political megalomania, remembered the killing wars. He opened his mouth several times to emit a bromide, but the words, "Play the game!" kept running through his head and prevented him. Whispering started, and the secretary of the committee was writing on his paper with deliberation.

Neil looked directly at McGrath and said: "I think the greatest problem in the world today is the concentration of vast, uncontrolled power in the hands of people who feel no vestigial glimmer of responsibility to exercise it to the benefit of anyone but themselves."

Everyone around the table quickly looked at his shoes, studied his nails, examined the ceiling, or gazed out the window. All moved their jaw muscles. Neil's words were precisely those used in the newspaper the day before by Percy Clapp with reference to McGrath. The industrialist looked calmly back at Neil for a minute and nodded to his blocky oddjob beside him.

This latter undid the button of his jacket and barked, "You better elluserdate that assertation for the bo—for these fine gentlemen, my friend." There were unconcealed sighs of relief around the table as the world re-balanced itself.

"For example," said Neil, "take the labour movement and trade unionism generally. Laudable in concept, yes, but totally insidious and unfair in the way unions have been encouraged by irresponsible political leaders, to operate in practice: answerable to no laws, and arrogating onto themselves ever more power with no commensurate responsibility. The laws should be as rigorously applied to unions, as entities, as to any other legal person or corporation. Then labour leaders would not be able, with the tacit approval of politicians, to wink at the illegal activities of their members, which risk destroying the life's work of an enterprising individual, and with it the best interests of the workers themselves."

By now, McGrath was nodding slowly and thoughtfully, and the rest of the table, particularly those whose research work or legal fees or subcontracts depended on his whim, looked like hens apecking. For the next twenty minutes, Neil and McGrath were engaged, to the exclusion of all the others (except for their chorus of concurring "ah's" and "mm's"), in a cordial dialogue on the legal and social climate requisite to the fostering of benign self-aggrandizement and enlightened opportunism.

Within the month, Wolfe Tone McGrath publicly announced that: "In the election of Mr. Neil Godwin as our first Better Roads Scholar, my fondest hopes respecting excellence of mind, body, and positive attitude have been fully realized." He telephoned Neil to ask him to dinner.

McGrath's home was unpretentious on the outside. Inside, Neil expected to find compensating splendour, but the interior seemed spartan to him. Only after several minutes did he realize that his eye could be made to see pleasing objects in agreeable locations in every room he entered. McGrath's wife welcomed him with an attitude that put Neil at his ease and then left the two men alone. She played clarinet in the fledgling symphony orchestra and had a practice to attend.

"What kind of music do you like yourself, Neil?" asked McGrath. "I assume your tastes there, as elsewhere, are catleek." He grinned as he gave a St. John's pronunciation to the word.

Neil chuckled and said, "Yes, sir. But some pieces move me more than others. Gluck's overture to *Iphigénie en Aulide*, for example." He'd heard this the day before in the university music room and hoped what he considered to be its relative obscurity would be impressive.

McGrath stopped on his way to the shelves of records and turned around. "My God," he said. "Neil, is that the truth?" He made the sound of the four upbeat notes and blinked his eyes. "Ah, those four brutal notes. Recurring, relentless doom. I haven't listened to it for fifteen years. But when I used to, it brought tears to my eyes every time. Not only the sound of the great music itself, but also what it evoked. Father Agamemnon's pleas to heaven to prevent the consequences of his own moral cowardice. All unavailing. Artemis' merciless heavenly wrath. Achilles' powerless love. Clytemnestra's maternal tenderness transformed to wifely hate. Iphigenia's innocent filial devotion. And her slaughter so that a mob of men could redeem their manhood in pursuit of a brazen whore. How true it all was! Jesus. Let's hear it."

Neil nodded, slightly amazed by how much had *not* been evoked in him on his first hearing of the short overture. No tears came to McGrath's eyes this time, though. He smiled throughout, alternately gazing at Neil and out the window into the dark.

During dinner, McGrath's manner was that of one man speaking to another as an equal. He was at least as interested in hearing Neil's views as in giving his own. Neil was greatly attracted to him. He had never before met a person so well-read, well-spoken, and clear-thinking, and so broadly and deeply knowledgeable in the arts and practicalities of life.

At the end of the evening, McGrath asked Neil what university he wanted to attend and Neil said he would like to read law at Oxford. McGrath undertook to work on his admission to a college there.

Neil spent a day or two each month with McGrath during the spring and summer, either at his house or flying in the small aircraft he piloted. And whenever McGrath got back from an out of town trip he would telephone Neil the same day for a chat.

At dinner together two weeks before Neil was to leave for England, they discussed local politics for the first time. "This question may be improper, Neil," said McGrath, "considering the great friendship between him and your father all these years. But if you will answer, tell me: what do you think of Percy Clapp?"

"Not improper at all, Wolfe Tone," Neil replied. "Not at all. My father's friendships are not necessarily my own. And as far as Percy Clapp specifically is concerned, I can say that I have never appreciated his style of political leadership in the least."

"You know, Neil," said McGrath, "I very nearly engineered the defeat of Clapp ten years ago. Then I was stupid enough to think I could effect salutary change from the inside. Christ! But let me tell you something in utmost confidence. The next time someone good takes him on, I will see to it that he *is* beaten. I believe profoundly that Clapp has got to be stopped, now more than ever. He'll destroy Newfoundland if he's ever able to get his hands on the kind of money that will become available from commercial offshore oil discoveries." Neil agreed without knowing or asking how.

"Neil, think of this," resumed McGrath, with a dreamy look in his eyes. "If the vast revenues projected from the offshore oil ever do materialize, we will have an opportunity here to turn our little island into a beautiful Renaissance bloom. I believe that the flowerings which took place in Athens, Florence, and Elizabethan London, for example, were not mystical, inexplicable happenings. I believe that if a reasonably large sample of humans is taken (the six or seven hundred thousand here would be enough), and if the conditions, opportunities, stimuli, leadership, sense of worth and excellence as individuals and as a group, cross-fertilization of ideas, and so on, are provided and fostered, a flowering of artistry and creativity will take place as necessarily and as logically as any other cause and effect relationship that we can perceive and understand. What could have been culturally lower initially than those first Venetians who took to the lagoons to avoid the Hun, or those wretched early Aztecs driven to a marshy island in Lake Texcoco? Our own doomed aboriginal Beothucks didn't *have* to perish without a whimper, leaving no fruit."

Neil and McGrath exchanged ideas on this subject for a while, becoming excited, over their fourth cognac, at the thought of using the offshore oil income to create a cultural jewel in Newfoundland, based on all the province's indigenous qualities. It would be much better than simply allowing the place to turn into a crass, middle-class suburb of Toronto as, they both agreed, would be Percy Clapp's inclination.

"I noticed in your application for the scholarship," said McGrath, as they lingered at the door and talked, "that you may be interested in going into politics when you get back from university. I have a lot of money, Neil. An awful lot. And I want to do something sensible with it. I'm not suited for political leadership myself. But I am prepared to spend all my money, every cent of it, in getting rid of Clapp and putting in a group of people who are interested in effecting the ideas we discussed tonight. I'd like to see you head up that group, become premier here in other words. Don't worry about being too young. It's a long term thing. I'm under no illusions about Percy's strength in the country. It'll take a couple of elections after you come back to get rid of him. You'll be old enough then. Give it some thought over the next couple of years. In the meantime, we'll stay in close touch and I'll do some spadework back here, starting with a few darts at Percy in the election I believe he intends to call this fall."

Driving home from Wolfe Tone McGrath's house that night, Neil felt he knew something of what Montaigne had written. Here was a friend. Their decade and a half difference in age was nothing. Neil loved the man. He could see the two of them in the distance together and he experienced a stronger sense of purpose than ever in his life before. The amorphous blob of his destiny had assumed a settled, concrete shape.

6

Percy Clapp strode into Ernest Godwin's house and his small, energetic form took over all the space. The other guests, it seemed to Neil, were jerked from their chairs to their feet and sucked into a circle around him. Neil hung back with Jane by the wall and noticed that Clapp's eye was on him as he said hello to the others. Then he broke away and came over to Neil. He openly studied him and his sister for a good thirty seconds, then said, fervently, over his shoulder: "Good heavens, Ernest, how blessed you are to have two such bright and handsome children! It's been years since I had a good look at them. I forget. Are they twins?"

"No, they're not, Perce, ah, Mr. Prime Minister," said Ernest. It irritated Neil that his father would feel constrained to use, after twenty-five years of friendship, a formal mode of address. "No, there's three or four years between them. Neil here is our bayman, born in Maggotty Cove Motion just after I began my preaching over there."

"Yes, yes, I remember, I remember," smiled Clapp. "Ah, Maggotty Cove Motion. Lovely authentic name. *So* superior to the Silver Surf or Blue Foam or Golden Sands or Green Glades, or whatever it was that the people there were petitioning the government to change the name to a couple of years back. A bayman, hey? Great political asset, that, being born out there in the bays instead of in here in the city. Nurture that start, Neil. Neil? Nurture that start."

"Neil is off to Oxford University in a week," said Ernest.

"Oh yes, yes, I know, I know. You won that scholarship set

up by the famous Wolfe Tone McGrath, didn't you? I don't blame you for accepting that, incidentally. Admired you, in fact, under the circumstances. Showed you were not small minded. The song, not the singer: a good philosophy to have in politics where you're flung in willy nilly with God knows what unedifying specimens of humanity from day to day. I assume on faith alone that some of them are human." Clapp took Neil and sister Jane each by an arm. "They look enough alike to be twins, though, Ern. They are virtually identical. They could be the male and female counterpart of the same person. Plato should be here. Truly handsome. A delight to the eye. And here's the triplet." He now took both of Neil's mother's hands between his own. The lines of annoyance in her face at his nearly spoiling her dinner by being an hour late disappeared. "There's no doubt about who has all the dominant genes in your marriage, Ernie, my friend. Your genes have been utterly effaced by those of your good wife in these bright and beautiful progeny. Fortunately."

Laughing, Ernest led everyone into the dining room. Neil felt he had just met Clapp in person for the first time. Clapp's nimbus of fame and notoriety since he had become premier made him a different man now from the one who had hung around Ernest's house when Neil had been a child. Although he had continued to drop by their home after having become premier, Clapp's visits had been not only much less frequent, but had involved merely a quick entry, a closed-door meeting with Ernest in the study for half an hour, and a quick exit, two or three harried-looking assistants chasing him to his car.

This dinner was the first purely social visit Clapp had made to their house during the past eight years. When his father had discussed it with his mother three days ago, Neil got the impression that the suggestion had come from Clapp himself. Neil had been happy to reply to Ernest's numerous requests for assurances that, yes, he would definitely be present at the premier's dinner. He had been curious to see and hear what the great man would be like at a small private dinner, anyway; and the thought that he was secretly planning with McGrath to take Clapp on in a few years would add a certain piquancy to the occasion for Neil.

It was not surprising that Clapp's three ministers and party president were eclipsed by the premier's conversation around the table, but Neil had not expected his father, who normally dominated a group verbally, to be so overshadowed as well. And, to his own chagrin, Neil found himself more than once groping clumsily for simple words with which to express an uncomplicated thought, feeling as if he were committing trespass on Clapp's ownership of the air. Eighteen-year-old Jane alone seemed undiminished in stature. As usual, she said what she wanted to say, clearly, intelligently, and succinctly.

The premier listed a dozen names of prominent men he would be approaching soon to see if they might be interested in becoming his candidates in the next election. Randolph Rute the labour leader and President Gorman of the university were among them, Neil noted. "And what I want from you, Ern," said Clapp, "is the name of one of your best men who – "

"Or best women," added Jane.

"Or best women, of course," said Clapp, nodding gravely at her, "who will become a candidate for me and go into a top portfolio in my Cabinet."

Ernest promised to think of a name and grinned towards Neil: "But if this were the election after the one coming up, Mr. Prime Minister, I wouldn't have to think long."

"You know, Ern," said Clapp without pause, "it's too bad Neil here is not yet finished his studies and ready to go right now. I am very much aware of his great interest in politics."

While Neil was wondering how Clapp had arrived at that awareness, a minister who had only simpered all evening now opened his mouth for the first time. "Talking about Wolfe Tone McGrath," he blurted, "do you think, sir, he intends to come out against us in the election, what with his millions?"

Clapp chuckled as if to dismiss the concept as irrelevant and turned icy eyes on Neil. "Give us *your* views on that, Mr. Godwin!" he ordered.

Caught off guard, and feeling that he had not acquitted himself well in conversation earlier, or perhaps unconsciously wishing to ingratiate himself by revealing impressive and novel information, Neil spoke out in one impulsive spurt. "McGrath's a very definite threat, I'd say, sir – he'll spend every cent to get rid of Percy Clapp, he says." Neil felt his face flush as he spoke, and when he'd finished he was overwhelmed by dismay at his breach of confidence.

Jane, who alone knew something of Neil's talks with McGrath, stared at him in amazement. Ernest Godwin darted his eyes from face to face smiling proudly.

Everyone else was looking at Clapp whose veins had just stood out briefly on his temples. He smiled wanly and said, with a chortle of amused contempt in his voice, "Wolfe Tone McGrath. I'll give him Wolfe Tone." He scanned faces to confirm that no one of Irish descent was present. "You can only admire the brass of these bogtrotters. Starving to death in the peat bogs back home. Lace curtain radicals no less over here. They should clean out their own political cesspool there before they smear their excrement on our faces here." Neil recalled that McGrath had told him about his forbears leaving Cork for Newfoundland in 1780. "Wolfe Tone McGrath should remember the time he took me on once before," continued Clapp. "I routed him then, and I was only a political babe. If he tries again, if he should dare to try again, I shall bury him!"

Clapp stood abruptly and went to the hall closet. His face seemed pale under his black hat when he emerged. He thanked Mrs. Godwin for the superb meal, apologized for not being able to take time from pressing public affairs to stay for coffee and, in the middle of saying goodbye to the others, turned to Neil.

"Oh, by the way, Neil, Clyde Ferritt dropped in to see me the other day. He's back from Oxford for three weeks and is giving me a hand with some of the political stuff. Doing an excellent job of it, I must say. We've got a speaking tour laid on for a few days this week, starting tomorrow. Come along with us."

Neil demurred. He felt more like crawling under a rock and staying there until he left for England. "I've got too much to get ready for Oxford, I'm afraid, sir," he said. But Clapp insisted, saying the tour would last only three days, would be a tremendous experience for him, and would give him a chance to talk to Clyde about Oxford. Neil looked away from his father's vigorously nodding head and agreed to go.

When the other guests had left, he called McGrath's house intending to tell him the cat was out of the bag, but the housekeeper said Mr. and Mrs. McGrath were somewhere on the mainland and not due back till late tomorrow. That night, Neil's dream was a blend of distorted faces and throttling tentacles involving Clapp, McGrath, himself, and the giant squid. There was a lot of anger and anxiety, but no discernible plot and no resolution of tension. Awake in the morning light, however, Neil felt that his disclosure to Clapp last evening had not really been as heinous as he had thought. He had, he reasoned, only restated what everyone already knew and what McGrath had not taken many pains to conceal.

Ernest drove Neil out to Paddy's Pond where the government float plane was kept. He told his son that, having been singled out by the prime minister like this, he had but to keep his nose clean and his political future was assured. Neil held his tongue, but he was irritated that his father would feel he needed help from Percy Clapp or anyone else to gain entry to something so contemptibly easy as local politics.

Six Ministers of the Crown were already assembled on the wharf by the small plane, each in his roomy black Homburg and heavy black overcoat. Neil had already taken off his own jacket because of the day's warmth. When Clyde Ferritt arrived with Clapp, he greeted Neil as an old buddy. But his affability did seem to decrease thereafter in inverse proportion to the attention the premier paid to Neil before the ministers.

The pilot announced that there was one passenger too many to comply with Department of Transport safety regulations. The ministers ignored him and moved towards the plane. "The captain is the boss on that, boys," said Clapp, and the ministers stopped in their tracks incredulously. They shook their heads in admiration of their master's large mindedness, his great man's acceptance of a small man's fiat. The pilot beamed. Everyone looked around to see who would be left behind. Eyes settled momentarily on Neil – Clyde Ferritt's stayed longest – and moved on.

"I'll stay," announced Neil, and everyone moved towards the plane at this obvious solution, finally articulated.

"Don't be silly, Mr. Godwin," said Clapp. "You're my guest. Jim, you don't need to go on this junket."

"Whatever you say, Prime Minister," replied the minister addressed; but Neil heard him whisper fiercely to a colleague after Clapp was on board, "Goddamn it, if the Minister of Forestry don't need to go on this trip, who do?"

A few minutes after they were airborne, Clapp took a pile of papers out and started to look through them. "Jim! Jim! Jim!" he roared over the engines. "What in the name of God does this gibberish mean? Jim!"

"You asked him to stay behind, sir," said Clyde.

"The Minister of Forestry stayed behind on a tour designed to explain the proposed development of a gigantic paper mill to the people?" bellowed Clapp. "What have I got myself surrounded with at all? Am I beset by imbeciles? Will someone tell me that?" He began to chuckle and then everyone laughed hugely.

During the next three days the plane landed at half a dozen communities. At each stop, there was a public meeting to which, apparently, all living souls in the place came. At every meeting, Clapp spoke for an hour and a half without a note in his hand: reeling off numbers and converting them back and forth between cords of wood and tons of paper; naming the twelve (only) pulp and paper mills in the world larger than this proposed one; listing the specific related industries which would inevitably be attracted, and the nature and number of jobs thereby created in each village; explaining the multiplier effect in the creation of even more jobs; and estimating with specific figures what the tremendous increase in population and property values would be. In each settlement, he was carried back to his seat in the audience by several stalwarts amid three cheers, and stout women seized him and kissed him.

While the Minister of Municipal Affairs droned out an explanation of maps, graphs, charts, pictures, and multi-coloured columns, showing astronomical increases in the *indicia* of progress, and architectural concepts of super-highways, massive government buildings, underground shopping malls, four tier parking garages, and ten thousand seat stadiums, Clapp paced the back of the hall. Scores of people went up to him with widely ranging requests for help. He spoke with all of them, dictating into his small portable machine the essence of each request and playing it back for the delighted supplicant to hear. All petitioners went back to their seats in satisfaction, especially since Clapp had prefaced each entry with an emphatic, "Action!" This informal court completely disrupted the remarks of the other speakers, since everyone in the place turned around and looked at Clapp each time his stentorian whisper issued from the back of the hall.

After one of the stops, Neil found himself seated next to the premier on the plane. "That municipal plan was a little elaborate for a place with a present population of two hundred and fifty people, wasn't it?" he suggested.

"Oh, that's just that bloody fool of a Sam," said Clapp, nodding and smiling at the Minister of Municipal Affairs who had turned to grin at hearing the mention of his name over the engines. "He's entirely in the grip of a mad planner from Ottawa he's taken on as Director of Urban and Rural Planning. Pay no attention to him, Neil. None. None whatsoever."

They spent the third night of their tour in a settlement identified as Falmouth's Hall on the map and called Famish All by its residents. Perhaps, surmised Neil, the realities of life here had corrupted, in their descendants, all the hopes of the original settlers. The next morning, another small aircraft landed in the harbour. Clyde came into the dining room of the boarding house and said to Clapp, "That must be Mr. Toope now, sir."

Clapp spent twenty minutes alone with Toope on the wharf, his head down, pacing about, sometimes gesticulating forcefully. Toope got aboard his aircraft again and departed. Clapp came quickly back to the boarding house. "The Minister of Justice reports some political slippage on the west coast, boys. Same old story. They feel ignored because of their distance from the capital. We need to do some shoring up.

Clyde, arrange a public meeting in Corner Brook for tonight. Don't worry, Neil, we'll have you back in plenty of time." Neil wondered why the Minister of Justice had to fly all the way there to have a long, private conversation with Clapp about something which could have been mentioned in a short telephone call.

Clapp and his party put up at a hotel in Corner Brook that afternoon. Before, during, and after dinner, Clapp consumed a surprising amount of sweet sherry, red wine, and colourless licorice liqueur for someone who was represented to the electorate as a near teetotaller: "Never touched a drop of liquor in my life. A touch of light wine such as is used at the altar, occasionally perhaps. But liquor? Not a drop in my *entire* life!"

At the designated hour after dinner, Neil went up to Clapp's suite. When he knocked on the door, it was immediately opened a crack to Clyde Ferritt's, "Shhhh! The skipper is having a nap." Neil crept in on tiptoe. There on the sofa was the premier, sound asleep, surrounded by six silent, motionless men in Homburg and overcoat. Clyde slouched around soundlessly in his pinstripe suit and light-brown hushpuppies. The ministers stayed in their positions for another half hour, making signs, mouthing words, and grinning at one another like orangutans.

Neil found it hard to hide his disgust. Why had Clapp not gone into his adjoining bedroom for a nap and allowed the others to talk in the sitting room? Could the man be that egocentric, imposing himself in such a way on his colleagues and friends, when he could have enjoyed the privacy of his bedroom while they had a relaxed chat? And why did the ministers put up with it? But as Neil observed the men around the room he began to realize that it was no imposition at all. They were only too delighted to be there like that. The imposition was on Clapp. It was just another one of the chores he imposed on himself to flatter his followers.

That night at the meeting in the overflowing hall, Clapp had Neil and Clyde sit on the stage with the ministers and some local notables. Several people spoke ahead of Clapp, who, Clyde said, always spoke last at purely political meetings. Neil mused on how easy it would be to speak to this crowd and what a poor job of it the other speakers were making. How exhilarating it would be to sway this audience, carry them along, make them yours! When Clapp got up to speak, he came over to Neil. "Would you like to say a few words?" he asked.

Neil's bowels turned alternately to water and stone. "Not right at the moment, sir," he muttered. "Perhaps at another meeting."

Clapp patted him on the shoulder and said, "Plenty of time to work yourself up to that. Okay, Clyde, you go."

Clyde made a speech about the new generation that was too long, Neil thought. And Clapp must have agreed because twice he compressed his lips and frowned at Neil.

Clapp himself was soon in full oratorical flight. He never once touched on a matter of government policy, but the spleen and humour poured out of him on every other subject. Twice he pointed out Clyde Ferritt and Neil Godwin as, "the living symbolic proof of tomorrow's great hope," and joked about having to watch out for his own job in a few years, what with brilliant young men ("near geniuses") like them around, impatiently waiting to take the bit between their teeth. The crowd roared their appreciation for everything he said, and Neil had to acknowledge to himself that he could have listened to him with enjoyment for hours.

During one dramatic pause, a heckler started up and continued to interject thereafter. Clapp skewered him several times to the immense delight of everyone, but he would not keep quiet. Finally, Clapp said, "I want to hear what you are saying, but I cannot. Come up here." Up swaggered a drunken young buck. "What you are saying is important," Clapp maintained. "Everyone should have the right to hear that. Come up to the mike." He reached down, took the other's hand, and literally lifted onto the stage a man nearly twice his own weight and one third his age. Neil could see the instantaneous bunching and relaxing of the muscles in his neck as he focussed his strength and made the pull. Clapp led the heckler to the microphone and held up his hand for silence. The hall became deathly quiet. The young man looked out onto the hundreds of grinning, expectant faces, uttered some sounds comprehensible only to himself, and then looked desperately to Clapp for help. Clapp lifted over his own chair and sat the frozen disrupter down; and he stayed there, immobile and red-faced, his hands clasped on his lap, his eyes on the toes of his boots, for the rest of the meeting.

The minister next to Neil leaned over, nodding his head sagely. "Percy goodens them like that every time," he whispered.

Clapp finished the sentence he had been speaking when last interrupted, and then launched into an attack on an old political opponent who still lived there in Corner Brook with his family, even though he had long ago retired from politics. For twenty minutes Clapp revived or manufactured a memory of the man and smeared it. Neil gazed in wonder and fascination at the audience, a mixture of the commonalty with a large sprinkling of business-suited men and wide-hatted women, nearly all of them with their faces flushed and their hands raised and their mouths wide open, applauding and cheering Clapp's rant of execration against a forgotten political opponent of the distant past. Simultaneously, Neil felt repelled by their loss of self-discipline and drawn by Clapp's total control. In the end, Clapp was hoisted by a dozen brawny men and carried out to his car through the cheering crowd.

In Clapp's suite afterwards, the premier said they'd better have a couple more public meetings down the coast tomorrow before going back. Neil apologized for having to leave by commercial aircraft in the morning. He must go home to prepare his things for his departure by ship in two days, he said. Clapp wouldn't hear of it. "You'll have lots of time," he said, "and I want to listen to you speak at tomorrow's meetings. I'm disappointed I didn't hear you tonight."

Neil spent most of the night, asleep and awake, mentally composing his speech. Early in the morning he got up and began to write notes on one side of an envelope. That showed the right combination of nonchalance and preparedness, he thought. By the time he finished (including the writing out of whole key paragraphs), he had covered seven envelopes. While he waited for his breakfast to be brought up to his room, he practised drawing the envelopes smoothly, inconspicuously, and quickly from his pocket.

Clapp held three meetings that day. Before the first, Neil could hardly talk to his companions for fear of forgetting his thoughts. But once he stood before the crowd on the stage and began to speak, he felt himself to be in his proper *milieu*. He pontificated with ease on the need for a government to combine the new and untried with the old and proved, the energy of youth with the wisdom of age. He made the morning crowd of mostly elderly men and women laugh at his quote of the hoary saying: "It's too bad youth is wasted on the young"; and revealed to them that in fact, rightly used, youth need not be so wasted. At the end of his peroration calling everyone to action, young, middle-aged, and old alike, he retired to his seat to a good loud clap.

Clapp praised both Neil and Clyde equally during his remarks. But two ministers whispered to Neil afterwards that the prime minister had thought young Godwin had a much better way with words.

The final meeting of the day took place after supper, which meant they would have to spend the night in the community. Neil didn't mind now. He was pleased with himself. He felt that his speech had become even better each time he had spoken, and the others confirmed it. Twice during their late night snack, he caught himself offering helpful advice to Clyde on public speaking.

In bed, Neil wallowed in his triumph for a while. Then he thought about how he would tell Wolfe Tone McGrath of his success as a political speechmaker and of his close observation of his future antagonist. He would also explain away his inadvertent disclosure to Clapp of McGrath's intentions – but that blunder seemed rather minor now.

During breakfast the next morning at dawn, the pilot phoned St. John's from the hall of the boarding house to check on the weather. He could be heard responding "Oh, my God," "Bad, bad," and "Don't tell me that," to the voice on the end of the line; and Neil cursed to himself, running over in his mind how long it would take to get home by car if bad weather forced them to drive.

The pilot came into the dining room. "Did anyone hear it on the news? A private plane crashed on takeoff from St. John's yesterday evening."

"I heard something on the radio about it late last night," Clapp admitted. "Who was it?"

"They haven't released any names yet," said the pilot. "I was only talking to meteorology. One person hurt bad, they said. Do you want me to call the tower and see what I can dig up, Mr. Prime Minister?"

"What on earth for?" replied Clapp. "What's the weather like in St. John's?"

"Good."

"Then let's go."

"Lord Jesus," said Neil. Blighted hopes, guilt, suspicion – a vision of Toope and Clapp alone on the wharf – all surged through him in an instant. "Wolfe Tone McGrath!"

"What are you saying, Neil?" blared Clapp. "How do you know it was McGrath?" The anger in his eyes was real.

"He has a private plane," murmured Neil.

"Would that we were so lucky! How many private planes operate out of that airport, Captain, in the run of a week?"

"Oh, my goodness, sir, dozens," said the pilot.

Half an hour after they were airborne, the co-pilot opened the door to the cockpit and passed out a note to Clapp. He read it and shouted, "The pilot of the plane that crashed was Wolfe Tone McGrath. He's alive but his injuries are critical. Precognition, Neil?"

Everyone stared at Neil. He did not reply. It was like old news. He experienced nothing beyond the numbness he already felt in his limbs. His mind focussed, not on the accident itself, but on Clapp's use of the wrong term to describe the presentiment he'd had earlier.

Ernest Godwin was waiting for Neil on the wharf when the plane put down. A number of ministerial assistants were standing with him. The talk was all about McGrath. Neil stood back and heard it flow.

"Plane was demolished."

"Eye witness thought it stalled from too steep a climb after takeoff."

"Stupid thing for McGrath to do. Been flying since he was a boy."

"He's in a bad way. Skull fracture. Broken legs. Lungs punctured by his ribs. That's only the first report."

"Good God," broke in Clapp. "I wouldn't wish it on my worst enemy. We'll bury the hatchet with McGrath because of this, boys. I want every minister to go and see him at the hospital. Ern? Where's Ern Godwin? Ern. Neil was marvellous on our tour. He made a tremendous contribution to our political meetings. We have a budding Lloyd George there, my friend. This news about McGrath took some of the pleasure out of it for him at the end, I'm afraid. By the way, Neil, I remember from the legislation I brought in that your scholarship is not affected by anything that might happen to McGrath or his company. It's an independent trust."

Neil got in his father's car and watched the black-hatted and black-coated ministers around Clapp move like a phalanx towards their cars, the premier's mouth opening and closing and his hands gesticulating all the while. They were, Neil noted absently, a comical sight.

"I called McGrath's house this morning as soon as I heard it was him," said Ernest, as they drove off the wharf. "One of his men was there. Mrs. McGrath was at the hospital. He's in intensive care. No visitors, yet."

"I'll go to the hospital anyway this afternoon," said Neil. He flicked on the radio, and after hearing on the news that McGrath was in a coma, his condition critical, he turned it off again. They drove in silence for several miles.

"Well, how do you like politics?" asked Ernest, with forced cheerfulness. "Percy thought you were wonderful." Neil raised his hand and let it drop to his thigh.

A few minutes later, his father spoke again. "I don't mind saying, Neil, the first thing that occurred to me was how very lucky we were that Percy had invited you on that tour. You might have been up there with McGrath, otherwise. It's a sure and certain sign. You have been spared for something."

79

Spared for something – by whom? Neil thought, his mind full of bitter conjecture. *You poor benighted fool!* He nodded at Ernest with a melancholy smile on his face.

Just before they reached home, Ernest took a deep breath. "Politics," he said softly. "There must be something to it, Neil. I've never heard tell of anyone yet who got out of the top spot in any political system without being prized and bludgeoned out with a crowbar. There must be something to it, Neil."

7

"Lord Jonathan Cantingsworth," said Clyde Ferritt. "I should like you to meet Neil Godwin."

"How do you do?" said Neil.

"Hodge do?" said Cantingsworth.

Clyde had invited Neil to dinner at his college, Christ Church, "to meet a few of my more amusing friends," and this was the third young man with a Lord or an Honourable prefixed to his name who had joined the group at Clyde's table in the dining hall. Judging by the familiarity and anima- tion with which they discussed their summer's adventures with Clyde, Neil concluded that his countryman was hob- nobbing with the circle of noble sons ensconced in that college.

During dinner, because he had no experiences in common with Clyde's friends, Neil could find little to say. Occasionally, between the fast-changing topics of general conversation, Clyde would throw cheery remarks in Neil's direction like: "You knew Wolfe Tone McGrath is still in a coma? Too bad. I don't believe there's much hope for him, to be honest with you, Neil."

After dinner, they drove in Clyde's car to his flat to have coffee by themselves. There, Clyde talked about nothing but Newfoundland politics. Neil wondered why, in view of Clyde's current niche in a high social level, he was still inter- ested in those insignificant events back home. Perhaps, he thought, remembering his own poor contributions to the dinner conversation, Clyde considered home politics to be the only overlapping fringes of their two lives.

When Neil could no longer keep himself from returning to his studies, he thanked Clyde and stood to leave.

"Christ," said Clyde, going to his desk, "I nearly forgot the main reason for bringing you here. Percy said to place this in the hands of Neil Godwin without fail. The world's greatest election manifesto. Here. Done."

Neil took the pamphlet and walked back to his own college. In his room, he skimmed down through the large, triple-spaced, multi-coloured words. Clapp had narrowed his election battle to two issues:

ONE. Years ago, this preyed-upon province was forced by the greedy-guts, dog-in-the-manger attitude of our neighbouring province, Quebec, to sell them all the electricity produced by *our* gigantic hydro development on the great Churchill Falls at a fixed price for nearly a hundred years – with no clause in the agreement to raise that price. Quebec was and is aided and abetted in that grab of our power by their handmaiden, the federal government. When the price of oil exploded into the sky, and with it the value of electrical energy, our good neighbour, Quebec, reaped all – not some – *all* of the benefit of the increase in value of our electricity, while we are left with a laughably small return which is often not sufficient to cover our costs. Good neighbour? Ha! After this election, we will put an end to that deal, my friends, even if it means that I personally have to pull the switch in the Churchill Falls power house, and we will take back the billions of dollars which are now being ripped off our backs by Quebec.

TWO. Tests show that there are deposits of oil off our coast equal to the known oil reserves of Arabia. In their usual way, that crowd in the federal government have insulted me, and through me, *you*, with an offer to enter into a deal which gives them all the control over these oil fields and most of the income. On your behalf, I have told the Prime Minister of Canada where to go, and where to shove his offer while travelling there. That oil is ours and will stay ours. It does not belong to that bunch up there in Quebec and Ontario, and it will not!

When Percy's manifesto went on to promise to make every man (and woman) in the province an oil sheik, Neil crumpled the pamphlet, threw it into the wastebasket, and went back to his page in the book on Roman law. The concept being discussed there about contracts between a paterfamilias and a manumitted slave, a point of law obsolete these fifteen hundred years, seemed no more irrelevant to him than what he had just read.

The only news from home that interested him at all during these weeks was contained in the letters from his family. His sister's extravagant and amusing descriptions of her "life as a freshperson" at the local university made him realize how much he loved her, and how sorry he was for having virtually ignored her, except for occasional chats, during the past four years. He saw Jane's lovely, bright face often, and wished he had time to find someone like her at Oxford with whom to exchange affection.

His mother's weekly letters revealed a side of her character which was at variance with his lifelong perception of her as a woman preoccupied only with conscientiously performing her chores around the house, content to leave the declamations to her willing spouse. Her thoughtful, caring lines, apparently written piecemeal over a period of days (sentences were often in ink from different pens), sometimes startled him by their terse perspicacity. "Make your life true for you, Neil," she wrote in one letter, "the instrument of no one else." And below, in ink of another colour, "I don't wish any ill on your father's friend, Percy Clapp, of course."

Ernest Godwin's letters were filled with guidance and lists of possibilities for some anonymous "intelligent, educated young man who ...." But Neil's main interest was in the regular reports he had requested his father to make on Wolfe Tone McGrath's condition. For weeks the prognosis of the doctors was guarded. Then it changed to cautious optimism. Brain wave patterns were beginning to give hope for McGrath's full consciousness eventually, with minimal mental impairment.

Neil was surprised at how quickly an interest in Newfoundland politics came back to him following his receipt of that news. When he ran into Clyde Ferritt a few days later, he asked to see his copy of the detailed results of Clapp's recent election, saying he had misplaced his own copy. In fact, he had thrown it away right after opening the envelope sent to him by the premier's office.

In Clyde's room, they went over the figures at length, and Neil carefully noted Clapp's many strengths and few weaknesses, adding and subtracting numbers and pushing blocs of votes around in his head to arrive at Clapp's defeat.

"To hell with this, Neil," said Clyde, finally. "Percy's support is so solid, one can only say he's made himself premier for life and let it go at that. The only question is, how long will he live? And that's for augury to answer, unless someone brings in a hit man from Montreal ... Good news about Wolfe Tone McGrath, I hear. I didn't realize you and he were such close friends until Percy told me after the accident. I had thought the normal relationship between benefactor and beneficiary applied to you two, i.e. the expectation by the one of grateful forelock tugging, and the display by the other of resentful ingratitude. I wouldn't have pulled Cecil Rhodes out of a nigger's privy, for example."

"Wolfe Tone and I turned out by chance to be kindred spirits," answered Neil. "I see that a Commission of Inquiry has been appointed by the federal government to investigate the cause of the crash. That should be interesting, especially when Wolfe Tone comes to and can testify." He watched for Clyde's reaction.

"Very," said Clyde, picking up a brochure from his desk. "Very. Neil, on the subject of crashes, how about your coming skiing with me over the Christmas vac. I've been meaning to ask you. The Oxford-Cambridge-Trinity College Dublin Ski Club has a trip planned to Lech this year. It's too late for you to go through normal channels now but I can get you a place if you'd like. Cantingsworth is treasurer of the ski club."

"I've never skiied before, Clyde."

"Excellent, excellent. I knew you hadn't. Nor have I. All my friends here are bloody experts on the slopes. They can't

84

understand why I'm not. They think we all live in igloos back in Newfoundland. They don't believe me when I tell them we don't have much snow."

"So your total uselessness in the snow, corroborated by mine, will prove to your friends that we don't live in igloos. Is that the plot, Clyde?"

"Right."

"Okay, get me a place through your abnormal connections." Behind his flippancy, Neil was flattered to be asked.

On the train to Austria, Clyde re-introduced Neil to his friend, the ski club's treasurer. "This is the man who has made your presence here possible, Lord Jonathan Cantingsworth. And here is what alone makes Lord Jonathan's presence among us possible, his *fiancée*, Victoria Montagu."

Everyone laughed. The sound of Victoria's laugh matched the beauty of her face. When Cantingsworth made it clear for the third time that he didn't normally travel in steerage like this, sleeping in these unspeakable *couchettes*, but that his position on the executive of the ski club had imposed the martyrdom on him, Victoria glanced at Neil and rolled her eyes upwards so quickly that Neil was not sure afterwards whether he had imagined the look or not.

In Lech, Cantingsworth lit out for the Olympic slopes, while Neil, Clyde, and Victoria joined the beginners class together under the same instructor. For the first two days, Neil was too shy to take the initiative in talking to Victoria. She, however, approached him frequently; and by the third day the two of them were invariably together as they skiied down the gentle baby slopes. Clyde stopped going to the classes because the large amount of time he spent on his side in the snow had given him a chill.

In the evenings, Cantingsworth and Victoria squabbled a lot. Their usual posture in the hotel lounge was to sit side by side, their heads turned away from each other, in prolonged pouts. And yet they always retired for the night together. It began to cause Neil pain that they slept in the same room.

On their last afternoon in Lech, Victoria bubbled about what good friends she and Neil had become, and made him promise to come round to see her in Oxford after the Christmas vacation. When Lord Jonathan swooped down from the Alps towards them at the top of their slope, she started to fall for no apparent reason and, grabbing Neil, pulled him down on top of her. With much crystal laughter she got up, using Neil's thighs, hips, waist, and shoulders for support. Twice, her face brushed his. It made Neil blush. He knew she needed no help to regain her feet. She was at least as stable on her skis as he was.

There was a deep flush on Cantingsworth's face as well. He wheeled on his poles and *schussed* to the hotel in a bound. Victoria suggested to Neil that they take the lift to a higher slope.

Neil passed most of the remainder of the Christmas vacation at the Bloomsbury Group Bed and Breakfast off Russell Square. At least once a day during his wanderings about the city he would go to a public telephone and look up Victoria's number, even though he knew it by heart. But he never phoned. Three times he hailed a taxi near Hyde Park Corner and had it make several passes by her family's townhouse in Kensington, but he never saw her.

Just before the start of the new term, he went up to Oxford and found a note from Victoria in his box at his college lodge. It was two days old. She would be in her room at Lady Margaret Hall every afternoon that week from three-thirty on, she said, and would be delighted if he could come round for tea.

Neil walked there that afternoon cursing himself for having missed two days. He went up the stairs to Victoria's room, breathing deeply to try to still his palpitating heart. Her door was open. As soon as she saw him she cried, "Oh, super, super, it's Neil!" and jumped up from her chair. She took both his hands in hers, kissed him on the cheek and led him in. She introduced him to her friend from down the hall and poured him a cup of tea. The eyes of both girls were fixed on him. Neil could feel his face burning and his hand shook so much that it was only on the fourth attempt that he was able to bring his cup to his lips.

"Isn't he lovely?" said Victoria. "I told you he was lovely."

"The improvement in aesthetics and personality is a quantum leap," agreed her friend, and laughed.

Victoria lowered her eyes. "Miranda is reading Physics," she murmured. "It's her way of saying that Jonathan is no longer my beau. I realized at Lech that it was simply not working. But, Miranda, to surmise a replacement at this point is a terrible presumption on your part."

"Physicists are trained to detect the presence of elemental forces, even between organisms," remarked Miranda. "Here! I'd better leave after that."

"I agree," said Neil, meaning to continue with a gallant comment on the presence of attractive forces. But then, feeling stupid when Miranda turned around at the door to pretend she was insulted, he stammered, "That is – I agree about the elemental forces between orgasms – I mean *organisms* –"

Both girls clasped their hands to their breasts, smiling with delight. Then Victoria came over, took Neil's face between her hands, and kissed his hair. "Lovely!" she repeated.

"I'm so glad to have met you, Neil," said Miranda. "I hope we'll see you often." She whispered to Victoria from the hall, "You lucky stiff!"

Alone with Victoria Neil felt less stultified, and engaged in an exchange wherein he pleased even himself with his sensitive insights and wry humour, cast deliberately now in a more coherent form of the boyish naturalness which had caused a hit earlier. That night they went to see *Pygmalion* at the Playhouse together, and afterwards, at the entrance to her college, they parted with a tender, delicious kiss that Neil could feel on his lips for the rest of the night.

On their third evening together, they had dinner in the dining room of Lady Margaret Hall and coffee in Victoria's room. Between visits from her friends who lived on the same floor, they hugged and nuzzled. Finally, after the last visitors had left, she locked her door. They stood pressed together in a long embrace and then, kissing each part as it became exposed and murmuring words of love and admiration to it, they undressed each other. There was a series of explosions in Neil's brain as he surveyed her whole body – the nipples jutting out nearly an inch from her breasts, the flair of her hips, the valley between the muscles along her spine, the long tapering legs, and the glistening pink between the firm girth of her thighs. He seized her more violently than he had intended. She giggled happily and pulled him towards her bed, taking a plastic bottle from her dressing table *en route*.

"Lie on your back, you savage beast," she said, and squirted skin lotion onto his belly. She smoothed it over his chest and neck and down over his abdomen, between his legs and onto his balls. She kissed and tongued the top of his penis while rubbing lotion on the shaft between her palms. By concentrating on the image of a wind-whipped, mist-swept, sea-battered, craggy cliff of home that he forced into his mind, he managed not to spurt.

Her eyes unnaturally bright, Victoria passed the bottle to him and lay on her back. He gently massaged every inch of her body. His heart thumped so hard as he caressed her vulva that he had to steady himself with his hand to keep from falling on top of her. When he kissed her labia and licked between them, she caught two handfuls of his hair and guided his head up and down, moving her pelvis against his face. Then she hauled his body up over hers. After they had bounced around on the bed for a minute, she said, "Leave it in, leave it in!" And he came with such a force that the squeal he heard sounded far away ... though it may have been his own.

They clung together for a time, panting, and then Neil's penis began to twitch of its own accord. Victoria noticed. Surprised that it had not become flaccid inside her, she eased it out for a gleeful squeeze of confirmation. "Oh, crackie!" she grinned. "Blimey, my wild colonial boy!"

She turned over, rested her face on the pillow, took a firm grip on the top of the headboard with both hands, and thrust her backside high into the air. At the sight of her peachblow vulva and roseate anus, both freaked with strings of semen, Neil got to his knees and plunged, not fussy about where he entered. For an hour or more, they sought (between brief respites) to exhaust the permutations and combinations of their apertures and protuberances: lapping, probing, sucking, thrusting, high and low, fast and slow. Finally, they collapsed in each other's arms, their lips touching, murmuring sweet words of mutual approval and appreciation ....

Neil awoke with a start. The light from the bedside lamp was shining in his eyes. Disentangling himself from Victoria's limbs, he reached for his watch on the bedside table. It was twelve twenty-five: nearly an hour and a half after the deadline for all male visitors to be out of the college! He woke Victoria up and told her. She responded by kissing him and stretching across to turn off the lamp, grazing his face with her breasts. Then she straddled him and took hold of his penis. It sprang up in her hands, and she settled herself down over it.

For an eternity, as Neil was pushed and tossed about like a dry leaf in a baffling wind by the strong body that had already made Victoria the fourth best female tennis player at Oxford, waves of anxiety pounded through him. The windows of the room were too high above the ground to permit his escape in hale condition in the event of discovery. And just one girl on the floor need inform on him to the college authorities to make that discovery certain. He strained his ears over what sounded like the terrific commotion they were making in the bed, to listen for the trooping jackboots in the corridor. His blood stopped flowing every time he heard the whisper of slippers and the rustle of silky feminine night-time fabrics passing by the door .... Hope! Perhaps his excellent results in his college tests would soften the moral indignation of the Proctors. No. Just last term, two exceedingly promising students had been booted out by these enforcers of university discipline for an identical breach of the regulations. All through the night, between fitful snatches of sleep in Victoria's arms, Neil's certainty that this delightful gambol meant the ignominious end of both of their Oxford careers swept his body with nauseous dread.

Whistling his way along Norham Garden and through the university parks late the next morning, marvelling at his escape from detection and recalling every coo and yelp of passion with its accompanying action, Neil felt an impulse to talk to Clyde Ferritt. He made the detour to his flat and found him in.

"To think, Clyde," he said, after describing the night's

events without mentioning Victoria's name, "that a dozen girls knew I was in that room all night and every girl in the college must have learned about it from hearsay, and not one of them said a bloody word. This England is a civilized spot." He rasped his hand up and down his unshaven face as corroboration of his adventure.

"Or," suggested Clyde, "alternatively, all the other inmates of that cunny-warren were too busy at their own dim occupations all night to bother with informing on you."

"Perhaps that's it," chuckled Neil. "The so-called chastity of the female sex is a pure fiction invented by men's own hopes and fears." He felt expert enough about women now to boil them down to an epigram.

"Victoria, eh – speaking of fictitious chastity." Clyde grinned. "Lord Jonathan Cantingsworth will not be amused."

"Shag Cantingsworth," said Neil. "Assuming, without admitting, that it was Victoria, they've broken up, anyway."

"Ha, ha, ha," said Clyde. "Well, I suppose I'm entitled to some vicarious pleasure from all this. I'm the one who introduced you."

For three weeks, Neil and Victoria did not miss an afternoon or evening together. Every day they made wild and prolonged love, and Neil's studies quickly lost importance. Early in the affair, the Senior Law Tutor at his college had detained him after a tutorial to praise the quality of his first term's essays and tests. The tutor suggested that Neil should work for a first class degree in his final examinations. Neil showed no enthusiasm; an Oxford "first" seemed minor compared to the thought of Victoria waiting in his room.

When the tutor began a speech of encouragement, Neil twisted his body about impatiently, erotic images of Victoria tumbling through his mind. Finally, he interrupted. "I'm not going to study fourteen or fifteen hours a day all the while I'm here, I'm afraid." The tutor frowned in disbelief. "If I wanted to live the life of a celibate monk," continued Neil, "I wouldn't have come to Oxford. I'd have gone up on the Hindu Kush. I'm sorry, I simply cannot do it."

"Your proclivity for smart hyperbole is not attractive, Mr. Godwin," the tutor replied sharply. "You 'simply cannot do it,' indeed! And I simply cannot comprehend how anyone, let alone an overseas Commonwealth student like yourself, can be content with mediocrity when – with a modicum of planning and effort over a minuscule span of time from your life – you could be among the top 5 per cent of the foremost university on earth!"

Neil closed the door of the study on the tutor's disgusted face, and was glad to neglect the law in Victoria's arms. When he did open his books it was only to scribble down essays which earned plaudits from no one.

The afternoon that Victoria did not show up at his room as agreed, after she'd spent the weekend home in London, he walked and jogged to her college, concerned about her well-being. She met him on the college grounds before he reached the door and kissed him on the forehead. "My," she said, "you're all overheated. I'm glad you came because I have to tell you something. Jonathan and I are back together. Funny, what. But you know how these things work. Have to run." She squeezed his arm and walked away, turning her head once to smile beautifully. "It was lovely, Neil. You were super."

Dismissed, Neil slunk back to his room, fervently wishing he were still under a silly delusion that the intense devotion he felt was mutual. He had not realized before that mere words could cause such physical pain in one's solar plexus and at the base of one's skull.

For days, he tried to escape into his books; but whenever he leafed back through a chapter or a case he had just read, he found he had absorbed little. He took to staying up much of the night, frequently re-reading during those lonely hours his father's latest reports on Wolfe Tone McGrath, who had been flown to Montreal a month before and who was said to be making steady progress in the hands of prominent neurologists. He wrote and re-wrote a dozen times a letter he would send to McGrath when he regained full consciousness. He made plans to fly to Canada to see him this summer. He mused every night on the time when he could leave Oxford for good and go back to Newfoundland, where he and a restored McGrath would begin their political and artistic activities together. Those nights, that thought was his only solace.

8

The notice in *The Cherwell* listed Lord Jonathan Cantings-worth and Clyde Ferritt among the speakers in the next Oxford Union debate.

So that's why Clyde hadn't been around to see him for a month, thought Neil. He'd made his choice of friends. God-damned Ferritt! Everywhere he went, whatever he did, he oozed to the top .... Neil read the motion to be debated: "Resolved that this House urges severe legal restrictions on the immigration of citizens of Commonwealth countries into the United Kingdom." Cantingsworth and Clyde were to speak in support of the motion .... That toadying tuft-hunter of a bloody Ferritt! No wonder the gang of grandees he had insinuated himself into thought so much of him.

Neil threw the newspaper down and walked across the college to the sherry party for Fellows and students being given by the college head. On the way there, he looked again at the familiar plaque on the college wall commemorating a former student – Field Marshal Douglas Earl Haig. Once at the party, Neil wandered about the room restlessly, unable to pay attention to any of the small talk or to contribute to it. He swallowed several glasses of Amontillado. To avoid the Fel-low whose tutorials he had missed during the two weeks since Victoria had dumped him, he joined the group of stu-dents around the principal of the college who was sitting in an easy chair in front of the fireplace. Neil listened to the principal mumbling around the pipe in his mouth and the fruity, responsive laughter of the students. Suddenly, he couldn't stand the sounds.

"Do you know how sickening it is to me to have to pass by that plaque to Douglas Haig every day?"

The principal looked surprised. Not only had Neil interrupted him in the middle of a sentence, but the question had nothing whatever to do with the story he was telling. "*I* beg your pardon, Mr. ah ... "

"Haig!" repeated Neil. "Why is there a brass plaque to the memory of Haig in the wall of my college?"

The principal removed his pipe and displayed his dental juttings in a smile. "Lord Haig was an eminent *quondam* student of this college," he said. "It's true that a certain school of historians has endeavoured to place his contributions to the First World War in a less than heroic perspective, but this college is too firmly established to pitch and sway in the breeze of every historical fad that blows in our direction. You're not reading History, are you? No, I should scarcely have thought so. Where were we, gentlemen?"

"We were talking about Haig," said Neil, louder now. "Our illustrious alumnus, Lord Haig. Our very own military genius who murdered hundreds of my fellow Newfoundlanders at Beaumont Hamel. Haig!" he shouted. "Who had those brave and silly boys ordered out of their trenches and sent naked into a blanket of German bullets. Haig! Who did that for no strategic or tactical purpose except to test how coldblooded the Huns were, at slaughtering defenceless boys at close range." The principal was on his feet now, visibly alarmed at the vehemence of this unhinged student before him. "Field Marshal Douglas Earl Haig!" Neil concluded with a roar. "He and his brass plaque make me puke!"

"Quite!" muttered the principal; and moved away smartly.

Though Neil's comments caused a noticeable increase in the conversational buzz, he participated little himself and soon left for his room. As he went, he wondered if he'd done the right thing. He didn't care much if he hadn't.

When the first knock sounded on his door he didn't answer, assuming that it was probably the porter under

93

instructions from the principal to help him pack his bags and get out. The second knock, he realized, was much too timid for that. His heart leaped. The meek, apologetic tapping was entirely appropriate. He knew it was Victoria. His premonitions on such things were always right.

"Come in," he called cheerily. The door opened but he could not make out the figure in the dark doorway. "Who is it?"

"Boo. Boo Mansingh."

"Oh. Boo. Come in, Boo. I couldn't see you in the dark."

"Natural camouflage, man."

A tutorial partner of Neil's, Abu Mansingh was a South African coloured. He and Neil were not close friends, but they liked each other and had spent time together during their first term. Mansingh had told him that although he held no hope (without a skin graft), of ever achieving the status of "European" under the apartheid system in South Africa, he did aspire, once he had his Oxford degree, to become an "*Honorary* European" like the Japs. After they had laughed at that, Mansingh had been impressed at the way Neil had fulminated against "the pigment-oriented slots lying at the root of all man's inhumanity to man."

Mansingh put a magnum labelled "Spanish Burgundy" on the table now, and Neil got glasses. This was the first time they had sat down for a chat since Neil had started his fling with Victoria. He was glad of the company.

"You haven't been very sociable since this term began, Neil," said Mansingh. "But I had to come round tonight to congratulate you. That Haig business was a superb gesture on behalf of your own people."

"Well, I've made up my mind to put up with no myths that seek to ennoble evil ever again, Boo. I'll doubtless catch shit from the principal, though, for my rudeness."

"That's what some of the other chaps thought, too. There'll probably be a kangaroo court requiring you to show cause why you shouldn't be disciplined, suspended, or sent down for insolence to your superiors. But to me that's what makes your gesture so great."

Neil nodded. But he wished he had his time back.

Two nights later, Neil was in the Buttery with dozens of other students watching a program in John Kenneth Galbraith's television series on money. He found himself wonderstruck. There on the screen, Galbraith was strolling through the memorial park at Beaumont Hamel and describing the slaughter of Newfoundlanders in that place as *the* egregious example of callous stupidity in a war caused and maintained by capitalist greed.

Neil felt his whole body suffused with the happy glow caused by that most pleasant of unexpected events: serendipitous vindication. The accolades of the students around him, most of whom had heretofore considered his outburst on Haig tiresome in substance and discourteous in form, he received now without gloating.

In the morning, he got a note from the principal asking him to come to his office. Neil entered the room with a bearing of polite dignity and accepted the principal's apology for his inexcusable display of indifference to Neil's strongly felt conviction. After Neil had answered two or three questions on Beaumont Hamel, which went dangerously close to exhausting his knowledge on the battle, the principal offered to establish a committee to discuss the possible removal of Haig's plaque "now that modern historical research has placed his military role in better perspective."

Walking back through the college quadrangles, Neil felt lucky. He'd always been lucky, he realized. And although he would never be so foolish as to count on it as a certainty – he knew he'd always be lucky in the future.

At noon, the porter at the lodge summoned Neil to the telephone to take a trans-Atlantic call from his father. After they had exchanged pleasantries, Ernest Godwin said quickly, "Neil, Wolfe Tone McGrath is dead. I wanted to tell you before you got it in dribs and drabs. Pneumonia and meningitis, apparently. It struck suddenly and killed him before they could control it with antibiotics. It happened over the long weekend. I don't know if the hospital was short-staffed or not. There'll be an autopsy and an official report and – "

"Gee, that's too bad," said Neil.

"Pardon?"

"I said, gee, that's too bad," Neil repeated, as blandly as before.

There was a short silence and Ernest said, "Well, I'm glad you're able to take the bad tidings so well. When I was putting through this call, I was worried to death about hitting you with it."

"It's only what I expected, Dad, really, deep down. Thanks for letting me know. This call is costing you a lot of money. Give my love to Mom and Jane. I'll write soon."

Neil walked back to his room. He felt astonishingly unaffected by the news. It was strange, he thought, how unpredictable and independent one's emotional reactions were. Perhaps he was endowed with torsibility. Napoleon had that. Perhaps he could bounce back from anything ....

Late in the afternoon, Boo Mansingh came to his room. "Shaacles was wondering why you missed another tutorial," he said. "He asked me to see if you were ill."

"No, I'm all right, Boo," answered Neil. "I got a message from home that my best friend, my mentor I suppose, had died and I wanted to think about him for a little while. He and I planned to –" The flood of tears and half a dozen sobs were out before Neil could stop them. When he had himself under control again, Mansingh's arms were around him and his handsome, tan face was close to his.

"I know, I know," Mansingh whispered, his eyes dry but commiserating. "I know how it feels. During the Christmas vac, my best friend in South Africa accidentally fell off the roof of the police station. I wish I could have let it out of me as you can."

"I didn't know that, Boo," said Neil, releasing himself from Mansingh's arms and drying his eyes on his sleeve. "Was he killed?"

"Yes. Every bone broken." Mansingh smiled. "Funny thing what a three storey fall can do. It was the fall that had removed all his fingernails, the police said."

About to blow his nose, Neil looked at Mansingh. Somehow the statement made them both laugh. It reminded Neil of the fits of laughter he and Muck Barrows used to have when they were trying to escape from a predicament.

They went down to the Buttery for a beer, and then later to the Hall for dinner.

"We'll go to the debate together, if that's all right," said Mansingh.

"What debate is that, Boo?"

"The Oxford Union debate on restricting immigration of Commonwealth citizens."

"Oh, yes. I don't think I'll be going."

"But your fellow countryman is speaking."

"I don't think I'll bother."

"I certainly understand if you don't feel up to going, Neil. But I have to go. It's important to me. For 'citizens of Commonwealth countries' in that resolution, read 'wogs.'"

"If it's important to you, Boo, I'll go with you."

When they entered the auditorium, Neil looked through the crowd for Victoria, but he did not see her. He spotted Cantingsworth and Clyde though, and said to Mansingh, "I'll just say hello to Clyde, even if I can't wish him success." He had a vague idea in his mind about re-establishing friendship.

Clyde noticed him approaching and said something to the three or four men with him. Cantingsworth turned his back and walked away, but the others faced Neil with twinkling eyes.

"Well, well, well," boomed Clyde's resonant voice. "How's our Better Roads scholar. Our street, road, curb and gutter scholar." There were chortles. "Marvellous to see you once more, Godwin." Clyde twitched his lips into a quick smile, his eyes scanning the crowd. Then he patted Neil's arm and moved to the front of the room.

Neil had said nothing. He rejoined Mansingh, who had found two chairs, and told himself, as he sat down, that his inability to reply to Clyde had been caused by his surprise at his erstwhile friend's perfect – better than perfect – Oxford accent. It hadn't been in evidence the last time Neil had seen him.

Jonathan Cantingsworth led off the debate. He spoke of the obligation of superiors to succour unfortunate inferiors, and of the equally urgent duty of these superiors to resist by all available means, unkind as they might sometimes mistakenly appear to be, the lust of self-centred mediocrities (psychologically crippled by their attempt to hide from themselves their fated roles in life), for the precious possessions of the great men of this land. That principle, he asserted, was true for all native-born Britishmen. Then how much the truer was it indeed for former colonials? For there was an insidious danger lurking in that most despicable of mediocrities, the colonial mediocrity, who, actuated by a spirit of grudge-bearing revenge (the basest of all motivations, and ill-founded in any event), sought to take over the institutions and property of the mother country.

This was not snobbery, Cantingsworth stressed. He needed only to refer to that remarkable British tradition of rewarding superior merit by elevating excellence into the high social status and honour represented by the House of Lords. This age-old practice ensured the flow of new, deserving blood into the aristocracy, constantly strengthening it, and at the same time providing access to the upper reaches for individuals of all classes in all parts of the empire. In truth, continued Cantingsworth, he was at some pains to acknowledge the greatness of superior persons from colonial countries whose merits had gained them entry to that exalted chamber. And in the present day, Commonwealth men of quality and intelligence, such as his colleague tonight, Mr. Ferritt, were still thrice welcome in this land. "But that sentiment cannot and should not apply to mediocre colonials, who in final and conclusive evidence of their petty meanness, think that because individual Englishmen possessed the virility, stamina, and parts to civilize their lands, they in turn can now overrun ours by numbers alone, committing profane trespass on the things and the persons, especially the persons, we love and hold dear."

Some people in the audience considered this to be a nifty little speech, a deliberate caricature of itself, and they laughed and applauded. Others saw nothing funny in it and booed. Neil's reaction was strictly personal. *That prick is talking about me!* he thought. He looked at Mansingh, but his companion was staring straight ahead and would not meet his eyes.

The first speaker for the negative had now started. During his speech, Neil decided what to do. He waited till the speaker had finished his peroration ("... and like the German youth of today, we of this generation in Britain are not to *blame* for the sins of our fathers –but, also like the German youth, we have no choice but to *atone* for the sins of our fathers!"). Then Neil stood up while the audience clapped the speaker. He took deep breaths.

"Boo, my friend," he said loudly, as soon as the room had become quiet. "I'm listening to no more racist crap." He started to walk out, thinking that his words had not sounded as impressive in delivery as they had felt in conception.

"Aw, come *on*, man!" shouted a deep voice in an American accent. "It's only a debate. What happened to freedom of speech?"

Neil glanced over and confirmed that this speaker was black. He felt silly at his outburst now, but saw no alternative to his walkout. As he turned, he caught a glimpse of Victoria's lovely face looking back at him in mild disdain. He halted and pressed his elbows against his ribs to stop his hands from shaking.

"Freedom of speech!" he snarled back. "There are freedoms *of* and there are freedoms *from*. Let Cantingsworth and Ferritt have their freedoms *of* speech. But I'm freeing myself *from* their spew of racist vomit." There were murmurs and a wide sprinkling of claps at this. Mansingh and a half dozen others followed Neil out. From what Neil could hear at the door, Clyde seemed to be getting off to a faltering start.

"Neil," said Boo Mansingh outside, "I'll never forget that. Walking out on your own friend from your own home on a matter of principle! I'll always remember this night: March the Fourth."

"It was nothing, Boo. It might have been better to stay and argue."

"No. Others will stay and argue. What you did was dramatic. It's what I should have done. The remarks were directed at me. Instead I was glued to my seat, just as back in

South Africa I accepted the official half-existence grudgingly accorded me by the government so that I could win my bursary to Oxford."

"My God, Boo, there's no comparison! If you had bucked that system, you'd have ended up as a raspberry smudge on the veldt, reduced to one suck of an aardvark's tongue." Neil meant him to laugh at the exaggeration.

"All too true," Mansingh said earnestly. "What an appropriate image! I must remember that for when I go back."

"Boo, you're not going back to South Africa! You said you weren't."

"I've changed my mind, Neil."

"Look, Boo, you know what you should do? Fall on your knees and thank the bastard-in-the-sky for inadvertently letting you get out of there in the first place. Then forget that whole goddamned mess and stay here in England, or better still – in view of Cantingsworth and his like – go to the States or Canada. That's what I'd do in your place."

"You wouldn't do that, Neil. If you were me you'd go back and fight, no matter what risks came your way. And that's what I'm going to do now, as well."

Boo was wrong about him, thought Neil as they went into his sitting room. He pulled out a bottle of Newman's Port, aged in the caves of Newfoundland, and poured a glass for Mansingh and himself. He wondered why people were always raising him higher on the scale of virtues than he felt he should be. Did they see a quality in him that he himself was blind to? Or was it that he was forever emitting credible bullshit? It must be the latter, he thought, because he heard himself say, after he had emptied his glass of the delicious liquid in one swallow: "Ah, this is beautiful stuff. The quiet, uninvolved life has many beautiful things like that to make it worthwhile, Boo. But I think you're right all the same. If I were in your place I think I would risk the loss of my life, with all its beauties, to see justice done."

He put Mozart's Quintet for Clarinet on his record player and refilled the glasses. They listened for a few minutes and then Mansingh broke in with fervour. "Neil, do you know why I, an intelligent and articulate man, did not take up my own cause when I was growing up in South Africa?"

Neil turned reluctantly. He'd rather listen to the music. "Why not, Boo?"

"Fear and cowardice, that's why. Not physical fear and cowardice. *Moral* fear and cowardice. Many think that because there's a tint in one's skin, it automatically makes one brave ....

"Do you know that even now when I get on a train at Paddington to go up to Oxford, I am shaking inwardly with fear? I always look around for a compartment with no one in it, and when none are empty, and I have to approach one with, say, a single white man in it, I actually begin to tremble. I open the door to go in and I can physically feel the trepidation come over me. If he glances up, I almost collapse with dread. I want to cringe before him and beg him not to give me a dirty look or to say anything unkind. After a while, I do regain a little courage. If he speaks to me first, I can engage in polite conversation – in which I am mostly deferential. All during the train ride I know rationally that, if put to the test, I am superior in every way to the other man; but the initial trepidation and dread is there, and even when it finally goes, the feeling of diffidence and inferiority remains."

Fascinated, Neil listened to Mansingh's eloquent explanation. Typically, his friend's words were rather formal; but they were forceful, too – as if he'd thought them out long before.

"The whole point," Mansingh went on, "is that this feeling I have *isn't* rational. It seems to originate in my blood. For all I know, it may be genetic. Certainly, uppitty coloureds had a much better chance of having their genes eliminated over the past few generations on the Cape. It may be a combination of a conditioned reflex of fear, diffidence, and ingratiating obsequiousness, together with a genetically inbred *sense* of inferiority.

"I could say now to you that, when I get back to South Africa with my education and training and exposure, I'll be able to talk reasonably with the whites, face to face, on an equal basis, stern, forceful, and strong. But I know, I *know*, Neil, that back home in the familiar *milieu*, the same fears and diffidence will rise up, and be multiplied a hundredfold with every superior movement, gesture, and word of the white man before me. But I am going back. And I will be a leader of our cause!

"Aha! you say. Good old Boo. What courage! He's going to force himself to overcome those feelings and become a leader of rational action on behalf of his people in spite of, perhaps even because of, his fears. And I say, yes that would be nice. I'd like to do that. But I know that I won't. I know that my moral courage may fail me at the crucial time because of these Hormones of Cringe and Scrape, flowing through my cells. So I'm going to take the path of force and violence. The physical risks are much greater to myself, but I welcome those risks because courage of another order comes into play. And when the time comes for me to claim what should be mine, I'll talk to the men I cringe before now from a position of remote, fear-inspiring physical superiority – atop a heap of their battered brains and guts!"

Neil remained quiet for a time, but now he wasn't listening to the music. He was absorbed in the thought that while Mansingh had been talking about a sense of diffidence in his cells, he had been describing a nearly constant feeling of Neil's since he had come to Oxford. Even his outbursts at the sherry party and tonight at the debate were reactions to that feeling. He had felt truly at his ease during the past six months only when he was in the company of Boo Mansingh.

The next afternoon, Neil saw Clyde coming through the college gate. He was not eager to explain to Clyde his performance at the debate, and he headed for the chapel, hoping he had not been seen.

"Neil!" Clyde called. "May I talk to you?" Neil waited impassively for him to catch up. "I want to apologize to you for last night, Neil."

Neil said nothing. He was glad Boo Mansingh wasn't there, as he was never confident that he could match Clyde's sarcastic putdowns, and one was sure to follow now.

"That was a terrible thing I did last night, Neil, and I –"

"What is this, Clyde? Your cute idea of reverse psychology?"

"No. I'm sorry, Neil, you have every right to be angry with

me. That must have struck you as a terribly callous thing for me to say to you. But I had no idea that Wolfe Tone McGrath was dead or, I assure you, I wouldn't have talked about your scholarship like that. I don't blame you for walking out on me last night. I deserved it. I thought you had over-reacted at the time but when I heard about McGrath this morning, I was surprised you hadn't punched me in the face. My sincere apologies."

"Thanks, Clyde," said Neil, turning to walk to his room. "See you."

"Uh, Neil?" Neil looked back. Clyde was fidgeting with something in his pocket. "Let's have a coffee."

"Sure, Clyde, we must get together sometime."

"Have you got a minute now, Neil?"

What in the name of God was wrong with him? Neil wondered, as Clyde's hand continued to move in his pocket. Did he have crotch-rot? But out loud he said, "Let's have one in my room now if you'd like."

Back in his room, Neil put the kettle on and turned around to see Clyde pulling a folded sheet of paper out of his pocket, feigning great surprise. "What's this? Oh, yes. I must have stuck it in my pocket absentmindedly." He faked a movement to return it to his pocket and then said, "Oh, here, Neil. You may find it amusing."

It was a letter to Clyde from Percy Clapp. Neil skimmed the page:

.... Based on our close and valuable association in the past, I believe the best position for you would be secretary to the Cabinet. You will be responsible to no one but myself alone. You will be my eyes and my ears and my mouth. You will be designated "Chief Confidential Adviser to the Prime Minister and his Cabinet" and, as such, will be considered the senior man in the Public Service.

On the political side, I shall be instructing my Cabinet that all ministers are to regard your word on any matter as emanating from me. Your salary will be negotiable with me, commensurate with your seniority and heavy responsibility.

It is a position replete with unparalleled opportunity and bespeaks a glorious political future ....

Passing the letter back, Neil said, "Sounds great, Clyde." He turned his back to put coffee in the cups. Clyde was on his way to power. Neil made the joyless moment pass by saying to himself: Power over what, for Christ's sake? When he faced the room again, he saw that Clyde was examining his gestures and features closely.

"Do you think so, truthfully, Neil? I'd like your frank advice."

"It's certainly something to cut your eye teeth on, Clyde – before you move on to something perhaps a little more significant in the scheme of things."

"Yes, I might take it for a while on that basis, ha, ha." But Clyde was not fooled. "What about you, Neil? What will you do next year when you go back yourself?"

"*If* I go back," said Neil. "I have by no means decided that I will go back. Every time I look at a map of the world from this perspective abroad, Newfoundland looks like a little speck of flyshit, with about the same degree of importance. I love it here in England, Clyde, and I may well stay."

"I think you're on the right track," commented Clyde. "I'm sorry in a way that Percy has made me this very attractive offer." He took one sip of coffee and got up to leave. At the door, he added, "I'm sure your plans to become a cosmopolite will work out, Neil. But if you should decide to come back home, remember you can count on me for help."

Through his window, Neil watched Clyde crossing the quadrangle. Clyde suddenly twisted his head around and looked up at him with a smug smile, knowing he would be there. Neil waved and made the thumbs-up sign, irritated with himself.

During the rest of the academic year, the number of Neil's friends greatly increased. Many of them at his college had approached him to express admiration of his stand on Lord Haig at the sherry party. Others considered his attack on bigotry at the Oxford Union debate gutsy. Two women students at St. Ann's College stopped him on the Broad one day to congratulate him. They'd seen his courage at the debate, they said. This encounter led to friendships with them and to amiable liaisons with several other girls. It delighted him that whenever Clyde Ferritt came round for his now weekly visit, he usually found four or five friends sitting in Neil's living room with him.

"I was talking to Percy on the phone yesterday," said Clyde in June, not long before he left. "'How's young Godwin making out?' he wanted to know. 'What time is he coming home for a visit this summer?' I told him you weren't. Coming home, that is. Christ, he considered that to verge on *lèse-majesté*. 'Doesn't the man know I want to see him?' he said."

"The gentleman Clyde is referring to," said Neil to the other friends in his room, "is the Honourable Percy Clapp, the premier of our province. A retiring, unopinionated man, wouldn't you agree, Clyde? He considers Newfoundland to have gone from eldest ugly step-daughter of the British Empire to youngest fuckee of the Canadian Federation, without getting so much as a kiss during the transition." The British boys hooted. Neil was pleased with his easy ability to formulate the lines his friends, always poised for laughter, had come to expect. "Anyway, Clyde, the Honourable Mr. Clapp will just have to try to run his circus without me this summer, I'm afraid."

Neil's summer was full of travels. He and Boo Mansingh went on a tour of Russia sponsored by the Labour Party at the university. Then he spent a month at the homes of college friends in Cardiff, Edinburgh, and Maidenhead. After that he passed nearly six weeks by himself in London. He had intended to spend only a week there before going to Exeter, Cork, and Canterbury to stay with other friends. But in his room in the Bloomsbury Group Bed and Breakfast, he wrote his friends to tell them an emergency would keep him from accepting their invitations as planned, and he wandered throughout the city alone for five weeks and five days, seeing no one he knew and speaking to no one except waitresses and ticket-sellers, until the approach of the new fall term made him go back up to Oxford. All alone or among others he was equally self-sufficient, he exulted.

By the middle of his second year, the statement that had been false when he made it to Clyde had, he believed, come true: he loved England, especially London. He had a girlfriend now, Jennifer Mersey, pretty, bright, curious, and devoted to him. They went everywhere together in Oxford and, owing to her father's habit of having his office in the City get tickets for them to plays, symphonies, and ballets, they missed little of interest in London. They spent several pleasant weekends at her home in Guildford and, during week days and nights at Oxford, she was seldom out of his digs on Museum Road where they talked, studied, and made love.

It was a comfortable, enjoyable affair. If he'd had Jennifer during his first year, he often thought, he'd have had no trouble going for that "first." The fact that she had another year at Oxford after this one was a factor in his decision to stay on for a graduate degree in Law and obtain the standard of excellence which he would miss on his first degree here. Now, most of the news from Newfoundland he read from a lingering sense of duty alone. His sister's letters were the sole exception. He was glad when they came. Jane's latest letter gave what purported to be a verbatim report of a monologue she'd overheard Percy Clapp giving their father:

> I'm going to show those Quebec Frogs how this separation thing is done. Did you ever see anyone so Gallic as the French, Ern? With their endless theorizing at the ends of swords, lopping each other's heads off over whether evil is the absence of good, or good the absence of evil. And your Quebec Frog is worse again. Sovereignty-association! In but out. Up but down. Wet but dry. Defecate and stay *on* the pot!
>
> Ernie? Latins are all alike. Choose at random any banana republic – one governed by total anarchy and lawlessness or one ruled by iron totalitarian dictatorship (it has to be one or the other, no other kind exists) – and you will find that it contains more academic lawyers spouting concepts and writing *the* definitive textbook on international law than you will find in all the Anglo-Saxon democracies lumped together. Then go to any other Latin nation and look at the list of political scientists and philosophers of

political theory babbling away there and you'll find the same thing. More in Nicaragua, more in El Salvador, more in Paraguay or Ecuador, more in each, in *each* I say, than in all the British Commonwealth countries and the US combined.

Bloody Quebec Frogs. I'll teach them how to separate. I'll show them how pragmatic Anglo-Saxon people – I omit the Irish among us for the sake of argument – exercise their political will. Frogs! It must have been a Frog who contrived the Trinity: one plus one plus one equals one. Clyde, find out if it was a Frog who first invented the Trinity. There's your Latin logic for you. No wonder they can neither separate nor stay in.

Jane had certainly captured the flavour of Clapp in her quote, thought Neil, whatever it was she had him talking about.

The next batch of newspaper clippings from Ernest Godwin clarified the matter for Neil. Percy Clapp was asking the legislature to grant his government the power to hold a referendum on two questions:

Do you want us and our children and grandchildren here in Newfoundland to get a better deal from our own hydro power and offshore oil? If the answer is yes, and if you want your Newfoundland Government to have the power to threaten that we will separate from Canada if we don't get a better deal, mark your X here.

Or, do you want the mainland governments (*eg.* the Quebec Government in Quebec and the Quebec Government in Ottawa) to keep walking on our faces and on the faces of our children and grandchildren in their hobnailed boots? If so, mark your X here.

In introducing the bill into the House of Assembly, Clapp said that the enabling legislation was needed to strengthen his hand in negotiating greater benefits from the federal government and Quebec regarding Newfoundland's resources. "Not necessarily separation," Clapp was quoted as saying, "but separation if necessary."

After a two day debate, the law giving Clapp the right to hold a referendum was passed unanimously. Even the Opposition members agreed that such a power would be a strong string for the government's bow in its negotiations, although, of course, it would never have to be used.

The newspapers reported that within a week after the law had been passed, Clapp put the referendum machinery into motion, with a three week campaign to precede the vote. Under one picture of Clapp making a speech, he was quoted as saying: "Because of modern Anglo-Saxon technology, we don't need that transmission line across Quebec for our power anymore. We can now bring the power by undersea cable across the straits to the island, then across the gulf to the mainland again, bypassing the Gallic grab-alls, with a resulting revenue to us of one billion two hundred and fifty-five million three hundred and twenty-five thousand dollars a year at the start, and rising at the rate, compounded annually, of thirteen decimal four seven per cent every year thereafter. A pure Anglo-Saxon route for our power, bringing billions to our people."

Under another later picture, showing Clapp bellowing to a hall jammed to the rafters with people, the quote was: "They get a great kick up there in Canada out of telling Newfy jokes. Oh yes, a great kick. Unspeakably foul and malicious jokes about us, their erstwhile fellow-Canadians. Will they laugh, I wonder, on February seventh when I will have the right to turn off that switch and they will have to light their kerosene lamps with frostbitten fingers?"

When the clippings on Clapp's lopsided victory in the referendum reached Neil, he leafed through them shaking his head. He saw a picture of Clapp at his victory celebration, flanked by Ernest Godwin and Clyde Ferritt, "both of whom played prominent parts in the referendum campaign." Neil looked at the picture for a long time, but not at his father. Ernest Godwin seemed to be a peripheral figure there. The centre was Clapp and Clyde and the subject was Clapp's arm around Clyde's shoulders. He was about to crumple the photograph and say, "Aw, so what?" when he remembered that Boo Mansingh was sitting behind him, reading. He changed the first word to what he intended to be a laugh.

Mansingh looked up from his Prosser "On Torts" and said, "Bad news from home, Neil?"

During the following week, Neil told his girlfriend, Jennifer Mersey, that he could not see himself ever returning to Newfoundland where time and energy was wasted on such lunatic antics as that referendum. He knew she liked to hear him talk like that. And then he noticed that a surprising number of commentators had something to say on the event. An editorial in a Canadian magazine called the referendum "but another, this time home-grown, Newfy joke." An American periodical thanked Newfoundland "for providing light and zany counterpoint to the usual ponderous turgidity of Canadian politics." An English newspaper beseeched the Almighty "to tell us why it is that so many of the oil discoveries crucial to the world's needs have taken place in areas of the globe where the method of government is as painful to an observer steeped in British tradition as if Plato himself were forced to watch the concepts of his Republic being implemented by a colony of Macaque monkeys."

Neil laughed at the first few of such commentaries and joked with Boo Mansingh that he might have to return to Newfoundland for good after all since pure shame at his origins would now keep him from showing his face elsewhere. But as he read more opinions of writers who took notice of the referendum only to dismiss it and his homeland contemptuously, his reaction changed. He began to rage at the ignorant and stupid notions of know-alls who insulted or patronized a place they neither knew nor understood.

"Oh, you'll be going home all right, Neil," said Boo Mansingh. "Just as I will be."

"I don't know, Boo," said Neil. "I just don't know."

"I wish the bloody newspapers would bloody well belt up about it," said Jennifer Mersey.

They soon did. The referendum had no aftermath and Clapp attempted no follow-up. It had simply been a crass show of political strength on Clapp's part, Neil concluded; and his feeling of defensiveness on the part of his homeland died.

It was that spring, near the end of the academic year, that Clapp came to London with Clyde Ferritt and asked Neil to become a candidate in the next election ....

We must take the current when it serves ... Or lose our ventures. During the sleepless night he spent after meeting Clapp, these lines rolled often through Neil's mind. Staring at the ceiling he reviewed the day's interesting events: Clapp's dazzling performance at lunch in Lord Smythe's merchant bank; his unexpected disdain for Clyde's political ability; his intimation that Neil himself appeared to have the qualities to succeed him as premier in a few years; his enthusiastic agreement with Neil's idea of the direction Newfoundland's development should take. The thought of taking over from Clapp – of having unlimited money for his purposes; of travelling everywhere; of mingling with the successful, the intelligent, the learned; of kindling talent; of effecting progressive concepts; of raising the downtrodden to a station of dignity; of becoming a figure of history, greater than Pericles, acclaimed everywhere for all time – made Neil shiver and leap up from his springshot bed often during the night.

Why not? he asked himself. Wolfe Tone McGrath was gone forever, dead from "medical complications consequent on injuries resulting from misadventure of which the specific cause was unknown," according to the report of the Commission of Inquiry. It was only right that Neil should carry on alone with the plans they'd made together. True, he'd have to play along with Clapp for a few years, but thereafter he could make sure of the fulfilment of their plans himself (if Clapp did not turn out to be as co-operative as he had indicated today).

And what was there to be said against his going home in a month right after his exams? Nothing. The idea of getting a "first" in another Law degree was a combination of intellectual vanity and escapism. He could see that clearly, now. He didn't need it to practise law anywhere. Jennifer Mersey? A friend who was exceedingly valuable to him, without doubt, and a relationship that he would like to continue indefinitely, perhaps permanently. But after his experience with Victoria, he would (thank you very much), countenance no further neurotic longings of the heart or loins that would palsy him into a failure to realize his potential. Besides, if there was a question of permanency involved, a few months separation would be a good test of the strength of their love. She'd be disappointed about the cancellation of their summer travels together, certainly – he would be, as well. But that was a trivial self-indulgence when stacked up against this political opportunity.

No, there was nothing which prevented him from going home next month. It was not even an all-or-nothing thing. No bridges were being burned behind him. He could always pull out again if he wasn't satisfied. He fell asleep and in his dreams he saw his father's happy face.

In the morning, he decided not to call Clapp's suite to let him know yet. He wanted the question to bounce around in his own mind for a few more days, just in case he'd left an important element out of his deliberations. But he knew his mind was made up when he had trouble all week keeping political speeches and strategies from forming spontaneously and mingling with his thoughts on the law.

He sent Clapp a telegram: "The answer is yes, my kind regards, Neil." He wrote Ernest Godwin and received an ecstatic phone call from him in reply. His mother then came on and said, "We're looking forward to seeing you, Neil. You can really make up your mind when you get back whether you want to stay or not."

"Shush, mother," Neil could hear his father in the background.

Jane took the phone. "I'm dying to see you, Neil. I've *really* missed you. Your letters were nice but, you know ... I love you. See you soon!"

He told Jennifer Mersey of his decision and consoled her as well as he could. She asked if she could go with him. He said she had to get her degree first and then they'd rejoin one another next year.

The night before his examinations started he had a dream

of fleeting images: Goofy Newfies, Percy Clapps, and giant squids in black Homburgs. It made no sense and was more amusing than frightening. He attributed it to his long hours of study.

Neil wrote his exams, said goodbye to Jennifer and Boo Mansingh and other friends, and boarded an airplane for home.

9

"Yes, I believe I did want to talk to you, Neil," said Percy Clapp over the phone. "I understand you are interested in running in the ... Didn't we discuss this in London? Anyway, you'll be running in Great Bona District. That's where your father comes from. It's always good to have a connection of some sort with the district in which you are seeking election. We were thinking of running you in Twillick District where you were born, but that would have meant retiring old Captain Josh, and the poor fellow needs the work, useless as he is. Besides, he might have yelped about it and put the Opposition crowd wise to our plans. Get a list of contacts in Great Bona District from Clyde Ferritt. Watch him, though. He can be tricky. He's got a subtle and busy head on him. We *did* talk about this in London. I remember now. Spend some time in the district this summer. Make yourself known personally if you can. I don't mean kill yourself. I know you have a legal career to consider. Spend a few weekends there. Come and see me whenever you want. My door is always open to everyone. No need to waste your time coming up right now, though. Say hello to your dad for me."

Neil sat listening to the dead line. Clapp's reaction to the homecoming of his star *protégé* was not what Neil had expected; but then, of course, he *was* busy planning the election, and did not have time for chit-chat ...

Jane came into their father's study where Neil was sitting, saw that he was still on the phone, and went to the bookshelves. He looked at her from behind. Since his arrival home

113

four days ago, he had found it difficult to take his eyes off his sister. She had fully matured during his twenty-one month's absence. Now, at twenty, she was so beautiful, so quick-witted, and so lively that she caused an ache in his chest. She stood on her toes to reach for a book. It made her lovely legs perfect. He followed the lines of her curved hips, small waist, and slender back under her light summer dress. The two or three wisps of fine hair which had escaped since she put her hair up that morning curled down over the nape of her slim neck and made her suddenly seem so vulnerable that he shivered.

Realizing he still held the phone to his ear, he said, "That's fine then, sir, goodbye," into the silent receiver and hung up.

Jane pushed the book back on the shelf, turned, and smiled at him. Lovely, he thought. He felt a bitter-sweet pang of perverse gladness that she was his sister, for otherwise he'd surely lose his heart to her.

"Did you finally get hold of old Percy?" she asked, coming towards him. She knew he had left a message at Clapp's office the day he had arrived home and had mentioned to Clyde Ferritt at their lunch together the next day that he wanted to see the premier.

"Yes," answered Neil. "Of course, there was no urgency."

"Old Percy," said Jane, putting her forearms on Neil's shoulders as uninhibitedly as a lover or a child and looking into his face. "Do you remember the time he thought we were twins?"

"Yes. The male and female counterparts of the one Platonic person." Neil smiled and looked away. He could not gaze frankly into her eyes for more than a few seconds without wavering, as he used to be able to do years ago.

That summer and fall Neil alternated between articling at the law firm he had joined and making long visits to the district he was going to run in. His initial reception by the people he met in the district was one of hospitality, but at a distance. Only when his relationship to his father, and thus, to his grandfather, Arthur Godwin, became widespread knowledge, did they accept him as one of their own without qualification. Neil was glad when that happened. Before, as a

114

stranger, he had been served up store-bought stranger's food as a matter of *politesse*: canned klik, kam, or bully beef, canned pears, and canned cream. As one of their own he got their regular homely fare: fresh salmon, lobster, venison steaks, homemade bread, jams, and dainties.

It was the guffers which had the greatest effect on Neil during that summer, guffers which he began to hear more frequently, the more he became part of the people of the coast. He was unnerved when his first guffer was sprung on him. He thought the teller of the tale had gone mad. It was late one evening in Handy Harbour. About twenty men were sitting or standing around in the gloom of the large store, the only direct source of light being the orange flame from the pot-bellied stove that had been lit to take the late-summer nip out of the air. There was a sudden lapse of conversation. Neil was just picking up the thread again when he noticed that no one was looking at him.

A voice boomed out from behind the stove. "I minds the time one mawsy night when the sea was strange, and the Cape Cove wreckers done their deed, their dirty deed that won't die out. We won't forget, thank God there's ones that tells this tale and keeps alive the thought that hell and hell alone is the resting place of the Cape Cove men." Those words spoken, the man walked with slow and giant steps out into the middle of the floor, ignoring everyone before him, forcing men to scramble out of his way. With larger than life movements of head and limbs he resumed. "I slewed around when I saw the lights on Cape Cove Head where until then no lights were seen …" He went on to tell the story, in a loud and controlled voice without ever searching for a word, of how the men of Cape Cove had extinguished the light in the lighthouse on Handy Harbour Point and had put a light up on the next headland, thereby luring a vessel full of passengers and freight to death and destruction on the rocks. The depraved purpose of the wreckers had been to salvage the flotsam from the doomed vessel and strip the valuables from the dead bodies as they washed ashore.

Cape Cove, the place of villains referred to in that guffer, was next to Handy Harbour and of a different religious persuasion. When Neil went to Cape Cove, he heard the same guffer told in identical words, with one exception. There the villains of the tale were the men of Handy Harbour who had "douted" the true light and lit the murderous one, and had thereafter done their ghoulish work.

Not being able to find any historic reference to a ship wreck or the operation of wreckers in either place, Neil asked around for the origin of the tale. He learned from an old retired schoolteacher that Arthur Godwin, his own grand-father, had made it up – in both versions. According to the teacher, who said he remembered the exact occasion well and chuckled at the remembrance, Arthur Godwin had spoken to him one day about the two antagonistic villages. "They're getting too tolerant to suit me," he had said. "Next thing you know, if we don't watch it, there'll be no religious strife at all, and religion will get a good name."

In Pickeyes and in neighbouring communities for miles up and down the coast, Neil found that the highest praise anyone could bestow on any entertainment, whether television, movies, school concerts, or books, was still: "Nearly as good as Uncle Adder's guffers." Many of the oldtimers in the area decried the decline in the quality of guffers since Arthur Godwin's day. One old man commented: "All the slewing around and swinging arms and yelling and bawling and huf-fing and puffing: your grandfather never had to do that. Uncle Adder only had to sit there and open his mouth and speak. Oh, my sonny boy, what words! What words!"

During his travels through the district, Neil recalled that when he was a child his father had made only vague referen-ces to his grandfather or to his home community. He also noticed that there were no churches of the Gazers on the Goodlike Glory of God's Full Fair and Fearful Face in that region.

"Father," he asked, on one occasion when he returned from his rounds, "why don't you have a few churches in Great Bona District?"

"Oh, I didn't bother," answered Ernest; and went on to another topic.

Later, Neil told him, "They certainly remember Grandfather Arthur Godwin on the Great Bona shore. Uncle Adder's guffers – "

"My God, they still remember!" Ernest Godwin's face was aglow for a moment. "How they loved him for lightening their hard lives!"

"The memory of him and his guffers has certainly brought me a lot of goodwill as I've gone around down there."

"I was only fourteen when he died in Pegasus – Pickeyes we used to pronounce it in those days," said Ernest, reflectively.

"They still do," replied Neil.

"Only fourteen." Ernest's face had darkened. "But it didn't make much difference. I never knew your grandfather to bring home a shred of food in his life. In fact, he never did anything all day except sit around reading or scribbling or staring in a trance. And at night he would drag himself over to the general store, flop down on the bags of flour and talk without let-up for hours. Men and women used to flock in to hear his yarning, while mother was home trying to keep us from starving and trying to hide from us the blood she was coughing up by the cupful. It forever turned my – " Ernest abruptly came out of his bitter reverie and formed his mouth into a smile. "I remember a routine some of the older boys used to use whenever they saw me. 'How did little Ernie and his sisters come to be born?' one would say; and another would reply, 'Uncle Adder is in a daze from daylight to dark, but, my son, he must be some wide awake in bed!"

Neil began to chuckle but stopped when his father didn't join him. "Grandfather wasn't very old when he died, was he?" he asked.

"Forty-three, I think. He died about a month after your grandmother's death from 'consumption of the lights,' as they called it."

"What did he die of?"

"Laziness, I believe. He told me a couple of weeks after mother died that he was fed up with constantly trying to keep his skinful of guts upright, and that, even when he occasionally succeeded in doing so, he was overcome by the useless vanity of the achievement. I don't know what he died of. The people of Pickeyes took a guilty pride in his death. They claimed they caused it by encouraging father to over-exert himself on the night of the visit of Joey Smallwood to, quote, 'this historic, this hardworking, this Godfearing town of –where am I? –Pegasus.' For three hours, after Smallwood had begun a speech on the benefits to be received by New-foundland if we joined Canada, your grandfather impaled him from the audience while Smallwood did the dance of anger on the stage. The only time Smallwood had ever met his match, the people of Pickeyes told each other at Arthur Godwin's funeral that same week. Your grandfather despised professional politicians as much as he despised professional men of God. What was it he used to rant about them? Oh, yes. He used to call politicians and preachers 'traffickers in the same noisome holy-poly nostrum.'"

"He would have been very proud of what you are and what I'm trying to be," said Neil with a laugh, trying to lift his father's unwonted gloom.

Ernest looked away for an instant, his forehead wrinkled and his eyes unfocussed, as if struck by a thought. Then he pushed himself out of his chair. "Well, anyhow, there you are. The great Arthur Godwin."

Late that fall –by which time Neil had expected to be sitting in the legislature – no election had been called. He had telephoned Clapp's office three times but had not been able to reach him. Clyde Ferritt was also busy whenever Neil rang his office. The one time he did return Neil's call resulted only in their having a quick drink together in a bar, and Clyde didn't want to talk about the election in so public a place for fear that word would leak out. He shrugged when Neil pointed out that the newspapers had been full of election speculation for months as a result of Clapp's broad hints.

Neil finally coerced Clapp's secretary into giving him an appointment to see the premier. On his way to the Govern-ment Building he ran through his mind some of the points on which he would wring definite commitments from Clapp: the exact date of the election; when, thereafter, he would be appointed to Clapp's Cabinet; and what portfolio Clapp was prepared to give him. If the premier equivocated on any of these things, then Neil would simply tell him he would not be running. God damn it, he thought, it was Clapp who wanted him, after all!

Neil introduced himself to the premier's secretary right at the appointed time. She told him he would have to wait just a few minutes.

He strolled along to the outside waiting room which was filled with about thirty people of all types: fishermen, delegations from municipal councils, men obviously looking for jobs, several women with small children, and a dozen smartly dressed businessmen with bulging briefcases. The businessmen were subdivided into two distinct groups: those sitting and staring at the floor, and those pacing the floor like caged animals, unable to master the energy of their avarice.

After two hours, the secretary came into the room and announced that the prime minister had been called away to an important luncheon engagement but would be back this afternoon. It was an afternoon that Neil spent in more useless waiting – and in nursing a growing sense of outrage to his pride. Who the hell did Clapp think he was, keeping him waiting like this? Then Clyde Ferritt sauntered into the waiting room. He said hello to the few with the fortitude or desperation to be still there. Noticing Neil, he drew him into a corner and boomed out, "I understand the prime minister has big plans for you in the next election. Our districts will be adjacent to each other. I'm already starting to call your end 'Kiddies' Corner.' Good luck." When Neil answered, his voice seemed small in comparison. Clyde walked on through the waiting room, spoke a brief word to the secretary, ostentatiously opened Clapp's door before completing his perfunctory knock, and disappeared behind it.

At five o'clock, the secretary came through with her hat and coat. "Oh! Mr. Godwin, is it?" she said. "My goodness, you've missed the prime minister. He left an hour ago with Mr. Ferritt. Didn't Mr. Ferritt ... ? Come back tomorrow morning, then. I'll fit you in as soon as humanly possible."

In the evening, Neil railed to his father: "Famous open door policy. Access to the People's Premier. 'Come and see me any time. My door is always open. Anyone can talk to me at any hour – the great of the land, the little of the land – I am no respecter of persons.' Like shit! Sorry, Dad."

Ernest smiled and picked up the telephone directory. He found a page, put his finger under a name, and thrust the open book towards Neil: "Clapp, Percy, res." followed by a number. He dialled.

"I'll see if he's home. Hello, Perce? Neil wants to talk to you." He placed the phone next to Neil's ear.

"Uh, hello, Mr. Clapp?"

"Hello, Neil, I hear good things from your district."

"Thank you, sir. I'd like to see you tomorrow morning if I could."

"Of course, my son. Come up mid-morning. I have a Cabinet first."

"Thank you, sir. I'll see you –" The line went dead before Neil could say "then."

In the morning, Neil arrived at Clapp's office at eleven o'clock. "The prime minister was just asking if you were here yet," said the secretary. "He's in a meeting now, but he should be able to see you in a little while."

At twelve-thirty she rushed out to the waiting room. "Which one is Mr. Godwin?" she said. "Mr. Godwin. You might be able to catch the prime minister before he leaves for Labrador City if you hurry. Through that door." Neil heard twenty groans of disappointment behind him as he loped towards the office.

He pulled open the heavy door, nearly losing his balance in his hurry, and with a pretence of casualness walked jerkily into the office. No one was there. Then he sighted Clapp's back through an open door on the other side. He had his coat on and a bundle of papers under his arm.

Neil coughed, but although Clapp turned around he made no other motion. Neil walked tentatively towards him and Clapp said, "Is that you, Mr. Godwin? This is a pleasant surprise."

"Thank you, sir. I was wondering about the election this fall."

"One has to have a sense of fine tuning in this political racket," said Clapp. "Where's that goddamned elevator? It doesn't hurt to be a little bit cute, either, Neil. I'm going to

120

have to stop letting the ministers use this private elevator. It's never here when I want to get away fast. I had the Opposition crowd thinking we were going to have an election this fall by putting a word there and a word here. They got all geared up for it. Here's the elevator now, thanks be to God. Now they're thrown off their stride, *and* they've actually spent most of the money they've been laboriously collecting over the last two years." Half in and half out of the elevator Clapp paused, grimacing in irritation as the buzzer sounded. "That's the moral here," he continued. "Keep the enemy off balance. Stay in touch now, Neil. Say hello to your dad. Good luck in your legal career and watch that district of yours." He removed his hand from the edge of the elevator door and disappeared.

Neil stood there alone and dumbfounded. "Fuck that district of mine and *fuck you, too!*" he said, with rising volume. But he doubted that Clapp heard him.

Seeing the secretary peeping around the door at him, Neil strode out past her and left the building for his law office. As he went, he toted up the disruptions caused in his life as a result of his belief in Clapp's weasel-words. He had thrown away his plan to work for the "first" in a graduate law degree – and twice, during the past summer, Clapp had referred to Clyde Ferritt's Oxford "first" as further evidence of his assistant's near-genius. He had neglected his articling duties at the law firm and his studies for his Bar examinations because of his protracted visits to his district all summer and fall – and the principals at the firm were beginning to make it pointedly clear they had no use for a dilettante lawyer, no matter how clever he might be. He had left behind in Oxford a woman whose qualities would be difficult to match, even if he felt inclined to try to do so. He pined for Jennifer Mersey now, for her loving face bent over his, her auburn hair held behind her ears away from her eyes and mouth so that she could look at him and kiss him, her body pressing, her limbs encircling .... Bastard Clapp! he cursed.

What grated on Neil most was how stupid he himself had been. He had not reflected once on the fact that a general election had been held only two years previously, or asked himself why, with two or three years to go in his present term of office, Clapp would be contemplating an election now. That he had allowed himself to be sucked in by Clapp was what maddened him.

"Henceforth," Neil said that evening, impatiently interrupting his father's attempt to explain that in politics one's plans did not always work out to the last detail, "I'm going to stay as far away from Percy Clapp as the laws of physics will allow."

Neil hardly stirred from his law firm all winter, researching points of law for senior lawyers during the day and catching up on his studies for his Bar exams at night. He did visit Great Bona District several times to attend weddings or funerals, at the invitation of friends he'd made there. But the visits were without any political motivation whatever.

He never saw Clapp during these months, though he received a note from him saying that the reports from Great Bona District continued to be excellent and that Neil should feel free to drop in on him or call at any time. He saw Clyde Ferritt once, at a large Christmas cocktail party given by Clyde at his parents' opulent home. His chief pleasures were reading letters from Jennifer Mersey and Boo Mansingh in Oxford, and talking with Jane about her university work and advising her on the problems of a life made complicated by her attractiveness to men.

For his own part, he had not been attracted to many women since arriving home. There had been carnal interest, but he only pursued a few of them for that purpose, preferring to abate most of the tensions that arose, alone. He sometimes wondered whether a basic short-coming in his character might be that he was not a self-starter.

A week after he was admitted to the Bar in early spring as a practising lawyer, a partner of the law firm handed Neil a case that was set down for a hearing in the Supreme Court in five days' time. Neil was already familiar with the file. It involved a man, their client, who had worked in the asbestos mines for twenty years and had contracted asbestosis. He was now dying of cancer of the lungs. The Workmen's Compensation Board had turned down his claim for compensation for himself and his family. His asbestosis had never been serious enough to disable him and prevent him from working at his job, the board had said in its judgement. And, as for his lung cancer, the claimant had not proved that it had been caused by his working in the mine: "The law clearly states that the burden of proof is on the claimant-employee to show by convincing medical evidence a definite cause-and-effect relationship between conditions in the workplace and any lung disease causing disability or death in the claimant. This, the claimant, who admitted he has smoked all his adult life, has not been able to do."

"Neil," said the partner, "there's no hope of winning that case, so there's no way you can bugger it up. That makes it a good one to give you some experience in appearing before a Supreme Court judge."

For the five days and nights before the hearing Neil constantly thought about the case, studied pertinent literature, and wrote long notes. He knew a more experienced barrister would not have wasted ten minutes on it. He appeared before the judge and argued for two hours. The Department of Justice lawyer, acting for the Workmen's Compensation Board, seemed ill-prepared and taken very much by surprise by Neil's presentation.

Within two weeks, the judge, stressing the urgency of the matter, handed down his judgement. It overturned the decision of the board and granted the miner full compensation. Neil was as amazed as anyone else. He didn't know then that this judge, appointed by the Government of Canada as a loyal party supporter years ago, was considered stupid by leading barristers for his childlike susceptibility to arguments founded on pity.

The judgement was hailed by labour organizations everywhere. Randolph Rute, the labour leader whom Neil remembered from the time his unfortunate satire had brought him before the University Discipline Committee, termed it a landmark in the development of human civilization which created in the mind of the ordinary worker a little faith in the possibility of justice from the legal system.

These reactions caused much to-do in the news for a few days. Newsmen descended on Neil's office and he saw himself interviewed on the television newscast for two nights running. Jerome Finn, a fraternity brother of Neil's for a year at the local university before he had dropped out, and now a television news reporter, spoke on camera from the steps in front of the Courthouse about Neil's aggressive style of advocacy, his vigorous and fearless cross-examination (of which, in fact, there had been none), and "the sudden emergence of this bright new star, this legal luminary, on the horizon of justice in this province."

When Jerome Finn came by his office to interview him a third time, Neil asked, "What is going on, Jerome? Is it the combination of ingredients in this story? 'Idealistic young lawyer, acting for dying underdog, takes on big business villains and callous bureaucracy in courtroom and, holy shit, wins the case!' Is that it? Or is it the public memory of all those agonizing deaths of miners from lung cancer caused by the radon gas down there in the St. Lawrence fluorospar mines? Is that why there's all this interest?"

"Go 'way, Neil," said Jerome, "for the love and the honour of fuck. It's because you look good on film. And listen here. You'll be premier one of these years, just watch – and you'll be needing a good PR man. I only act stupid."

The Workmen's Compensation Board immediately appealed the judge's decision to the Court of Appeal. Because it was a question of grave public importance, the Court of Appeal agreed to give the case priority. They also gave Neil a rough ride, barking at him to direct his arguments to an interpretation of the law as it applied to the facts, rather than to a consideration of morality as it applied to a hypothesis, and ordering him to forbear from attention-seeking histrionics.

The judgement of the Court of Appeal was soon handed down. It was short. The judges decried the way in which a judge had substituted his tender sensibilities for established law, found the arguments of counsel for the dying miner wholly immaterial, and reinstated the decision of the Workmen's Compensation Board.

Neil flung the judgement at the wall. It was so light and flimsy it made a loop in the air and fell several feet short. What a bunch of mean-minded little men, devoid of all humanity and compassion and innovating courage! he thought. Where do they come from?

Into his office came the senior partner of the law firm bearing a file folder. "You're finally rid of that asbestosis case, I see," he commented.

"I thought we might appeal it to the Supreme Court of Canada," said Neil.

"What in the world for?"

"We might win. You never know. And even if we don't, we might get one of the judges there to call upon the legislatures to remedy a manifest injustice in the law."

Bemused, the partner regarded Neil. "Good heavens!" he said. "We're lawyers not Nader's Raiders. And who's going to pay for it? Even the labour organizations would know there's no chance of success. Look, Neil, that case was good for publicity and to let you get your feet wet, but there's no money in it, unfortunately. And we've got to keep that out there going." He indicated with a sweep of his hand the room of word processors, dictating and transcribing machinery, books, telephonic equipment, foodstuffs, buff deed backings, embossed letterheads by the thousands, electronic devices, and the battery of smartly dressed women fiddling with it all. "This is where the money is. Not too sexy, perhaps, but the real bread and butter stuff." He opened the folder in his fingers as tenderly as a lover would have parted the portals of his heart's delight, and exposed to Neil the sale note, the survey description, and the mortgage document inside, its blank spaces still virginal.

Neil took the file, knowing what intellectual delights it held in store for him: connect the chronological chain of title to the property by tedious searching in the index in the Registry of Deeds, make sure his secretary filled in the blank spaces in the deeds correctly, check his secretary's typing of the description of the land for typographical errors, get tax certificates and sheriff's certificates, argue with the lawyer for the seller over a ten dollar adjustment on the furnace rental-sale agreement .... His mind jammed on the litany of clerkish scutwork, which, he thought, required the attention of a trained lawyer, only to justify the exorbitant fee. He asked himself how two lawyers could meet on the street and pass each other without bursting out laughing. He tried to remember the name of the Italian writer who had made that remark about two priests meeting, but could not. He *would* be able to remember the name, he told himself, if his brain was not so blunted from this dehumanizing drudgery. He lay back in his chair to the limit of its spring.

Perhaps he should get into politics after all, he mused idly. He wouldn't have to do scutwork then. And he'd be able to state his views without some arrogant prick on the Bench reining him in with his absolute power every two minutes. Besides, in politics he might be able to effect some general and substantive changes for the better – instead of temporarily circumventing a quagmire for one person and filling him with false hope (like in that asbestosis case) while the quagmire in fact remained, ready to trap more victims.

Moreover, hearing his own name on the news and seeing himself interviewed on television had not been unpleasant; and politics lent itself more readily to that than did real estate transactions. But then, Percy Clapp! For the first time since his return home, Neil felt unmanned by the loss of Wolfe Tone McGrath. He was dejected at the thought of what they might have done together – something that it was impossible for him to do alone.

Neil made a show of looking through each new file as it was passed to him, and then piled it on top of the others in front of him on the desk. He used the pile as a prop for Black's big law dictionary and spent hours savouring various terms and concepts he encountered by opening the tome at random: violent presumption, neck-verse, dedititii, springing use, impubes, waveson, the accursed morsel, driftway, avowtry, jetsam, bill of pains, eminent domain. Not the technical meaning of each word, but its sight or sound evoked in Neil thoughts about his own past, present, and future. None was relevant to any of the files on his desk, but they were so inherently evocative, these words, that he might have gone on searching, sounding, and profitlessly contemplating until booted out of the law firm, had he not received a message from Percy Clapp's office. It arrived just after "master of the moots" and just before "clerk of the petty bag," and it said that the premier was about to announce a general election.

Neil slammed the big book shut, jumped up from his desk, and ran.

10

During the election campaign in Great Bona, Neil discovered the source of the articulateness of nearly everyone he had earlier met in the district. It was the practice the people got from harassing political candidates. What these occasions lacked in frequency, they more than made up for in intensity. There were unceasing complaints, fantastic demands, and attempts at every turn to trip the candidate up verbally and to make him look foolish.

In Neil's district, it was even worse than in most of the others because of the high standard of politician-baiting established by his own grandfather, Arthur Godwin, fifty years before. It was a tradition which people still strove to maintain. In the stores and on the wharves where Neil had enjoyed many friendly conversations during the past summer and fall, he was now the sole subject and object of vituperation. He was unpleasantly surprised on many occasions to be made the butt of a saucy jest by men whom he had earlier considered his close friends in the district.

Once he was surrounded by twenty men on a wharf in Consumption Cove, engaged in a spirited argument on what good the Queen's recent visit to the province did to the development of the fishery, when his very best friend in the place ended the Hegelian dialectic by reconciling all contradictions with a synthesis on a higher level of truth: "You knows as much about a codfish, Neil Godwin, as you knows about the Queen's cunny." The line would precede him to distant settlements, Neil discovered; and he would not be able to open his mouth about any aspect of the codfishery without a local wit asking him how close he'd been able to get to the Queen while she was in St. John's, and everyone within hearing joining in a huge laugh.

As he trudged door to door, hitherto quiet, friendly, and soft-spoken women became harridans, broken boils of bitching, complaining, and demanding. Everyone he met on the road described every pothole in sight with tedious detail and accusing terminology. Private misfortunes altogether outside of government ken or control – matrimonial difficulties, problems with wayward youngsters, legal squabbles between siblings – were narrated at length to him by both sides to a dispute, and action demanded, or else. People whom he had previously considered to be his closest political supporters now publicly gave him only a slim chance of getting elected.

Neil finally figured out why he was coming in for so much more invective and ill-use than his unprepossessing and virtually unknown opponent. It was the basic precept of life around the bays. The unostentatious exercise of a talented skill – boatbuilding, navigating, filling in unemployment insurance forms – was appreciated and admired by the friends and neighbours of the person possessing the gift. In fact, it imposed a burdensome duty on him to use it for the benefit of all. But aggressive people, whether talented or not, elicited a reaction from their neighbours that was the opposite of appreciation and admiration. This negative reaction was doubly severe for anyone who was at the same time seeking a position of power over his fellows. Then the criticism and ridicule would be brutal. Strangers were generally exempt from this treatment, however. They were accorded a distant courtesy and hospitality no matter how unlovable their behaviour. The treatment was reserved for those who were "one of us." Thus, if Neil had arrived in the district as a stranger when the election had been called, he would have received a cordial welcome everywhere throughout the campaign, and, simply as Percy Clapp's catch-fart, his election would have been assured. But, having made himself one of them by revealing his ancestry and by closely associating himself with the community during the past year, he was considered a grasper, and received maltreatment that was frequent, cruel, and vehement. As a result, he spent most of the campaign period genuinely believing he was going to lose this formerly safe seat.

In bed at night, Neil would wonder why Percy Clapp, who had gone to great pains to identify himself with the people of the bays, and who was considered one of them – and who had also aggressively set himself far above everybody – was not subjected to abuse or attacks. The baymen were Clapp's political strength and his unwavering supporters. Anyone on the coast who referred to Clapp in any terms but the most extolling was considered eccentric.

Towards the end of the campaign, Neil discovered the reason for Clapp's preferential treatment. He had been wondering why there were no political repercussions during the campaign from Clapp's failure to follow through over the past year on his farcical separation referendum. None of Neil's prospective constituents considered the matter to be of much consequence. At last, Neil's curiosity drove him to ask a group of men their feelings on the referendum and the lack of action on it. They said: "Listen, my son, that was a good bit of fun while it lasted, and knowing Percy, it might be a good bit of fun again yet." Now he knew Clapp's secret. The only people who were not expected to conform to the unostentatious norm of behaviour were either those whose antics made them fit subjects for guffers or those who were talented at the telling of guffers. Any kind of outrageous conduct from them was tolerated, indeed, expected, as an implicit part of the exercise of their skills. That, then, thought Neil, was the reason they loved Clapp. It had nothing to do with good or bad government. He entertained and amused them brilliantly with both his *words* and his *actions*. It was a discovery worth remembering, Neil decided.

On election night, Neil waited nervously for the results to be reported on television. He was incredulous as the counts were given and astounded when the station proclaimed him the first candidate elected. At the end of the night the final results showed that Neil had received 87 per cent of the votes cast in his district, a return second only to what Percy Clapp himself had attained, and a good 15 per cent greater than the vote for Clyde Ferritt in the adjoining district. The discrepancy between prognostication during the campaign and performance at the voting booths in his own district struck Neil as remarkable. All the people who had playfully encouraged him to run during the months before the call of the election and who had turned on him like a rabid pet thereafter, had, in fact, voted for him. The abuse and ridicule had obviously been a matter of ritual. At twenty-three years of age, Neil was a Member of the Legislature, the youngest ever elected.

Back in the city, everyone complimented him on his victory. He was sought after for radio and television interviews. Even the anti-Clapp newspaper was flattering, for, while the editorial decried the re-election of Clapp's government, it took some solace from Neil's and Clyde's appearance in politics as "the hoped-for front wave of a future political high tide which will swallow the flotsam, derelict, and wreck still littering the political low-water mark, a legacy left from Clapp's litany of past lunacies."

Neil felt good, even after he heard from some newsmen that Clyde was spreading the rumour that Neil had insisted on running in one of the safest seats in the country, while Clyde had insisted on running in one that looked as if it would otherwise be lost. This was Clyde's colleague-like way of acknowledging Neil's higher percentage of votes.

While waiting for the legislature to reconvene in the fall, Neil went back to his law practice and worked desultorily. He chafed to get into politics full-time. He let it be known to Percy Clapp that he would welcome an invitation to join his Cabinet as a minister. As the weeks went by and no such invitation was forthcoming, he mentioned his desire to his father, and asked him to put the pressure on Clapp. Ernest agreed to bring the subject up at the earliest opening. More weeks went by and still nothing happened. He saw Clapp at several caucus meetings and even had lunch with him and two or three other members on one occasion, but Clapp paid no particular attention to him and did not even obliquely bring the matter up. The lack of response from Clapp started to get on his nerves.

When the House of Assembly opened in early fall, Neil found that his seat was directly behind that of Dr. Gorman, the former president of the university. Before long, as a result of their chats in the House and Gorman's invitations to drop down to his office for a coffee, Neil overcame a lingering sense of resentment over Gorman's treatment of Muck Barrows and developed something of a friendship with him. What interested Neil most about him was the contrast between his previous stature at the university, and his stature now in the eyes of the political colleagues around him. Gorman still tried to be authoritative, but it cut no ice here. He was considered pompous and vain. Other members joked to his face that Clapp had appointed him to the Cabinet only for religious balance and for his distinguished head of splendid white hair, which looked good on the stage at school graduation ceremonies.

Dr. Gorman was still Minister of Education, theoretically a senior portfolio, but Neil soon discovered what Gorman had learned shortly after his appointment three years before – that he was very much on the outer fringe of Clapp's government. Most of their talks in his office centred on Gorman's resentment at not being taken seriously by Clapp. He held Clapp in secret contempt and considered him far below himself intellectually. Neil was astonished at how politically stupid Gorman was, and although the minister tried to cover up this fact with well-chosen words, he himself must have felt out of place in the government *milieu*, for he kept plumbing Neil's mind for his political and economic thoughts. And, while he listened, he did not disguise a surprise which approached awe at one or another of Neil's insights into the politically obvious. "I always knew at the university that you would take off with flying colours once you settled down and extricated yourself from the unedifying company you kept at first." He smiled with what looked to Neil like pride. But he never mentioned Muck Barrows' name.

As time went on, and Neil remained uninvited into the Cabinet, he frequently let his irritation at Clapp overflow into these conversations with Gorman. He would sometimes tell the minister of his fears of the country's imminent bankruptcy if Clapp were permitted to continue his irresponsible spending practices. Gorman would agree enthusiastically, stating that he'd had similar misgivings for nearly three years now, but that Clapp would stick his head in the sand every time he raised them. Eventually, Neil began to repeat to Gorman all the stories he had ever heard (inventing a few as he went along) in which the constant theme was the suspicion that "Clapp had his fingers in the jam jar." Gorman's doubts about Clapp's incorruptibility came to the surface immediately, and he drew on his own hoard of similar tales.

"Knowing these unsavoury facts, as you do, Neil," probed Gorman one day, "why are you in Clapp's party at all?"

"Well, Dr. Gorman," said Neil, "I am in politics to try to effect beneficial change. The quickest and best way to do that, considering Percy's strong political support in the country and the slim likelihood of his defeat by the electorate in the near future, is to effect change from within. That may offend a moral purist, but it has the pragmatic advantage of perhaps achieving some change in the right direction."

Gorman rose from his seat. "Neil," he said, "how often in the past three years have I longed to hear someone of ability in our caucus say that? Those are my sentiments exactly. I've been waiting for someone like you to come along. Change from within. That's it precisely. We can accomplish that. And there are others in the caucus, the weaker ones with no leadership abilities, who believe that as well, and would be willing to follow a strong person's lead."

One morning in late fall, Neil was called by Clapp's secretary and told to come immediately to his office. At last, thought Neil happily. The old bugger had finally got the message. When he arrived at Clapp's office he was shown in right away. Clapp and Clyde Ferritt were there, as well as Toope, the Minister of Justice, and his deputy minister.

"Mr. Godwin," said the premier, without preliminaries, "everyone admired the brilliant manner in which you conducted your case on behalf of that poor man afflicted with asbestosis and lung cancer. Even Toope here, the Minister of Justice, and his deputy, whose legal department acted for the compensation board and who were therefore theoretically

133

against you insofar as the adversary legal system is concerned, cannot hide their grudging admiration of your skilled and inspired advocacy." Toope seemed willing to try. He cleared his sinuses with a long, vibrant snuff, and his lungs with a resonant hawk, a look of disgust on his face.

"I understand your speech to the judge was superb," continued Clapp. "I read about it in the papers, of course, and it was good there in print, but not a patch, they say, on the real thing delivered by you in person, in court. The fact that the Court of Appeal was not persuaded later does not detract from your initial success.

"Thus, Mr. Godwin, already you've displayed superior legal abilities and superior political acumen, both of which are necessary for the proposition that I'm now going to put to you. You are aware that there has been an ongoing dispute between my government and the Federal Government of Canada over the ownership and jurisdiction of the continental shelf off our coast. Largely academic heretofore, this question is now of utmost importance to us, compared to which no other question rises above insignificance. Exploration and analysis show the shelf to contain vast, perhaps unprecedented, reserves of oil and gas. Advancing technology and rising prices have made feasible the commercial exploitation of these offshore resources. I'm speaking now only of the oil and gas because those are the glamour products which seem to seize the imagination. I am mindful as well, however, of the value, in a protein-starved world, of the fish which swim in the waters above our continental shelf.

"Now, there has been palaver for years about having the offshore ownership question settled definitively by the Supreme Court of Canada. The best constitutional lawyers in the world, Mr. Godwin, advise us that our case is legally sound, far superior for good historical reasons to similar claims by any other coastal province. But I know, and you know, even Toope, the Minister of Justice over there, knows – everyone with the most minuscule grain of sense knows – that the Supreme Court of Canada will not decide the dispute between us and the Government of Canada on law. Those judges were all appointed by the Government of Canada.

Most of them are from central Canada, steeped in the long tradition of gouging the hinterland for the benefit of their Bay Street clients, and will make a decision in favour of Canada, that is to say, Toronto. Those judges were once practising lawyers after all, and the fact that a whore has become the madam of the brothel does not *ipso facto* imply any great sweeping alteration in her outlook and philosophy. Oh yes, they'll couch their decision against us in the noble language of keeping Canada strong and united, but we'll be robbed of our riches as certainly as if we were rolled in the cathouse privy. That's what we are up against there. So the Supreme Court of Canada is out. Out!

"A political settlement between us and the federal government has proved impossible. God in heaven knows how we have tried, Mr. Godwin. But those greedy-gutted, grasping bastards want to keep this province on the federal welfare rolls, as gratefully cringing recipients of Upper Canadian largesse. Pack that! Screw that! Piss, shit, and puke on that!" The Deputy Minister of Justice's head sank between his shoulders by degrees during these concluding ten words of Clapp's policy towards the federal government. Neil himself marvelled at how singularly free from bureaucratese the premier had been able to make his summary of his policy position on the question.

"No." Clapp paced. "No." He straightened a curtain at the window. "No." He abruptly stopped and sized up his large mahogany desk, shoved it with tremendous effort an inch to the side, sized it up again, showed satisfaction with its new location, and resumed his pacing. "No, Mr. Godwin, our government is going to submit the dispute for resolution to the International Court at the Hague.

"Oh, they laughed at my referendum to have us separate from Canada. They said it was for negotiation purposes only. They even say now that my lack of serious intent regarding the referendum has been proved by my allowing the matter to lie dormant ever since I won it. They'll learn after a while. It's no use getting old if you don't get cute. Right, Toope? That referendum result, Mr. Godwin, gives us status to appear as an entity before the World Court, a *locus standi* to use lawyers'

135

mumbo jumbo. That's what the Government of Canada has failed to realize.

"My Cabinet colleagues, on my own firm recommendation, want you, Mr. Godwin, *you*, to form part of the team of lawyers who will be representing our interests before the World Court. Not just another member of that team, mind you, but as the lead local counsel of that team. We are retaining, naturally, the services of the foremost international lawyer on the face of the earth, a gentleman based in Great Britain." He gave the name of a man whose textbook on international law Neil had studied at Oxford. "He will provide overall leadership in preparing and presenting our case, so, in effect, you will be second-in-command to him, which, of course, I know you would want in any event, since, in spite of your astonishing abilities, you are young and just embarking on your legal career, and your association with a prestigious international legal name will do neither your cause nor your career any harm. But I stress that you are the lead counsel of whatever team of local lawyers you will be putting together here.

"It is estimated that the preparation of our case for presentation and processing through the World Court will take two to three years – the most exciting three years of your life. Now, tell me, Mr. Godwin, how does my proposal strike you?"

Neil, who had been standing and swivelling from side to side to keep his eye on the mobile premier throughout this discourse, now sat down unbidden. He was staggered, partly by the attractiveness of the offer and partly by the inherent stupidity of its premise. What was the point of going to the International Court of Justice on such a dispute? If Newfoundland were to separate from Canada, its offshore resources would belong to it automatically, as with any other independent nation. If Newfoundland did not separate, the World Court would not rule on an internal dispute between a country and one of its own provinces. Neil put this analysis to Clapp in the form of a polite question.

"That is a question, Mr. Godwin, of striking acuity," said Clapp. "I told you, Clyde, my friend, that Neil Godwin was *not* a dum dum. Didn't I tell Clyde that earlier, Toope? The answer to your question, which we have on the best authority, is one which you will remember from your legal studies: equity deems to be done which ought to be done. By that referendum, we expressed our national will to separate. The fact that we have not yet formally negotiated separation is irrelevant. The court will not allow justice to be perverted by the shenanigans of one of the parties before it. The Government of Canada may drag its feet for years on the separation. They may even send in their gun boats to try to prevent it altogether. The court will not allow such unilateral actions by our adversary to deprive us of our rightful place in that court. Right, Toope?" The Minister of Justice rolled his cigar between his rounded lips with his fingers and nodded gravely.

"Moreover," continued Clapp, "we are not unmindful of the prevailing favourable climate of world opinion regarding aspirant, emerging nations, or, *or*, Mr. Godwin, and more important, of the total domination of all global institutions by third world countries and Soviet satellites. They won't be able to resist a chance to hurt the US, and what better way than to take a kick at that pile on the American anus – Canada? Oh no, Mr. Godwin, I have no doubt, none, that you will win a place for us in the World Court, and once there, will carry the day for us. Not a *bad* little start to your future legal and political prominence – national hero and founding father of your country in your mid-twenties. What do you say? I must know now."

Where in the name of Christ did he dredge it all up from? thought Neil. Still, it made *some* sense. He accepted the proposition for further research, dousing the sparks of doubt in his mind. After all, a far lesser plum – the taking of the province's case to the Supreme Court of Canada – had been the constant talk of the legal fraternity for years, with much speculation over which firm would ultimately get the job. And here he was: the ONE! And going to the World Court to boot! What better kick-off to a life of riches, power, fame, honour, and the love of women could he reasonably expect? He shook hands with Clapp to the accompaniment of much enthusiastic verbiage. Leaving the office, Neil wondered why Clyde Ferritt would hang back in his corner and grin like that.

Clapp made the announcement of Neil Godwin's retention on this case of "unprecedented importance to the future wealth of ourselves personally and of our beloved country." Everywhere he went, people said that Clapp had made an excellent choice and gave Neil their very best wishes in this tremendous responsibility. A few people even called him on the telephone. A woman caller said that she and her family had seen his interview on the news about the offshore oil case and they had loved it. All her family and friends were of the one opinion, she said; namely: that Neil would become premier, "and we're not talking about the distant future, either."

At the luncheon club where many lawyers gathered, Neil had expected to be greeted with their usual scepticism of anything involving Percy Clapp, but instead, most of them made known to him by a private word their interest in becoming part of the team he would be putting together.

"Judas Priest!" T. Alexander Touchings, the President of the Law Society, said to him over their club sandwiches. "A case in the Supreme Court of Canada ... " (Neil had given notice of appeal on the asbestosis case despite the disapproval of his senior partner) "... and another case in the World Court, all within your first year of practice – either one of which is something that nearly 100 per cent of the lawyers practising in St. John's will never have happen during their entire lives!"

Carried away by thoughts of a great legal career, Neil spent most of his time now either chatting with people about his two cases or doing what he liked to do best alone in his office: "conceptualizing." Every so often, the need to get cracking on the organizing and research for both of these cases would occur to him. Then he would see a vision of himself hunched over his desk reading from one book and writing notes in another, and his enthusiasm would wane a little. Once, when he was conceptualizing about his cases, three or four tomes lying unopened before him, he saw a vision of himself in that same hunched-over, copying position, and his hair was grey and his dark suit very expensive looking. The shock of the image stood him up.

While he was gazing out his window at the ships manoeuvring in the harbour, he got the first of several phone calls that morning from newsmen wondering if he knew anything about the rumours from Clapp's office that there was soon to be a Cabinet shuffle and that Clyde Ferritt was slated to go in as Minister of Industrial Development. Neil feigned both cheerfulness and a secret knowledge which he would not divulge.

That afternoon, Neil went to the legislature to confront Clapp on this rumour which omitted any reference to himself.

Dr. Gorman turned as Neil sat down. "How are you enjoying the practice of law," he asked. He listened as Neil gave his usual description of his two most important cases and his absorption by them, then nodded. "Yes, I thought you were totally immersed in your law practice and that's why you don't stay in the House much. That's also why I can't understand Percy's remark to Clyde ... I accidentally overheard it some days ago."

"What was that?" asked Neil.

"Come down for a quick coffee," said Gorman. "We'll be back before Question Period is over. I never get any questions from the Opposition, anyway."

Clapp was not yet in the House, so Neil left with the minister. They were in the elevator waiting for the door to close when Clapp went by. His eye caught Neil's.

"Yes, a funny thing for him to say," whispered Gorman, and Neil, on the point of following the premier, decided to stay.

"What did the premier say, Dr. Gorman?" inquired Neil impatiently, as they entered the office.

"Well, he said something like – you'll have to pardon the language: 'Finally got that bloody nuisance of a young Godwin poked away for two or three years. Pushy little bastard. First, he had his father pester me to let him run in the election, and then he had Ernie driving me right off my head again tormenting me to put him in the goddamned Cabinet.' I'm morally certain that's what he said. I remember because it struck me as peculiar. You're not interested in going in the Cabinet, are you? Not yet, anyway. Not until you get yourself well established in your law practice."

"No," said Neil. "I'm not interested in full-time politics for a few years yet."

"I didn't think so. Knowing how you feel about Percy, I thought you'd want to make yourself independent financially, before you force your changes from within, as you said. I must have been mistaken about exactly what Percy said …."

But Neil knew that Gorman had heard Clapp's words correctly, and Clyde's ugly, grinning face as he had accepted the offshore oil case came into his mind. Afraid he might reveal his anger and disappointment to Gorman, Neil turned the conversation to other things. Soon, however, he was impelled to start in on Clapp, and threw out anything nasty and damning that he could think to say about him. The minister listened, nodding and murmuring his agreement. Neil ended his denunciation of the premier with a snarl: "That goddamned Percy Clapp has got to go!"

Dr. Gorman sat bolt upright. "You know, you are absolutely right! And do you know something else? I've talked to a few of the boys in the back benches, especially those who are frightened they will not get in the Cabinet again this time around, and I am convinced that it would only take the thin edge of the wedge to bring Clapp's whole house of cards tumbling down."

Neil certainly didn't agree with that analysis. But he said nothing to the contrary. In fact, he indicated that the minister was not far wrong, so annoyed was he with Clapp's shifty ways.

As Neil was about to leave the office, Gorman nodded sagely. "You go on up to the House. No need to say another word about this. I know where you stand. I'll be along shortly. I just have to get a few papers."

About ten minutes after Neil had resumed his seat in the House, and was wondering how to grapple with Clapp, Gorman came in. "This is it," he whispered, as soon as he sat down. "Let's go!" Rising in his place he demanded recognition from the Speaker on a point of personal privilege. He thereupon announced his resignation from Percy Clapp's government on the grounds of the utter financial irresponsibility of the prime minister and his "well documented corruption, based on information that has come to me from several unimpeachable sources." He was reading his words from his sheaf of papers, obviously prepared some time before. "There are many other persons in the prime minister's Cabinet and in the back benches who share my views," he finished. And half-turned to Neil.

A deep silence fell over the assembled members. Clapp gazed placidly at the clock. Expectantly, Gorman looked around at the members on his side. Several in the back benches slunk down in their seats and avoided his eyes. Obviously, the minister had thought he was the centre of a great conspiracy, and that Neil was one of his followers (judging from the raised eyebrows he now showed him). In his foolish vanity, Gorman had taken the normal, pervasive grumblings about leadership at face value, and had expected many supporters in this act of lunacy. Incredulous, Neil wondered how such a combination of scepticism and gullibility, dignity and ridiculousness, could exist together in one man.

Dr. Gorman now stammered and fumbled and sat down. Clapp stood up and said, "Before I speak to the point of privilege of the Honourable Gentleman, Mr. Speaker, perhaps there are other members on this side who may wish to say a word in support of his point." He looked slowly and confidently at every face on his side of the chamber. Neil could only admire the sure style of the man. When Clapp's eyes reached his, and stayed a few seconds, Neil wagged his head once to the side and made a grim smile – both gestures designed to show his disbelieving contempt for the minister.

Ending his survey, Clapp went on to say how happy he was that the minister had at least done the honourable thing by resigning, but how sad he was at the low and scurrilous manner in which the minister had chosen to do so. "The minister's action in resigning today has saved me the truly painful task of removing from office in public disgrace a minister who, in spite of the complete trust I had reposed in him, had coupled to his forgivable incompetence, a personal greed and lust for graft of unforgivable proportions. In spite of this, I had given him a way out which would have allowed him to retain some last tatters of self-respect. But regrettably, this Honourable Member has chosen to add to his attributes of stupidity and cupidity and malignant self-esteem (in the celebrated old phrase of Joey Smallwood), the further equally unwelcome but consistent traits of craven cowardice and moral dishonesty. Instead of resigning with grace, once I had privately disclosed to him my knowledge of his pilfering from the public chest, he now seeks to cover his vile breach of public trust with a tissue of state matters of pretended public importance, which, even if they did exist in reality, and even if the Honourable Member had the wit to understand them, would only be used by him for his own financial self-aggrandizement. No breach of public trust and no act of dishonesty or corruption has taken place in my administration, but that this minister was either at it himself or privy to it."

The former minister made a pathetic attempt to protest that his honour and integrity had been impugned, and moved that Clapp either withdraw the charges or set up a select committee of the House to investigate their validity. The Speaker, however, ruled against the procedural propriety of every request, demand, or motion. Gorman's remedies were now at an end. Everything said in the House was privileged, and could not be made the subject of an action for slander in a court of law.

The Minister of Justice, Toope, rose in his place and moved that the former minister be suspended from the legislature for the remainder of the year's session for "his unfounded allegation of corruption against the prime minister." The motion was debated and passed with much protestation of loyalty to Clapp. Neil's erstwhile sounding board for political annoyances was escorted out of the chamber in humiliation and defeat between the Sergeant-at-Arms and a police constable. That evening, Neil found a handwritten note from Gorman in his mailbox. It politely inquired when Gorman might expect Neil's public denunciation of Clapp, so that he could work out his own future political moves around that date.

That evening as well, Neil received a phone call from Clyde Ferritt, the first for months. As soon as Neil picked up the phone Clyde began to speak; and he talked on without giving Neil any chance to comment. "I am calling you against my better judgement," said Clyde, "but our friendship requires me to do so, Neil. I feel I must advise you that your fraternization with Gorman has not gone unnoticed by Percy. He means to take action with respect to you tomorrow morning, and I am forewarning you of that for your own sake. It's up to you what you do about it. Apart from our friendship – in case you have any doubts about that – I also have a selfish motive in calling you: we are both young and we will be around long after Percy is gone. When a populist leader such as Percy finally falls it will be in a swirl of popular revulsion against him. The intelligent young man who opposes Percy now, on real principle, may not win immediately; but at the time of Percy's fall in a few years, that young man will be remembered and revered for his courage. It will be a tremendous political asset, and, quite frankly, Neil, I would want to be remembered by that man as having done him a favour. That's all I can say now, but I hope you make the right move – bearing in mind that forewarned is forearmed. Goodbye for now, Neil. And good luck."

Neil thought and thought for most of the night. He wished Ernest were there to advise him, but he was on a coastal boat somewhere, visiting Gawker churches in remote communities. He knew he had ruined his chance of going into the Cabinet; but he could not see how Clapp, in view of his father's support, could take any punitive action against him.

The following morning, a message awaited Neil at his law office. The prime minister wanted him to go immediately to the Cabinet room; the whole caucus was asked to be there. Was Clapp planning to bounce him out of the party? Neil wondered, as he drove. He made himself alert and ready to jump the gun on Clapp if need be. When he walked into the room, he saw that most of the Cabinet Ministers and members were assembled, together with an unusually large number of press people. Clyde came over to comment, "Percy is about to heap an awful load on you." Neil swallowed, but said nothing. Going to the entrance of the premier's office, Clyde announced in a stage whisper: "Godwin's finally here, sir. You can proceed with the execution, now."

Neil saw Clapp laugh and then wipe the levity off his face before coming out. He came towards Neil grim-faced and with the energetic stride that he assumed to propel himself out into waiting crowds. Tense and uneasy, Neil nearly jumped towards the mikes to erupt into a spiel of denunciation, but while he stood there, undecided, Clapp told him to sit in a chair at the table. Neil hesitated. "Clyde *did* call you last night?" said Clapp.

Neil's head snapped towards Clyde. "Yes, he did, sir," he allowed, finally. And moved to the table with the premier's arm around his shoulders.

Clapp sadly announced the immediate resignation of two additional senior ministers for reasons of ill health, and then, much more cheerfully, the immediate appointment of Ferritt and Godwin and one other man to the Cabinet. Clyde was to be Minister of Industrial Development and Neil would be Minister of Health. When all eyes in the press corps turned to look at him on hearing this news, Neil tried hard to give the impression that he knew what was going on.

"Yes," said Clapp, finishing his praise of Clyde and moving on to Neil. "Besides Mr. Godwin's mental abilities he also happens to be a physically healthy young specimen of a man." He broke into the grin that the press loved to see, presaging, as it always did, good copy. "It's about time we had a Minister of Health who isn't mentally or physically moribund, threatening to pass on all the time, casting doubts in the public mind on the efficacy of this government's health system!" The former Minister of Health, whose place Neil had taken, had suffered a stroke several weeks before and was now mostly bedridden. The press laughed uproariously and scribbled.

At noon, the other minister, whose resignation for reasons of health had been announced, objected vehemently on the news that his health had never been better. The press began to play it up, speculating on whether or not Clapp had uttered a public untruth, and whether or not there was a serious political rift in his government. A crisis situation was painted in the newscasts. That evening, Clapp was on television saying, "He says he's not sick, does he? Well, that's all right. You know how the old joke goes: the other one is sick enough for both of them!" Thus passed that political crisis. The remaining stories on the Cabinet changes admired Clapp's moves in ridding the government of some deadwood and bringing in fresh talent in the persons of Ferritt and Godwin.

Clyde approached Neil at the swearing-in ceremony that evening. Neil had pointedly ignored him after the press conference.

"I'm glad you got the drift of my remarks on the phone last night, Neil," Clyde said. "I had to be a little ambiguous because Percy didn't want it to get out. He doesn't trust the phones, he says. I think he just loves a cloak-and-dagger atmosphere around everything."

Neil was irritated to realize that he was warming to Clyde once more, that he was finding it impossible to sustain his grudge against him. He let the time for a sharp reply pass and they chatted in a friendly way until Clapp joined them.

"Well, Clyde," the premier said to the roomful of ministers. "I hope you didn't have your heart really set on becoming the youngest Cabinet minister in our history, as your mother told me the other night. Neil will have that status in a moment – not to mention that, at twenty-four, he will be the youngest Minister of the Crown presently serving in the entire British Commonwealth! A record for Newfoundland. A great achievement, Neil. Come over boys and congratulate Mr. Godwin on that achievement."

"Who deserves congratulations more, sir?" said Clyde, trying to be light. "The one who possesses the talent, or the one who recognizes talent in others?"

"What does the one who dreads talent in others deserve, Clyde?" asked Neil.

Clapp studied Neil's face intently and chuckled, bringing on a general laugh. "Well done, Neil," he said. "Very well done! But let's go in and see the governor now, boys. These questions are long, and life, especially political life, can be all too short."

As Neil was being sworn in, the oath of office requiring him to report directly to the Queen any "intestine insurrections" brought Muck Barrows to his mind. He hadn't seen him since their swift drink together during Muck's visit home the summer before Neil had left for Oxford. And he hadn't replied to any of Muck's letters afterwards. But he thought he might write him now to describe Gorman's ignominious political rout as having been plotted by Neil to avenge the underhand treatment Muck had received from the university.

He never got around to it.

For in the middle of all this – Neil had met Gillian.

11

Soon after he had arrived back from Oxford, Neil had become a good occasional friend of T. Alexander Touchings, the President of the Law Society. Touchings was a third generation lawyer and leading Catholic layman, and was reputed to be wealthy. Their friendship was nearly exclusively restricted to the luncheon club where he and Neil went daily. The difference in their ages did not make any difference to their growing relationship, and it was not long before they were treating each other as equals in every respect, and exchanging funny, usually lewd, personal experiences.

One day, after Neil had been admitted to the Bar, Touchings came to lunch as usual; but this time he was accompanied by his daughter, Gillian. Neil had never seen her before, but he had heard about her from Touchings and knew that she had just come back from several years of study at universities in London and Paris. She was intelligent, attractive, and knowledgeable, and blessed with a sense of humour similar to her father's, though, Neil thought, gentler.

She and Neil started to go out together, and he found that although her attractiveness may not have been striking, like that of Victoria Montagu or his own sister, Gillian had an undeniable beauty about her. It seemed to come from within. She exuded an inner repose and a sense of security about herself; a resigned indifference to life's unavoidable buffets combined with the attitude of an activist for the occasions when action might be useful, lovely, or moving. She was open and frank about her ideas and opinions, but she seemed to

147

possess an inviolate core of privacy. It was not strenuously guarded; it was just there. It was clear that she would never be property.

The trait Neil noticed most about her was that she completely filled and owned the space she occupied, wherever she was. She was never showy or obtrusive; but her presence was always felt, impossible to ignore. When she spoke, she usually brought a novel approach to the subject. She was not an intellectual bully, but she accepted fatuities from nobody, unless as a conscious act of mercy. Neil quickly came to the conclusion that he'd never met anyone who was quite so balanced, mature, aware, and unillusioned, or who possessed such well-defined but unopinionated desires, aspirations, tastes, and needs. Having come to grips with what she was, Gillian wasted little time or fruitless anxiety on what she wasn't.

Religion was not a usual topic of their conversations, but when it did come up, they were both relieved to discover that despite the indoctrination of their childhoods in divergent tenets of faith, they now shared, as adults, a similar undoctrinaire view of theology. They would both be atheists if that did not imply a dogma of its own.

They knew, as they continued to spend lengthy periods of time together, that their initial attraction to one another was developing into a strong mutual attachment. Its physical expression, however, had not yet gone beyond kissing and snuggling. Gillian was very affectionate but gave no encouragement to Neil to proceed further. He put it down to inexperience on her part and asked a few oblique questions about past boyfriends, as a guide to his own future conduct.

"Neil," she said, with a smile of amusement at his probes, "I lived with a man for nearly a year in London. I ended our relationship, without regret then or now, when I judged that it was detracting from, rather than adding to, the worth of each of us. Right. Have a couple more of these brandied peaches. I'm after your heart."

The heart she was after was sore that night as Neil lay sleepless on his bed in his newly acquired apartment. He would have sworn with total conviction – before Gillian's revelation – that he possessed no vestigial remnant of the male double standard towards sex. Then he began to wonder why, in the light of her sexual experience, she had never given the slightest impression she wanted to go to bed with *him*. Just two evenings before, when they had been arranging the furniture in his apartment, he had jocularly suggested she stay the night. She had replied, with equal jocularity, that she was only now getting reacquainted with all the subtle nuances of her own bed at home after years away from it, and that she didn't want to break practice until she had them totally mastered. Perhaps her rational or joking approach to everything (a trait that, until now, he had found so appealing), was in fact a manifestation of, or a cover for, sexual coldness.

Without wanting to, Neil juggled conflicting emotions and absurd postulates all night. When, hanging between sleep and wakefulness just after dawn, he found himself wondering how long it took skin cells to die and to be replaced by new ones, and whether Gillian's vagina was yet lined with cells entirely different from those which had last enveloped her former lover's penis, he leaped off his bed in disgust at himself. He got ready for work growling curses at his own compulsive reflections. Nevertheless, he was compelled the next evening to ask Gillian some crabwise queries designed to elicit her attitude on sex.

"I have a purely selfish morality about screwing for its own sake, Neil," she told him. "It's based on the following consideration. If the sole end in view is the celebrated female orgasm, then self-congratulatory studs should be made to realize that it is easier and better achieved with the tip of one's own index finger than with a man's phallus, which is about as delicately engineered for that purpose as the forefeet of a hippopotamus, seized by a hormonic urge to pound out a piece on the harpsichord, would be for producing the music of Bach."

Neil had to laugh with her but the thought, "Oh Jesus, don't tell me she's one of *those!*" went through his mind.

"What I'm trying to say, Neil," continued Gillian, taking his hands, "is that I'm not very interested in the simple fuck, zipless or zipped, that is not bound up with loyalty, friendship, self-esteem, and deep physical and emotional devotion on *both* sides." Her face was serious though the corners of her mouth seemed to be twitching.

"Sounds like we have to work our way through Roget's Thesaurus," said Neil. "Interesting concept in foreplay."

Her eyes prepared for another laugh. One was never far away. "You're lucky," she said. "I was about to add 'dignity,' too, until the image of the two of us bouncing and grinding on your bed in there popped into my head. The dignity of the beast with two backs, humping along, going nowhere."

Neil hardly knew what to make of her. He did know, however, that the thought of getting back to her after the election which was called by Clapp the next day, made the campaign of abuse and declining hope bearable. He telephoned her every night, no matter how late he returned to his hotel, and every night she was waiting for his call, answering on the first ring, saying how much she missed having him there with her, and allaying the fears he expressed about the outcome of his election by telling him she hoped he'd win but that she couldn't care less if he didn't.

The evening after his election he suggested to Gillian that they have dinner at a restaurant to celebrate; but she asked him to take her to his apartment, instead. Bustling around his kitchen as they cooked the meal together, they kissed and hugged often. He showed all his joy and vigour at his victory. She responded with delight to his antics. Warmth and love and charming silliness filled the atmosphere, and they found it impossible to keep their hands and mouths off each other, even when they sat down to their meal.

This is the night, thought Neil, as he kissed her breastbone and felt his head encircled and squeezed by the hug of her arms. It had to be. A disappointment tonight would finish him.

She did nearly finish him by slowly whispering, her lips touching his ear anew at each word, "I sense on both sides a deep physical and emotional devotion and ... to hell with Roget's!"

Neil amazed himself by wordlessly sweeping her off her

chair – just like in the movies. She only had time to scoop up one more spoonful of her favourite *crème caramel* before being borne away. Kicking off her shoes and clinging to his neck as he jogged into the bedroom, Gillian giggled, "And, Neil, don't go looking for no dignity."

It hadn't occurred to him to do so, but once they were on his bed something akin to quiet dignity and reverence did come over them. They gently touched each other's faces and necks with their fingertips, and then undressed each other with slow delight. With his hands and his lips, Neil softly sculptured every inch of Gillian's curved smoothness. He forgot all about his own desires. He strove only to please her, and discovered that his own excitement increased the more pleased she became. He had never before experienced such pleasure as at the sight and sound of the joy he was now giving. And he knew that Gillian, eagerly returning every kiss and caress, was experiencing the same powerful feeling.

During the final minutes, when Gillian's image of their bouncing and grinding on the bed came true, the beast they created seemed sublime and self-sufficient. No outside fantasies to improve the reality had to invade Neil's mind this night. The rapturous face he saw and kissed, his awareness of what he and she were *doing* to one another, and his understanding that she was transported like him, was everything.

Neil and Gillian passed seventeen consecutive nights together like that, giving and receiving great love. Then Neil had to leave for his district to turn on the pumphouse switch that would officially start the flow in a newly constructed sewer line.

He was going to be away for three days. The night before he had to leave he had said goodbye to Gillian; and so he was surprised when his secretary came into his office at noon, just as he was about to set out on the long drive. "A Ms. Gillian Touchings is out there," she said. "I told her you were leaving to go out of town. Will I give her to one of the articling students? I think it's one of those marriage-breakdown things you hate."

"Why do you think that?"

"She wrote it down here .... " The secretary glanced at her notebook. "She wants me to tell you that she's after a suite for hippo and harpsichord in a flat."

"In that case I'd better see her," said Neil. "Bring her in."

He closed the door behind Gillian and they kissed. "I came to take you back to your flat to eat and help you pack," she said, giving him three or four big winks. "Get it?"

"Oh God, Gillian," Neil moaned, "I have to leave in a few minutes or I'll be late for the shit-pump ceremony. I put my suitcase in the car this morning."

"Don't you want to eat first?"

"There's a cold turkey supper with the dreaded purple salad after the ceremony. I'll wait till then."

"But that's a five hour drive. I will not have you going without your sustenance." She put her hand on his crotch and whispered, "Neil, lock the door."

He reached for the doorhandle and then remembered that the knobs had been put on backwards and that the door locked only from the outside, like a room in a lunatic asylum. He began to tell Gillian that, but she already had his fly undone and her hand inside. Without removing her raincoat, she held on to his erect penis for balance and hopped up and down on one foot, peeling her panty hose down and off one leg with her free hand. Then she stood on her toes and wound her bare leg tightly around his waist. Feeling her heel digging into his back and the hot wetness of her vagina at the tip of his penis, Neil directed a silent prayer to his secretary, who was under instructions to enter and remind him whenever he was being detained beyond the time for another meeting: *Give me thirty seconds. Please.* Then he put his hands under Gillian's coat and skirt and lifted her up by the buttocks.

"Am I too heavy for you?" she asked for form, as she hung from his neck and clasped her feet behind his back.

"I'm like the Rock of Gibraltar," he said. He couldn't feel her weight.

"Oh, Mother of God," breathed Gillian as she settled down over him and let her head fall back. "Oh, Blessed Mother of God!" Her convent upbringing sometimes came out during moments of passion.

He did feel her weight now, especially since she'd begun to move up and down like a piledriver. Eyes half-closed, he had a delightful sensation of floating free, just before he heard his head thud against the carpet on the floor. In his attempt to adjust their oscillating centre of gravity, he must have leaned back too far. His face was covered by Gillian's skirt and he felt her pelvis swivelling against his chest for a few seconds before it abruptly stopped. He hoped her thrusts hadn't been a headless-chicken reflex and that he hadn't broken her neck. At least she was breathing.

"Gillian," he whispered sheepishly. "Gillian, are you all right? Gillian!"

"Ah," she said finally, "my very own Rock of Gibraltar."

He helped her to her feet. "You would have been in a fine pickle," she said, laughing, "if they found us on the floor unconscious, you in your three piece suit and your dick out through your fly, and me, your client, with my coat and skirt up over my back, my panty hose ripped off one leg, and my bare bum in the air." Struck by a thought, she stopped laughing. "Was it an hallucination or did I see your secretary peeking in here while you were ravishing me? Just before you collapsed. No. You had the door locked."

"The door doesn't lock, Gillian."

"Oh, lovely!" She pulled the top of her panty hose up to her waist and let go of the elastic with a violent snap. "Well, it's not a total disaster. At least I know you won't be up to hanky-panky at work, not in this room, anyway."

"I have to confess something, Gillian. I planned it all this way. You'll have to marry me out of pity. If you don't, they'll disbar me when word of this gets around – for taking advantage of a client's trust to violate her." It was the first time an idea so irrational and unfunny as marriage had passed the lips of either of them. Neil felt his heart make a thump.

"Most romantic proposal of marriage I've ever had," said Gillian. "Oh, well, they say pity lasts longer than lust. The answer is yes. But mention it again when you get back just in case one of us has a concussion at the moment." She embraced and kissed him. "Now I'd better scoot out of here before this gets soppy." She opened the door an inch and pushed it shut immediately. "Oh, my Jesus! They're all out there like a bunch of Gawkers. Sorry about that, Neil. I mean, the secretaries are kind of looking at the door intently."

"Let's do this right, then," grinned Neil. He pulled the door wide open and took Gillian in his arms. "Goodbye, my love," he said, kissing her cheek. "I'll see you when I get back after seventy-two of the longest hours of my life."

"Farewell, dearest heart," said Gillian. "Till your safe return." She kissed him, abruptly tore herself from his embrace, and moved at a disconsolate half-trot into the unprecedented silence of the typing pool. She stopped by Neil's paralyzed secretary and confided in a whispered aside, loud enough for all the other fascinated secretaries to hear, "It's *all* right now, girl. Sure he wants to marry me and everything after that, my dear!" Her St. John's accent was faultless. The widened eyes and spreading smiles of some of the women communicated, "Well done!" Most of the younger ones, however, turned pained eyes on Neil.

Neil was not able to stay in his district for the three days he had planned. The next afternoon he succumbed to the urge to head back to Gillian and that night, in his apartment, they confirmed their decision to get married. In the morning he told his parents.

His mother was pleased. She liked Gillian. Jane, too, seemed pleased. She came towards him with a wide smile saying, perhaps a little too fervently, "Congratulations, Neil. Congratulations!" He put his arms out for the hug he expected, but she stopped short, leaned forward, and gave him a brief kiss on the cheek. He tried to look into her eyes, but she'd already turned to move away, the fixed smile unchanged.

"Gillian Touchings," murmured Ernest, lost in a fog of thought. "I don't know how my people will ... " He cleared his throat. "Will anyone be changing anyone's religion, Neil? I'm just curious."

"No."

"What about the children?"

"What children is that, father?"

"Your children, Neil. Touchings is a past Grand Idolater or

Grand Inquisitor or whatever of the Knights of Columbus."

"Oh, *those* children," Neil said. "Gillian is a Catholic in the same way I'm a Gazer on the Goodlike – not very orthodox." Ernest still looked dubious. "By the way, father, and first things first, we'll have a nice ecumenical service if that's all right with you."

"The Catholic Church of Rome," said Ernest, brightening, "and us? At the same service? Yes, that's all right with me, Neil. Grand."

That night, Neil went to see T. Alexander Touchings. As he walked into his study, a sudden memory of all the graphic sexual tidbits he'd given Touchings from his life during the months before he'd met Gillian made him feel momentarily unworthy. He bolstered himself.

"Alec," he announced, before sitting down, "Gillian and I want to get married."

"You had a Wasserman lately, Neil?" asked Touchings.

"Heh, heh, heh," said Neil.

"What about the children?"

"What children is that, Alec?"

"Gillian's children. The issue of your marriage."

"Oh, *those* children. Thanks anyway, Alec, but we already know how to do that."

"Not funny! Jesus, I hate this. The Pope'll probably take back my medal. What religion will your children be?"

"Oh, all of that will be entirely in Gillian's hands."

"Jesus, Mary, and Joseph! That'll finish me altogether. She went off the rails somewhere along the line. Her mother and I had our hearts set on her marrying a good mick who would whip her back into shape. Now that's all shagged up, too. You won't reconsider this blunder, Neil?"

"No."

"Well, all right. I saw this coming anyway, after you stopped laughing at my dirty jokes at lunch. Got right pure on me. I knew I'd be here one day consenting to this. I thought it would be sooner than now. She *is* a jewel. That's how I made my money in the first place, anticipating the worst and the best. So, to atone for this sin of consent, I changed my will last week to leave *all* my money to the Church. I hope you don't think you're marrying an heiress, my son."

"I wish you'd told me that before I committed myself, Alec."

Their chuckles brought Gillian and her mother in from their lurking place in the dining room. They wanted to share in the silly men's sentimental delight over this romantic moment.

The wedding date was set and Neil went back to his apartment for the unpleasant task of writing a letter to Jennifer Mersey in England. Since Neil's return home, she and he had been corresponding regularly. Her letters were more in the nature of *billets-doux* than Neil's had been, although he had to admit to himself now that he had done very little in his replies to discourage her outpourings of love. This would come as a severe shock to her. He wished that he had not so often taken the path of least resistance in his relationships.

Neil sent off his letter and he never heard from her again. But not for the reason he had expected. Instead, within days, he heard from Boo Mansingh. "You have no idea," wrote Boo, "how happy we are to hear the news of your engagement and impending marriage. Jennifer was so afraid of hurting you terribly. You see, Neil, Jennifer and I became engaged to be married some weeks ago and we were searching frantically for some gentle way to break the tidings to you. Needless to say, your letter was like manna from heaven. I love Jennifer very much, Neil, and I congratulate myself on knowing that she is very fond of me. Rest assured that I will take care of her in a manner befitting the profound love I bear for her and for you. We intend to live in London in view of Jennifer's job at the Tate and in the hope that my recent application to the BBC will be successful. Come and see us when you are next in London."

Was there in fact nothing but fickleness, if not downright treachery, in this world? Neil wondered. He would have placed his very life in the safekeeping of either of those two. And here was caprice, irresolution, and disloyalty. Gradually, however, Neil was able to replace these thoughts with satisfaction that everything had worked out so well for everyone;

and finally, he managed to smile to himself over how endearingly and charmingly human everyone was.

Only once during their preparations for the wedding did Neil have doubts about his marriage to Gillian. Two days before the wedding day, they were walking along the sidewalk together after work. It was late afternoon, and they were hand in hand, nuzzling each other, chatting, and laughing, when Neil saw a familiar shape from the past coming towards them on the sidewalk. Gillian said, "Oh, God, there's that poor woman they used to call the Hump."

Neil looked with surprise at Gillian. He had not expected her to recognize the woman, let alone apply the appellation descriptive of her bent body and irremovable burden. "You've seen her before?" he asked. For some unthinking reason, he had considered Gillian to be outside, or even above, such knowledge.

"Years ago," said Gillian. "Everyone in town used to see her all the time. Don't you remember how she used to march down the street surrounded by taunting children? There was someone else with her in those days. A fellow who would beat on a tin can as they marched."

"The Goofy Newfy," offered Neil; and Gillian nodded.

They remained silent as the Hump came nearly abreast of them. Her eyes were downcast. Neil looked at her in the hope that she would glance at him. He wanted to smile at her, to convey some sentiment of friendliness and understanding. He was about to look away when, just as she passed by his side, she turned her soft, wrinkled face up to his. Their eyes met – and immediately she thrust her fists straight down towards the ground. The tendons bulged out on her horizontal neck. Her head jutted even further forward than usual and, without any intermediate expression, her face changed abruptly from quiet vacancy to shocked horror. She appeared to be emitting a terrified scream, but no sound whatever emerged from her wide-open mouth. For a stunned moment, Neil could not move his eyes from the horror-struck face with its silent scream of terror. And then the unexpectedness of the expression, its apparent purposelessness, and the dread he had of suddenly hearing a soulless shriek, all startled him into impulsive movement. He twisted away from her, his violent action toppling Gillian into the long grass beside the concrete walk. Managing to stop his own fall with one hand, Neil swivelled to keep his eye on the Hump. She had resumed her previous calm and now looked straight ahead, walking away from them as tamely as she had come, her old, black vinyl coat swaying at the hem, one brilliant highlight on her back glistening in the sinking sun.

"Neil!" said Gillian, regaining her feet. "Why did you do that? I'm getting a little bit tired of being flung down on my ass every two minutes."

"Didn't you see the way she looked at me?" asked Neil.

"No, I did not see the way she looked at you." Gillian smelled the arm of her coat, her nose wrinkled in disgust. "You mean you pushed *me* down in the dog piss because the poor old Hump looked at *you*? That action portends great chivalric protection for me during my matrimonial career!" She walked on ahead, brushing at her coat with irritated gestures.

Neil lagged behind. He knew she had a right to be annoyed but it made him feel that he should not marry her, that their relationship would impede what he had to do with his life, whatever that was. She turned and waited for him to catch up, smiling now. Why hadn't she been looking at the Hump as he had? Perhaps he had misread her nature: the most attractive thing he had previously found about Gillian was that, like himself, she always noticed little details of people's actions or words which reduced pomposity to absurdity or raised simplicity to grandeur. His discovery of that trait in Gillian was what had brought him so close to her at the start. And there she was, totally oblivious of a gross and frightening expression directed against him by the Hump. This doubt about marrying Gillian faded before they had walked another hundred yards together, arm in arm, but while it lasted, he wished a telephone pole would fall on him – or her – to prevent the forthcoming union.

The wedding took place amidst much public comment over the fitness of the match. "The service was simply inspiring," Clapp blared at the reception afterwards. "How very far we've come! A moving ecumenical wedding performed by the clergy of two of our *great* denominations. Civilized and decent. Shakespeare is lucky he's not alive now, for he'd have no models in our broadminded land upon which to fashion his Montagues and his Capulets!"

Jane stole more than her share of attention at the reception, first by looking so beautiful as a bridesmaid in the receiving line and later, after a number of glasses of champagne, by being a little too saucy to some of the stuffier guests.

"I must say," said Touchings (looking a bit lubricious, Neil thought, but that might have been the champagne), "I do like that sister of yours. I welcome her aboard, so to speak. But as for that sacrilege you perpetrated on me today .... Look here!" He pulled a page from the morning paper out of his pocket and showed Neil and Gillian where to read. He had underlined the typographical error:

Marrying today are E. Neil Godwin, the young and coming Minister of the Crown and son of prominent evangelist Chief Elder Ernest Godwin, and Gillian Maude Touchings, freelance writer and only daughter of T. Alexander Touchings, the foremost <u>layer</u> in this city.

"I have no idea how they found that out," sighed Touchings. "But I'm resigned to it. Nothing will ever go right for me again. Why should it, after I violated my lifetime of devotion to the Church with that backdoor apostasy today?"

"Relax, Daddy," said Gillian, with a grin. "I'm reasonably certain it's not an accurate description. I have another notion altogether on who's foremost in that field. Now, if I can only get him to stop politicking this bunch of old Tories and take me on my honeymoon .... "

12

"It was I," roared Clapp, "*I,* I tell you, *I,* who had Randolph Rute appointed to the Board of Regents of our university! The first labour man ever appointed to that board in our history. And he with a grade eight education. I did that for Rute. No one else did it. I did it. I did it!"

Neil was at his first Cabinet meeting after his honeymoon. One of the ministers around the table had brought up the activities of Randolph Rute, who was attempting to organize the thousands of widely scattered fishermen and fishplant workers throughout the island into a union. Neil, with no evidence, but feeling a sense of gratitude towards Rute dating from the time the labour leader's confrontation with President Gorman had saved him from the righteous wrath of the University Discipline Committee, had chimed in: "Rute seems to be making some headway." It had been this that brought on Clapp's bellow about all he had done for Rute, his political friend and supporter. The premier did not like it when one of his close supporters gave evidence of flying out of orbit onto a tangent of his own, Neil knew. Still, his attitude towards Rute's activities was puzzling, since Clapp himself had tried to unionize the fishermen long ago.

"It's not that the *concept* of a unionized fishery is not a good one," Clapp began again. "But I have to say to you, gentlemen, in the secrecy of this Cabinet chamber – and remember your oaths when you were sworn into your high offices: 'the secret debates of Council, *I will not reveal!'* – I have to say that our fishermen friends, sturdy and independent souls that they are, are not capable of seeing where their best interest lies. I know, gentlemen, I tell you, I know. I tried for five years to penetrate that murky obtuseness with a shaft of light."

"If *you* couldn't succeed at it, Mr. Premier, then it's flogging a dead horse. That's all I can say," said a minister, rising out of his chair under the energy of his convictions and looking from face to face with jerky, belligerent, conclusiveness.

So that's it, thought Neil. Clapp was afraid Rute would succeed where he failed .... It gave him an idea for solving a problem of principle that had been bothering him.

The day after he had arrived home from his honeymoon, a partner of his former law firm had telephoned him to ask about the appeal to the Supreme Court of Canada on the asbestosis case. "We'll have to withdraw that appeal now that you're out of the firm, Neil," he had said.

"Can't someone else there take it?" Neil had asked.

"Yes. If we get a retainer of five thousand dollars. You remember the policy of our firm. Failing that, someone would have to do it as charity and have the time spent taken out of his own income. Who here is going to do that? You'll either have to withdraw it or do it yourself, Neil."

"I'll leave it in for a while and think about it."

Neil had thought about it; but his thoughts had been full of the skull on the pillow groaning, between morphine stupors, about his faith in Neil, his belief that Neil would see to the welfare of the half dozen pale-faced kids around the bed. Neil had asked his senior officials in the Department of Health what the consequences would be of changing the law to require the Workmen's Compensation Board to assume that any miner's lung disease was caused by working conditions unless the employer could prove the contrary. They didn't know, the officials had said, but they certainly *thought* such a change would open the floodgates and bankrupt the compensation fund. They could not in conscience recommend the change to him as minister.

Now, after the Cabinet meeting, Neil followed Clapp into his office.

"Times have changed, sir," he said. "I'm not so sure as the others that Randolph Rute will fail."

"I gathered that from your comment," responded Clapp. "Rute is a friend at the moment. But in politics, everyone is a potential enemy, Neil. Everyone. I would ask you to remember that the next time, before you give comfort to the enemy in full Cabinet."

"Whether Rute stays friend or becomes enemy, I have an idea that will help keep the labour movement as a whole friendly to us. Remember all the accolades from the unions when the judge first found in favour of the miner with lung cancer and *against* the ruling of the Workmen's Compensation Board?" Neil went on to explain how the law should be changed.

"That's it?" said Clapp.

"Well, at least it's a symbolic gesture in the right direction."

"It puts us on the side of the gods all right. But what if it turns out to be an empty gesture? Won't the companies hire an army of doctors to prove a disease wasn't caused by mining conditions, Neil?"

"Proving a negative is virtually impossible in cases like that, sir."

"That's good. I like that. You've got a brain, Neil. How much will it cost?"

"Not much, I'm told. But anyway, it's a contributory fund. It won't cost the government anything. The only argument against it is superstitious fear of change."

"I tell you, I like it, Neil. Why stop at mines? Why not extend the idea to all workers who contract lung disease?"

"Well … " said Neil. But Clapp was pacing, his chin between thumb and forefinger.

"Neil, draft it up. We won't wait for the legislature to reopen. We'll put an order-in-council through Cabinet immediately and ratify it later in the House."

Within two days Neil brought a draft order before Cabinet, and Clapp rammed it through. The only dissenting voice was that of Toope, the Minister of Justice. "This is not some fancy scheme to get politically what you couldn't get judicially for that client of yours, the miner, is it?" he asked, with a sleek

162

grin. He turned to Clapp. "I remember *Ernie* Godwin was crafty like that in the old days when he was an articled clerk, before he got religion."

"That miner is no longer a client of mine, Mr. Toope," said Neil. "He may still be a client of my former firm, but I, unlike perhaps others" (he meant Toope) "resigned from my law firm when I entered the Cabinet, so there'd be no possibility of a conflict of interest on my part."

Toope glared, and leaned forward to speak, but Clapp laughed. "Boys, boys, look at the clock. It's lunch time. That kind of talk on an empty stomach will give you both gastric ulcers." Clyde Ferritt regarded the scene in silence.

Clapp and Neil made the announcement jointly, and they were hailed by workers' organizations as liberal and progressive. At the next Cabinet meeting, Clapp said, "Mr. Godwin, your political acumen on this thing was simply astonishing. Gentlemen, there's a young man I'm glad is with us and not against us." Neil could see Clyde slumped in his seat pretending to be asleep; but he was observing Neil through slitted eyes.

The reactions of two people close to Neil contrasted with one another. The miner in his modest home, saved now from foreclosure, to whom Neil made a special visit by government helicopter, said he could at last die in peace. His spidery fingers gripped Neil's hand and did not let go until he passed out. Gillian's father, who was a specialist in corporate law, and whose mansion on Circular Road Neil visited the same night, inveighed against the irresponsible action of Neil and the government in piling another financial burden on business. Touchings was genuinely angry for the first time since Neil had met him.

And then Rute stated on television that he took Mr. Clapp's enlightened new workmen's compensation regulation as an indication of support for his own equally progressive attempts to unionize the fishery. During the Cabinet meeting the next morning, Clapp said nothing at all on the matter. But he did not give the impression of being overjoyed. Twice Neil caught Clapp looking at him in a thoughtful way, for no reason connected with the topic under discussion.

Soon the organizing activities of Rute were the main topic of conversation throughout the land. Rute's cause was strengthened considerably by a strong propaganda campaign against him on the part of the Fish Merchants' Association. He continued to style himself a great supporter of Clapp wherever he went. He even included in his speeches to the fishermen a statement to the effect that he was following in Percy Clapp's footsteps in trying to form a strong union of fishermen. Clapp liked to hear people talk about following in his footsteps. What he did not appreciate was anyone going far beyond the point where his own footsteps had faltered and stopped. And Rute's success in signing up members indicated that he was doing just that. Within a year, most of the fishermen and plant workers had joined as contributing members of the new Fishermen's Union.

During that year, Neil and Gillian settled into a pleasant married routine – when he was home. After she became pregnant, he regretted even more keenly than before his frequent absences from her. And the nature of his travels – rapid tours of rural hospitals, long drives to one-night speaking engagements in remote communities, hopping from harbour to harbour by float plane at Clapp's request "to show a constant political presence" – did not make it convenient or enjoyable for Gillian to accompany him. She seemed happy enough to stay home, although she often sought reassurances that he shared her contentment over starting a family so soon. When he was away, she spent most of her time writing articles on Newfoundland cultural and literary activities for local newspapers and occasionally, for mainland periodicals.

Gillian had her own friends, some of whom Neil found hard to take. They usually began a tiresome criticism of the government's failure to adequately support the arts, the moment he came into their presence. But Neil said nothing to her about that, in the same way that she stayed silent about the crass shallowness of many of the political backroomers with whom Neil was often obliged to socialize whenever he was in St. John's.

Touchings was no longer Neil's cordial friend. Gillian joked to him that if her father was able to visualize even a fragment of what Neil subjected her to in bed, then it was no wonder that being a father-in-law was incompatible with friendship. But Neil knew that the change in their relationship had nothing to do with his marriage to Gillian. It was caused by Touchings' sudden awareness, after Neil had talked Clapp into ramming through the new workmen's compensation regulation, that his son-in-law's political philosophy was dangerous to the positions Touchings himself represented and believed in. They had several shrill and bitter arguments after that, and Neil's less frequent visits to Touchings' home were now always made in the company of Gillian.

Since Neil's marriage, Jane and Gillian had become close friends. They seemed to spend hours talking together at the kitchen table over their coffees. Sometimes, when Neil was in his den reading reports at night, he would hear Jane ask Gillian how on earth he could stomach Clapp – how he could stay in a government whose sole policy was to cling to power by any means, never directing any money towards the things that needed to get done, but always ready to spend wildly in order to extend its own political grasp. Gillian's soft replies, too low for Neil to catch, did not sound like strenuous arguments against Jane's points.

It was Jane who drove Gillian to hospital when her labour began. Neil was four hundred miles away. He had intended to stay home all that week because the birth of the baby was imminent. That morning, however, Clapp had handed Neil a government cheque for fifty thousand dollars. It was payable to a town council on the other side of the island, and designated for the start of construction on a hockey arena.

"Deliver it to them yourself, in person, Neil," ordered Clapp. "The flight out there leaves in an hour. What's wrong? You'll be gone less than a day. Don't you understand how much goodwill there is for you in that one goddamned cheque? This opportunity would be wasted on the Minister of Recreation. He's got no political future. You go, Neil. You're the Minister of Health. Hockey is healthy, isn't it? Or will I get Clyde to do it?"

That night, Neil had just handed the cheque over to the mayor (who expressed his disappointment to the crowd in the town hall over the small size of the grant), when he was called urgently to the telephone. It was Jane. His wife was in very difficult labour there at the hospital, she said, and calling out his name. Would it be too much of an imposition on him to come the Christ home for a couple of minutes?

Contrite, Neil could not take offence at Jane's words or tone. He went to his hotel room to await further calls. He felt guilty all night about not having set out immediately to drive to St. John's, even though he knew the early morning flight would get him home sooner. Then, at four in the morning, Mrs. Touchings telephoned: Gillian had given birth to a healthy daughter and was now resting comfortably. Till he left for the airport at six, Neil walked constantly around his room. He only stopped from time to time to apply a wet facecloth to his aching, red-rimmed eyes.

Once at the airport, Neil pestered the attendants for information they could not give on how long the plane's departure would be delayed by the fog in St. John's. He cursed himself continuously for having decided not to drive back last night. It was mid-afternoon before he arrived at the hospital and walked into Gillian's room.

"All hail!" remarked Jane, from her chair beside the bed. "The putative father deigns to survey the scene." She broke into a smile when Gillian patted her arm and beamed at Neil.

He spent the rest of the afternoon and evening with Gillian, mostly apologizing for his needless absence. Finally she made him laugh by saying, "Look, will you stop? Sure, what good would you have been to me here, anyway? What would you have done as a masculine gesture of sympathy? Pass a pumpkin?"

When Neil got home from the hospital that night, he watched a television documentary on the Fishermen's Union. Rute's clear sense of direction impressed him. He was so happy about the birth of his daughter, so delighted with Gillian's joy in her, that throughout the program he could not stop himself, alone in the house, from uttering loud and strong words of encouragement to Rute's image on the television set.

At tomorrow's Cabinet meeting, he thought, he would

propose a policy of government assistance and benevolent legislation for Rute's union. Why not? The union was a positive force for good. (His daughter was well-formed and healthy.) What was he doing in the government, anyway, if he did not support progressive causes? (Gillian was strong and feeling good.)

The phone rang. Someone else to congratulate him on his astounding feat of paternity, no doubt. "Yes, I am pleased with the outcome, but I'd just like to say that I would not have been able to do it without a great deal of help from my wife," he would say again, mimicking the sanctimonious politician's style in a way that everyone found so witty, applied to these circumstances.

"This is the prime minister calling .... Uh, who's this?"

"Neil Godwin, sir."

"Oh, yes, Mr. Godwin. I just saw Rute on television. Did you hear what he said? He said – I heard him say it – he actually said that if, as the fish merchants pretend, the fishery cannot afford to pay decent wages or prices, if that is truly the case, then the fishery is better off destroyed, and the quicker the better. Those are his very words. That bastard is going to ruin this country, Sam. Surely to God Almighty he can see that half a loaf is better than no loaf at all!"

This was the first time Clapp had phoned him at home since shortly after his entry into the Cabinet. Listening, Neil recalled how Clyde was forever telling him about his late night chats with the PM.

"Yes, and not only that, sir," said Neil, "but this Fishermen's Union has the smell of a combine about it. Here are the fishermen, banding together, conspiring to fix the price of their product, and – "

"By God, you're right ... you're not Sam. Sam would never think of that .... Mr. Godwin! Neil! By God, you know you are absolutely right."

Clapp hung up. Neil sat there, wondering why he had not voiced support for the union, as he had intended, instead of throwing out the specious point that he had argued against when Touchings had made it a few nights before.

The next morning at the Cabinet meeting, Clapp said,

"Gentlemen, this Fishermen's Union business has the stink, the veritable stench, of a combine about it. Everyone would be up in arms altogether, if General Motors and Ford conspired to fix the price of their cars. Everyone *is* up in arms because the Arabs forced a cartel to dictate what the price of oil would be. This Fishermen's Union of Rute's is doing precisely the same thing. What are we going to do? Make chalk of one and cheese of another? Gentlemen, if we are not clear and logical in our thinking, then we are lost. This is nothing short of a conspiracy by the fishermen against, not only the fishplant owners – that we could live with – but against their fellow countrymen, their own flesh and blood!"

A few months later, Rute announced the union's first boycott. The fishermen in Pinchgut refused to sell their fish to the fishplant there or allow anyone else to do so until they were paid a stated price per pound. Again, Neil exulted privately over this development, once again determined to support the union's activities at the next Cabinet meeting.

Clapp called Neil at home that night. "I just spoke to Clyde on this strike business," he said, "and his comments were not very penetrating. Now you are a lawyer, Mr. Godwin, as well as being a Member of Her Majesty's Government, so you are more aware than most of the gravity of this situation. There is no legislation which permits fishermen to go on strike. As primary producers, they are expressly excluded from the operations of the labour code. That strike called by Rute is entirely illegal." Clapp stopped, and waited for Neil's comments.

"Yes, and not only that, Prime Minister," said Neil. "There is a very serious, perhaps fatal, conflict of interest in this union. The fishermen and the plant workers are members of the same union, but their interests are completely different. We now have a situation where the plant workers, who are not on strike themselves, are certainly going to be laid off and thrown out of work as a result of the actions of the fishermen who are boycotting their fishplant."

"Neil," said Clapp, "it is always a pleasure to discuss vital issues with you. Do you know that when I spoke to Clyde Ferritt on this very question a few minutes ago, he could offer nothing by way of a real analysis of the situation, as you just did, in spite of his reputed brilliance? The exceedingly great contrast between his political skills and yours has become very, very apparent to me, Neil."

Clapp hung up, and again Neil sat there, telephone pressed against his shoulder, wondering what in the name of Christ was wrong with him, why he couldn't resist the sycophantic urge to advance technical sophistry to support a position he knew Clapp wanted buttressed. Had his legal training drained him that dry of principle? Or was it simply that he carried in his genes the same dog-like desire to please his master, the same built-in, obsequious deference to a perceived superior that Boo Mansingh had feared was in himself? Whatever the reason for his gutlessness, he made up his mind to overcome it in the future. Henceforth, he would support Rute's union on principle, no matter what Clapp or anyone else wanted to hear him say.

The next morning, Clapp called an urgent Cabinet meeting on the strike. "Yes, gentlemen," he said, addressing the gathering, "we are about to see the last of this fishermen's combine. There is simply no way that it can stand the strain of its inherent, wrenching, and deadly conflict of interest – the savage conflict of interest between fisherman and plant worker – a conflict of interest as savage and as deadly as that which has existed since time immemorial between tillers of soil and keepers of sheep. It is the same irreconcilable conflict which caused Cain to brutally murder his only brother, Abel. The fissures and cracks in this union will soon expose themselves to public scrutiny!"

Neil was about to jump in and argue against his own idea as just expressed by Clapp; but Toope, the Minister of Justice had already asked for the floor. This, in itself, was sufficiently unusual to pique interest around the table, for Toope never hid the fact that he did not consider himself to bear any part of the collective responsibility of the government. He treated his justice portfolio as a vehicle for keeping him close to the premier. He still spent part of each day at the office of the law firm of which he was supposed to be a non-active partner. Usually, his sole comment at Cabinet meetings, whenever he was asked his opinion on some crisis facing the government, was: "You fellows are buggering this up."

Now Toope launched into a well-prepared and skilfully delivered plea on behalf of the Fish Merchants' Association, his thesis being that whatever hurt them, hurt the government and the public generally, because the government had lent or granted so much money towards the construction and operation of fishplants. He pointed out the manner in which the Fishermen's Union was breaking the law by going on strike to begin with, and by preventing anyone else from bringing fish to the plant. Toope's peroration was: "If the fishermen will not obey the law, then they must be *made* to obey the law. If they are permitted to flout the law of our land, then you fellows cannot call yourselves a government. I am Minister of Justice and I say to you, give lawbreakers the cold steel. You'll be respected the more for it. Because, gentlemen, your first duty is to uphold the law. Remember your ministerial oaths to act against intestine insurrections. This is an insurrection, gentlemen, deep within the bowels of our society which threatens to rip out the very guts and vitals of our beloved land."

In the silence that followed, Clapp paced the floor behind his chair. He was muttering, "You're right, you know, Toope. The Minister of Justice is right, you know, boys."

Neil exploded without volition. "Premier, this makes me want to puke! Who the hell does Mr. Toope represent around this table, anyway? The people who elected us or the medieval-minded clients of his own goddamned law firm? Talk about conflict of interest! That was the worst example I've ever heard tell of in my life." He wanted to go on and say that the union should be given legislative sanction to withhold their labour and their fish and to negotiate fair wages and prices, but he had come to the end of his breath. By the time he had gulped in another lungful, Toope had joined issue with him.

"Now listen to me, young fellow! No, no, Mr. Clapp, he had his say, let me have mine." As Toope spoke, Neil could see Clyde hiding his grin with his hand. "I haven't lived on the face of this earth for nearly all my allotted span of three score and ten in order to be subjected to the insolent yelping of a mongrel, crackie pup!" New life stirred around the table. "I only answer you at all, Godwin, because I have good friends in this room who might think less of me, not because of anything you have said, or could possibly say, but because I failed to provide them with the gratifying spectacle of deflating an outsized head.

"Conflict of interest! You fling that in my face as if you actually knew what the words meant. Conflict of interest! I, who forty years ago drafted for the Law Society the rules governing conflict of interest on the part of practising lawyers – rules, by the way, which have not been altered one jot or tittle since. Conflict of interest! I, who have been an Officer of the Supreme Court of this land for nearly five decades, and a King's Counsellor for nearly thirty years. *What* conflict of interest?" he roared. "Have you ever heard me utter one word about government policy around this table? Has anyone? Have you ever heard me say a word about education in this Cabinet? Have you? Have you? Have you ever heard me emit one sound, one way or the other, about Health, Transportation, Welfare, or any other field of government. Has anyone here?"

"No, never!" said some ministers, with conviction.

"Have I ever said yes, no, or kiss my arse to any proposal raised by any minister here? Never! Not once! I opened my mouth today during a general discussion on the state of the country to give these, my friends, the benefit of my knowledge of the existing laws of the land and some jurisprudential theory on the necessity of legal sanctions to prevent the law from falling into disrepute. Which, I humbly submit for your lordship's consideration, is the bounden duty of one who is a King's Counsellor, a Master of the Supreme Court, and a past Treasurer of the Law Society.

"Conflict of interest! What an insult to the prime minister, who had me appointed to this Cabinet over ten years ago and who has requested me on several occasions since, without solicitation on my part, I might add, to remain as his colleague herein. What an affront," boomed Toope, "gratuitously spewed at the head of Mr. Clapp, our highest and most esteemed statesman, by a puffed up bladder of piss and wind!"

There were one or two murmurs of, "He's right," started, Neil thought, by Clyde. It was difficult to be sure since they were all whispered behind hands.

Neil opened his mouth to offer a rebuttal, entirely without words to say, and although he flung himself back in his seat as if in irritation, he was grateful when Clapp held up his hand for silence. "Nothing whatsoever is to be gained, Mr. Godwin, Mr. Toope, by protracting this fruitless internecine battle. It has served the purpose of pointing up the extreme dangers inherent in this whole situation – one which even threatens to rent apart the seamless garment of Cabinet solidarity." Clapp, who had eyed Neil throughout these remarks, now terminated the Cabinet meeting and called Neil into his office.

"I know what you're like, Neil," commented Clapp. "You think the thrust and parry of powerful, contrary forces are good and necessary in a free society. When you are premier (which you will no doubt be, and sooner, much sooner, than you may think), you will not find powerful or competing disturbances and disorders quite so attractive. Unless, Neil, unless they are caused and fomented and controlled by yourself, in order to do and see done what you know is right for our people."

Clapp now called the Minister of Justice in from his nearby office. Grasping Toope and Neil each by the right hand, he forced a handshake and the words "No hard feelings" from both. Neil smiled confidently into the hard face of Toope. And from that time on, he found himself a member of Clapp's inner group. Consisting only of Clapp, Toope, Ferritt, and himself, this was the group that decided on all issues before they were ever raised in Cabinet.

That night, far from being laid off because of the boycott of the fishermen, the plant workers voluntarily went on strike themselves in sympathy with the fishermen's position. And, during the days that followed, far from impaling itself on its inherent conflict of interest, the union throve.

At the informal meetings of Clapp's small inner group, both

172

Neil and Clyde would argue for legalization of the union's status in order to force the plant owner to negotiate in good faith, something he now refused to do. Toope would make no comment, and Clapp would say only, "You might be right. We'll see, we'll see." He appeared to be waiting for something.

The town of Pinchgut, in which the fishplant was located, seemed to be divided down the middle on the issue, in much the same way that the general population was. The television news reports gave the impression of near violence on both sides in the town, as the jostling camera caught quick glimpses of the grim faces of both the strikers and the supporters of the plant owner. But the sole injury suffered to date was a broken leg sustained by a young man who, *coitus interruptus* by the unexpected late-night approach of some picketers, among whom was the father of the object of his affections, slipped on some fishguts under the wharf when he tried to make his escape.

After the strike had held its position at the top of the news for several weeks, its aura of constant tension maintained by daily inflammatory statements from both sides, Rute succeeded in having his union join up with a powerful international union based in the United States. This ensured financial support and strike pay and greater organizational expertise. Clapp had assumed no public position on the strike, but privately he had taken to calling the Fishermen's Union, "the F.U.," his contemptuous tone and snarling lip suggesting that he was saying "Eff you!" He now began to refer to the international union as the "murderers' union," owing to the fact that it had been involved in assisting prisoners of a maximum security prison on the mainland in a well-publicized sit-down strike to gain better prison conditions.

It soon became apparent that the propaganda of the Fishermen's Union and its organizing strategies were in the hands of professionals. Clapp's irritation went up commensurate with the union's exercise of greater skills in the conduct of its strike. Rute was now appearing on paid telecasts with expertly prepared statements. He called upon the government to give direct support to the union's cause and to the

173

strike itself because the plant had been constructed largely with the money of the people.

Public opinion seemed now to be polarizing in favour of the union's position, helped, no doubt, by the reactionary words and recalcitrant attitude of the plant owner and his cronies in the Fish Merchants' Association. Clapp seemed to be very concerned by the success of the union's popular appeals and by the skill of their propaganda. Whenever a film clip of the strike was shown on television, he would scan all the faces in the background, trying to pick out unfamiliar mainland faces from the "murderers' union."

Rute's latest television address had been very effective. He ended it on a new note. He called upon the government to help the fishermen and plant workers in their great struggle against oppression, and to stop siding with the forces of evil and fascist power and with the attitudes from the dark ages as represented by the plant owner and his associates. He went very close to condemning Percy Clapp for having fourteenth-century concepts of social justice. He invited the more forward-looking elements in Clapp's government to support the union publicly, to prove that their track record of helping the ordinary joe was not just a flash in the pan of political expediency. Neil knew that Rute meant him. And he also knew that the labour leader was right.

Neil and Gillian had been watching Rute's appeal together in their living room. She was holding their daughter, Elizabeth, on her knee and, seeing Neil's concentration on the television, she kissed the baby's face and hair and bounced her gently to keep her from distracting him. After the speech, Neil slumped back in his chair and dangled his leg over the arm. Gazing at the old, second-hand sofa opposite, he was aware that Gillian's eyes were on him.

"Neil," she said at last. "This man Rute. What's he like?"

"Good," murmured Neil. "He's a good man."

"Well, then, since his cause is also good, you should be supporting him in what he's trying to do, I think."

Neil was nodding thoughtfully when the telephone rang. He went into the kitchen to answer it. Percy Clapp was on the other end, and this time the premier did not ask for Neil's

174

opinion. He raved for five minutes about the slander and calumny perpetrated by that insidiously dangerous turncoat Rute – and hung up.

"Clapp?" asked Gillian, when Neil came back.

"How could you tell? By my cauliflower ear and atrophied tongue? The gist was that he does not love Randolph Rute."

"That puts you in a bit of a bind," said Gillian. "What will you do if he takes on Rute? Get out?" She brightened.

"And do what, Gillian?" asked Neil, showing a little irritation. "I can't jump back and forth between government and law practice like a bloody yo-yo. I'd have to start at the bottom again in practice, *if* I could find a firm that would take me. I wouldn't make enough in the first year to heat this house. Standing on principle is great if you're not too hungry to stand up at all. And just run your eyes over the furniture, Gillian. It won't take long. Christ, the room looks like a salvage shop after a bankruptcy sale!"

"The furniture *is* scarce," laughed Gillian. "But that's only because it'll all be rare antiques in another fifty years." When Neil didn't smile, she went on: "Look, Neil, you'll recall that I didn't want to buy this house in the first place. I wanted a small apartment. We should sell this ancient mausoleum to some other upwardly mobile couple with a fetish for millstones."

Neil didn't answer. He was reflecting on the desire he'd had when he married Gillian of ensconcing her in a dwelling suitable to her previous station in life under her parents' roof.

"And Neil, my love. Do me a little favour, please. Don't under-rate yourself to me like you did just then. If you went back practising law, you'd be at the top of the profession in no time. If it's money you want, which I don't deny would be nice some day, you'd be making it hand over fist before too long. So don't let that enter into your decisions at all. Just use your own judgement on what's right. And whatever you do, I'm here with you."

Neil walked over and kissed her. He took Elizabeth in his arms, played with her for a while, and cooed her to sleep. An hour later in bed, with Gillian pressed warmly against his side and breathing quietly on his neck, he worded in his mind the ultimatum on the Fishermen's Union that he would give Clapp in the morning.

But next morning, waking up to the early news, Neil heard that the Minister of Justice had dispatched several hundred policemen to Pinchgut with orders to stop the illegal boycotting activities of the union and permit the fishplant to recommence its operations in keeping with its rights under the law. Clapp's voice came on, saying that it was the government's first duty to restore law and order. Once that was done, the whole question of the Fishermen's Union would be looked at and, if deemed necessary, changes would be made in the law.

Neil talked to Clyde by telephone during the morning. Both expressed outrage at not having been consulted by Clapp on the police action. Neil did not broach the subject of resignation with Clyde, however, as he was not certain how such information would be used. Secretly, he made his own plans to resign following the Cabinet meeting which Clapp had called. Not only was he against what Clapp had done as a matter of policy, but he wanted to disentangle himself from the disastrous consequences on public opinion which these strong-arm methods were sure to have, especially since they had been used against fishermen who had successfully projected themselves as underdogs in the labour strife.

As he walked along the corridor to the Cabinet chamber, Neil felt a strong grip on his shoulder. He turned to see the gnarled old face of Toope, the Minister of Justice, about two inches from his own. "Listen, you – you little fart who thinks he's king shit," spat Toope. "I hope you're not entertaining any notions of practising law again while I'm still alive. As long as I'm on the executive of the Law Society, which I'm entitled to be, *ex officio,* for the rest of my life, I'll be after your balls: starting with a raid on your books for suspected misuse of trust funds. That'll look nice in the newspapers, won't it? And don't think Touchings will protect you, either. He won't be on the executive forever – and he's as disgusted with you as I am, anyway."

The old man lunged ahead and went into the Cabinet room where he was greeted affably by colleagues. Clapp came in from his own office, followed by Clyde, and while he was giving his rationale for the police action, Neil sat quietly, waiting for the meeting to end so that he could give the premier his resignation. He'd made up his mind to risk the vengeance of old Toope, as well as that of Clapp which was sure to follow. The meeting was winding down and Neil was beginning to feel dread at what he was about to do, when Clapp's intercom buzzed.

After listening for a moment, Clapp roared, "Are you sure? Bring me in a radio!" He slammed down the receiver savagely, and stood as if he were struggling for self-control. Then he turned to his colleagues and spoke in solemn, measured tones. "Gentlemen, this is a day of infamy. That was the Chief of Police. He's in my office now ...." Clapp paused. "This morning, when the police confronted the strikers and asked them to disperse in the name of the law, the men turned into a violent mob. During their riot, they knocked down a pregnant woman and her three-year-old daughter. The woman is in hospital and – my friends, my friends, you will not be able to make yourselves believe this – the child was trampled to death!" Murmurs and curses went up around the table. Neil groaned inwardly.

The radio news story confirmed the report of the child's death, as the breathless on-the-spot reporter described the bedlam that had occurred in Pinchgut. Brief mention was made of Rute, who had sustained an injury to his back during the violent outbreak.

Clapp switched off the radio. "Gentlemen," he said, his manner icy and determined, "I am going on country-wide television tonight. I am going to condemn this senseless, unprovoked, brutal murder – yes, murder – of an innocent little girl by a violent mob defying the attempts of peace officers to prevent the total breakdown of law and order. I am also going to say that this government will not tolerate acts of violence, heretofore unknown to our peaceful people, perpetrated by foreign, big-city gangsters, as represented by this murderers' union from the mainland. I'm announcing our intention of calling the legislature together immediately to pass legislation outlawing from our country this murderers' union for introducing alien methods of unlawfulness, butchery, violence, and murder to our peace-loving, law-abiding land. We'll soon be clear of that murderers' union from the mainland, my friends. We'll send those bastards packing!"

Neil's thoughts were in turmoil. He knew he should shout at Clapp: "Wait! Let's find out exactly how it happened first." But he said nothing. The union was finished. Rute was finished.

That evening on television, Clapp's performance was the best Neil had ever seen. He had added to his script, at the insistence of Neil and Clyde, a statement that the government also intended to introduce legislation to legalize the activities of a legitimate Fishermen's Union and to accord it the right to negotiate within the labour code on the prices to be paid for their fish. "It is not the principle that we are against," intoned Clapp. "We are all for fishermen organizing to protect themselves. That is why we did not take action sooner regarding this illegal strike. But we are immovably against the methods employed by that murderers' union from the mainland which have resulted in the vicious killing of a blameless little child. And I shall remain unalterably opposed to the murder of children for as long as a breath remains in my body." Tears welled in Clapp's eyes and overflowed onto his cheeks.

During the night and the following morning, news stories reported more details about the encounter in Pinchgut. It was revealed that the child who had been killed had been playing in the road behind the strikers, and that when the men had been driven back before an unexpected police advance, she had slipped and fallen unnoticed beneath their feet. One of Rute's lieutenants claimed that he had seen a policeman use his stick to strike Randolph Rute across the back when the labour leader had stooped to pick up the fallen child. The girl's mother had not, in fact, been physically hurt. She had been hospitalized for shock.

No one seemed interested in the details, however, or in the analysis of conflicting reports. Everyone's thinking appeared to be paralyzed by one thought: a child had been killed by a mob of illegal strikers under the control of a big-city union run by gangsters.

The next day, high school students in the hundreds demonstrated, carrying signs with messages of hate towards the murderers' union. The university students paraded throughout the streets of St. John's. They burned effigies of Randolph Rute in four places, each effigy having a sign around its neck proclaiming "Death to the puppet of the murderers' union."

Clapp called Neil and Clyde together for a discussion on who to get to organize a new union of fishermen. Clapp had said on his telecast that the government was so much in favour of the idea of a fishermen's union that he would be seconding one of the most prominent and senior labour leaders in the land for the job of helping to organize it properly. He now told his young colleagues that he'd already received offers from a dozen union officials and had narrowed the field down to two. "Who," he asked, "will I choose for it: Cook or Raff? Cook is the better man by far, but it boils down to the question of what slogan sounds best: 'Pick up your hook and follow Cook,' or 'Pick up your gaff and follow Raff.' What do you think, Neil?"

Neil thought about the man, Raff, who visited him unannounced every two or three days at his office to talk tedious trivia about his Hospital Workers' Union, and who had breath like a mixture of ammonia and cat shit. The temptation to be rid of that foul air was too great to resist. "I like, 'Pick up your gaff and follow Raff.'"

"'And rip out Randy's Rute,'" added Clyde.

Neil's stomach contracted. He felt like kicking Clyde in the face. He joined in the laughter of the other two.

"Good, good," said Clapp, wiping away a tear, "only, like so much that you've come up with lately, Clyde, we can't use it."

"I'll slip it to some university students I know," put in Neil. "They'll use it."

"Excellent!" said Clapp. "We three make a pretty good team. Remember. In spite of the stresses and strains of possessing political power, we must always stick together. Remember that always, boys, and we'll be all right. Now the only outstanding question is what to do with the goddamned

179

fishplant. There'll never be any peace with the fishermen as long as buggerlugs owns it. Think about it, boys, and we'll discuss it later."

Neil thought about the fishplant and decided that the government should nationalize it and turn it over to a co-op of fishermen and plant workers to operate. It could serve as a pilot project leading towards the day when the whole fishing industry would be controlled for the benefit of the fishermen and workers. He would wait for an opportune moment to spring the possibility on Clapp.

After lunch, Clapp called Neil to his office. As he sat down, Neil could see that the premier was half drunk on the sherries that he habitually consumed at lunch, and concluded that this was no time to open discussion on the nationalization of the plant. Clapp paced the floor.

"What do you say," he began, "to our nationalizing the fishplant?"

Neil laughed out loud in surprise.

"I know what you're thinking," resumed Clapp. "It would make us look like a banana republic. It might affect our ability to raise money on the bond market. Too Marxist, and so on. But we can avoid all that. We need only negotiate a sale with the owner and pay an agreed price and get a statement from him that he was not forced in any way to sell and that he is completely satisfied. We could give that to our financial syndicate in New York and London to pass around."

"Negotiate an agreed price,hmmm ... " said Neil. Clapp's negotiated and agreed prices were well known, and he did not have a reputation for being parsimonious with his friends.

For a few minutes, Clapp continued to pace back and forth in silence. "Neil," he asked, suddenly. "What do you truly want to do with your life?"

"Well, I –"

"Surely to the Lord Jesus Christ, you do not want to grub around in this penny ante, poopy-arsed, minor political league for the rest of your days. What are you now? Just twenty-six, right?"

"Yes."

"You don't see yourself in this bloody racket for the next

forty-five years! You have more vision than that, Neil. Ten or fifteen years will be more than enough, even including your time as prime minister, which is not far away, even now. So, there you are at thirty-five or forty years of age. A lifetime ahead of you. What will you do? You're far too intelligent to scrape around practising law here in St. John's, filling in blanks in mortgage deeds and leases, taking off copies of divorce petitions on the Xerox. If you are as brilliant as I know you are, you have something else in mind to make your life worthwhile."

"Well, yes, as a matter of fact, I do. I've always wanted to write, to have the time to spend my days writing."

"How similar we are!" exclaimed Clapp. "How very similar we two are! That's exactly what I liked to do and I would gladly have spent my life at it. But the need to keep some soul within this 'skinful of venom,' as Wolfe Tone McGrath used to call me during my first campaign, was forever interposing its grim self. It's a desperate heartbreaking business, this writing. The chances of making a living at it are slim. I've written a couple of books on our history. The happiest time of my life. If it weren't for the fact that I could count the dollars I made at it on the fingers of one cramped hand, I would have kept at it."

"Yes," said Neil, "I guess that's what keeps me from – "

"Christ, everyone imagines he's a thinker these days," continued Clapp, "and what's worse, everyone believes he has within himself, as a result of pathetically mundane experiences, the stuff upon which to build great insights, novel commentary, galvanizing stories – "

"Yes," offered Neil. "Everyone thinks he has it in him to produce a literary opus destined to make posterity cream her drawers in an endless series of multiple orgasms." He was startled by his own imagery, apparently forced out of him by an unconscious competition of metaphors with Clapp.

"Come again?" asked Clapp, his face contorted with irritation at having been interrupted. "Oh, I get you." His eyes gleamed with mirth. "What a pleasure it always is to chat with you, Neil! You have a way with words that Clyde Ferritt will never have. And you're right. Everyone doesn't have it in him.

181

Perhaps you do. But why starve trying to find that out. Get yourself set first. No hunger pang ever stimulated the creation of one brilliant thought.

"No, Neil, for the present, at least, you must be a doer. You cannot waste your time on useless vicarious sublimation. Your deeds and exploits must be such as to provoke other recorders and scribblers. You have only one chance in a million of making a living at writing unless you become a hack drudge, filing copy, perhaps criticizing bitterly the writings of someone else who, unlike yourself, may have become prominent enough to be noticed. But then you're back to the same thing as grubbing at law, except for measly, uncertain pay. No." Clapp shook his head. "No. The real answer is to become financially secure enough to do what you want, what you are really made to do."

By this time, Clapp's ceaseless pacing had become almost mesmerizing. Wearing the bedroom slippers that he always put on in his office, he moved soundlessly, gracefully, quickly, with boundless, overflowing energy. He stopped suddenly right over Neil, forcing him to settle back in his chair and look up. "Neil," said Clapp, "there's a hundred thousand for you in this plant takeover deal."

"Jesus Christ, Premier!" If Clapp hadn't been looming over him, Neil would have stood.

"I sincerely hope, Neil, that you are not thinking in your mind that this would be a bribe or anything even remotely resembling it. The day I hear of anyone in my administration of Her Majesty's Government accepting a bribe, that's the same day he gets flicked out on his arse. There will be no bribes in this government. There was enough of that in the past. All I'm saying is this. When the deal goes through, the plant owner will make a pure and simple contribution to our party. A political contribution. My bagman will arrange all that. Normal, legitimate, above board. After a decent interval, the party will pay you one hundred thousand dollars. The payment will not be able to be related to anything, not by the plant owner, not even by the party treasurer. You will pay income tax on it as legitimate income, thus avoiding the trap that has snared many a greedy man. If you want, you can spread the payments to you over several years, to cut down on the total tax payable. Don't look so goddamned dubious, Neil. I thought you were more sophisticated than that. What are you making as a member of the House and as a Cabinet minister?"

Neil named a figure which was the same as Clapp was supposed to be making. Clapp obviously didn't know how much he was making from that source, either because of his total lack of interest in money, which was what he said publicly and frequently, or because it was so small a portion of his total overall income.

"Is that all?" he asked. "Any moderately successful carrion-eater, any lawyer or businessman downtown, pisses that much up against a tree in port wine and cognac during his weekend rambles around his country estate in the run of a month. And he gets the money for less work, less worry, less responsibility, and more security than you have in your job. Consider the one hundred thousand as a salary, an honorarium, from a respected political party in grateful return for your substantial contribution to its success. I believe the takeover of that plant is the right thing for our people. But not a word yet. Think it over. I've got to go now, but keep in mind, Neil, that there will be plenty of other occasions over the next few years for a payment of salary from the party. There's absolutely no need to be anxious or greedy. Slowly build up a little nest egg of three, four, five hundred thousand. Enough so that you will be able to live off the income, beholden to no one. Options wide open. Write. Become premier. Become prime minister of Canada. Travel. And you will have earned the money legitimately by the sweat of your brow. A proper and legitimate payment on a regular basis for hard work done on behalf of a political party, grateful for having the use and advantage of your superb talents."

Clapp smiled benignly at Neil as he led him to the door, but Neil saw the smile die on his face before the door was quite closed. His mind was on other things already – since this matter had been successfully tied up.

At home, between the recurring misgivings about Clapp's proposition, delicious anticipation coursed through Neil's body. He said to himself that he would never take the money offered by Clapp, of course. He wished, nonetheless, that the premier had not so closely intertwined, in the same conversation the two legitimate things: the plant takeover and the salary from the party. Three or four times, the vision of himself five years from now, with several hundred thousand dollars discreetly tucked away, made him jump up from his chair and exuberantly toss baby Elizabeth high in the air. Gillian smiled and chuckled at the delightful domestic scene.

"Neil," she told him, "you're happier tonight than I've ever seen you since you went into the government. Have you made up your mind to get out of politics?"

"Not for a while yet," he said. "We'll see how it goes ...."

During this period, when Neil would sometimes see Gillian looking at him searchingly, he would say to himself that he would prove to her one day soon that he was not under Clapp's thumb like the rest of them – that he *had* to put up with a certain number of distasteful things if he was ever going to reach the position where he could effect the reforms he talked to her about. Of the hundreds of people with whom he had spoken after the outlawing of Rute's union, Gillian had been the only person who had completely disagreed with Clapp's actions. He had argued against her at the time, while knowing that she was absolutely right. He looked ahead to the day when he could say to her: "Gillian, you were right. And I *knew* you were right. But I had to go along with it for the moment, so that I could arrive at the point where I am now – the point where I can make up for it one hundred fold to thousands of people! To have acted other than I did would have put me in the wilderness with the other anti-Clapp would-be's – impotent, bitter, and shrill."

Neil longed for the day when he could say that to Gillian.

184

13

"For any political leader to call an election on the issue of our recent labour strife," said Percy Clapp to the cameras and the scribbling reporters, "would be the mark of the blatant political opportunism which very nearly destroyed Newfoundland in the past. I therefore wish to dampen the election speculation which has followed on the heels of the dramatic events regarding that so-called union of the fishermen. I would rather be defeated than take advantage of the heightened emotion of the electorate to maintain myself in power.

"*If*–not *when*–if, indeed, I again seek power from the hands of our people, it will be for the sole purpose of doing a job of work for their future benefit. My forthright and decisive stand on our labour problems was popular, yes, and perhaps deservedly so, but there will be no election at this time on that issue. Those wounds will be bound up and allowed to heal. Whenever an election is called, it will be called on a substantial and well-thought-out program of policies for the *future* good of this land."

After the press conference, Clapp called Clyde and Neil to his office. Neil arrived first and said, "I've been giving a lot of thought to this plant takeover."

"The what?" said Clapp.

"The takeover of the fishplant."

"Oh, yes. Right."

"And I think it's a good idea, Prime Minister, as long as the price negotiated is fair – fair to the government, that is, which may not necessarily be in complete accord with the owner's notion of fairness."

"Of course, Neil, of course. I'm in complete agreement. That will all have to wait until after the election now, though. But you won't have to wait long for your part of our deal, a couple of months or so, that's all. We can't rock the boat at the moment since a sizable portion of our election financing will come from the other plant owners."

Neil pretended he had not been fooled like everyone else into thinking there would be no election. "We'll have to get some good extraneous issues and a series of programs to present to the electorate as a smoke-screen."

"Neil, it's a pleasure to work with you. You miss nothing."

When Clyde came in, Clapp told him to get the lead time on printing a party manifesto for an early election. "In the meantime, let's think of some issues."

"Let's run on the one we have," suggested Clyde. "Law and order, plus a reformed fishery."

"I'm surprised at you, Clyde," said Clapp. "Weren't you at my press conference? I didn't see you there. You had something more important than your prime minister making a crucial statement on behalf of the government? For all your reading of history and your obsession with politics you haven't read this one very well. Neil had the right idea, as is becoming usual, before you got here. You should know that every emotional upheaval contains within it the seeds of an even greater reaction against it. Do what you suggest and a couple of years from now, public opinion may be exactly the opposite on this very issue. Are you proposing that I pursue a course that would very likely make me appear in the future to have taken flagrant advantage of a situation which may well have people puking with disgust in a year or two? Maybe you are not so lacking in political acumen as it appears. Perhaps you *do* wish me to lock myself into an irreversible position now. But I intend to be in politics five years from now and I'm not about to preclude the realization of that intention by screwing myself in advance." Clapp's eyes twinkled at Neil as Clyde's jaw sagged a little. Clyde liked it much better when the premier spoke of his imminent retirement and letting the young fellows take over.

Clapp now dictated the election platform non-stop for two

186

hours, and when he got to the fishery program he said, "Any talk of the plant takeover will have to wait until after the election. There'll be time and enough then to complete all aspects of that matter." Neil glanced at Clyde and was startled to see his big, ugly face crack like shattered concrete into a rare smile. He squirmed happily in his chair, like a child being tickled.

A week after his public announcement that there would be no election on the labour issue, Clapp called a meeting of Cabinet to announce that he had just had an election called by the governor for a date three weeks hence. One or two ministers were so put out by the thought of a three-week-long slog through their districts that they even raised questions.

"Why now, Prime Minister? Sure, we've still got more than two more years to run in this term?"

"Anything can happen in two years," said Clapp. "It's been over three years since our referendum to separate from Canada was passed. People are starting to ask when we are going to separate in fact. Others are beginning to say it was all a big bluff." (Neil had not heard the separation issue mentioned for two years.) "But we cannot separate yet," continued Clapp, "because we would then lose all the revenue we presently get from the federal government. We must wait until the revenues from offshore oil start to roll in. The commercial development of our offshore oil has not come so quickly as I was told it would. I was badly deceived by our advisers on that. Heads will fall after this election, I will guarantee you that, my friends. We are stymied in the same way on the Upper Churchill power. We cannot pull the switch on that either, because it would be a violation of the trust deed, making all money borrowed for that project due immediately. Bango, we're bankrupt. Let me see if I can get this across to you in baby talk: do you want five more years of clear sailing or do you want two more years of being boxed into a corner?"

"I see your point now, Mr. Prime Minister," said the new Minister of Education, "but didn't you say publicly last week that there would be no election at this time?"

"I said: no election at this time on the fishermen's strike issue!" roared Clapp. "By the bowels of Christ, must I be so badly disappointed in my twilight years by my own colleagues – subjected to the calumny of friends for whom I have sacrificed so much? It has been hard enough on me being misquoted, misinterpreted, and accused of double talk by an ignorant and blinkered press day after day, year after year. But by my own political colleagues? Has it then come to this?" A guilty silence prevailed around the table for a minute.

"Besides," resumed Clapp, "as a result of my statement about no election last week, the Leader of the Opposition slipped away yesterday on a three week cruise by ship. The election will be half over before he can come back. I know that because, gentlemen, I took the precaution of checking."

Everyone around the table perked up and laughed heartily. How could you even think of being irritated at this man who thought of everything? He was a genius. What a leader!

The election was easy and dull. The only bit of colour besides Clapp's speeches, came from the one perennial Communist Party candidate, who some suspected of being financed by Clapp to keep before the people the idea that the menace of being overrun by Communist hordes was by no means dead. At his news conference, the Communist Party candidate was asked by a reporter, "In view of the fact that this is your seventh attempt to get elected, what will you do in the event that you are not elected this time around, either?"

The Communist, who apparently understood the substance, if not the tactics, of the cause he represented, was quoted in the papers as answering: "If in fact the people do not elect me this time, then I say, f★★k the people!"

During the election, Rute was interviewed for television from his hospital bed. He was not recovering well from what had turned out to be a broken back incurred during the *mêlée*. It was doubtful, he said, if he would ever walk again. The camera closed in on his face, which appeared to be withered, gaunt, and old, and caught the welling tears in his eyes as he said in an uneven, hesitant voice, "I can't understand why everyone thinks I was wrong. I just don't understand it." Neil nearly got sick from self-disgust as he watched.

He spent most of the next day in his hotel room pleading an upset stomach when his campaign workers came for him, and brooding to himself about the opportunity he had lost to take the right side.

When the election results were declared, Clapp had won 75 per cent of the votes cast and all but one seat. Neil took note of the fact, however, that the turnout of voters was the lowest in forty years. *Not everyone believed you were wrong, Rute,* he thought.

Clapp's sole loss had been sustained by Fagan, a St. John's businessman who, because he was a successful retailer, went by the nickname "Socks." He had apparently visited the rural areas of his district wearing yellow doeskin gloves, a paisley ascot, and a matching puff hankie, while drawing through an eight inch long cigarette holder. Word reached Clapp after the election that the people of the district had said they were not going to elect a man who more than likely wore silk undies. And that was that! Socks Fagan had lost by sixty votes against an opponent whose sole platform was that he only needed to be elected this one more time to qualify for his pension from the legislature.

Clapp tried to hide the fact that he was more hurt by this one defeat than pleased by the forty-nine victories. In Cabinet, he frequently said: "I ran Socks Fagan in that district in the fervent hope that he would be defeated. I'm very conscious of the need, under our system of politics, for an Opposition. It would have been too bad altogether if we had made a clean sweep of it. Too corruptive of the parliamentary system." And always, as Clapp spoke these words, Neil could see his hands tighten into fists at his sides, as if one of Socks' testicles was in each.

Several months after that election, as Clapp and Toope were having a nap after lunch in their chairs, and Neil and Clyde were conversing about Mao's Long March, Clapp suddenly spoke up. "Jesus Christ," he said. "Trying to get Socks Fagan elected was like trying to poke a soft cock up a dry cunt, and just as heartbreaking."

"I'm of your mind on it, Perce," said Toope, awakening with a jump.

Clyde and Neil could only look at one another.

After much dickering with the fishplant owner, a price was tentatively agreed on, which was one million dollars above its replacement cost. The extra amount was supposed to be for goodwill. Neil told Clapp and Clyde: "One million dollars goodwill for a plant that fishermen and workers alike still avoid like the plague. I don't know, Prime Minister."

"That's what I think too, although, now, he may have in mind something a little different from the normal meaning of the term 'goodwill,'" said Clapp. "What do you think, Clyde?"

"It's too much. But certainly peace and quiet, not rocking the boat in the financial markets, together with other necessary expenses in connection with the sale," smiled Clyde, "they're all worth something."

"Okay, then, let's go with it," said Clapp. "Neil, you bring the matter up in Cabinet as vice-president of the treasury board, and we'll get it through."

At the next meeting, Neil entered the Cabinet room with Clapp. Clyde, who had called to say he would be a little late, came in through the outside door. Neil explained the need for the takeover and the acceptance of the price by the owner. There seemed to be a general agreement with the proposal around the table. But then Clyde leaned forward. "The takeover is an excellent idea in principle," he said, "and I commend Neil Godwin for presenting it so well. But the price mentioned seems way too high. According to my calculations, the value of the plant is much less than the figure mentioned." He looked at the secretary of the Cabinet taking notes. "I must go on record as disagreeing with the price unless I am shown additional reasons and considerations why it should be so high."

Neil looked at Clapp, and the premier's eyes blazed back for a second, before he said calmly, "This is what makes the Cabinet system of government so infinitely superior to all others – independent and intelligent men expressing strong views until a consensus is reached." He dropped the subject and went on to other matters.

After the meeting, Clapp motioned to Neil to come into his

office. As Neil went in, he heard the other ministers congratulating Clyde for having the guts to stand up and protect the public purse like that. In his office, Clapp was furiously pacing the floor.

"Bastard wants more," he said. "Just like his goddamned grandfather! Did you know his grandfather? Sold the same stockpile of crushed stone to the government three times. Went to jail. He's not getting one red bloody cent more. He agreed. I'd fire him out of the Cabinet today, only it might cause too many ripples now, just before the deal is clued up. I wouldn't mind forgetting all about the takeover, but I gave you my word and I'm not going back on it, even to get sweet revenge on a miscreant like that. What a goddamned misbegotten creature Ferritt is to be sure! Have you ever seen anyone so ugly? And stink! Did you know his shoes always rot off his feet before they wear out? No wonder no one has ever seen him out with a girl. He must be a fruit. I won't get him up here now for fear that the sight of him might make me turf him out! We'll meet on it again tomorrow."

The next day, Neil opened the outer door to Clapp's office at the agreed time and heard laughter inside. He knocked on the inner door and went in. Clapp was pacing the floor and appeared to be halfway through a lecture to Clyde on Cabinet solidarity. He glanced at Neil and said, "And what about that display in Cabinet yesterday, Clyde?"

"I'm sorry if I upset anybody," said Clyde. "I didn't mean to. Look, Premier. Everyone in Cabinet knows that we, ah, three make all the decisions. I watched faces as Neil was explaining the takeover and price yesterday and I saw some looks of doubt exchanged. I don't want anyone to think we are on the take or anything, which would be a normal suspicion. It wouldn't mean much to you, but my grandfather was falsely accused of selling the same lumber twice to the government. He was tried and acquitted. But it comes up now and then. So I want to make sure, not only that I am clean, but that I appear to be clean as well. I felt I had to jump in there yesterday, like that, and I believe we will all be better off as a result."

Clapp looked at Neil. "Satisfied? Okay, we'll have another

Cabinet on the question. Clyde, you lead off and say you're now content about the price, having looked at all the relevant documents and so on."

Neil got up and said he would be leaving if that was all. He kept on his mask of annoyance and glanced scornfully at Clyde as he reached the door. As he opened it, he felt Clapp breathe in his ear, "Don't worry. That prick is not getting one more cent." Neil closed the inner door behind him and stood there for a moment. He heard Clapp say, "Don't worry, Clyde, Godwin is not getting one goddamned cent more than ... " Neil noticed Clapp's receptionist looking at him and hurriedly closed the outside door.

At home that night, Neil's mind drifted over each member of Clapp's Cabinet in turn. At one time they were able men for the most part, whose promising political futures were now long and far behind them. They had been divided and ruled by one man whose energy and intellect and motivation would have greatly exceeded their combined total even if they had been able to act in concert. They'd been neutralized by being pitted against one another wastefully, thought Neil: lulled into impotence when their incipient greed had been stimulated into obsession by occasional flashes of largesse from Clapp's limitless funds; immobilized by jealousy and watchfulness until worn out by those demands on time and spirit; praised publicly by Clapp, but humiliated by the undisguised contempt his treatment displayed; sent on frequent, pleasant trips abroad on manufactured government business; talked into a state of stupefaction; sucked into a setting where Clapp made all the decisions, took all the responsibility when things went wrong, and took all the praise when things could be made to appear to have gone right. They were given no crumbs of credit, unless they were expressly bestowed by Clapp – but then they had no share of the blame, either. They were relieved of having to face any painful issue squarely – because all their elections were won for them singlehandedly by Clapp. And, thought Neil, they had grown to love it. Clapp was trying the same technique with him and Clyde, he realized. Why not? They were two young smart-asses and potential threats.

Neil pondered the hundred thousand dollars offered to him by Clapp. The fishplant would be taken over in due course. The donation to the party would take place. The relationship between the money and the transaction would weaken in Neil's mind as time went on. Whenever Clapp had obliquely mentioned the salary from the party since first making the offer, Neil had just as obliquely disclaimed any interest in it, causing the premier to form his lips into an O and give him a sidelong look. But Neil wondered what in fact he would do when Clapp slapped his palms with a bundle of hundred dollar packets.

If he had a grain of sense, Neil thought, he'd remove himself *now* from Clapp's machinations and soul-destroying temptations. But did he have to be swallowed by this quagmire? Were Clapp and Clyde better men than he? Was he to concede, by running away, that he had been defeated by the likes of them? The thought of leaving the field open to Clyde galled something inside him sorely....

And so Neil stayed on – and continued to meet with scores of peripatetic promoters who had *the* answer to Newfoundland's industrial development needs. "When the oil starts flowing," Clapp would say every week, "and when the hydro power becomes available for our own use, are we going to remain just hewers of wood and drawers of water? Are we going to content ourselves with being simply the conduit pipe to industrialized nations for our oil and our power? Not on your life, gentlemen! We are going to prepare an industrial base here now! We will be ready to make use of our vast natural resources ourselves when that glorious day dawns."

The latest and most impressive of the promoters was Mr. Plopnicoff. Clapp dragged him before the full Cabinet (an honour reserved for the more grandiose schemers), to allow him to enunciate his idea for converting the island into another Ruhr Valley. The concept appeared to be multifarious, if not all-inclusive, ranging from the manufacture of incandescent bulbs and light-weight electronic parts, to the local mixing and packaging of tons of orange juice brought back in empty oil tankers on their return trips.

"Genius is simplicity, gentlemen," announced Clapp. "Mr.

Plopnicoff has made a simple but epoch-making discovery. He has discovered that this island, stuck out into the middle of the Atlantic Ocean, is equidistant from all the large industrial nations of the western world and, therefore, equidistant from all the western world's major markets for goods to be manufactured here. A simple but brilliant discovery."

"Oh please, please, your excellency," beamed Mr. Plopnicoff. "I can take no credit for my gift. Some people happen to have a good eye and can shoot straight. I happen to have big-picture-ability and can turn it into wealth for my friends and associates. That's all."

"Come, come, Mr. Plopnicoff, you're far too modest," chided Clapp. "A remarkable man, gentlemen: an entrepreneur; a lover of fine art – I've seen pictures in his basement in New York that you simply would not believe; a man of action – he was a member of the Stern Gang in Palestine when he was only seventeen, reputed on good authority to have killed six British soldiers with his own bare hands!" Plopnicoff pursed his lips and dropped his face towards his chest in a gesture of embarrassed modesty. "And," continued Clapp, "you're not even a Jew, are you, Mr. Plopnicoff?"

"No, your excellency," agreed the promoter. "Jewishness is purely a matter of religion. I resist all narrowness of thought. Since my spirit embraces the whole world, my personal beliefs are therefore worldly as well."

Neil interrupted. "Speaking of the whole world, Mr. Plopnicoff ... " He was irritated by the fact that Clapp had not had him and Clyde, who was absent from Cabinet today, fully briefed on Plopnicoff's proposals prior to the Cabinet meeting, as he ordinarily did. "If," said Neil, "we are equidistant from all major world markets, as you say, then that can only mean that we are as far away as geographically possible from all of those markets, as well. Pardon my narrowness of thinking, but I am unable to see the advantage of being located at the furthest possible point away from all the markets for your proposed products."

Plopnicoff glanced at Clapp in alarm. Clapp said, "Thank you, Mr. Godwin. Now you can see, Mr. Plopnicoff, that I spoke the simple truth when I told you that I had surrounded myself with brilliant, educated young men." His face had flushed and the veins were standing out on his temples, but his voice was controlled. "Gentlemen, let me say this: men who have had breakthrough ideas, and have made money, big big money, as a result, and who have had to carry small-thinking men along with them – kicking, screaming, and scratching all the way – do not waste time on petty, obstructionist details." He turned his eagle eyes on Neil and glowered for the shortest instant. Which irritated Neil even more.

"I would assume, Mr. Plopnicoff," said Neil, "that you will naturally be looking for the normal government guarantees if your proposal goes ahead. But tell me, sir, if you don't mind a saucy question, how much money do *you* yourself propose to put into these projects?"

The promoter was unfazed by the indelicacy. "That, young sir, will of course depend on the outcome of the final feasibility reports, but, ballpark at the moment, say, several big ones and perhaps more."

"There you have it, gentlemen," interjected Clapp. "A man who not only has the brains and drive to conceptualize projects like these and to put them into operation, but who has the faith in them to risk his own money to prove their viability to the world."

After the Cabinet meeting, Clapp called Neil into his office alone. "I had hoped," he said, "that you would understand that I had no opportunity to discuss these projects of Plopnicoff's privately with you before the Cabinet meeting and that, with Ferritt absent in his district, there was little point anyway. I had hoped that I would not have been subjected to such embarrassment from you, Neil, of all people, before my guest and before the whole Cabinet." Neil remained silent. "Naturally, Neil, we'll do nothing at all until we have an independent feasibility study done by the best firm in the world. Only then, and not before then, will we act. Only when we are satisfied that, financially and socially, it is in the best interests of the country, will we make any kind of a political or financial commitment. Now of course, Neil, we, as a government, will have to assume *some* risk, in the nature of things. No risks, no progress. But once we are satisfied on this thing, then and only then, can we think of awarding you and Clyde a small stipend for your work and your responsibility, a recognition of the benefit to our people of having you in the government instead of out making money in private life. The same method as before – through the party as a straight, above-board payment of salary so clean you can pay your taxes on it. Two hundred thousand each."

"What about the other hundred thousand?" asked Neil. He meant to suggest, not that he wanted the money, but that (since nothing had been forthcoming so long after the fish-plant takeover), these offers of cash were actually hollow bluffs. Before he could explain himself, Clapp cut him off.

"That's coming, Neil, that's coming. You have lots of time to poke that away. Don't worry. And for the love of Christ don't get greedy and impatient. That has been the downfall of many a good man who did not have so far to fall from as the great height which you will shortly attain. And I'm talking politically as well as financially. Relax, Neil, relax. Don't start getting as bad as Ferritt on me. Spare me that at least."

Clapp still tried to play Neil and Clyde off against each other, but Neil approached Clyde after the Plopnicoff proposal and initiated an understanding between them regarding Clapp's methods. As a result, they now found themselves tacitly arrayed against Clapp and particular promoters, in an effort, usually successful, to prevent a government commitment of money on mad proposals. The understanding grew over the months into something close to a new friendship.

Neil and Clyde travelled around quite a lot together in connection with the various industrial development areas. Their burgeoning relationship suffered a serious strain during one of their trips and progressed no further. It occurred in Paris in early fall. Neil had asked Gillian to come along on this trip: she had just found out she was pregnant again, and Neil wanted her with him. The three of them were ensconced at the Crillion by their promoter-host, Plopnicoff, and spent the week being chauffeured around Paris and its environs in a Cadillac limousine, and being brought to hot spots during the nights.

One evening, they had dinner at Le Vert Gallant with their host and several financiers, including a seventy-seven-year-old, one-eyed Italian duke who kept trying (clandestinely, he thought), to give Gillian a diamond pendant in exchange for one night of delirious lovemaking. Gillian declined by saying she had no training in external heart massage and she did not find the thought of having to apply mouth-to-mouth resuscitation all that appealing. The duke's empty eye socket – a war wound that he displayed proudly – had given Gillian the willies. "If he says *Alla vostra salute, mia bella'* and fixes that socket on me once more, I'll have my morning sickness now – all over his evening clothes!" she told Neil. So they begged off visiting the Lido and the Scheherazade again. Clyde went with the rest, and Neil and Gillian returned to their hotel.

Later that night, the two of them heard a female voice in Clyde's room, which was next to theirs and had an adjoining door. They could not believe such a thing was possible, so Neil tapped on the door. Clyde opened it, saying, "I'd like you to meet Marie-Thérèse. She seems to have joined our party *en route*." Neil, clad only in his short pyjama bottoms, had not expected to be brought in the room and introduced so formally. In his surprise, he walked over to the girl and held out his hand. It was then that Marie-Thérèse made a statement which caused the dispute between Neil and Clyde later.

Neil went back into his room and told Gillian what had happened. Within three minutes, they heard the corridor door to Clyde's room closing, and the sound of receding female footsteps. Then Clyde knocked heavily on their common door, and Neil opened it. "You owe me a hundred bucks, Neil," said Clyde.

"What for?"

"For half the two hundred bucks I had to pay Marie-Thérèse. You heard what she said when you came in."

"Yes," answered Neil. "She said, *Les pricks il les pleut.'*"

"No," said Clyde. "I goddamned well heard her! Excuse me, Gillian. She said, *Le prix il est plus.'* Now come on, Neil, give me my hundred dollars."

"Clyde, I wouldn't mind if I had done anything with her. Not that I would have in any event." Neil looked sideways at Gillian.

"You did as much with her as I did. Come on. The hundred!"

Gillian laughed outright. "If Marie-Thérèse was speaking French," she stated, "I can assure you that she didn't say either of those things."

Clyde stopped his negotiations and turned to leave, muttering under his breath. "You still owe me a hundred dollars, Godwin .... "

After that, he seemed to consciously try to keep a distance between himself and Neil.

One scheme that was finally given approval in principle by Cabinet was the proposal by Plopnicoff to establish a group of industries to manufacture small electronic components, light bulbs, and other lightweight gadgets of which the transportation costs to market were said to be relatively insignificant. The orange juice mixing factory, Clapp did not press for the moment: "Have your way, boys. But, I tell you, the juice idea is a natural for this place, what with all those five-hundred-thousand-ton oil tankers that will be returning to our shores empty. I only hope for your own sakes that you are not making the blunder of your political lives."

Neil and Clyde had finally agreed to approval in principle of the gadget factories because they had opposed many of Clapp's other maggots in the past and because they knew that the financing would never be arranged for these projects, anyway. Already, the Parisian financiers had refused to become involved without an unconditional guarantee of 100 per cent repayment by the government, which was something Clyde and Neil could not accept. The Export Credit Guarantee Department, (ECGD), of the British government also resisted any involvement without the same full guarantee by Clapp's administration. This was in accord with Neil's and Clyde's predictions.

Then, without warning or reason, ECGD reversed its position and agreed to guarantee all but fifty million of the two hundred million dollar project in return for a first mortgage on the plants and the use of British materials in the construction. Neil and Clyde attributed the turn-around to an unfavourable balance of payments condition in the British export markets much greater than publicly acknowledged. Still, they were very surprised at the reversal, as ECGD had already been badly burned on the bankruptcy of the Come-By-Chance oil refinery – a collapse that ranked among the largest in the world and caused ripples in unlikely places; (it had brought down one of the great giants of Japanese industry).

A few days before Christmas, Clapp left for a month's holiday in Hawaii, while Clyde took off for a couple of weeks in Toronto and New York. On Christmas Eve, at five o'clock in the afternoon, Neil received a call at home from the comptroller of the government treasury. He'd just heard, he said, that Plopnicoff was in the process of trying to raise money from Saudi Arabian sources on the authority of some Newfoundland government document.

Neil thought for a moment. The deal with Plopnicoff was that only after he himself had actually put his twenty-five million dollars into the project would ECGD issue its guarantee for one hundred and fifty million, or the Newfoundland government allow the remaining twenty-five million to be raised on its own guarantee. Plopnicoff had not yet put in his money; ECGD had not yet concluded its formal agreement; and the Government of Newfoundland had not yet given its guarantee. So what was Plopnicoff up to? Neil told the comptroller to meet him at his office.

As guests began to arrive at the house for a Christmas Eve cocktail party, and as Gillian, standing beside a sardonic Jane, glared after him in exasperation, Neil left to join the comptroller in an attempt to track Plopnicoff down by phone. By the time they reached him in Rome, at the residence of a bishop high in the Vatican bank, it was late at night – and they had already pieced together most of the story through additional phone calls to the comptroller's overseas acquaintances. It had nothing to do with the gadget factory. And it was worse than Neil had thought.

Apparently, Plopnicoff was travelling about oil-rich Arabian countries waving a letter signed by Prime Minister Percy

Clapp – a letter authorizing him to enter into a scheme to raise seven hundred million dollars on behalf of the Government of Newfoundland. The money was to be used to repay the bondholders of the Churchill Falls hydro project in Labrador; and the lenders would be entitled to a half-interest in that project. The idea was that the Newfoundland government would then be able to turn off the flow of electricity to Quebec without having to worry about going into default under the bond. This would bring Quebec to her knees, forcing her to offer a market price to Newfoundland for the power, instead of the skimpy sum now being paid. When Neil spoke to him on the telephone, Plopnicoff was quite open about everything.

"May I ask how you obtained that letter?" inquired Neil.

"Prime Minister Clapp gave it to me," replied Plopnicoff. "Forced it on me, in fact. Just before he left for his holiday."

"Well, I should tell you that he overlooked the need to get a Cabinet order for any such commitment on behalf of the Newfoundland government. The letter is not legally binding in any way."

"He's your prime minister, Mr. Godwin, not mine. And a very excellent prime minister he is. I would have assumed that, since you are in his Cabinet, you considered yourself bound by the normal solidarity and mutual support of colleagues in such circumstances .... Please tell me if I am mistaken in this."

"It has nothing to do with Cabinet solidarity," said Neil, struggling not to lose his temper at Plopnicoff's unctuous tone of voice. "It has everything to do with proper legal form. Please tell *me* something. Why are you involved in this? What's in it for you?"

"Very little, I'm sorry to say. Just the normal finder's fee. I'm doing it out of friendship and respect for Mr. Clapp."

"How much is the finder's fee, Mr. Plopnicoff?"

"The usual. Just one per cent."

"Seven million dollars! For you?"

"Alas," sighed Plopnicoff, "would that it were so much. But there will be certain expenses in connection with the raising of the money. Moreover, excellency, as you will be aware from your talks with Mr. Clapp, there are certain other ... shall we say, unorthodox ... expenses associated with my own project in your fair province, which cannot be covered from audited sources of funds."

Neil felt his face redden as the comptroller looked at him quizzically. "You've lost me there, I'm afraid, Mr. Plopnicoff," he said stiffly. "But I should tell you that the comptroller of the treasury is listening on the extension."

"Yes, of course." Plopnicoff did not miss a beat. "I naturally assumed that you would not be holding this conversation without the advice of a high official. I was referring to a personal reserve for contingencies in start-up and operation which might not be foreseen in the auditors' projections – but which I must nevertheless provide for. You see, excellency, I am totally committed to my Newfoundland project. Its failure would destroy me personally. I must be prepared for every eventuality."

"Yes. Well. On your efforts to raise seven hundred million for the Upper Churchill ... I don't have to tell you that now that you know your letter is not properly authorized, it would be illegal and fraudulent for you to proceed. I just mention this for your own protection."

"I understand completely, Mr. Godwin," murmured Plopnicoff. "And I thank you for your thoughtfulness in giving me the benefit of your legal training."

"This is not for you personally, of course," Neil went on, "but if one of your associates or employees inadvertently continues to act on that letter – if we hear of any further activity along these lines – the comptroller will have no alternative but to alert Interpol."

"I understand completely, Mr. Godwin," Plopnicoff repeated, although this time his tone was distinctly unpleasant. "I understand *everything* completely .... And henceforth I shall govern myself accordingly."

Neil hung up, relieved that the conversation was finished. The comptroller came over and shook his hand vigorously, expressing admiration for his superb handling of the problem.

When Neil returned home early Christmas morning, three

drunken, jovial men were all that remained of the original forty guests. As he tried to explain the urgent reason for his absence to Gillian – whose coldness was supplemented by cutting remarks from Jane – the men interrupted with droll irrelevancies: "A *real* friend would have stayed in his office *all* night, Godwin; we were just starting to make some headway with the girls, here!"

Neil hustled them, protesting, into their coats and out the door, then made for the stairs in exasperation and exhaustion.

"Neil needs his rest, now, Gillian – after all his men's work," said Jane, beginning to carry glasses and plates into the kitchen. "Let's get at the women's work."

"Christmas Jesus Eve!" muttered Gillian. "Leaving me here alone with all those political turds! I just can't *believe* ...."

Clyde arrived back home in the New Year, after Neil had given him a quick phone call. Shortly thereafter, Neil began to hear from some press people he knew. The word was that Neil had very nearly allowed a breach of the seven hundred million Upper Churchill Bond by botching his responsibility as acting Minister of Industrial Development in Clyde's absence, and that Clyde had saved the day by forthright action immediately upon his return. The premature termination of Clyde's holiday had been necessary when he heard about the fumbling which was going on at home.

Although he was angry, Neil bided his time. He would get Clyde later. He went instead to see Toope, the Minister of Justice, and asked him if he had approved the letter Clapp had given Plopnicoff without Cabinet endorsement.

"Yes," said Toope, without looking at him. "Why do you ask?"

"Mr. Clapp had no authority to make the commitment in that letter, Mr. Toope."

"Not formally he didn't. But it was just a matter of having it retroactively approved by Cabinet later. Pure formality."

"What are you talking about – pure formality? That letter had ramifications that could have bankrupted this province! The whole concept needs careful analysis. And I certainly would have objected to Plopnicoff having anything whatever to do with it. So would Ferritt."

"Is that right now?" queried Toope. "I was given to understand from an impeccable source that the only two in Cabinet with more lip than brain, you and Ferritt, had been bought – rather, *brought* –around (I sometimes get those two words mixed up, always have, my sole linguistic idiosyncrasy), bought around –there I go again –to a favourable view of Mr. Plopnicoff in all respects. You're in a government, young man. Teamwork, resolving internal conflicts, united front, solidarity, tolerance of colleagues. God knows what I had to tolerate from you during that fish strike. But I'm not prepared to resign over every little piece of scratch-ass nonsense I don't happen to agree with, like some fellows with more lip on them than a rubber dinghy."

Neil let his anger towards Clyde cool. He understood Clyde's overvaulting ambition, he told himself, and was only sorry it precluded any chance of a real friendship between them. He was even more sorry and rueful, he realized, that he could not seem to galvanize *himself* into practising countervailing slyness and deceitful trickery. But, he thought, great political leaps forward did not result from mean knavery, after all. They resulted from circumstances and the brilliant gifts to take advantage of them. To hell with Clyde!

When Clapp got back late in January, Neil and Clyde agreed to go and see him together in order to lay down a few unalterable rules for the operation of any government of which they would remain a part. "You give him both barrels, Clyde, and then I'll jump in and confirm our immutable conditions," said Neil.

In Clapp's office, Clyde began his carefully thought-out remarks in a restrained and slow manner. Clapp paced the floor without interrupting. His face was tanned from his holiday and exuded vitality. Neil remained silent. As Clyde listed the conditions on which the continuing presence of Neil and himself in government depended, Clapp straightened pictures on the walls or re-arranged chairs. Then, when Clyde was about halfway through his speech, Clapp suddenly stopped in mid-pace and looked sharply at him. Without warning, he lunged across the room as if he were ready to commit assault, and Clyde, aghast, plastered his back and both palms against the wall. He threw a look of terror at Neil – just as Clapp reached out, straightened his tie, and pulled the knot tighter under his collar. That done, Clapp resumed his pacing.

Forcing a smile, Clyde recommenced his speech; but now his voice was too loud, almost hysterical in sound, and his choice of words was too strong. He faltered to a finish and looked to Neil to deliver the *coup de grâce*. In the pause, Clapp walked over to within a foot of Clyde and stared into his face. "Clyde," he said, "listen to me. When are you going to get your goddamned hair cut?"

"Pardon me?" stammered Clyde.

"Are you still trying to attract the sloppy vote? You have already captured that constituency, Clyde. Believe me, now, you have. I'm telling you, you have! My firm advice to you is to make an all-out effort to attract the neat and tidy vote. When, for example, are you going to start wearing your bloody Homburg hat like all the other ministers?"

Clyde glanced at Neil, who was red-faced from trying to keep his laughter silent. "Godwin over there never wears his Homburg, either," he sulked.

"Neil Godwin is only a young man in his twenties," Clapp roared. "You can't expect him to wear all the accoutrements of gravity yet, for Christ's sake! Where's your sense of appropriateness? Haven't you learned a goddamned thing from the tens of thousands of dollars your father spent sending you to schools for sow's ears?"

"I'm only seventeen months older than Neil Godwin!" Clyde shouted back.

"Clyde, Clyde, Clyde," said Clapp gently, pityingly. "Most of you was fifty years old the day you were calved, and some of you never got born at all. That's your basic problem."

Clyde turned and started to stride out of the office in his heavy, bobbing way. When he reached the door, Clapp said, "Clyde, do I now assume that you will not be accompanying Neil and myself on our round-the-world industrial fact-finding tour in March? Fifteen European and Asian capitals. Meetings with top statesmen, financiers, industrialists. Let me know within the hour. I'll have to choose another minister to go in your place."

Clyde stopped abruptly with the door already half open. He stood with his back to Clapp for ten seconds as his eyeballs flicked from side to side, then he turned. "I'll give you a call in a few minutes about that, sir. Thank you for seeing us today at such short notice."

Neil followed Clyde out, exchanging grins with Clapp as he went.

"Thanks for all the help in there!" said Clyde bitterly, as they walked back to their offices.

"How could I help anyone who was so frightened, the diarrhea was dripping out from under the cuffs of his pants?" Neil demanded.

"I never knew that the little fucker could *be* so frightening. Physically, I mean," answered Clyde. "What's all this about a round-the-world tour?" Resentment and humiliation had evaporated in his unconcealable curiosity to know what was going on behind his back, what he was in danger of missing.

Neil knew no more about it than Clyde, but he said, "It involves our travelling to ... Look, Clyde, you'd better check the details out with Percy. I thought you knew all this. Percy told me about it before Christmas."

Clyde's face was grim and apprehensive. "Yes, he did try to tell me about it, but I wasn't paying much attention."

Neil knew that he was lying, and was gratified to see his colleague trying to cover his jealousy and worry with nonchalance. The past half hour had balanced somewhat the scales of justice, he thought.

When Neil went home for lunch that day, he found Jane and Gillian playing with Elizabeth on the living room floor. Jane hadn't been around for a couple of weeks and Neil greeted her cheerily. She got up and, for the first time in months, hugged him warmly. He immediately felt close to her again.

"Hey, you two will enjoy this," he said with animation, "knowing how much you admire Clyde Ferritt." He described the morning's episode in Clapp's office. The women laughed till he reached the end, and then they exchanged glances.

"You figure you really got one over on Ferritt, do you, Neil?" asked Gillian. "What about the reason you went to see Clapp in the first place? How was that resolved?"

Neil suddenly realized that there was not much satisfaction in his "triumph" over Clyde after all; Percy had merely succeeded in flummoxing them both once more. He made a shrug of annoyance.

"Jesus, Neil," said Jane. "Is that what you guys do up there all day long? Go around trying to one-up each other?"

"And what do you *girls* do all day long?" Neil shot back. Some of the warmth he'd felt earlier had already departed.

"Oh, we get married and so on, don't we, Gillian?" The women grinned in delight at one another. Like two conspirators, thought Neil. Against him.

"And we have babies," added Gillian. "Speaking of which, Neil, how long will you be gone on that global rampage with Clapp in March?"

"Oh, not long," said Neil hurriedly. "A month at most." He'd forgotten when he'd mentioned the trip that Gillian was due to deliver that spring. "*If* I go at all, I'll be back long before the baby is born." He quickly figured out dates and was relieved to find that a return home in mid-April did in fact leave a month or six weeks before the expected date of birth.

"But what about if Gillian's calculations are off?" asked Jane. "Or what about if the baby arrives before it's due? Don't tell me I have to play surrogate husband again." She beamed at Gillian. "I'll already have my hands full, I'm afraid, playing the role of a real wi –"

"What about if you stop playing the prick around here?" Neil cut her off with a shout. In recent months the two women seemed to have combined forces against him – badgering him whenever they were together – and Neil had suddenly had enough of feeling over-defensive about both his domestic and his political performance. "Listen here, Jane! I'm getting goddamned well pissed off with your snotty comments all the time. If you can't come to this house without poking your nasty little snout into my private life, then you just get the f –"

"Neil, Neil, Neil!" yelled Gillian. "Jane was only joking, in the name of God! She came here to tell us she's getting married."

"Oh," said Neil. For a moment, the only thing he could do was wonder how the characters in second-rate novels got out of the contrived traps of humiliation into which they always blundered. "Shit! I'm sorry, Jane. Uh, who's the lucky man?"

"Roland," said Gillian when Jane, on her way to the coat closet, didn't answer.

"Roland Maidment?" Neil went after Jane, trying to hide the surprise on his face. He knew Jane had been going out with him for several months, but he'd never thought it would lead to marriage. Roland was the son of a prominent St. John's neurosurgeon. He was a quiet, unassuming student of chartered accountancy and, to all appearances, he loved the work. Once or twice, Neil's friends had joked about the contrast between Roland's stodginess and Jane's vivacity: champagne and porridge, they described it.

"That's wonderful, Jane," Neil went on, trying to make amends. "Roland's a nice guy." Then, as Jane continued to put on her coat, he asked, "Ah, are you sure he's right for you?"

Jane swung about. She pointed at Neil and said to Gillian, "Ah, are you sure *he's* right for you?" She turned back to Neil. "Listen, my concerned big brother. Roland is kind and considerate and caring. He won't say or do anything to hurt me and he won't leave me in the lurch .... Goodbye, Gillian. Better take good care of yourself."

Still trying to detain his sister, Neil followed her to the door. "That's good, Jane ... there's no hurry .... Jane, when's the big day? Roland doesn't have his CA yet, does he?"

Now, when it was too late, Neil wished he could talk to Jane about marriage: give her good advice, be sure she was making the right decision .... But with a slam of the door she was gone.

14

When the week finally arrived in which Clapp, Clyde, and Neil were to leave for London on the first step of their six-week industrial fact-finding tour of the globe, Clapp, as usual, made a public announcement of the time of their departure. Clapp enjoyed the way friends and supporters always gathered at the airport to cheer him on such occasions. This time, however, the three of them were given a different sort of welcome on the day they arrived at St. John's airport. Instead of getting a rousing send-off, their flight was actually delayed.

The trouble was caused by a small, but noisy, demonstration of university students. What exactly they were protesting was not clear. There were shouts about foreign giveaways, about the need for more money for university students, and about the destruction of the Newfoundland way of life. The undercurrent of feeling among them was, however, quite obvious: they were sick and tired of Percy Clapp. In general, the demonstrators ignored Neil and Clyde. Only infrequently would one or another of the students divert his or her attention from Clapp in order to particularize to Clapp's "running dogs" the holes or appendages on the premier's person that were going to be stopped up or sliced off.

After a while, Neil noticed one student at the edge of the crowd. He was carrying a bucket from which steam was rising and seemed to be awaiting a proper moment. Finally, the moment appeared to have arrived. "Horseshit, Clapp!" the student yelled. "Horseshit!" And as the demonstrators between him and the premier immediately melted away, he dipped into his bucket and began to throw great handfuls of the stuff at Clapp. Right in front of the television cameras a lump struck Clapp in the face. He let most of it drop from his cheek to the ground while he gazed with dignity into the camera. Then, slowly and deliberately, he took out his handkerchief and wiped the smear from his face. The student was arrested on the spot.

That evening, the television news showed a film of the incident. It ended with Clapp making a more-in-sorrow-than-in-anger statement about not pressing charges against the student. Media commentary was full of admiration for Clapp and condemnation of the demonstrators' gutter tactics. One journalist did wonder, however, if the blush was not starting to disappear from the premier's political rose. Later that night – after dark, and without public announcement – Clapp and his two young colleagues took the government plane to the mainland to catch another flight to the United Kingdom.

Once in London, Neil and Clyde had lunch with the English solicitor for a consortium of merchant banks in the City from which Plopnicoff was negotiating a loan for his projects in Newfoundland. "I'm a concepts man myself," Clapp had told them that morning, before leaving Claridge's for Foyle's Bookstore. "Details bore me. You boys talk to the limey lawyer."

Across the table from them now, the lawyer said, "Kleinwort-Benson, the lead bankers in the syndicate, are not all-fired hot to trot on this little Plopnicoff number. They got a hosing on that Come-By-Chance oil refinery bummer, and they're still uptight about Newfndland."

Ordinarily, Neil would have been delighted to hear that the banks were not eager to lend Plopnicoff the capital, but he had taken a dislike to this lawyer who, from the beginning, had given the impression that he'd rather have been anywhere else but there. His attempt now to display the cosmopolitan scope of his English by speaking his concept of American made Neil feel no warmer towards him. "But ECGD of the British government stood behind every penny your banks put into the oil refinery. The banks will lose nothing," Neil remarked testily.

"That doesn't lay my clients back one whit," said the solicitor, savouring the morsel of baby lamb from his third chop. "They have to think of the image ramifications of doing another deal with Nfoundlnd where you chaps conduct that slaughter of baby seals every spring. Our prime minister recently passed along to the president of the Board of Trade a copy of a *personal* letter received from Brigitte Bardot, demanding that the UK government crush that infamy in our colony. These are all considerations for my clients to take into account."

"Kleinwort-Benson's image ramifications?" inquired Neil. "Kleinwort-Benson! The gutless wonders who caved in to Arab blackmail and refused to do business with Jewish companies! Yes, of course, they have a sterling reputation to uphold as men of principle."

The lawyer snorted. "Apart altogether from my clients' views, old chap, I would remind you that I am a British solicitor. Unlike your American advocate, I and my colleagues will have no part of lobbying on behalf of our clients' wrong causes before the government or the legislature. We are prepared to champion something as solicitors only after we have first determined, according to the dictates of our own consciences, that it is in the best interest of our country and the public at large, as well as of that of our clients."

"Public-policy-first lawyers," said Neil. "That's comforting to know. I suppose you are doing your best to solve the root problems causing the tensions in your cities. How many solicitors of African or West Indian extraction are in your firm, for example?"

"I am afraid, sir, that I have to disclaim personal responsibility for the fact that none of our dusky brethren with the ability to rise to that rarefied atmosphere of the law has yet presented himself."

"Or herself," chuckled Clyde. "No sexual preference, please."

"Or herself," responded the lawyer, with an answering chuckle, before turning back to Neil. "You, sir, don't have any blacks or tints where you come from. Your ancestors managed, as I understand from my research into your glorious

210

history, to push into extinction the only off-whites you were blessed with, the original Red Indians, the Beothucks. So I should imagine you were able to restrain yourself from weeping too profusely at everything you read as a boy in *Uncle Tom's Cabin*."

Clyde laughed. Sensing from the burning feeling in his face that victory was unlikely here, Neil retreated with a Parthian shot that he knew was idiotic even as he uttered it: "Newfnd*land*. Not N*found*lnd. And not *New*fndlnd. It's pronounced Newfndland. Under*stand*?"

"Whatever," said the lawyer. "A rancid turbot by any other name smells as, well, foul."

Clyde laughed again. For a vivid instant Neil knew that the one act which would give the most purpose to the remainder of his life would be the act of finally nailing Clyde Ferritt.

"The irrelevancies of international politics and race relations aside for a moment, if Mr. Godwin will not object too strenuously," said Clyde, dusting off his Oxford accent for the occasion, "and getting into a topic perhaps more germane to our discussion, do you happen to know why, precisely, ECGD dropped their insistence that our government guarantee the repayment of all loans raised for the Plopnicoff projects?"

"Well, obviously," answered the lawyer, "the comfort letter from your Attorney General, Toope, is, for all practical purposes, every bit as good as an outright guarantee by your government."

This time, Clyde did not laugh. He exchanged a startled look with Neil and said, with pretended thoughtfulness, "Yes. I suppose the comfort letter is just as good. Ah, Neil, is there any aspect of that comfort letter you, as a lawyer, would like to ask about?"

"Yes. I'd like to ask how Mr. Toope's comfort letter is as good, legally, to ECGD, as a government guarantee would be."

"I said nothing about it being as good *legally*," said the English solicitor. "It's a piss-poor lawyer who knows only the law. As it happens, we are not talking about legalities here. Assuming we had your government's guarantee and sought to enforce it legally, how would we do that? By taking an action in your courts? I certainly wouldn't advise my clients to trust their lives to obtaining a favourable judgement from your courts against your own government. By taking an action in the English courts, then? And how would we ever succeed in enforcing our judgement in your province against your sovereign government? You see the difficulties. This is not a question of legality at all. It's a question of supra-legality. A higher law than mere law applies. The law of fear of utter ruination. If your Mr. Toope's comfort letter to ECGD, signed as Attorney General, the highest law officer of your province, and stating that his government would never allow this government-sponsored project of Plopnicoff's to default on its financial obligations to the banks, is not lived up to by your government, then you blokes might just as bloody well shut down your little island, because you would never be able to raise another penny anywhere in the world ever again for any purpose whatsoever. My clients would see to that."

"Yes, of course," said Clyde, "that's the precise situation as I've always understood it." He sat back and remained quiet.

The solicitor half rose while finishing his coffee. "Must run," he said. "Thank you for lunch, gentlemen." He smiled superciliously at Neil. "I shall report to my clients that despite a rather feisty, so to speak, conversation, all parties appear to be *ad idem* on this transaction, and that there are no insuperable objections to proceeding if they are able to overcome their moral qualms."

After he left, Neil and Clyde sat without speaking for a moment. "Are we on the hook with this deal?" asked Clyde, finally. "Is there any way we can get out of it?"

"It's subject only to financing," said Neil. "And it seems clear that the financing is all arranged, despite that bastard's hard-to-get attitude."

"I'm sorry I laughed at his belittling bullshit, Neil. I was actually only delighted that the banks seemed to have cold feet."

"Forget it, Clyde."

"Are you going to resign and repudiate Toope's goddamned comfort letter?"

"I might. What about you?"

"I should. Let's have a cognac and talk it over."

They discussed the fact that the government of which they were much-touted members was now committed to the two hundred million dollars which the factories were estimated to cost, and to any overruns in construction, start-up, and operating costs as well. With Plopnicoff possessing the construction supervision and management contracts, they concluded, such overruns were highly likely to occur, perhaps in the scores of millions of dollars. They also decided that they'd been utter fools to ever let Clapp persuade them that his own letter authorizing Plopnicoff to raise seven hundred million dollars to pay off the Upper Churchill bondholders was exploratory only, and never intended to be binding on the government.

"Aw, shit," exclaimed Clyde, draining his snifter, "as soon as Clapp gets back, I'm resigning and going home."

They ordered another cognac.

"Clyde," said Neil. "I'm wondering if Toope's letter makes any practical difference. Suppose it didn't exist. Our failure as a government to stand behind the debts of another large project in the event of its collapse would be disastrous for Newfoundland anyway, comfort letter or no comfort letter. Listen, Clyde ... " Their heads were close together now in the manner of two intimates. "If we are fated to hang back to back, you and I, on this lunatic scheme, we'd dangle just as high if the madman never banged off that letter."

Clyde looked closely at Neil for a moment. "Point number one," he said. "And point number two: what's another three or four hundred million dollars on top of a present public debt of several billion, anyway?"

They tossed down their cognacs and ordered another.

"Besides," added Neil, "say we do get out now in a mess of accusations and counter-accusations. Would it stop Clapp? What effect do you think our resignations would have on his hold on power? I can't keep the picture out of my mind of the two of us pissing on an iceberg, hoping to melt it."

"You're right, Neil. You're right. It would be a pathetically useless gesture – and there'd be no one left in Cabinet to exercise a modicum of control over the raving lunatic. Oh,

Jesus, where's that bleeding offshore oil? I wish to Christ it would hurry up and come on stream!"

"Absolutely!" Neil agreed. "Being constantly buggered by the likes of Plopnicoff is all bad enough. But having Percy right there with him as well, applying grits instead of grease, is starting to get just a mite tedious, I must confess."

"My sentiments exactly. But another month or so to think this thing through won't hurt. I *am* looking forward to seeing Hong Kong, Peking, and whatnot, aren't you?"

Neil nodded. "Hong Kong, especially. An old friend from Oxford is there with the BBC. I wrote him and his wife about my visit and I don't want to miss seeing them."

But this was only part of the reason why Neil had argued against resignation. The moment he had heard of Toope's secret comfort letter he had made up his mind on what he was going to do. But he wanted to do it independently, and in his own time and way. Now, as they emptied their glasses, he and Clyde agreed to say nothing to Clapp about the letter for the present. They left the restaurant together, and went to see if the premier was back in his hotel room.

That night, after the three of them had parted company to retire to their respective rooms at Claridge's, Neil was met in the corridor near his door by one of Plopnicoff's lieutenants. The big man expressed pleasurable surprise in his soft voice at this chance encounter. They shook hands. "Oh, incidentally, Mr. Godwin," the man said gently, keeping an exceedingly firm grip on Neil's hand, "I wouldn't put down the Arabs or build up the Jews in front of our business friends here in London if I were you. I'm speaking in everyone's best interest, now. There are lots of Arabs here with lots of money for lots of deals."

"I carry no brief for any of the groups fighting for that particular desert," answered Neil. "My own is handful enough. But I did understand that Mr. Plopnicoff was once a member of the Stern Gang over there."

"Mr. Plopnicoff is not mixed up with gangsters, Mr. Godwin. That *Washington Post* story was the worst kind of muckraking journalism. As a politician, you know how the press

214

can smear an innocent man's reputation. One or two of us on Mr. Plopnicoff's staff sometimes get the silly idea that you and Mr. Ferritt don't like Mr. Plopnicoff very much, and are not always making your best efforts on this joint venture of ours. I'm sure that idea is wrong. Good night, Mr. Godwin. Enjoy your trip around the world, sir, but be very, very careful you don't go off the beaten path. That can be dangerous among people where the law means nothing."

Before disappearing swiftly down the hall, the man gave Neil's arm a parting squeeze with his large hand. The pressure seemed heartier than that needed between friendly business acquaintances – but Neil was not certain of that, and he didn't care. He'd soon be clear of all this.

The next morning they quit London and proceeded, in accordance with Clapp's itinerary, to Aberdeen, Oslo, Copenhagen, Hamburg, and Amsterdam in the space of four days. They saw only the interiors of taxi-cabs and the walls of the banquet rooms where Clapp expatiated to businessmen's clubs on "The Impact of Newfoundland's Offshore Oil on the North Atlantic Community." Then they flew to Karachi, where they were to change flights for Hong Kong.

During the flight to Karachi, Clapp was thoughtful and quiet. He didn't even respond when Clyde, bringing up the topic for the first time since the three of them had left Newfoundland, asked him whether or not he thought the students' demonstration was significant. Clapp himself had not mentioned the incident at all. When they reached Karachi, however, Clapp announced, without preamble or explanation, that he was flying back home immediately. Refusing the offers Clyde and Neil made to accompany him, he urged them to go on to Hong Kong as planned. As they left to board their plane, he barely looked up.

"The old bastard is worried," remarked Clyde happily, as the two of them settled into their seats.

"About what?" asked Neil.

"That demonstration."

"But it was nothing. Fifty or sixty arseholes. He handled it beautifully."

Clyde shrugged. "He thinks it's the start of something."

"The start of what, though? Sure, he doesn't have to call an election for three or four years."

"No. But the party has to have its leadership convention this fall."

"So what, Clyde?" Neil was a trifle impatient. "That'll only be the usual monstrous piss-up."

"We'll see," said Clyde, putting his seat back and closing his eyes. His cryptic comments and his equally cryptic dismissal of the subject irritated Neil.

That night, when they arrived at the Peninsula Hotel in Hong Kong, Boo Mansingh was waiting for them. He gripped Neil's hand and held it for several minutes. Twice he put his other arm around Neil's shoulders and hugged him. He had hardly been able to sleep, he said, since he had received Neil's message from the BBC in London. He was only sorry that Jennifer had already left for a visit home to Surrey before it arrived.

In their hotel room, Mansingh told them that he was due to fly by chartered plane to Saigon the next morning. Would the two of them like to come along? Since the regime permitted only a few western correspondents to visit Vietnam, there was still space on the plane. Only those people who could be trusted to be fair were allowed to go (among whom, Mansingh laughed, he himself was considered the fairest of them all). He could arrange to have Neil and Clyde travel with him as sympathetic western statesmen.

Slumped in a chair and looking half dead from exhaustion, Clyde began to shake his head. But when Neil accepted the invitation with enthusiasm – adding, mockingly, "Boo won't let the Commies get us. Will you, Boo?" – Clyde acquiesced.

"I just hope this won't brand us as pinkos," he muttered.

Mansingh grinned. "From my viewpoint," he said, "you already look quite pink."

Mansingh, Neil, and Clyde arrived in Saigon late the next afternoon. They were met by a cadre whom Mansingh embraced and whom he introduced as the man who was to guide Neil and Clyde during their stay. Mansingh and his cameraman took some footage of them among people at the airfield, and as the camera rolled, the cadre issued orders to the Vietnamese on where to stand and what to do. Then Mansingh announced that he had work to do and that he would see them the next morning for the return to Hong Kong. Neil was about to ask him where he was going, but Mansingh's expression had become hard and remote. He was probably putting into effect his Oxford plan of learning guerrilla tactics for use back in South Africa, Neil thought. And decided not to be inquisitive. "Comrade Ho will take good care of you," declared Mansingh; and left with several other comrades.

When Comrade Ho stopped his vehicle in front of the building in which they would be staying, Clyde asked him if it was the former Caravelle Hotel. "I have no memory for that name," Ho replied with a stony face. Once he and Clyde were inside together, Neil whispered: "Christ, talk about a hard-liner Commie – can't remember the Caravelle, he says. We'd better watch our step with that fellow." They lay down for a nap, planning to leave later with their guide to see a performance of what he called "culture pollution."

When Comrade Ho returned, however, Clyde was still in bed. He was exhausted, he said, from their mad leader's crazed peregrinations, and he refused to get up. With a few qualms, Neil went off alone with their guide.

For half an hour, Ho drove silently through the streets of the city. Finally, he parked his jeep near a dimly lit doorway, exchanged grunts with the man standing there, and led Neil through a tangle of alleys empty of both people and animals. They entered a room right off the street without knocking. After a few minutes of jabber in an adjoining room, Ho returned. He was followed by two females, an older one with her arms full of a variety of hardware, and a younger carrying a chair which she placed several feet away from the foot of the bed. She directed Neil to sit down.

Ho said: "Blowjob goes with the show. Only twenty bucks extra."

Neil rose from his chair. He must have misheard. "I beg your pardon, sir?"

"Young girl. She suck your cock while you watch show.

Only twenty bucks more," explained Ho.

"I'm sorry, I didn't realize what … " began Neil, but his attention was diverted by the movements of the woman, about thirty years old, who was standing on the bed. She had unwrapped the robe from her body, carefully folded it, and hung it over the headboard. Her naked body was as lissome and strong as a ballet dancer's. "Comrade Ho," said Neil, "I didn't know you were bringing me to this kind of show. I think we'd best leave if you –"

"Our friend Booman say bring you here. Show you capitalist corruption of our people by war mongers. The problems we have. Now about blowjob? Yes?"

"No! Say, no thanks. No blowjob."

Comrade Ho muttered something and sat on a box in the corner. The woman on the bed was now stretching and limbering up, taking an ankle in her hands by turns to bring each shin up to her forehead, smiling at Neil as she did so. She then crawled around the bed arranging the armload of implements and food-stuffs she had brought in.

The girl, about fifteen years old, hung back by the inner door with lowered eyes. The woman directed a soft word towards her, but she made no move. After two sharp syllables from the woman on the bed, however, she glanced up, went straight over to Neil, and started to pull down his fly.

"No, no, no – no blowjob," exclaimed Neil to Comrade Ho. "Tell her no blowjob!"

"I already tell her no blowjob," replied the cadre, with a shrug.

"Tell her again!" roared Neil, inhibiting the small hand at his zipper with both of his.

As Ho said something to the girl, Neil let his eyes wander over her slim body, her full, pink lips, her silky skin. She was blushing. She started to get up again; but at another, sharper, word from the woman, she patted Neil's cheek, regained her hold on his zipper, and pulled it down.

"No, no, no, no," whispered Neil fiercely, sitting down and struggling to free his crotch from one of the girl's hands – just as she skilfully undid his belt with the other. Twisting her wrist out of his grasp, she then used both hands to pull down the front of his underwear. As she took his penis in her soft fingers, Neil looked wildly around for his guide. Comrade Ho had disappeared.

The woman, however, was still on the bed. Squirming enthusiastically, she was simulating great passion while poking a variety of items into her orifices. *Surely God*, thought Neil desperately, as the woman writhed, and the girl sucked and tongued below, *if anyone catches me here like this, I'll be taken out and shot! Maybe it's all a set-up* ....

Putting his hands on the girl's head, he tried to push her away – but she wouldn't let go. Putting his hands on her shoulders, he tried to get up – but she held him down. Suddenly, and quite without warning to either himself or the girl, Neil began to ejaculate into her throat. Her eyes crossed at the unexpected shock, and she lurched away, gagging and sputtering.

While she rested against the wall, bent over, gulping in air and coughing, the woman looked at her in mild amusement. Neil yanked up his trousers.

"You still horny, big boy?" queried the woman. "You nearly drown her. You want me? Only thirty bucks more."

"Thank you, no," muttered Neil, reaching for his wallet. "I've got to go. How much do I owe you?"

"Oh, you same as GI's. They tink only to the monies," she pouted. "Twenty-five dollars for show, and twenty for blow-job."

Neil quickly counted out five American tens and put them on the chair. Without looking at either the woman or the girl he made for the outer door, pulled it open, and let himself into the street. Comrade Ho was loitering outside.

As the two men strode briskly and silently through the alleys back to the jeep, Ho was once more stony-faced. "Now you see what they done to our country," he pronounced. "Such spectacle for money. You enjoy the show?"

"Well ... " said Neil. He was wondering what loathsome disease he had caught. He hoped that, because of her young age, the girl had not done that with too many other men.

"Daughter suck nice, don't she?" remarked Ho. "I teach her myself."

219

Neil remembered the half-healed whelks he'd noticed earlier on Ho's shins and kept his eyes on the road.

In their room at the hotel, Clyde was still asleep, so Neil was able to go to the shower stall without any quizzing and scrub furiously. His sole wish was that he had not contracted a form of galloping Saigon syphilis sturdy enough to have survived the victory and the political change-over. Clyde was awake when he returned, ready to ask about the performance. Neil said that it was another one of those demonstrations of bodily agility that the Oriental Communists seemed to be crazy about doing, and changed the subject. He wanted to talk about anything that did not remind him of what he'd done tonight.

He positioned himself gingerly on his bed, as if his body had become brittle. "Clyde," he said. "On the plane you mentioned the leadership convention coming up this fall. You don't really think there's any chance that Percy can be beaten, do you?"

Under the constitution of Clapp's party, The People First Party, there had to be a leadership convention within two years after every general election. Any party member could run for the leadership – and Clapp used that provision to show how democratic his party was and how eager he was to put his own leadership on the line at regular intervals. In practice, the conventions were political functions of small moment. Each time, the re-election of Clapp as leader had been all but unanimous. The combined total of votes cast for the two or three perennial crackpot candidates, the only ones who had ever formally opposed him, had once peaked at seven out of the thousand or so ballots cast by the delegates. The conventions were staged as festivals of folk adulation for Percy Clapp.

"Neil, I'm glad you brought that up!" Springs creaked as Clyde turned towards him on the bed and began to talk, as if to a confidant, in the near darkness of the room. "That demonstration – and this trip – have been eye-openers for me. I don't know if it's because Percy is getting old or because, for the first time in a long while, I've been able to observe him closely in an alien environment, away from the familiar things that associate him with power and strength. But he's changed, Neil. I think that horseshit episode frightened him to death. And it *was* vicious. I saw the student demonstration against Rute's union. It was a lark! The kids were all laughing and joking about, delighted to have a day off classes. Not when they demonstrated against Percy, though. That was different. Small, yes – but those kids looked ready to kill. And Percy knows it will grow, Neil. The tide is starting to go out on Prime Minister Clapp.... That's why he rushed home like a scalded cat – to try and stop the flow before it picks up speed."

"There may be something in what you say, Clyde," agreed Neil. He actually thought the reasoning was a bit thin, but he wanted to see where it was leading.

The springs bounced in Clyde's bed. "I think there is, too," he said. "Do you remember how Percy tore around Europe like a lunatic after we left London: going to all those speaking engagements, trying to preserve the legend of his tireless energy in front of us? On the plane to Karachi he looked like he was beat to a snot. And his speeches were lousy as well. None of the old fire at all!"

"Yes. I did notice that they weren't up to par...."

"He's drinking more, too!" Clyde sat up in bed. "We've seen him snapped-up a dozen times on this trip alone because of all his wines and liqueurs. Isn't he one awful sight with the veins standing out on his temples? Manoeuvre him before a television camera like that a couple of times and use a few close-ups, and this famous teetotaller can only project the image of a madman to his spectators.

"I tell you, Neil, it's there for the taking right now! If Percy is opposed at the next leadership convention by people of intelligence and drive and political savvy, he can be beaten. The right person has never tried it yet, that's all. And the ones who beat him could share power for thirty years, when the oil and gas revenue starts pouring in. The alternative is that Percy will be there for thirty more years himself. Christ, did you know that both his parents and three of his grandparents were over ninety when they died? That old bastard will live to be a hundred. You and I will be sixty before he's out! This convention coming up may be the only chance for a long, long time."

Neil did not disagree with Clyde's analysis. He allowed that this could well be the right time for someone good to run for the leadership against Percy, "take him by surprise, and frighten the living shit right out of him." But he offered no suggestions when Clyde tentatively asked who he believed that someone might be. Clyde, he realized, wanted Neil to support him for the leadership of the party. That was why he had been so friendly since London. *You'll have a long wait for my support, Clyde, good buddy*, Neil thought, reflecting on every little act of unkindness directed against him by Clyde since they had first met. Neil visualized the boy who had jeered at him as a Gawker before the cheerleaders at the school soccer game, more than a dozen years ago. And Clyde had just had the face to say to him that Ernest Godwin's numerous followers could be a potent political force – especially if they were properly mobilized by a leadership candidate outside the sect who could avoid charges of mixing religion with politics! *Screw you, Ferritt*, thought Neil. But aloud, he said, "Good night, Clyde."

The next morning, Boo Mansingh came to take them to the airfield for the flight back to Hong Kong. He showed an adamantine visage on the way to the plane, especially when he would stop to get more film footage of Neil and Clyde in suggested postures among groups of people. On the plane, however, he grinned wickedly as he asked Neil if, after last night, he now fully appreciated the hybrid culture with which the new regime had to cope. During most of the plane ride to Hong Kong, Mansingh sat next to Clyde and engaged him in earnest conversation. Once he wrote something on a piece of paper. Neil wondered uneasily what they were saying.

Back in their Hong Kong hotel room, Clyde said to Neil: "That Boo character. He loves you like a brother. What did you ever do for him?"

"We were good friends at Oxford, that's all. Don't you remember seeing him in my room all the time?"

"No. And friends is not a strong enough word. I couldn't

shut him up talking about you and how great you are. I'd say it's a good thing his wife *isn't* here or he would probably offer her to you. What is he, anyway? A Pakkie?"

"South African coloured is his slot," said Neil, without expression.

"That explains it, then. I imagine he wouldn't have had too many white English friends at Oxford in that case. Do you know what the bugger is going to do? He told me not to tell you till we got home. He wants it to be a surprise. He's going to edit that film he took of us, put in a voice-over, and have it transmitted to our television stations. Said we're going to look like a couple of world-class statesmen when he gets finished with us." Clyde paused. "He told me to tell you he hasn't forgotten the fourth of March. What did he mean by that?"

"I'm not sure. Easterners are mystical."

A day later, Neil suggested to Clyde that they proceed on their tour. He was feeling restless and uncomfortable and wanted to keep moving. Accordingly, the two of them said goodbye to Boo Mansingh and left for Taiwan. By this time, neither of them were very enthusiastic. They cut short their stay in Taiwan and in all the other places that were on Clapp's original itinerary. Instead of being away for six weeks, they arrived back in St. John's only fifteen days after they had left.

Neil had examined himself minutely every day since the mother and daughter affair in Saigon, and he had found nothing yet. But he still could not be certain that the incubation period was over. Ordinarily, he would have been happy to have returned home so soon; from the day he had left Newfoundland, his main concern had been that he might be away again when Gillian had her second baby. Now that he *was* home, however, he felt like a carrier of plague.

Gillian welcomed him at the door of their house. Holding Elizabeth on her hip, she put her free arm around Neil and squeezed him happily. He pecked her on the cheek and released himself too soon. Glancing at his face, Gillian passed Elizabeth to him. He held the baby awkwardly, at a distance from his body.

"You're out of practice," Gillian chuckled. "You certainly

haven't held anything that small in your arms during the past two weeks." Neil laughed – but too heartily, judging by Gillian's bemused look.

He handed Elizabeth back and carried his bags up to their bedroom. While he was unpacking, Gillian came in and put her arms around him. She pressed her parted lips on his mouth.

"It's all right, Neil," she said, when he reacted weakly. "The doctor says we can crack right to it for another two weeks yet. Or is there something else wrong?"

"Oh, no," Neil assured her hurriedly. "No, no. Not at all. Nothing's wrong." He turned back to his suitcase. "I'm just a bit tired from flying halfway around the world, I guess. And somewhere along the line I picked up this intestinal bug or something. I'm going to have to hit the sack. No, don't bother turning down those covers, Gillian. I'll use the guestroom. I might have an accident. You wouldn't want to be in the same bed with me if that happens, I can tell you that right now."

He embraced her briefly and hurried to the other room. He was not going to risk infecting her or the baby in her belly. He couldn't go to a doctor locally, he thought, because word was sure to leak out. Later on, during a visit to the mainland, he would have himself checked over. In the meantime, he decided, he would hide for ten days in his district.

In the morning, he looked bravely across the breakfast table. "Gillian, I've got to either run against Clapp for the leadership, or resign and get out altogether. There is no other alternative. I'm going to my district for a few days to make up my mind."

"That's an easy choice," smiled Gillian. "I don't see why you need more data from your constituents. What will you do, practise law?" Neil did not feel flattered by how uncomplicated she found the question to be.

The following days in Great Bona District were a dismal time. His tours there were always worse in the early spring because of the high unemployment, and the demoralization of many of his constituents after a long winter. For Neil, the grimmest aspect of the visit was his knowledge that, in spite of his brave words, there was nothing, in the short run, that he could do to help. He solaced himself in an academic way by telling himself what a good system of government the parliamentary system was. As a minister, he might eat at the Tour d'Argent one week, but the next week, as a member for a constituency, he was sure to be drinking tea in the shack of a welfare recipient. It kept one's perspective balanced, he thought.

Near the end of this tour, Neil heard on the news that Premier Clapp had sent a formal letter to the Prime Minister of Canada to initiate definitive talks on the actual separation of Newfoundland from Canada within eighteen months. By that time, Clapp's voice said, revenue from the offshore oil would start to flow from the government's treasury. Neil tried to feel flabbergasted. Clapp had not mentioned separation publicly or privately for months. The thing was generally considered to be a dead issue. What was he doing reviving it now? But there was no real concern behind his thoughts.

At home, however, Clyde sounded agitated when Neil returned his call. Clapp had failed to consult with him on the letter of separation too, he said. "When I raised that failure with him, the old bastard said that the referendum results had given him the right to negotiate separation and he naturally assumed that since I and all the rest of his ministers and members had run under his banner in the elections since the referendum, we were all with him on the question. 'Forgive me, please,' he screamed, 'if I believe that my own colleagues actually *mean* what they say to me and that they actually support the policies they have helped me implement. Forgive me my silly innocence!' How do you dispute that kind of logic? Listen, Neil ... remember what I said on our trip about Percy's serious weaknesses and the probability of someone good being able to beat him at that leadership convention this fall. Don't say a word – but keep it in mind."

For three nights running, Neil woke up at exactly 2:58 by the blue digits of his bedside clock. Each time his face, neck, and shoulders felt wet and cold, and the bed clothes were twisted around his legs. Gillian, sleeping on her back, would be snoring softly. He could see the outline of her big, pregnant belly, darker than the room's darkness. His thoughts, now that he was awake, would be continuations of those he had when he was asleep. The staggering idea of actually taking Clapp on himself, the worry that he was too young for such a challenge, the lack of money for a campaign, the formidableness of his opponent, the certainty of defeat at Clapp's hands, the dire consequences of Clapp's inevitable enmity ... all these thoughts tumbled repeatedly, cyclically, endlessly, through his mind. Napoleon's 3:00 A.M. courage, he would think, in self-contempt. And the blue digits would show him 3:30, 3:50, 4:10, 4:25, 5:03, or later, before he'd at last fall asleep again, his head between his two pillows. At 7:30 on the third morning, when Gillian roused him once more by removing the top pillow from his head, she said, "I hate to disturb the world's greatest shit sandwich again." It made him laugh, dispelling the crankiness caused by a row of unrestful nights. As usual, the morning light made him wonder what he had been worried into palpitating sweats about three or four hours before.

That evening, as he lay in bed before going to sleep, Neil came to a decision about his future moves. Running for the leadership was quite out of the question, too ridiculous a notion to countenance. So was the thought of staying in Clapp's government. But the idea of practising law made his life ahead seem like a long, drawn-out, terminal illness .... He looked at Gillian, who lay at his side. The book she was reading jerked irregularly from time to time as a result of the movements within her belly. Sensing his gaze on her, she turned and smiled. "Trying to read this vibrating book is making me seasick." She took Neil's hand and placed it on her tummy.

"I," said Neil, "am getting the hell out. We'll go away for a year after the baby is born."

"Thanks be to God!" Gillian heaved and pushed to get close enough to embrace him. Then she pulled back and looked into his face. "Why?" she asked. "Is there any *particular* reason? Besides general and normal disgust, I mean."

Neil was silent for a moment. Why? What could he say to her? Was there a principle involved here or was it an escape? Was it simply because he wasn't good enough to cope with Clapp and Clyde? "When I was in my district last week," he

226

began, slowly, "I sat in this one house, a shack really, for an hour. The woman was there alone with four children. She begged me to try to get her welfare increased. Her husband had vanished. I asked her how much welfare she got a month and she named the figure. A thought staggered me: during the past three years, I have eaten literally hundreds of meals at government expense, and the food and drink for *each* of those meals in London, in Paris, in New York, cost nearly as much for *me* alone as that woman gets for herself and her children for *everything* for one whole month. I can't shake the thought of that, Gillian. And I can't live with it any longer."

Gillian moved close to hold him again. "You're doing the right thing," she told him, softly. "I'm glad you didn't shoot me the BS about doing it for your family." They made plans to use their savings and obtain loans so that both of them could spend the next academic year doing graduate work at Harvard or Yale.

The next day, when Neil told him of his decision to resign, Clapp was openly incredulous and suspicious. "Resign as a Minister of the Crown?" he gasped. "Throw away everything you have built up already? Not to mention the leadership of the party and the premiership of the country in the future, right after the next election? I cannot conceive of it! What about the three hundred thousand you are flushing down the drain? You want more, is that it?"

Neil merely smiled at Clapp's apparent belief in his naivety and assured the premier that he would be leaving on an upbeat note. He was merely taking a sabbatical. His announcement would be cast, he said, in positive terms, mentioning a short leave of absence from the government to learn further skills which would be of benefit to the country when he returned to public life. Clapp was considerably mollified at this disclosure. After Neil made his public announcement, stating that he'd be spending a year studying economics at an American university, Clapp heaped on the praise.

"Naturally," he concluded, "I lament the loss of so brilliant a minister. What leader wouldn't? But I draw cheer from the fact that it is only a short-term loss. My friends, Neil Godwin will return! And when he does, he'll bring with him long-term benefits for his beloved countrymen."

15

For the next few days following his resignation, Neil unhur-
riedly wound up his affairs at his office, and spent much of his
time relaxing in a chair or wandering around at his ease. Each
night he slept for eight or nine unbroken hours, and awoke in
contented peace.

He paid two visits to Jane and Roland Maidment at their
new apartment. Gillian had seen to it well before the wedding
that brother and sister were on speaking terms again. But it
was mainly because of Jane's husband that Neil made the
second visit. He found Roland at once appealingly earnest and
dryly humorous behind his unimpressive voice. Neil understood now what Jane had seen in him. What Neil liked most
about him, however, was that while he showed surprising
knowledge and shrewdness in his political opinions, he did
not carp.

One evening, the television news gave coverage to a press
conference called by the son of Socks Fagan and Dr. Gorman,
the former colleague of Percy Clapp. Fagan the younger
announced that he would be seeking the leadership of
Clapp's party at the convention called for the coming autumn.
Gorman was to be Fagan's honorary campaign chairman.
During his own remarks, Dr. Gorman looked and sounded as
distinguished and wise as ever while he extolled the virtues
of his young companion.

When the news story was finished, Neil laughed out loud.
He was well acquainted with Gorman's vanity and stupidity,
but he would have expected a little better than this from

young Fagan. He knew him fairly well, had even had dinner at his home on a couple of occasions. He was in his early thirties and as unlike his father, Socks, as two men could be. Where the father was dull, arrogant, aloof, and much attached to his retail business, the son was sharp, unconceited, ingratiating, and treated the family business as an evil which fed him. He had spent just enough time at the department store since returning with his Master in Business Administration ten years previously, to make the business flourish. Much of his time was spent travelling throughout the island, talking to people in the stores and on the wharves. Even in Neil's district, he had several good friends. That was why Neil could not fathom his actions now: Fagan would know firsthand of Clapp's insurmountable popularity around the coast.

The next night, after much advertising all day, a radio station carried live, as a paid political broadcast, the public kick-off meeting of Fagan's campaign. The man was certainly willing to shell out the money, thought Neil; and listened to the broadcast.

In his speech, Fagan was not gentle with Percy Clapp. He started with the need for revolutionary reforms in the party. He then called upon Percy to announce whether or not he himself had the guts to seek the leadership of the party again this time around. "What is Mr. Clapp waiting for? Why hasn't he announced his candidacy yet? What is the great Percy Clapp afraid of? He *is* afraid of something. Is he afraid because for the first time in his life he has to face competition? Is the formerly fearless Percy Clapp now shivering in his boots because he knows that someone who is not afraid of him is taking him on, head to head? Yes, my friends, *that* is what Percy is scared of! He's scared of anyone who has the courage to ask questions and to speak for the people. He's frightened to death of someone who has the guts and know-how to stop the corruption and the sell-out of the people that he has been presiding over for twelve or fifteen years! If Mr. Clapp had the guts of a louse himself, he would have announced his candidacy for the leadership by now so that the people of this great party could decide that they no longer want his kind for our leader. But he has no guts, my friends, except the guts of a bully – the artificial guts and bluster of a propped-up petty dictator, who is showing what real courage he has now that his iron-fisted control is starting to crumble. Tomorrow, or the next day, Mr. Clapp will announce that he is running, not because he *wants* to face me but because now he *has* to. Even Percy doesn't have face enough to slink away (as he would like to), from this challenge. And this time, Mr. Percy Clapp, the convention will not be three days of drunken revelry among your handpicked hangers on, culminating in your re-election by acclamation. I guarantee you that. This time we'll do it rightly and honestly, without your usual under-the-table shenanigans and vote buying. And this time, because it will be done rightly and honestly, I'll tell you this, Right Honourable Percy Clapp: defeat is staring you straight in the face!"

There was loud, prolonged cheering, followed by a five minute chant of, "We want Fagan!" Neil was astonished. This fellow Fagan knew what he was doing. The newscasts that night and all the next day gave the meeting gush coverage. More than seven hundred people had been present, said the reporters, by actual count.

Clapp's reply the next day was soft-voiced and contemptuous. "I am not surprised that the son of Socks Fagan has jumped into this leadership thing, prematurely and unprepared. His own father managed to be the only candidate for our party who lost in the last election. And that is why Son of Socks has jumped into the race now in the manner of a sewer rat diving into a baptismal font. His father's shame and humiliation must have been a terrific blow to Son of Socks as a youthful and prideful member of the rich establishment of the city. And he's been smarting under that unbearable shame ever since. You see, until I came on the political scene, rich men's sons here were not used to being thwarted in their whimsical abuses of the people.

"Unfortunately, Son of Socks has chosen the wrong way to redeem his family's shame and humiliation. Socks Fagan lost his *election* by sixty votes. Son of Socks Fagan will lose his *leadership* attempt by being buried sixty feet deep. I intend to see to that. Our party will not fall into the wrong hands, into

230

the sticky paws of a rich city merchant whose ancestors in the mercantile elite stood on the backs of our people for four hundred years.

"For fifteen years, by night and day effort, I have kept this great party, which I founded, free of lies and crookedness and deceit. I will not allow the likes of Son of Socks to blemish that proud record now by bringing into politics the same dishonesty that he applies to the price and quality of his calico, his toilet paper, and his bull's-eyes. I had not intended to seek the leadership at the convention this fall. I had intended to let the leadership of our party and the government go to another man of the people. But my mind is now made up. I must put aside my selfish personal wishes and I must run as leader. I must keep this rich merchant from power over our beloved land. Son of Socks will not prevail over our people!"

Two or three days after this, Neil received an invitation from Clapp's office to have lunch with him in his dining room. Neil decided to go, if for no other reason than to personally give Clapp a definite "no," when he was asked to be campaign manager leading up to the convention. There were rumours around that Clapp wanted him for that purpose.

Only Clapp and Toope, the Minister of Justice, were present. Neither seemed to know where Clyde was. After lunch, Clapp, who was half drunk on sherries, burgundy, and transparent liqueurs, was in an expansive mood. But he said nothing about the leadership convention.

"Neil," he asked, "why do you suppose I want us to separate from Canada?"

Neil made his answer as flat as he could. He was not in any frame of mind to debate the merits of the notion. "I would imagine, Premier, that you believe it would be in the best interests of the electorate who have given you the mandate to represent them."

For a moment Clapp stared at Neil, rubbing his empty liqueur glass between his hands, shifting his body and twitching his legs in a barely discernible way. This was how he gave the impression that he could only barely control his bursting energy. "You know, Neil," he said, finally, "I was well over fifty years old when I first got into politics; and I got in at the top. I could have gone in at lower levels any time before that, but I didn't. I would not be the vermiform appendix of another political leader. Some fellows can stomach that. Toope here, for instance."

Clapp waved his empty glass at the half asleep Minister of Justice, and the old man dragged himself out of his chair and eagerly hobbled over to refill the glass with anisette. With one gulp Clapp downed the contents and resumed his speech.

"Instead, Neil, I went into one thing after another. I spent a number of years in journalism – met Ernest your father, during that period, got him his first job at the law firm. I knew Ernest Godwin well before he ever showed any interest in religion at all. But as with myself, his vocation was there all the time: that irrepressible calling to save and build man's spiritual self, as mine was to save and build man's physical well-being and dignity. A great man, your father. We've been the best of friends for over thirty years. He wanted me to be his best man when he married your mother. I was only sorry I couldn't be. Spirity Cove was just too far away for me to go to at the time.

"I'd got married some years before, myself – after holding off as long as I could. Not," snorted Clapp, "that it made much difference!"

Clapp's childless marriage was a sore point, Neil knew; and he attempted to smooth over the topic. "Your children," he suggested blandly, "would probably have been the victims of the gigantic stature of their father. Like Churchill's children."

Clapp mulled that over for a moment then shook his head. "Naw. There's the wife, you know. The prize bull is wasted unless he shoves it into a good cow. I fear I am but a streak in the firmament, coming from nothing and leaving nothing. It's too bad we don't have the ancient Roman system where a great statesman could adopt a suitable heir. Of course, I can still do that in the political sense. I have often thought during the past two or three years how happy I'd be if I had someone like you for a political son, someone I could bequeath my political capital to when the time came. It's not too late to consider that as a distinct possibility now, or when you get back from your studies ...."

Clapp leaned forward to catch Neil's reaction to this, but when silence and a mild smile were the only response, he continued on hurriedly. "Anyway, I did this and I did that. I spent some years trying to organize our fishermen into the first semblance of a protective union. I would have been successful, too, were it not for the fact that the government of the day scuttled my efforts at every turn. I can tell you, and I have the scars to prove it, no one in power gave *me* the political tolerance that our friend, Rute, enjoyed when he was setting up his union!

"Then I started raising sheep. It was during those years, when I had plenty of time on my hands to think about myself, that I formulated my plans to take on frontally the Tory government that then held power. I began to hold what amounted to tremendous open air meetings in my meadow surrounded by sheep, men, and sheepshit. I was well known from my days as a journalist and organizer, so when I commenced to spout off, newsmen would come out and give wide coverage to my jeremiads. By the way, Neil, let me relieve you of any anxiety you may have on one score. Two fellows who would come out now and then from the city to these meetings had a burlesque routine which they would use to try to cast me in a ridiculous light. One would ask loudly as he surveyed the flock of sheep, 'Which one did you say was Percy Clapp?' And the other would answer, 'I told you, the ram on *two* legs is Percy.' The man who set up that routine was Clyde Ferritt's father. So you don't need to have any fears about Clyde getting ahead of you in politics while I'm around, Neil. I'm not about to do him any favours after what his father did to me. And he's just like his old man, right, Toope?"

"The very image, sir, the very image," said the Minister of Justice, struggling to get up as Clapp waved his glass for a refill.

"The point of all this," continued Clapp, catching with his sleeve the rivulet of liqueur on his chin, "is that I was good at whatever I turned my hand to. But, because I would not spend forty years at the same desk, many people thought I had no attention span, no staying power. In fact, I was a seal in the water, locked under the ice, twisting, turning, darting, swimming, stopping, starting – searching for my airhole. And finally, as a result of the Tory government having brought itself into general discredit, I found that airhole and I thrust my brazen snout up through it with a force that would have sent any reasonable political observer reeling back. But of course, as far as the establishment here in the city was concerned, I still was, and always would be, an erratic buffoon, a honking circus seal."

"Oh, come now, Premier," interjected the Minister of Justice. "You weren't considered to be a buffoon. Everyone had the highest opinion of you then, as now. It was more a case of the reputations of some of the friends you associated with obscuring your own great talents."

"You may be right, Toope," allowed Clapp. "Certainly, Fenny Sircombe's antics were not calculated to inspire confidence in himself or anyone remotely associated with him. Did you know him, Neil? Fenwick Sircombe." Clapp spelled out the last name. "He was the most brilliant man this place ever produced, I'd say – but crazy as a caplin. You must have known him." Neil shook his head uncertainly. "You were probably too young. Well, if you didn't know him, you never will now. They had to put him away for good, finally. You're probably right, Toope. He did nothing to enhance my reputation, for sure. I didn't realize how bad he was getting until he married that hunchback and started to march through town all the time, beating a goddamned drum."

"My God, you're not talking about the Goofy Newfy, are you?" blurted Neil.

"I believe that's what the youngsters used to call him when he took those turns, yes," said Clapp. "I thought you said you didn't know him."

"I didn't know Fenny Sircombe. I only saw the Goofy Newfy. The Americans gave him that name, didn't they?"

"Neil! Neil! My sonny boy, Neil!" Clapp was bouncing on the edge of his chair. "Everyone who ever came here gave all of us that name. I don't know why poor old Fen got stuck with it. Our British brethren, during the years that they were pleased to mould our fate, considered this island as the natural collecting ground for the empire's retarded. Why, man, it was a constant tradition of such ancient standing with them, that they founded their colonial policy towards us on that alone. Our Canadian cousins, for their part, were not backward in assimilating this lore when we joined them, especially after they were able to confirm it from their own first hand observations. And naturally, we never disputed the point with them, hospitably letting the empirical truth of the guest hold sway over subjective native pride. So, Neil, is there any wonder that our American cognates would also have formed the opinion that we are the goofiest of them all – despite the powerful, competing claims to that status made by their emissaries on behalf of the many other lands touched by their benignant hand? Well, is there?"

Clapp was obviously prepared to rave on for a while yet on this subject, so Neil answered by asking how he had become friends with Fen Sircombe.

"I met Fenny the first time he wandered into the city debating club," said Clapp, settling back. "I was delighted to find someone knowledgeable and brilliant again, now that your father had moved to Maggotty Cove to conduct his ministry. Fen gave marvellous speeches during subsequent debates, but had a tendency to get carried away. I remember one time when he closed his eyes at the beginning of a speech, the better to see the ideas flashing through his mind. It was the best speech anyone in the crowded hall had ever seen or heard. With one slight detraction. Somehow, in his extravagant gesticulations, Fen got himself turned completely around, and he delivered his remarks for twenty minutes to the wall two feet from his nose, his back to the audience.

"On another occasion, Fen and I were teamed up against a couple of women. It was ladies' night at the debating club. I had spoken first for our side and when Fen's turn came, he did brilliantly. Even the great number of women in the audience could not help but applaud him throughout his speech. I was both proud and jealous of his performance. Then, just before he was to sit down, he found himself struggling for a simple example of a leisure-time commodity in a modern consumer society. 'For example,' he said, 'suppose, for our enjoyment, we must have a, a, a, a, a ....' He could not come up with a specific leisure commodity. I started to whisper up to him: marmalade ... persian carpets ... a yacht ... cognac .... But he wasn't listening. 'Suppose we must have, for our pleasure, a, a, a ...' (his eyes were swimming upon the concentrated faces of the stimulating ladies before him), '... a, a, a-gross-of-french-safes!'"

"Why did they put him away?" Neil inquired.

"You mean the first time? It was – Didn't you find those stories funny?" asked Clapp. "I would have thought you'd enjoy them." Neil put on a wan smile and chuckled, and Clapp continued. "It was during my one and only job in a federal government department – the Post Office here in St. John's. After a while I managed to get Fen taken on as well, stamping postmarks. One day a new assistant director was sent down from the mainland. He had earlier been an officer in the Canadian Army, stationed in Korea with the UN. He and his men had been ambushed by some Communist guerrillas and slaughtered almost to a man. As he himself had lain on the ground wounded, the guerrillas had gone from soldier to soldier. At any sign of life, the Communists would cut off that man's testicles and ram them down his throat, thereby suffocating him. This new assistant director had played dead successfully and survived with his testicles intact.

"Back home, he had requested to be relieved of his commission and sent to a quiet job in the quietest corner of the nation for a while, before resuming active army duty. And this is where they sent him. He had been at his new job for about two days when the price of bread went up by one cent a loaf. Somehow, Fen got it into his head that it was all this new fellow's fault. I was at my desk when I heard unnatural shrieks coming from down the corridor. Venturing out for a look, I saw Fen Sircombe taking monstrous swings with a bloody great fire axe from off the wall, while the new assistant director fended off the blows with a now battered metal waste paper basket. All the while, Fen was thundering in his magnificent voice, like an Old Testament prophet, 'Raise the price of the very staff of life itself, will you, sir? I'll have your balls off for that, my good man!'"

This time, Neil laughed a little without prompting, and Clapp said, "I could tell you about some of my other early friends as well, but you've gone a bit sober-sided since you got out of politics, Neil. Are you having second thoughts? Toope!" He waved his empty glass without looking at the minister. As the old man pushed with his feet and pulled with his arms to raise himself from the chair, Neil got up to refill the glass.

"That's my job, you saucy young bugger!" roared Toope. "Young bastards always trying to take over, even after they've resigned from the damned government!"

Neil sat down again and studied the ceiling.

"I'd better get back to why I want us to separate, while I still have a live audience," said Clapp. "When the next election was finally called, I ran as an independent candidate in Often Pretty, where my now sheepless sheep farm was located. Beautiful district. Named after a huge rock offshore, lovely in the breaking waves in the bright sun, lethal at all other times, called –" (the local English name of the rock was closer to the French than Clapp's present attempt to pronounce Enfant Perdu). "Over the months, I had also cultivated the four neighbouring districts, and I put independent candidates in them as well. I won all five districts. I gained 87 per cent of the vote in my own district, which, I took note of much later, was the same vote that you received when you first ran, Neil. I judged from those returns that, just perhaps, the people liked my style. If I've had a fault during my political career – which I haven't – it would be that I've been a little too modest."

"Oh, I wouldn't go that far, Premier," said the half asleep Toope, coming to as he thought he sensed a cue.

"In any event!" Clapp stressed the words evenly and looked hard at Toope, to cut off any further contribution he might make. "The two major parties, the Liberals and the Tories, divided the remaining seats nearly equally between them. Neither had a clear majority. Each had to depend on me if either was to form a government. I sat back and watched the

237

butchery. Both parties went mad, threatening, blackmailing, and trying to buy off each other's members. I myself could have been a millionaire several times over, but I've never given one sweet goddamn about money. And never will. That's my strength. The public's guts were turned forever more at the spectacle presented by those two parties, the one viciously clinging to power by its fingernails, the other openly resorting to the basest means to grab that power. I quietly organized my group while projecting a statesman-like moderation to the people.

"At the opportune moment, I brought the incumbent government down and precipitated another general election. No one had any doubt that I would win a majority. The other two parties were washed up. They would have been lucky to get a half dozen seats each. All I had to do was invent a good name for my new party.

"It was all queered for me by" – Clapp drained his fresh glass of liqueur, wiped his mouth with his handkerchief, and bawled – "that *goddamned Wolfe Tone McGrath!* God rest his soul now, of course. He saw what was going to happen: give the devil his due. He got the leaders of the Liberals and the Tories together to try to persuade them that I – not each other – *I* was their natural enemy! Destroy Clapp first, he said, and then they could resume their alternating enjoyment of the spoils of victory as of the golden days of yore. He asked them if they really and truly wanted political power to fall into the hands of this yahoo, Clapp. They acknowledged that they did not. Well, he said, that was exactly what was going to happen, for he knew from his own experience in his father's fish plants how popular I was with the ragged-arsed artillery (to use Joey Smallwood's phrase). Toope here was at those meetings. He saw how McGrath poisoned everyone against me. Even Toope was against me at the beginning. You'd never know it now, would you?"

"I came to my senses quicker than most, Premier, you've got to say that," commented Toope.

"Yes! Right after I won," answered Clapp. "Even a cocker spaniel who's kicked in the head only once knows enough to stay clear of the boot. I woke up one morning to the news that the Tory and Liberal parties had been disbanded (McGrath had convinced them that the very sounds of the names were anathema to the people), and that an entirely new party was already organized and would be presenting a common front of candidates and policies designed to save the country from this petty populist up-chuck, me. Simultaneously, there was a flood of supporting statements from nearly every prominent individual and organization in the place. McGrath had done his work well.

"Naturally, my heart and guts sank like a grapnel into my boots. I was lost. How could I take on and defeat the whole united establishment, solidly arrayed against me? My one strategy had been to keep my opposition divided and sneak up the middle between them. I tell you, I could not believe what McGrath had achieved. 'The cowardly wave' had got me.... You know how our fishermen fear that rare wave, many times larger than the others, which creeps up unnoticed behind the trapskiff and hits it just as a man's doing his work, knocking him unexpectedly overboard into the sea where, often as not, he drowns. The cowardly wave.... Sometimes, a brave and hearty fisherman who has been hit by the cowardly wave several times – more often than random chance would seem to indicate he should have been hit – and who has barely survived each ordeal by some fluke, at last loses his nerve for the water. The other fishermen completely understand his failure to ever again go out in a boat. They describe it by saying, 'He was touched by his last cowardly wave and he finds the water strange' – which explains everything to those who know. Well, Percy Clapp had been touched by his last cowardly wave and he found the water strange. It seemed to me that for the fifty years of my remembered life, random little disasters of the universe which should have been shared by a score of other nondescript wretches had focussed their effects entirely on me. And this was my final foul buffet. I was finished.

"It was Ernie Godwin who saved me. I was astray and bewildered, and your father took me by the hand and led me back. He told me what I had to do: instead of running free, I had to tack and buck; instead of a straightforward appeal to facts, logic, and honest emotion, I had to resort to lies, half-truths, and the calculated assassination of character. I had to make blatant use of the religious position of your father – Ernie was a great influence in that alone. He was able to blunt the *sub rosa* campaign that Archbishop Wadman was conducting against me. Wadman was only a bishop then, the bastard. Even now, if I ran against the devil himself in the next election, Archprick Rodney Wadman would actively support the devil against me. But you remember all that stuff, Neil. You were eleven or twelve at the time."

Neil nodded. In fact, he had only the vaguest recollections of that campaign. He had been in the midst of his doubtful, self-absorbed period. But Clapp, satisfied, resumed. "I remember you well at your father's house. You and that lovely little sister. I stupidly thought she was your twin on one early occasion. She was so full of personality when I used to visit Ernie before, and you were a moody little bugger, darkly brooding off to yourself. But you had a lean and hungry look even then. It took my notice.

"Anyway, I won that election. But only barely. What finally clinched it for me was the name Wolf Tone McGrath chose for his new party: The God, Queen, and the People Party. This was clever – designed to appeal to a broad political spectrum. Ernie Godwin took one look at that name and said, 'The People Last Party.' With that I knew we had the election won. I dubbed my party The People First Party, and both names took off like wildfire. Thus was the issue joined in the public mind: The People First Party versus The People Last Party. But even then it was a close-run thing, a matter of two or three seats in my favour."

It had been a long time since Neil had heard the words "The People First Party" spoken. Except for formal party documents, the governing party had been called "Percy's Party" ever since Neil had been associated with politics. Clapp had not discouraged this usage. He continued his narrative now.

"After that election, the last bit of good that had been in them went out of the People Last crowd. As much as they hated me for my upstart origins, my unbridled slander, and my fox-like looks, they could summon up no further stomach for the fight. They crumbled until they reached the pathetic state they're in today. Wolfe Tone McGrath himself was the first of their leaders to see the utter futility of continuing to battle against the likes of me. His excuse to his associates was that he wanted to protect the country by getting on the inside. In fact, he realized the substance behind my facade. We remained close for years until his greed reached pathological proportions. I should have perceived the strain of lunacy in him earlier. Did you know that he had a big, strong younger brother who was insanely jealous of him? That brother held a knife to Wolfe Tone's adam's apple for two hours, threatening to slit his own throat every minute. He did make a couple of serious cuts in McGrath's neck. That's why he always wore that silly beard afterwards. Poor fellow. He didn't have what you would call good luck before he joined forces with me. And his luck went sour altogether after he turned on me again."

Clapp fixed his icy blue eyes on Neil for the few seconds it took Toope to refill his glass. "After I formed my first government, I immediately began to heal the savage wounds I had inflicted on our body politic. And in this city today, where the bulk of my opposition originated, I now get over 60 per cent of the votes cast." He abruptly jumped up and walked directly over to Neil. "Now beat that for doing it right!" he bellowed, as if Neil had offered bellicose argument against the point.

Neil also got to his feet, intending to take his leave. Clapp hadn't answered his own question on the reasons for separation, but Neil felt he could survive without another mad and drunken monologue on that subject.

"Where are you going, Neil?" demanded Clapp. "I'm not finished yet. Sit down for another minute or two."

Making an impatient gesture Neil sat on the edge of his chair, tilting his head with an exaggerated air of expectation. He noted that Clapp's demeanour had changed. It now appeared to be resigned and determined. And whereas his earlier talk had seemed to be tentative, as if he were inviting Neil to offer something, his words now had a ring of finality.

"You know, Neil, when I first became prime minister, I was

241

some stupid, as stunned as me arse, as my worthy supporters around the bay might say. I saw myself as leading our people, this land, into the mainstream of North American life. I saw myself ransacking the federal treasury to give our citizens the modern public works and social programs that people have in a middle-class suburb of Toronto. I saw myself as a public figure of great honour in my own province and across this nation as a result of my progressive works and concepts. My sonny boy, I was that good and pure and saintly in my own mind that I could not sleep nights, for that beatific vision. I was nuts.

"We don't count down here. This nation consists of Toronto, *and* (so that they can persuade themselves in Toronto how active, vital, interesting, and cultivated they are), that boring turd known as the Western Provinces, *and* (for their entertainment in Toronto), that amusing fringe of *terra incognita* known as Quebec. There the frontier ends. That is Canada. Nothing else exists.

"You never attended any federal-provincial conferences, Neil, because I had stopped going to them by the time you came on the scene. But when I went to them, I made by far the most intelligent speeches of all the leaders there. My ideas, my words, my delivery were the best of any politician present – but the central press treated my remarks like the grunts and gesticulations of a deformed and feeble-minded freak, rigged up in the nation's flag to act as the country's clown. In favour of the nation's unity and strength, I was able to poke holes in the arguments and positions of the federal government large enough to drive a coach-and-six through, and they regarded me as the nation's perennial gadfly, a pissy-assed, latterday Socrates from the boonies, too harmless to even threaten with the hemlock." Clapp glared. "Fuck that!" he roared. "Do you follow me? Did you hear what I said? What I said was: fuck that!"

Neil assured Clapp that both his auditory apparatus and his faculty for comprehending basic English were in fine working order. "Saucy young pup!" said Toope, as the premier sat back and chuckled.

"It's too bad you're leaving, Neil. I'm going to miss you.

Well, I'm taking us out. I'm going to do it, and I'm under no illusions about what I will be up against. Oh, sure, at first, I'll be the darling of the liberals in the US and Europe and even Canada. You know how that crowd take to a half-baked agitator heaved up from the guts of a people to lead a cause of buzz words: 'masters of our own destiny,' 'cultural self-determination,' and similar clumps of horseshit stuck with primroses. The next twelve or eighteen months will show, I'm afraid, how pitifully putty-like are reasonable men of goodwill – like them – when led on, squeezed dry, and then ultimately disillusioned by an unreasonable man actuated by malignant impulses – like me.

"After the first few months it's going to be a rough fight, far different from that foolish referendum. That was just a sniff at the breeze. Everyone knew, or thought they knew, that I did that for a bit of fun, strengthening my hand against the federal government. This time, it's for real. And once the federal government realizes that, they will come down on us like a piledriver. That's why I have to whip the people here into a frenzy of paranoid xenophobia. I shall be fostering every kind of prejudice: misguided patriotism; religious, racist, and linguistic bigotry; geographic animosities; cultural misunderstandings. You name the dirty deed and it will be done, together with a good many presently without names. I shall be sparking and fanning, until its flame leaps up, that bizarre form of pride of place possessed in embryo by all poor and isolated peoples (don't ask me why – it defies reason – I only use the material at hand), the belief that they are in some paradoxical way better than all the other peoples and countries to which they feel inferior. I shall be convincing the susceptible among us, and that's a good working majority, that after we separate we will be better off from our offshore oil revenues than if we stayed in Canada, swilling contentedly at the federal trough. What that balance sheet will not show, of course, are the horrendous rip-offs all along the line. And finally, in order to break the will of those public spirited do-gooders on the mainland who will *still*, after all that, want to keep us in the federation, I'll have to cause a few bombs to be tossed around.

"In brief, Neil, I shall be turning my back on what I know is right for our people and fighting viciously for what I know is wrong for them. Where I should be striving to broaden, I shall be seeking to narrow. Where I should be trying to free those who are financially chained to the rocks of deprivation, I shall be driving in the spikes with a bloody great maul. I will rule, by merciless fist, a strictured island and a remote headland. And instead of bringing honour to my people, historians, intellectuals, and journalists will associate me with Papa Doc, Idi Amin, and the Emperor Bokassa when they see what I have done." Clapp waved his glass at Toope, though he kept his eyes on a thoroughly startled Neil.

You senile old madman! You're loonier than I thought! Neil nearly yelled. But after a moment he merely commented: "You mean to say you sincerely believe that what you are going to do is wrong for the people here – and yet you are going right ahead with it? I find that a *little* hard to accept, Premier."

"Don't be too silly altogether now, Neil," responded Clapp. "I thought I was talking to a cosmopolite in cynicism here. I'm sure Kennedy and Johnson were perfectly sincere about Vietnam. I'm sure what's his name, the inquisitor (the only thing I notice about my advancing age, the only thing, is my memory for names) Torquemada! – was perfectly sincere. They were sincere and wrong. I'm insincere and wrong. Will someone please volunteer to explain the subtle difference to the fuckee at the other end of the shaft!

"Sincerity! Ernie Godwin, your own father, professed absolute sincerity when he helped me with the referendum to separate, and no doubt will protest the same sincerity again when he helps me, as he promised, with the actual separation. But I believe that Ernie is more clever than that. He knows that there is always the risk of his personal religious movement being wiped out overnight by some rich and dynamic theological cyclone from the mainland – unless he keeps his hand on the controls. Shrewd cookie, your dad. If you're as smart (and you may be, you just may be), and if you recognize the advantages he has created for you from nothing, and if you keep your nose clean, you might be able to make something

244

out of yourself yet. What are you now? Twenty-seven. You might get this job at forty-seven. When I retire."

"Ernie was much smarter than that young bugger," said Toope. "I remember Ern well at his law firm in the old days. At least he had half a clue."

"Toope here still thinks I'm not going to do what I just outlined to you. He's always looking for ulterior motives in my bombast. He's as blinkered as all the rest of the members of that fat, closed-shop, anti-competitive monopoly union – what's it called? Oh, yes, the Law Society. But he's as blind to my real motives now as he has been to my empty liqueur glass for the past five minutes. I've sucked you in a dozen times in the last ten years, haven't I, Toope?"

"You're a cute one, no mistake, Perce," agreed the Minister of Justice, testing his legs for the strength to fetch a refill.

"But why exactly are you going to do this?" asked Neil. "Do you have the idea that it's the only way to preserve our culture, our unique way of life here? Is that it?"

"Unique way of life! Our culture!" spat Clapp. "This is our culture: if a thing doesn't move, break it; if it does move, kill it."

"Then why? I know you're pissed off with the federal government. But by going through with this – if in fact you're able to do it – you'll be severely damaging a progressive nation. And you'll be setting this island back a quarter of a century in the process! What is the *point*?"

"Yes, yes, yes, I know all that," said Clapp impatiently. "Every schoolboy knows that. I know that our offshore oil, even if it is commercially exploitable, is a non-renewable resource that will only last for twenty years or so. I know that the revenues from it will be only marginally greater than what the federal government would be putting into this province in the normal course of events over the same period of time. I know that when I'm finished with this place twenty or twenty-five years from now – if there's anything left of it after that buffeting, alone out here in the middle of the ocean – we will be forced to go on our knees, hat in hand, begging to rejoin Canada or to become part of the US. And I know those countries will be poisoned against us by then for our selfish prodigality in the meantime. I am very conscious of all those considerations.

"Neil, I said earlier that I am insincere and wrong in what I am going to do to our people. The obverse of that coin, my friend, is that I am sincere and right – for me. I'm now sixty-seven. I intend to stay in power until I'm at least eighty-seven. Did you see my father when he was ninety-four? One day, he ran from Fort William up Signal Hill to Cabot Tower and back. He put a snarling cur that chased him into a coma with one kick on the way. These coming two decades of separation from Canada will serve one purpose only: to permit *me* to do whatever I want; to allow *me* to enjoy the exercise and get the fruits of power, absolutely unimpeded; to enable *me* to live out a life of quality and personal fulfilment, practising my talents to the utmost, unfettered by anybody in my deeds or my words.

"In other words, Neil, I will put in place here a glorious system identical to those which flourished in Athens or Renaissance Italy; ideal systems which would oppressively exploit the masses of scrabbling pismires so that enough power and money could be accumulated in few enough hands to allow the patronage of a Phidias, a Michelangelo, a Raphael. The analogy is not strained. I would strenuously argue that my political career thus far – its antics, its humour, its legends, its analysis, its stories, its guffers, and its example – has already enriched, enraged, provoked, amused, mystified, and stimulated the minds of many others (as well as afforded me *some* fulfilment), and will do so to an even greater degree over the next twenty years of uninhibited exercise of my talents. Who knows? In retrospect, I may turn out to be a genius. Wolfe Tone McGrath put the germ of that idea in my mind, years ago. Only bit of sense I ever got out of him."

Clapp got up, put down his glass, and walked towards the door. "Besides," he said, "I want to be called prime minister *all* the time. People still call me premier half the time – do you hear what I'm saying, Toope? – and the only way of ensuring that I will be called prime minister is by making a separate country out of this ridiculous provincial appendage. This is what I mean to do, Neil, by fair means and foul. And speaking of Wolfe Tone McGrath ... " Clapp turned at the door. "He was the most formidable opponent I've ever faced. But he soon discovered what can happen to anyone who cuts across my bow!"

Toope inhaled noisily, and Neil gave him a curious look.

"I'm talking about my first campaign for prime minister," Clapp said quickly. "Good luck in your studies, Neil." He closed the door behind him.

For the second time, Neil stood up to leave. He didn't feel comfortable alone with Toope.

"Percy was romancing, of course," said Toope, peering up out of the depths of his chair. "He's not serious about any of that. Perce is afraid of you. He's trying to impress on you how ruthless he is in order to scare you off any moves you may be contemplating against him. Maybe he'll scare you out of here altogether. Permanently."

"Afraid of me?" snorted Neil. "Percy Clapp? What a laugh! And why would he think I may be contemplating any moves against him, Mr. Toope? That's too foolish to talk about."

"Perhaps Ferritt put the bee in his bonnet. Anyhow, Perce thinks you bear watching more than Ferritt does. He thinks you are far more dangerous. Apart from your ability, he thinks you're lucky. Lucky, he says, as a shithouse rat. Percy fears lucky people. He likes people around who are personally unlucky."

Neil turned in annoyance from the meddling old man who was, he thought, probably under Clapp's instructions to try to foment a rift between himself and Clyde, even at this stage. He wished Toope all the best and left. And how happy he felt in the spring sunshine – free for good of the tiresomeness of those petty, Byzantine intrigues.

16

"Neil, you're a bad bugger!" said Jerome Finn over the phone. "Why didn't you tell me – I'm your friend – what you were up to in Vietnam when you went on that industrial tour with Percy?" Neil swallowed dryly as a vision of the mother-daughter team of orovaginal dexterity entered his head. "Man, oh man, talk about sexy stuff!" continued the news reporter, and Neil glanced around to see if Gillian would be in earshot when he made his vehement denials. "Six and one-half minutes of film and voice from the BB bloody C. We're showing it in its entirety on tonight's news."

Boo Mansingh's film.

"Hang on a minute, Jerome," said Neil, relieved. "I want to see it first."

"Too late for that, now. We've got the newscast put to bed. I've been trying to get you since noon."

"I was having lunch with Clapp."

"We'll get you on that, tomorrow. We've got enough for today. Clapp a perv or what? Told me the other day he expects Ferritt to be premier one of these days. Later. What I want you for now is an interview right after the news. Live. You can watch the film here at the studio when we run the news."

"Clyde must be in it too, isn't he?"

"Yes; but you're featured more or less, Neil. What are you worried about him for? I did try to get him when I couldn't find you, but he's holed up somewhere. His office won't say where he is, which is good. That ugly conk of his would only have the viewing audience switching channels on us. See you at the studio."

The film showed Neil and Clyde surrounded by Vietnamese who were looking at them – especially at Neil – in hope and admiration. There were many close-ups of Neil, speaking or observing earnestly. Between shots of himself and Clyde, some fighting scenes had been spliced in, with a description of dangerous Chinese incursions. The commentary throughout the film had the style of a television adventure documentary on a trek into the unexplored interior of a South American jungle. Twice, while the camera focussed on Neil's face, the unknown commentator spoke, in the intimate tones of a lifelong friend, of brave men keeping the spark of freedom alive. Clyde was on film as much as Neil, but it was Neil who was clearly the leader of this expedition.

As the film rolled, Neil gave special attention to the footage taken the morning after, searching for any immediate signs of ravages from quick-acting Asian venereal diseases. But he looked fine, looming tall and strong over the Vietnamese, his face reflecting his relish of danger for knowledge's sake, his pity for the oppressed, and the international breadth of his wisdom.

During the interview with Jerome afterwards, Neil downplayed personal risk and disavowed personal heroism. He said, in reply to a question, that he'd not mentioned the visit to Vietnam before because it was simply a fact-finding trip arranged by a friend, concerning which he neither expected nor desired this kind of publicity, and certainly not praise. It was merely one of life's experiences. No glory should be attached to it, as he deserved none.

Jerome argued against him and concluded the interview with: "Is there any wonder that people are heartbroken that Mr. Godwin has left politics, however temporarily, and that a strong groundswell is already beginning to build for the entry of this man into the leadership contest?"

Throughout the television station, people complimented him on his bravery and humility. At home, a dozen phone calls conveyed the same sentiments. Then Clyde phoned: "That was beautiful footage, Neil. Your interview was good, too. I wouldn't have understated our personal risk quite so much, though. We took our lives in our hands there. They wanted me to go on first, but couldn't reach me. That's all right. Unavailability lends a certain mystique in politics.

"By the way, Neil, I don't know what Percy said to you this afternoon to your face; but behind your back the other day he said: Godwin is no goddamned good, anyway. No staying power whatsoever. Two years or so at something is his absolute maximum and then he ups and collapses on you. You know, Clyde, he said, I've known other people like Godwin. Smart (he's downgraded your intelligence from brilliant in your absence), apparently energetic, temporarily single-minded, come on like a hurricane, going to take the world by mere force of personality, and then, a couple of years later, fart at them and they tumble down in *ennui, weltschmerz, angst*."

Neil laughed. "At lunch today, Percy told me that that was exactly what everyone thought of *him* before his first campaign for the premiership. No wonder he's worried."

"Oh," said Clyde. "Well, it's a change from having Socks Fagan compared to a soft cock, anyway. Percy also said: Godwin is just not a leader, that's all. Even if Godwin had leadership *thrust* upon him he would lead like a Labrador retriever – way out in front of everyone, *apparently* leading the way, but always looking back nervously to see if his master is coming in the same direction. If his master happens to swerve off onto another path, he'll gallop back to him and bolt out in front again, looking back anxiously once more to see if he is still being followed …. That's a flattering analogy, isn't it?"

Neil tried to make a comment, but Clyde was off again.

"Listen, Neil, I've been under a lot of pressure – even more since that film on me tonight. The phone hasn't stopped ringing. There seems to be a draft building up. Now I want you to bear this in mind. Think about it. If Clapp should happen to go from the scene, you catch my drift, then you would be as welcome as the flowers in May as far as I am concerned, and can feel assured of a prominent position."

"Clyde," Neil said patiently. "Percy thinks I'm far more

dangerous than you are. He's frightened to death I'm going to make a move."

"What? He thinks you're more ... Oh, I don't believe ... " There were several seconds of silence before Clyde burst out, "That proper bloody prick! We'll soon see who's more god-damned dangerous than whom around here. Work your fuck-ing butt off for that prick and that's the thanks you get – insults behind your back!" He composed himself. "Keep in mind what I said, Neil," he finished hastily. And hung up.

Neil sat by the phone for a minute.

"Deep reflections on the sayings of would-be Premier Fer-ritt?" inquired Gillian, from the doorway.

He gave her the contents of the phone call and laughed. "The only reason I was sitting here was because I was racking my brains trying to remember if I've ever seen Clyde look at a flower in May. Or at any other time."

"No, you haven't," Gillian answered cheerfully. "No one has. It's nature's way of allowing the survival of defenceless, pretty things."

As they wandered into the living room together, Neil told Gillian about his lunch with Clapp, and about the premier's intentions for the future.

"God, what a tribe they all are!" Gillian slipped an arm about his waist. "Neil, when we leave this fall, let's stay clear of here, forever."

They spent the rest of the evening studying a map of the eastern seaboard, talking over the best places in which they could live and work and bring up their children after they had finished their year at university. But in bed, before dropping off, Neil had to admit to himself that during the short time between his resignation and the Vietnam story, he had missed hearing the daily mention of his name on the news. And at the thought of waking up tomorrow morning after yet another solid night's sleep, he felt fatigue.

In fact, he did not sleep solidly after all. When he woke and looked at his clock it was 3:01. He had not been dreaming, but in the last moment of sleep there had been a painless, white explosion in his brain that had left him wide awake and clear-headed. A cascade of certainty flowed over him in the

dark: a profound certainty of self-disgust. The word "mediocrity" kept forming in his mind like a rolling drum beat. And
between the bursts of percussion appeared various aspects of
his life, all of them characterized by that one, relentless word.
There was his shame as a boy, following Clyde's jeer about his
father's life's work – mediocrity; his playing second fiddle to
the likes of Muck Barrows for several years – mediocrity; his
readiness to let Muck be booted out of the university rather
than acknowledge his own silly peccadillo – mediocrity; his
weakness in allowing his involvement with Victoria Montagu
to keep him from attaining the marks he was capable of at
Oxford – mediocrity; his willingness to be a follower except
when Wolfe Tone McGrath had been around to galvanize him
into thoughts of leadership – mediocrity; his readiness to join
up with Clapp, his natural philosophical enemy, in the hope
of preferment – mediocrity; his squelching of his own principles regarding Rute and his union because he wanted to be
on the side of public opinion – mediocrity; his willingness to
let Clapp toy with him over the promise of "salaries," and his
readiness to allow the thought of money he never intended to
take to be destructive of independent spirit and judgement –
mediocrity; his participation in that filth in Vietnam with two
pathetic whores, which had nearly poisoned the one good
thing in his life, his relationship with Gillian – mediocrity.
And now there was his readiness to run away from Clapp's
corrupting grip on power and Clyde's vaulting ambition.
Mediocrity. Imbecility. Craven, gutless cowardice!

Neil felt himself lifting off the bed from the energy flowing
in him. He walked about the bedroom and thought of the
weaknesses of Clapp that he and Clyde had talked about and
had considered exploitable by someone good. There were
other weaknesses, too. The turnout of voters in the last
election had been one of the lowest in history. Obviously, a
great many people, while not voting against Clapp, would not
vote for him, and therefore boycotted the election. What
would happen if all those people, in addition to the regular
anti-Clapp faction, sensed a champion in Fagan or someone
else? Then there was that demonstration of students against
Clapp at the airport. Not exactly an uprising, but certainly the

spark of something to be taken advantage of by someone good. Clapp's overwhelming victory at the last election – all but one seat…. That kind of victory always contained within it the seed of the victor's downfall, Neil reasoned. There was always a massive reaction against it, whatever the cause. He listed examples to himself. Lyndon Johnson's lopsided victory over Goldwater in 1964: he didn't dare even seek the nomination three years later. Nixon's record breaking victory over McGovern in 1972: he was harried out of office within months. Trudeaumania in 1968: the man was barely able to hang on by a hair against a dullard four years later. It had happened in Neil's very own province: a leader had taken all but five seats in one election, and was defeated by a clown, whose brain hemispheres hung from his crotch, in the next. And it was going to happen in Quebec. Neil just *knew* that Bourassa, who had won 105 out of 108 seats in 1973, would be defeated next time around – even though over 60 per cent of the province was anti-separatist. It was always the same, Neil assured himself. The germ of hubris within multiplied and conjoined with shooting tendrils of revulsion without, and together they soon dragged the great victor down, strangling.

Neil stopped short and stared in front of him. Clapp, he concluded, *could* be beaten! He resumed his pacing again. Son of Socks or even Clyde Ferritt might be the one who would beat him at the convention. And here Neil Godwin was, skulking around in the wings, finger up the ass, waiting for some *deus ex machina* to pull him out onto front stage centre. He had more to offer than either of those two tools. *He* was someone good, for God's sake! What a blind fool he'd been! His destiny stretched out before him ….

"Hi, love," murmured Gillian from behind her belly. "What are you doing marching around the room in the dark? Sublimating the impulses of your manly hormones?" She patted her stomach. "*Hélas, le pauvre mâle!* But we've got another month till delivery and another two months after that before you can practise *all* your quirky dirt on my svelte body again." She snuggled the blankets around her and said, sleepily, "Ummmm, I can hardly wait."

Neil was too preoccupied to respond. Perhaps it was the

absence of the lewd reply he invariably made to a suggestive opening gambit of hers that made her eyelids suddenly come apart as if she had been struck by lightning. She craned her neck and stared at him over her belly. He could see the whites of her eyes gleaming at him in the gloom. "Oh, my shit," she groaned, and let her head fall back. "Shit, shit, shit, shit!" She grabbed one of his pillows and placed it on her face.

Neil was sitting at the kitchen table writing out his plans when Gillian came down in the morning. He asked what she thought of his decision to run for the leadership. "Excellent," she said. "If you want to run for the leadership, then there is absolutely no reason why you shouldn't run for the leadership."

"What do you think of my chances?"

"I think that's a different question, Neil. Perhaps the best way to look at it is this: win or lose, neither outcome is likely to have much impact on events twenty billion years from now, when the contents of this galaxy are being sucked and squeezed into a plasmic gob half the size of Clapp's mouth."

Gillian's continual *reductio ad absurdum* was starting to get under Neil's skin.

Right after breakfast, he went to discuss the matter with his father. Ernie Godwin was extremely dubious. He talked about his long friendship with Percy; told Neil he was not old enough; suggested that when Clapp got out in a few years, Neil could become premier (if that was what he really wanted), with Percy's own blessing, and advised against going through an ordeal of certain defeat now to gain nothing but Clapp's animosity, which might be crippling to Neil in the future. Poor father, thought Neil as he listened. Ernest obviously believed that becoming premier was the end rather than the beginning. But finally, Neil's reaction was angry. "For ten years you've been pushing me into politics and then, when I make my own move, you spout defeatism. Why can't I win this time?" he demanded. Their discussion was not a long one, for when Ernest gave him half a dozen reasons why, Neil left in a rather abrupt and surly manner. He knew, though, that his father would help when the die was cast.

The sceptical attitudes of his wife and his father helped to make his decision final. Daylight doubts had not formed. His mother's attitude affected him neither one way or the other, for he didn't know whether it was pity or encouragement. When he told her she hugged him wordlessly, smiling up at him through moist eyes, and he felt no inclination to clarify the ambiguity of the gesture. He knew his running for the leadership now was a move in the right direction, the beginning of the realization of that sense of destiny which had crystallized at the time of his friendship with Wolfe Tone McGrath, but which had been allowed to lose its cutting edge and become nearly amorphous again thereafter. He felt like punishing himself for the time he had wasted already.

Before Neil's press conference started the next day, the gathered reporters speculated on whether or not he was going to be Clapp's campaign manager. Some advised him not to, saying he should lie low for a few years, become his own man. When he finally called the conference to order and announced his candidacy for the leadership of The People First Party – which he intended to win, and thus become premier that fall – the newsmen appreciated his sense of humour. One said that since representatives of all the media were now present, Neil could begin the press conference whenever he was ready. Neil repeated his statement and saw the awareness dawning on the faces before him. The furious scribbling started. Jerome Finn looked at him thoughtfully, without the enthusiasm Neil had expected.

Neil went home and waited for the television news. Both he and the report itself sounded good, he thought. Immediately, the phone began to ring. By midnight he had received thirty-five phone calls. All wished him well. All congratulated him on his gutsy move. All said they would help him. All referred to their delicate job situation, or their licence to sell liquor, or their public carrier licence, or their civil service position, or their contract with the government, which would prevent them from coming out front. They would work behind the scenes, however. All requested Neil to keep their calls confidential for the moment.

Neil went to bed visualizing Clapp pacing up and down, raging to Clyde and other supporters about disloyalty and treachery. He forced out the picture of the long road ahead. The loneliness.

The morning news carried Clapp's reaction to Neil's announcement: "I've said repeatedly that anyone was welcome to enter this open and democratic competition, even merchant princes and their lawyer hirelings from St. John's, who wish to carry on into the new generation the wholesale robbery of our people that I put a stop to. That rich clique of big city merchants and parasite lawyers has never been noted for its political intelligence. But this time they have sunk below the already low estimate of their brainpower held by ordinary people. This gang of mercantile pirates and their hired mouthpieces cannot even get together long enough to field just one candidate to stand behind. They are all so filled with disunity and grab-all greed that they have now put out two candidates to represent them! They have already pushed forward two gaping maws of a Hydra-headed monster – and before long there will be a dozen of them kicking, biting, and scratching at each other for the spoils. I am flattered that they feel they need so many of their kind to take on just one of me. They will find, however, that a hundred wreckers and body robbers are still not nearly enough!"

"That bastard," said Neil, annoyed, "putting me with Fagan, and painting me as rich and aristocratic!"

"What did you expect from the likes of him?" asked Gillian.

Later newscasts showed Clapp responding to a reporter's question about what he thought of the leadership race to date. "Very disappointing, quite frankly," replied Clapp. "I had hoped that by this time my great party would have put forward some candidates of high calibre to contest the leadership. I am very disappointed – ashamed, in fact – at the low quality of candidates who have announced against me. So far, we have only this merchant-lawyer, double-barrelled pop gun, stuffed with fluff. I want it known that I welcome all comers. I earnestly hope we will see candidates come forward of the quality and fibre which I know exist in my great party!"

Privately, Clapp was also circulating contemptuous descriptions of Fagan and Neil which were spreading rapidly and making people laugh. One of the many in general currency was: "Political victory is to Fagan and Godwin as an ox is to his testicles – distantly separated." The short form of this became: "Those two ox nuts."

In the meantime, Neil had been calling on friends in St. John's. The ones who were actively interested in seeing Clapp defeated told him that they had already committed their support to Fagan. Some told him straight out that, by entering the leadership race, he had seriously diluted the chances of defeating Clapp. After a week of strenuous effort, Neil had – among the promises – been able to collect only seven hundred dollars. Five hundred were from Touchings, Gillian's father, who said, "I hope I can count this as an outright loss for capital gains tax purposes"; and two hundred were from Roland, Jane's husband, who also agreed to become his campaign treasurer. Ernest did not offer any money. Neil took his and Gillian's savings out of the bank, depleting their joint, higher education account, and began his campaign in earnest.

He began to take perverse solace from the lowness of his starting position, a fact he had finally recognized. He preferred to believe that the brightness of the faces he encountered was caused by smiles of friendship and support, rather than by grins at the memory of some of Clapp's well-known lines about him, now evoked by his presence. In the face of Clapp's devastatingly humorous and contemptuous onslaught he maintained a serious dignity and sincerity.

A small victory was achieved when he arranged for Clapp, Fagan, and himself to appear on television together for an informal discussion with a moderator. On Neil's suggestion, Jerome Finn had the program take place live at an hour after dinner when Neil hoped Clapp would have had his usual allotment of sherry and liqueurs. It worked well. Neil watched the tape of the program later and was impressed by the contrast between his own calm reasonableness and the close-ups of Clapp's face: the bulging veins, the savage look, and the magnified over-reaction to everything that was said. Neil thought about writing Clyde a letter of thanks.

But it was Clyde who contacted Neil – giving him a phone

call that night. The conversation began amicably enough, but Neil's studied lack of interest in every proposition put to him about rejoining the team, forgiving and forgetting, or accepting Clapp's offer to resign right after the next election, finally drove Clyde to say: "Listen here, Godwin! You knifed me in the back and you knifed Percy in the back. But when the shiv goes in you it'll be right in the guts, because Perce and I will be there laughing in your face."

While Clyde talked, Neil searched for an appropriate Churchillian or Wildean rejoinder, but none was forthcoming. He therefore said: "Go fuck yourself, Clyde."

The next day, Neil gave an edited version of the conversation to the media and claimed it was a fear-inspired attempt to bribe and blackmail him. Clyde was outraged by this breach of honour among politicians. He came on the television blurting: "You should have heard what Godwin said to me! He told me to go eff myself. Now, is that the kind of leader we want for our country?"

Following Clyde's silly outburst – and for the first time since Neil had announced his candidacy – everyone that he met was laughing *with* him, telling him how much they had enjoyed hearing what he had said to that prick Ferritt. Neil heard through the grape-vine that Clapp had told Clyde: "From now on, stay in a back room or under a rock somewhere. And in the name of the lordliftingfuckingjesuschrist, stay off that idiot box, which must have been named, if not created, in your image!"

Neil confined his campaign to an area within an hour's drive of home for the first month of his candidacy. He was determined to stay close to Gillian until the baby was born, and for a reasonable period afterwards. But he soon developed severe anxiety over limiting himself in that way. Fagan, he discovered, had a network of service club contacts and a well-established organization in the city which Neil realized he could not match. The only hope of beating Clapp was to undermine the premier's strength around the coast, far from home.

The constant, nagging feeling that he was wasting his time in St. John's became a dreadful strain on Neil's relations with

Gillian. It led to words between them which, for the first time, went beyond mere momentary irritation.

"Go!" she screamed at him one night, after he had been chafing and fuming for an hour. "Leave! Get out! You *knew* I was about to have a baby when you got into that goddamned leadership. Go! I said. I'll look after Elizabeth by myself. I'll have this baby by myself again. I'll bring it home from the hospital by my –" She put her hands to her face.

Neil was struck with immediate remorse at the sight of Gillian, racked with sobs, standing alone in the middle of the bedroom. He walked towards her, arms outstretched.

"Don't!" she said fiercely, turning away from him. "And don't start getting ready to use me as your convenient excuse, brother, when you lose that fucking leadership!"

Some of the words they fired at one another stuck like splinters in their hearts for days. But when the baby was born, and Neil was there with Gillian throughout the labour and birth, all harsh words were forgotten.

"They say it's the husband's fault if his wife doesn't produce any sons," Gillian said in the delivery room, as she examined her second daughter. "It's because the husband is full of bull-headed sperms. I believe it." Everyone laughed. And before he left the hospital that night, Neil received as many congratulations for marrying his wife as for fathering his child.

Neil was about to leave St. John's for a coastal speaking tour when Jane delayed his departure by two more days. She came to their house late at night and asked him and Gillian if she could stay there for a while. She was not going back to that bastard, Roland.

"What the hell is going on, Jane?" asked Neil in anger. All he could think of was that while he was away for two weeks, Roland would be preoccupied with a marital spat and not be able to concentrate on the campaign's desperate need for funds.

"Shh," whispered Gillian, putting her hand on his back. "What happened, Jane?"

"Until one day ago," said Jane, speaking across Neil to Gillian, "I thought Dr. Maidment was against Roland and me getting married because he wanted Roland to get his CA first. Then, yesterday, I heard that he had been going around the curling club for weeks before our marriage, saying that his fool of a son was tangled up with, and (for reasons that passed all understanding), engaged to marry, an earthy daughter of a preacher of some primitive species of evangelical theology. He was even asking lawyers at the club if there was any legal way of stopping a son from marrying disastrously beneath himself!"

"What has that got to do with Roland, for God's sake?" asked Neil. "He married you, didn't he?"

Jane turned further away from Neil. "We had dinner at Roland's parents' place tonight, Gillian," she continued, swallowing several times. "And I told the old prick right off. Roland didn't like what I said."

"Good for you, Jane!" declared Gillian. She put her arm around Jane's shoulders.

Neil glared at his wife. "For Christ's sake, Jane!" he said. "You don't have to love your in-laws, but you've got to try to live in some harmony with them." He pushed a vision of Touchings' face, contorted with anger, out of his mind. "What did you say to Dr. Maidment, anyhow?"

"Why should I tell you?" she shot over her shoulder. "You'd only side with him and Roland, whatever I said!"

"Let's go to bed," Gillian interjected quickly. "We can talk this over in the morning."

By morning, Gillian had persuaded Neil that, since Jane *was* his sister, he should go to see her campaign-treasurer husband and straighten things out. When Neil got to the apartment, Roland was still in his pyjamas, grey-faced with worry. Neil asked him for an outline of the previous evening's events.

"It went really well, at first," Roland told him, as the two of them sat side by side on the sofa. "I thought Jane had decided to just forget about what she'd heard. And then she started making little remarks about neurosurgery and about neurosurgeons who slice bits out of people's brains .... The old man didn't catch on right away – but when she began saying things about *me*, he could hardly miss it."

"What sort of things?" asked Neil.

Roland stared miserably at his clasped hands. "She said that maybe he'd used me for practice. 'Did you try a crude lobectomy on Roland?' she asked. 'He's a bit slow off the mark all the time, and as his wife, I'm entitled to know why.'" Neil smothered a grin just as Roland looked at him appealingly. "We had to leave after that. 'You'll regret this, my lad,' my father said .... And everything had been so great up till then, Neil."

"Jane says that the two of you had a bad fight."

"Jesus .... I only asked her what the point of all that was. We've got to try to be a bit friendly with each other's parents, I said."

"Exactly what I told her, Roland."

"And then I asked her if there was really any need to make fun of me in front of my family. Next thing I know, she's ranting and raving, Neil, calling me everything under the sun: I'm a coward, I never stand up for her, I let everyone walk all over my own face. Well, you know, one thing leads to another, and finally she wangs me across the head and takes off out the door." Roland was looking at his hands again. "She's four months pregnant, Neil."

Neil's combination of amusement and impatience faded. Why hadn't Jane told him? he wondered. So she was pregnant before she got married: big deal! He was her *brother*, for Christ's sake! Becoming aware of Roland's waiting silence, he smiled quickly. "Pregnancy," he said. "That must be the cause of it all, Roland."

Another full day of Neil's shuttle diplomacy finally brought the parties together again in an uneasy truce. Just as he was leaving their apartment, free at last to go on his tour, Jane said sarcastically, "When the men stick together, all's well with the world!"

Neil mentioned the comment to Gillian. "Jane's pregnancy has made her go kind of strange .... " he finished off.

"You knows as much about a pregnancy, Neil Godwin, as you knows about the Queen's – about a codfish," Gillian replied. "Just thought I'd prepare you for your encounters with the bay folk. But, I must say, she does not look well."

261

For sentimental reasons (suggested by Roland), the phoneyness of which Neil dismissed from his thoughts, he began his speaking campaign in his birthplace of Maggotty Cove Motion in Twillick District. It was the first time he had been back to the place since he had left with his family at the age of four. And even now he did not see it, because he arrived after dark by boat and left later that same night. The community was still very isolated, with no road connection to the outside.

Neil spoke to an eager crowd in the Gawker's Hall that had been built by his father a quarter of a century before. He was surprised, after he had finished, at the articulate, intelligent utterances of speakers from the floor. All his life, the name of the place of his birth had turned his mind against any thought that there could be anything good there. When he mingled among them afterwards, it was a pleasure to hear their realistically cynical comments on Clapp, and their independent, open-eyed, fearless outlook on life generally. One or two said to him, "You're nearly as good as your father was."

Neil travelled ceaselessly, endlessly making speeches to bigger and bigger crowds as his name preceded him. He had caught on. Young girls began to scream at his meetings. He got standing ovations and long, firm, handshakes from the men, and heartfelt hugs from the women. Young boys, reported one newsman who had accompanied him on a tour, were starting to comb their hair like Neil's. One learned commentator had taken to referring to him as "the indefatigable and ubiquitous Godwin." Another wrote, after attending one of Neil's meetings: "If Godwin does not kill the giant, he will stagger him."

Neil sent spies to see exactly what Clapp was saying at his own meetings. It was reported back to him that one of Clapp's themes was: "I love this land. I've given my lifesblood for this land. I am totally devoted to this land. I'd lay down my life for this land. No man was ever more devoted to his wife and family than I am to this land. I am married to this land. And her people are my children."

Neil's spies reported that these remarks, which Clapp would build up to a crescendo, were bringing his audiences to their feet as one. Neil primed a stalwart follower, bass-voiced and fit for anything, on what to say from the back of the hall at one of Clapp's future meetings. They rehearsed it to perfection.

Two or three nights later, at a meeting which Neil had earlier learned was to be attended by a television crew, Clapp went through his "this land" litany. When he had roared, "I am married to this land!" and was in the middle of his dramatic pause prior to taking his audience out of their seats, Neil's Stentor boomed out near the television mike that had been placed to catch audience reaction: "I hope to God you *are* married to this land, Clapp! You've been screwing her for fifteen years!"

The film clip of the sequence of events, shown on the news, was good: Clapp's litany, the unexpected bellow from nowhere, clearly understandable, Clapp's dumbfounded look – the audience, somewhere between sitting and standing, about-to-clap hands frozen, silent mouths open – then a few titters, women sinking down in their seats to bury their faces in their laps and shake with laughter, men openly guffawing – and finally, Clapp's blustering attempts to regain control.

Neil was told the story of Clapp's meeting a dozen times everywhere he went during the next week. Seeing the beneficial effect a light interlude could have on his fight against Clapp, Neil began to make up stories to be spread around by means of his network of supporters.

He concocted one which dealt with Clapp's sheep-raising days, a period of his life which Clapp kept fresh in everyone's memory by his frequent references to that noble occupation of the common man. During his spell at raising sheep, Neil told a group of followers, Clapp was called to go on a jury in a case of a man accused of having sexual relations with a sheep. A witness for the prosecution took the stand and told how he had watched the defendant introduce his penis into the sheep's vulva and that, as he did so, the sheep's bowels moved. "What?" said the judge, in disgust. And Clapp took it for disbelief. Jumping up from his seat in the jury box, irrepressible as ever, Clapp shouted, "Oh, yes, Your Honour, that's absolutely true. My own experience is that a sheep will shit every time." Again, the results were so salutary and pervasive that Neil used most of the time he spent travelling between communities making up scurrilous guffers to tell about Clapp. Another of his fabrications showed how the shallowness of Clapp's knowledge, together with his know-it-all attitude, had brought the country to the brink of disaster. This one had the merit of slandering Clyde Ferritt as well.

"Let me tell you what I mean," said Neil, to his closest friends. "Not long ago, Clapp and Ferritt and I were on a boat trip along the coast when we had to put in for the night at one of the smaller settlements. There were only two beds available at the boarding house and they were in one room. I had to sleep with the skipper from the boat and Clapp had to bunk down with Ferritt, who had never before in his life had anyone, male or female, share his bed. During the night, Ferritt, in his sleep, apparently mistook Clapp for one of his usual fantasies and climbed aboard him. Clapp had once heard somewhere that it was dangerous to wake someone up who was in the middle of a dream. So profound was Clapp's faith in his own shallow knowledge of psychology that he would not wake Ferritt up. That night, by my count, Clapp got it in the ass four times."

Everywhere he went, Neil heard these stories repeated. It became monotonous to be drawn aside everywhere and told a bit of smut about Clapp which Neil himself had manufactured the previous week. Then he noticed that new stories he had never heard before were being told about Clapp. And finally, old worn-out stories previously told as nigger jokes or Pakkie jokes or Polack jokes, and most recently, as Newfy jokes, were being resurrected, with Clapp as the main character. The genre now became known as a "Percy joke," and friends vied with one another to tell the latest. The more despicable a light it cast the premier in, the better the tellers and listeners liked it.

Neil stopped making up his own stories when he was told the one about how Clapp, who had worn out his anus because there was so much crap in him all the time, had been forced to have an anus transplant. Clapp, the punchline went, was

264

pumped full of anti-rejection drugs, but even so, two days after the transplant, the new asshole rejected Clapp! After hearing that one, Neil concluded that the Percy joke was now painfully self-perpetuating and needed no assistance from him.

On one of his periodic visits to St. John's, Neil entered his headquarters at midmorning for a quick vetting of campaign literature before departing again for the coast. Sitting on a desk in the middle of the main room, dressed in an army uniform and delicately sipping from a glass of amber liquid was Muck Barrows.

"Neil, Neil, Neil," he said, sliding off the desk with great concentration on his movements. "How's the kid?" He wove unsteadily across the floor, hand outstretched. Several of their common acquaintances had told Neil in recent years that Muck was well along in the process of ruining himself on inexpensive Sergeant's Mess liquor, and Neil could well believe it. "I helped myself to some of your traditional political hospitality while I was waiting for you," Muck went on, "with the aid of your lovely and efficient assistant, here."

"He said he was your best friend," murmured Neil's secretary guiltily. She had been under firm instructions to allow no one to bring liquor into headquarters and to give out none of Neil's private stock in his office unless he expressly requested her to do so. Muck had obviously not lost the knack of dealing successfully with his fellow human beings when he wanted something.

"He is," said Neil. "He is my best friend." They shook hands warmly. The others in the room, envelope stuffers and sealers, looked up at hearing this, and Neil thought it best to lead Muck into his office and close the door. God knew what he had been saying or doing outside already.

"Neil, old pal, I haven't laid eyes on you since that last time. God, five, six, years ago. And I never got any of your letters. I've been beating around a lot. They never reached me. Did you get mine?"

"Up to a couple of years ago, I did," answered Neil. "I'm surprised the army never forwarded mine on to you."

"Oh, well, you've been awful busy, Neil. That's okay. You've been really making something out of yourself. Jesus. I've often thought about how you and me – oh, shit." Muck became absorbed in trying to wipe a splash of liquor from his glass off his shoulder. "I looked around for you when I got home a week ago." He pulled open the credenza door and poured himself a drink. "But your sister told me you were on the campaign trail. I had a nice long gab with Jane at the Grapnel, I must say. She's still a queer hand, Jane. Kind of hyper, though. Yes, she says, she goes out every night so that her husband can work in peace and quiet at home to keep her in the style to which she's grown accustomed. Ha, ha, ha. Something else. 'What are *you* doing back here looking for Neil?' she asks me. 'Trying to get in on the graft, too?' You and Jane on the outs or something?"

"No, not that I know of," Neil said easily. "Why?"

"I just sort of got the idea. Neil, listen." Muck swayed forward for emphasis, holding his drink carefully so as not to spill it again. "I've been around." He patted, with his drink hand, a piece of military insignia sewn to his chest, slopping half his glass over the front of his uniform. "And, oops – fuck – I'm telling you, Neil, even though she *is* knocked up, I'd still eat a yard of Jane's shit." This highest praise of beauty from Muck's stock of armyisms made Neil push back his chair; but Muck remained unfazed. "How about you, Neil," he inquired. "You getting any strange tail these days?"

"David, I've been married for over two years," said Neil, and he slid a copy of his latest campaign newspaper across the desk, on the front page of which was a picture of himself, Gillian, Elizabeth, and the new baby, Anne. Muck pretended to look at it, his diagonal grin showing how irrelevant he found Neil's reply.

Neil wanted to get on the road again. He didn't want to hear this stuff, either, about Jane's nocturnal solicitude regarding her husband's work habits, or her opinion of his own political motives. He stood up as casually as he could.

"I heard that that bastard Gorman is against you," commented Muck. "Remember him when he was president of the U.? Bastard had me flicked out. Remember that? Jane told me you told her years ago it was because Gorman thought *I*

266

wrote that thing you wrote about Clapp and the rest. Remember? That true, Neil?"

Neil stopped on his way to the door of his office and walked quickly back to his chair. "Well, I didn't have any proof, David," he said. "But when I was thinking about it afterwards, it was the only conclusion I could come to." He sat down and looked at Muck earnestly. "Listen, David. I wasn't going to tell you this, because I didn't want any credit for it and I didn't want you, as an old friend, to feel you owed me anything. But three years ago, I nailed Gorman for what he had done to you ... " Neil described Gorman's idiotic, self-imposed downfall as if Neil himself had manoeuvred him into it in order to avenge Muck.

At the end of the account, Muck remained silent; and Neil looked at him uneasily. The pull of gravity seemed to have mastered the other man's facial features completely, so slack were the muscles from the booze. He could have been a superior type, thought Neil, intelligent, attractive, strong. Now, not yet thirty, he was crippled by alcohol: useless, an inebriated pain in the ass, with an automatic flow of drunken patter. Neil stood, readying himself to say goodbye; and Muck's expression focussed.

"Well, that settles it," he announced. "I've been in and out of your headquarters here for the past few days, and what you need, Neil, is organization. I already had half a mind to offer you a hand but, foolish as it sounds now, I didn't know where I stood with you these days."

"Gosh, thanks for the thought, David," said Neil. He moved hastily to the door. "Most of my efforts are out in the bays, far from here. I couldn't impose on a friend like that. The latest poll shows that I'm nearly equal to Percy in popularity now. Well up from the last one. We still have weeks to go. We think I'll pass him on the next. We've got lots of bodies here at headquarters. You can't disrupt your military career. I couldn't ask you to do that."

"Yes, I *know* you're popular, Neil. Even here in the city. But this is not a popularity contest. It's numbers. One, two, three!" Muck waved his fingers in the air. "Only numbers of delegates count. You need organization. I had to decide this week whether to stay in the army for another hitch or not. I'm a sergeant; and there's not much hope of becoming an officer without a university degree .... That prick Gorman! Thanks for what you did, by the way .... " Muck's shoulders straightened. "I'm going to get out and come back and give you a hand with organization. It may be too late, already."

"I've got no money to pay you, David," countered Neil.

"I'll sponge off the old man for a while. He's not so pissed off since I paid him back for the car I totalled on him." Muck fingered the small scar near his temple. His head still looked slightly skew. "I'll leave for the mainland this afternoon. I'll be back in a week or less. I hope we're not too late, Neil. We'll do the best we can with the short time left." Muck put down his half full glass, shook hands with Neil, and walked out of the office, his body militarily erect.

Terrific! fumed Neil on his way out to the car. An alcoholic lout who knew all about the leadership contest after a four day visit home, and who would use his former friendship with Neil to intermeddle everywhere and screw the works up. Lovely. *And all because I handed him that yarn to cover up my slip ten years ago,* Neil chastised himself. *You weak, soft, stupid bastard!*

Halfway across the island, Neil had to interrupt one of his organizers – who was telling him yet another hoary Percy joke – to listen to what sounded suspiciously like a little joke of Clapp's own. It was an announcement on the radio by the president of The People First Party, a hand-picked Clapp man, that the party executive had now drawn up the rules governing the election of delegates to the leadership convention. Only registered party members would be permitted to vote at the meetings to elect delegates, he said. This was normal and caused Neil no anxiety. What the president said next, however, forced Neil to strain mightily to conceal his misgivings from his men in the car. The president announced a cut-off date a week hence for the registration of party members. It was true, he said, that in previous conventions, people were permitted to register as party members right up to the day of each meeting to elect delegates – and indeed, at the meetings themselves. But this leadership convention was being so hotly contested that the executive deemed it necessary to impose some order on the election of delegates well in advance, to make sure that everything was fair and square and that no candidate could complain of irregularities after the convention. Therefore, only members of the public who registered before the cut-off date and who were in possession of valid membership cards would be able to vote at the district meetings to elect delegates.

So that was what all of Clapp's members in the legislature had been doing in their districts during the past month! They had been searching out, and signing up as party members, supporters of Clapp who would vote for slates of delegates favourable to him. Christ, thought Neil. He should have been more alert to Clapp's wiles. Neil himself had intended to use the same technique: putting together slates of delegates committed to him, and then lining up droves of supporters from the general public to come to the meetings to vote them in. But he had meant to do that much closer to the dates of the meetings themselves, when he had built up an optimum amount of public support to draw from. Now he had only one week to find and register party members to vote for his slates of delegates at the meetings.

The president of the party concluded his list of rules by saying that, owing to the great number of district meetings that would have to be held to elect the delegates, the executive had been forced to pass a regulation giving it the right to call meetings to elect delegates at any time, on twenty-four hours notice, between the cut-off date and the day of the convention. Whenever feasible, of course, much greater notice would be given, he said. Neil knew that in no case would greater notice be given, and that each meeting would be called on the basis of one criterion only: Clapp's organizers' convenience.

Shortly afterwards, the other candidate, Fagan, came on the radio and exposed all the fears Neil had been hiding. He verged on hysteria in an effort to make an issue out of the party executive's prejudicial use of power to stack the cards in favour of Clapp. But Neil knew that no one would pay any attention to his protests. Abstract rules were not the kind of thing that worked people up in advance of their concrete application. The leadership contest would now have to be fought in accordance with the new rules, no matter how unfair. In fact, Clapp was probably hoping that Neil would waste his time trying to have them altered. No. Muck Barrows had been right. This thing had become an organizational battle, pure and simple. The greater or lesser popularity of candidates would have only a marginal effect.

At another huge, enthusiastic Godwin rally that night, a man stood up following Neil's speech and said: "The prime minister told me to tell you this, Mr. Godwin. Tell little Neily Godwin, he said, that all this clapping and bawling would be just ducky if this was a beauty contest. But in politics, he said, rather than being young and pretty, it's better to be old and cute. The PM said you'd know what he meant."

The man was booed down and a chant of "Godwin! Godwin!" began. But up there on the stage, overlooking the bright faces, Neil knew what Clapp meant.

Neil immediately set his organizers to work signing up party members and providing them with membership cards, concentrating on his best districts. He realized he needed help from some already organized source, some person or institution with the influence and membership to get large numbers of people signed up throughout the country quickly. Ernie Godwin, to his son's aching disappointment, had already announced his strict personal neutrality in the contest, pleading a conflict between friendship and kinship. Privately, he had freed his chief lieutenants to do as they pleased. Understandably taking their chief's neutrality towards his own son as an implicit lack of support, large numbers of Gawkers displayed the same loyalty to Neil's cause that he had shown to theirs over the years, and had gone with their traditional political leader, Clapp.

Neil decided that part of this battle had to be conducted at that level. He hurried back to the city and arranged to see the Right Reverend Rodney Wadman, who for years had not striven sedulously to hide his lack of appreciation of Clapp. Neil was pleasantly surprised at the ease and celerity with which Wadman agreed to see him; and assumed it was because the reverend realized that the Gawkers, as a group, were not behind him. He felt out the matter by saying that he assumed his lordship would naturally be remaining neutral in this intra-party struggle.

"No," said Wadman, "I'm afraid I cannot stay neutral in this particular political altercation."

Delighted, Neil formed his hands into a church and steeple, and leaned forward with a smile.

"No, I'm very much afraid I'm going to have to suggest gently to my people that for the good of the country, they should support ... " Wadman sipped his sherry, apparently relishing the moment, "... Mr. Clapp."

Instantly knowing he was serious, Neil exclaimed, "But, sir, in case there's some misunderstanding, you should be made aware that I am not a practising Gawker and that a great number of Gawkers are behind Mr. Clapp."

"I know, I know. I shall have to live with that disagreeable fact. Incidentally, you are not attempting to divide religious denominations along political lines, are you? Such attempts dissolved us into civil war a hundred years ago."

"No, of course not, sir, but ah, sir, for some years now you have not hidden from public knowledge your distaste for Mr. Clapp's policies and methods."

"I know, I know. I shall have to accommodate my conscience to that minor reversal." Wadman got to his feet.

"Sir, my lord, excuse me, sir, before we part ... I should tell you that Mr. Clapp once informed me that in a contest between him and the devil, you would support the devil."

"Mr. Clapp said that?" Neil's hopes rose as Wadman paused at the door. "Mr. Clapp was quite right."

"Yet you are prepared to support him over me?"

"Yes."

"May I ask you why you are doing this, sir?"

"Much is asked. You may ask. Unto the third and fourth generation of them. I live by the word. You are not attempting to deprive a man of the right to keep his innermost thoughts inviolate, are you? Goodbye, Mr. Godwin." He said the name as if the sound of it made him sick.

Neil left, pretending to wonder what was wrong with this

cryptic old fool, but knowing he was in the worst of all possible political worlds: his own father's Gawkers weren't with him, and anyone who had reason to despise the Gawkers' encroachments, like Wadman, was against him. Soon, however, he was lost in his plans for the continuation of the organizational drive he had put into motion. He hoped that Muck Barrows – who had come back from the mainland within two days, rather than one week, after he had heard of Clapp's membership ploy, and who was already out "organizing" – wasn't doing too much damage.

When the meetings to elect delegates to the convention actually started there were several near riots. Hundreds of supporters of Neil came to the meetings, but were unable to vote for the delegates because their names were not on the party membership lists and they possessed no membership cards. Neil attended personally as many of these meetings as he could, and got a tremendous ovation at each one. Most of his fears now left him, even though, theoretically, slates of Clapp delegates were elected at most meetings, owing to Clapp's workers having registered so many of their own as party members. The welcome he was receiving was too genuine not to be trusted. In a few districts, Neil was able to get his own slates elected as delegates. Son of Socks was reported to have made similar gains in some city districts where he had concentrated his efforts.

Most of Neil's remaining misgivings about the election of Clapp's slates died when he started systematically to visit the homes of the elected delegates. In nearly every kitchen there was one of the big glossy pictures of himself that his workers had distributed. In Catholic homes, it had been placed alongside pictures of the Pope and John Kennedy. In Protestant homes it was next to ones of the Queen and King William on a white horse. Even in the homes of Clapp delegates, his picture enjoyed equal prominence with that of the premier.

Towards the end of the campaign, independent polls showed that throughout the country, nearly 60 per cent of the population said they liked Neil Godwin more than Percy Clapp. The percentage who said they would rather have Neil as prime minister was only slightly less. Although the slates of delegates who were supposedly elected to support Clapp at the convention outnumbered Neil by nine or ten to one, this caused no concern among Neil's supporters. Nobody considered these slates as conclusive, by any means. Many delegates said that there was going to be a secret ballot at the convention and they would vote in accordance with their consciences. Some Clapp delegates were quoted anonymously as saying they had agreed to be elected on a Clapp slate because that was the only way to get to the convention, seeing that Clapp had everything rigged – as usual.

In the final week of the campaign, the wide extremes between Neil's daily highs and lows about the likely result of the convention averaged out to ambivalence. Late at night, again and again, he would count up the number of delegates committed to him, and then add enough from Clapp's slates to arrive at a saw-off between the two of them on the first ballot. He knew that if he and Clapp were reasonably close on the first ballot, and if, after Fagan was dropped as last place finisher, his votes came to Neil on the second ballot, he would have the majority he needed. It was a possible scenario; but whether it was probable or not, he could not say. All he knew was that it would be very close on that first ballot.

Neil's supporters, however, had no doubts. And their spirits were buoyed even higher by an amusing event that took place during these last days. Clapp's headquarters had just put out a newspaper filled with photographs of the premier in every conceivable posture. One picture showed him exchanging an extremely tight embrace with a well-constructed young woman whose scanty dress inadequately covered her tumefacient form. The caption below the picture read: "Despite the long, exhausting hours put in by our prime minister, he still has an appreciative eye for Miss Wanda Jones, one of our country's many beautiful girls." Muck Barrows, Neil learned later, got some henchmen to run off several thousand copies of this picture, but with the caption removed. Drawing on his compendious knowledge of pornographic films, Muck had a new caption printed under the picture: "The Devil in Miss Jones?" The pictures received wide-spread anonymous distribution to delighted recipients.

Delegates were treating their copies of the photograph as a collector's item. Demand for the picture was clamorous. A new spate of Percy jokes began.

The party executive arranged for the last dozen meetings to elect delegates to be held in widely separated towns two days before the convention. Neil chose to attend the meeting in Spirity Cove, his mother's home community. His workers assured him that enough organization had been done in this district to elect a Godwin slate of delegates.

That day, Neil drove through Spirity Cove. He had never been there before and his mother had seldom talked about it. There was not much to the place. It was situated about halfway out on one side of a small peninsula. Between the settlement and the end of the headland was a long, sloping, treeless expanse, the Folkly Rooms, which rose up from the beach near Spirity Cove to the cliffs and sea on the other side. The most prominent feature of the community was a grassy knoll, incongruously located on the flat part of the beach where the Rooms began.

On impulse, Neil stopped his car near the beach and asked a teenaged boy if the hummock had a name.

"That's Ecky's Fish," the boy told him.

"My God, Ecky's Fish," said Neil. "That's Ecky's Fish! Do you know why it's called that?"

"Something about old Eck Priddle or something, I think," offered the boy. He didn't know.

Neil was starting to think about what he himself knew when Muck's car drew up alongside. The two of them went on to spend the rest of the day as they had planned, campaigning in the neighbouring communities together, making sure that people whom their workers had registered went to the meeting that night. Muck had been working hard in this district because of the initial advantage of Neil's family connection here, and he expected their slate to get elected *in toto.*

At the end of the wearisome day, during which Muck's energy and spirit had been unflagging, they parted. "I'll go to the hall to make sure our floor committee is ready for action, and you go to the hotel and pretty up for the meeting," Muck grinned.

Neil reflected as he went on how he had warmed to Muck during this day together. Their friendship had picked up where it had left off ten years before. Neil was already aware, from discreet questions he'd put to workers on the subject, that Muck had not been known to take a drink since he had started his organizing activities in this campaign. The one annoying trait of Muck's (and it was inconsequential), had been his continual use of the words "*if* you win the leadership ... " rather than "*when*" like Neil's other workers.

In his room, Neil found that he was worn out. He dozed twice over his sandwich. He decided against a short nap, since it would merely aggravate his exhausted state. After all, he had only this one last meeting to get through tonight. Leaving the motel, he drove down to the beach. He parked his car and wandered up the rise of the wide, moory Rooms, breathing deeply the moist breeze that caressed his face. He walked and walked until he came to the edge of the cliff, where he stood looking down at the heaving swell far below, listening to its dull moan. Then he moved back a distance and sat on a natural chair of stone. In the waning evenglow, he ran his eyes over the terrain he had covered, glimpsing the speck of Ecky's Fish and seeing the mist-draped channel that led, gradually widening, from Spirity Cove to the ocean outside. He sighed and then groaned. Visions of defeat and failure at the convention crept into his tired and vacant mind. When he heard Muck shouting his name far away, he was momentarily torn between silently hiding and responding to the call. Eventually he got up and hurried back, surprised at the number of sombre valleys and rocky ridges he'd travelled over. He met Muck halfway down the slope.

"That was a good idea," said Muck, anxiously sizing him up. "I saw your car parked there and I figured you went for a stroll to relax. You were saying today how you wanted to walk on the Rooms. We won't be too late for the meeting if we hurry up."

At the meeting that night, as a result of the efforts of Muck and other workers in the district, all of the twenty delegates elected were from Neil's slate and pledged to vote for him at the convention. They left the meeting amid cheers and shouts of impending victory from the several hundred people present. Muck was very high in Neil's esteem.

As they headed for the city to prepare for the leadership convention, Muck was more sanguine than he'd been all day about the likelihood of victory. Even the newscasts predicted a close and exciting race. Neil himself felt good: he'd either beat Clapp or come close enough to be considered the second most powerful politician in the province. Either way, his political future was assured.

17

On the first day of the convention, Neil moved among the delegates for hours. He was mobbed, continuously surrounded by a crowd twenty deep on all sides. Every time he came into the main hall, the cheers and chants would start for him. The outcome became a foregone conclusion for Neil's supporters when it was announced, just before the deadline, that Clyde Ferritt had entered the leadership race. His feeble reason for doing so was to give the youth of the country a representative candidate, as none of the other two young candidates had caught the imagination of the youth at all. But Neil's workers knew the real reason for Clyde's entry: Clapp did not want to risk coming last on the first ballot, which would mean being automatically dropped.

The candidates' speeches were delivered that first night. Fagan had drawn first place in the speaking order; and he was politely applauded by all when he finished. Neil noticed that he had a small core of shouting, placard waving supporters.

Neil got up to speak next, in accordance with the draw. There was a standing ovation and, when he finished, the crowd rose to their feet once more.

Clapp was next and he was met by good applause. Many stood. But there were sprinklings of laughter and chuckles as well, as when an audience greets a favourite self-deprecating comedian. At the end of Clapp's speech there was a long standing ovation for him, but little by way of cheers or placard waving. It was a farewell clapping of hands, mixed with sorrow that he had to go like this. Clyde's speech was in praise of Clapp.

That night, most of the commentators made Neil the odds-on favourite. One respected analyst said that he had randomly asked so-called Clapp delegates confidentially if they were really going to vote for Clapp, and a great number of them replied that they were going to do the right thing. He had asked what they thought of Godwin and more than half said they liked him best of all the candidates. "This committed slate thing is very much over-blown," the analyst concluded. "I predict a second ballot win for Godwin. There will be some sympathy votes for Clapp on the first, and then Fagan will drop and his votes will go to Godwin."

The votes were cast the next afternoon. The results would be announced in the order of the speeches, said the chairman. A total of one thousand and eighty votes had been cast. "Fagan: one hundred and eleven votes." A roar went up, and Neil heard a chant, "Godwin! Godwin!" The chairman brought the hall to order. "Godwin: eighty-nine votes." The place went deathly silent. *How many?* people muttered. Neil heard "eight-ninety," "nine-eighty," from around the hall. He himself knew the chairman had slurred the first numeral; he waited to hear "four eighty-nine." Fagan's votes would give him the majority on the next ballot .... The chairman continued, "Clapp: seven hundred and sixty-six votes. Ferritt: one hundred and eighteen votes. The new leader of The People First Party – the Right Honourable Prime Minister, Percy Clapp!"

There were a few scattered shouts of joy. A round of applause started. Neil's heart felt as if it was being squeezed in a fist. "Climbing mother, climbing mother," bounced about his head. Gillian embraced him and tried to put his head on her shoulder.

Clapp passed through the crowd to the podium to make his victory speech. Clyde and Toope were with him. At the end of his short speech, Clapp passed the microphone to Clyde, who called upon Fagan and "that valiant, young, *last* place finisher, Neil Godwin," to come to the stand. Fagan walked to the microphone, moved that the vote for Clapp be made unanimous and called upon Neil to second the motion in accordance with tradition.

Muck took one look at Neil and tried to accompany him to the podium, but Neil told him to stay with Gillian. Before the mike, he started to say that the party had in its wisdom made its decision and everyone must now abide ... But he faltered in the middle of the sentence. The sound of his *clichés* rasped on nerves in the back of his head and neck. He paused and spoke softly, not expressing the defeat and humiliation he felt, but the lines he would have put in the mouth of a character in a script under these circumstances. "I will not smother my conscience for that species of political expediency and cowardice called party solidarity," he said. "I will fight evil where I see it, even if I have to fight alone. But I'm not alone. I've seen what the people in their thousands across this land think of this would-be dictator – this little Mussolini, all bluff and bluster, who mistakes his own maniacal energy for great genius, and his addle-brained scheming for statesmanship – whose courage consists solely of that brass mace in the House of Assembly which, up till now, he has wielded with impunity at every head with a tongue to speak its mind – and whose conscience is carried around in his bloated billfold.

"Your votes here today have kept this man in power. But I know and you know and he knows that outside this hall, throughout this country, I have poked a hole in the corrupt carcase and have shown it to be filled with rattling bones and foul gas, merely. We know it is dead, for the stench has reached our nostrils. I intend to bury it!"

There were sharp intakes of breath all around, as Neil stepped down to the floor. He expected to be booed for this gracelessness. Instead, there was absolute silence while he walked out of the auditorium alone.

At home he turned on the television. Clapp was being asked what he thought of Godwin's exit, so unusual for a political convention. "What can one say about a person who is such a poor loser, such a bad *last* place loser?" queried Clapp. His face looked strained and tired.

Gillian and Muck arrived, and Gillian stood with her hand

on Neil's head while they watched a wrap-up of the convention. "What is amazing," said one of the commentators, "is that the votes which each candidate got on the convention floor – counting Clapp's and Ferritt's votes as one, since they were all Clapp's – were nearly exactly the same as the slates of delegates which were reported earlier as having been elected for each candidate. This proves that the vast majority of people will remain faithful to their public commitments of support even when there is a secret ballot, and even if they feel that they have made a commitment to the wrong candidate, as my polls consistently showed."

"You'll find that kind of loyalty useful someday when you have some hard decisions to make," said Gillian.

"That information is useful only to a poli sci course, now, as far as I am concerned," responded Neil. "I'm out of this goddamned political racket for good. It's too painful .... Not for me – I can take it. But you saw my workers and supporters around us after the results were announced. Men and women sobbing like babies. They *knew* we were going to win. But win what? Crying like a mother who had lost an only child – for losing. For *losing* what? I despise it all utterly."

On the television screen, an interviewer put his mike in front of a group of delegates. "You seem to be Clapp supporters *and* Godwin supporters, judging by the lapel buttons you're all wearing. Tell me, were you surprised by how badly Godwin lost?"

With the agreement of his companions, one of the delegates replied: "A little bit, but that's nothing. I'd say that nearly everyone at the convention liked Neil most of all. But sure, he's only young yet. This was like kind of old Percy's sendoff. Neil will make it in a few years, guaranteed."

"Belt the bejesus up, you stupid bastard!" muttered Neil, and switched off the set. He wanted to go off by himself, but Gillian had already offered Muck a drink and he had accepted a soda water and ice. Neil said to him, "Muck, I'm very much aware that every delegate vote I got, with the exception of those in my own district, was the result of your organizational work. You knew I was going to lose badly – Christ, last place, eighty-nine votes, 8 per cent of the total – and you still stuck with me. I'm doubly grateful to you for that. Anyway, you can get yourself a job, now, and make yourself some money. We're all finished at last with this crap."

"Oh, my God, Neil," said Muck. "Whatever you do, don't force me into the position where I have to get a job." He chuckled. "Listen. Relax tonight. Tomorrow we'll talk." He finished his soda water and left.

Neil went into the den and slumped in his chair. Elizabeth pushed the door open wide and climbed forthrightly, as usual, into his lap. He kissed her hair but his gaze remained on the window opposite. He paid so little attention to her chatter, and played their habitual games so absently, that she complained. Finally, she climbed down and toddled out, puzzled disappointment on her small face. Neil began to push himself out of the chair to go after her, but let himself drop back when the phone rang.

Gillian came in. "That's your mother and father," she said.

"I'm not taking any calls this evening, thanks, Gillian."

"Not even from them?"

"No."

"My goodness, Neil!"

Two hours passed and there were no other calls. People had better things to do on a Saturday night, he thought, than to phone up a loser. He got up, declined Gillian's offer of a bite to eat, and walked up the stairs to go to bed. In his abstraction, his legs carried him automatically to the doorway of baby Anne's nursery before he realized where he was. He turned around without going in and went directly to his own room.

In the morning, Neil wandered around the house in his dressing gown for a couple of hours, looking out of windows and thinking about nothing. At one point, Gillian put her hand on his arm. "That was the bank manager on the phone, wondering what we are going to do about the overdraft on our account," she told him. "He waited until the outcome of the convention was known before pouncing. I don't want to bother you with this stuff now, but I have to, Neil. We're completely out of money. We've been living on my little income, credit cards, and the bank overdraft for months. We owe thousands. We need to sit down and make plans."

"That's all right, Gillian. I'll sign a note for the overdraft first chance, and I'll be back practising law in two or three days." Neil's throat tightened as he said it. He hadn't told Gillian about the sizable notes he had signed personally at two other banks to cover the expensive last push of his campaign .... He *had* to take off for a while .... "But first, I need to pay a short visit to my district," he went on, patting Gillian's hand. "Remember I said when I resigned as minister, that I would be resigning my seat in the House this fall as well? I have to go out and check on that, see if I should stay on."

Gillian's quizzical face showed she did not understand Neil's logic for having to rush off to his district now. "But you only said you would be resigning to study. Since then you've run for the leadership and ... " She paused, then finished calmly. "Well, of course, Neil, you should stay on; if for no other reason than that we'll need that sessional pay when the House opens again in the new year."

At noon, Neil dressed and carried a small overnight bag out to his car. He drove towards his district. For several hours, with increasing depression, he thought of the future. He had none that he wanted. Those few more years before he took over from Clapp, the years that people used to talk about, were a joke now. Even if the possibility still existed, he could not stand the thought of those tedious years of waiting. The idea of practising law day after day, year after year, brought on nausea. And he couldn't pursue his studies as originally intended: the university year had already started, he had not applied anywhere, and he had no money, anyway.

More and more, the large debts he had incurred and his inability to pay them off without years of unloved work lay heavy on his mind. His other choices of going personally bankrupt, or of going begging to Touchings for help, were equally burdensome. His devastating defeat – his idiotic diatribe, in the place of a gracious concession speech, on Clapp's victory – his certainty that Clapp would be after his hide – his months of flat-out effort to accomplish nothing but the exposure of his puny political weakness ... all of these were individual, crushing weights. On top of it all was Gillian's lack

282

of any real interest in what he was trying to do, and Jane's growing (but unwarranted) animosity. And there was his father, who failed to support his only son, simply because he considered that son's action stupid .... By the time Neil saw the road sign indicating the turn-off to his own district, the thought of listening to a constituent had become unbearable. He passed the intersection at full speed and drove on. He was going to Spirity Cove.

Neil stopped only three times during the eight hour drive – twice for gas, and once for a soft drink that he asked an attendant to bring him. He never got out of the car. At last he came to Spirity Cove and parked on the edge of the Folkly Rooms. On shaking legs, he began to walk across the moor in the dark, scarcely breathing the buffeting wind. Sometimes, in the valleys, he slipped off the firm ground and sank to his ankles in mud. After his foot once touched the ground half a yard below where he expected it to be and he fell hard on his side on stones, he proceeded in a crouch, feeling ahead with his hands for detritus and scree, using the occasional break-through of moonlight for the long view.

He was trying to remember how much time had passed since his start across these barrens, when he realized he had lost all sense of direction, as well. Gravity was no help because there were so many small ups and downs in the general slope. He kept still for a minute and waited for the moon to come out again. It did not appear and he decided to press on in the direction he faced. A few halting steps later, in a lull between gusts of wind, he heard the roar of the sea directly beneath his feet. He looked down into the black and saw, in a sudden short flash of light, the broken reflection on distant waves below of the clouds that were scudding wildly past the moon. He concluded that this was the end of his life, as obscure and meaningless as the death of any of the extinct Beothucks who had used this high head of land to look out at the islands, the Inner and the Offer Bons Phoques, for signs of their own prey. And he did not care.

These thoughts did not endure beyond his realization that he had not tumbled over the cliff. Automatically, he had dropped backwards to safety. In the next burst of moonlight he saw the place near the cliff where he had sat in the natural chair of stone. He made his way to it, slumped down, and leaned his head back against the rock. An abysmally defeated past and an odiously dark future filled his mind. When there were breaks in the wind he listened, but he could not distinguish the beat of the sea below from the pulse of blood surging in his ears. A kinship called. So easy, he thought, to avoid the hard. So easy to reach restful, soft oblivion. The one way so hard and so hard. The other way so soft and so easy. To float blissfully down. He closed his eyes and emptied his mind of these attractive why-not thoughts. An image of Gillian with Anne in her arms and Elizabeth clinging to her leg, formed and faded.

Ecky's Fish down over the Rooms. Neil reflected on the conversation he'd had with his father several months before, when he had first begun to fear that Ernest was not going to get behind him on his leadership attempt. He had not been able to fathom the basis of the bond to Clapp which would keep Ernest from supporting his own son, and had gone at the subject indirectly, including in his question a slap at Clapp's loyalty:

"I've always been curious, father, about why you played such a prominent role in Percy Clapp's separation referendum. Was it just your old friendship with him or was it, as Percy told me, because you're frightened of some powerful evangelical group from the mainland taking over here?"

"Ha, ha," Ernest had said. "Good old Percy. Always looking for the ulterior motive. No, it was neither of those reasons. It was just sentiment on my part. Pure nostalgia.

"You know how I met your mother. I had left Pickeyes when I finished school and came to St. John's alone with a little money from a summer's fishing. I wanted to train to become a teacher but I didn't have enough money and I would have to spend a year working first. I fell in with Percy Clapp while I was going around looking for a job. He was a reporter for the paper then, and wanted to help, he said, this young kindred spirit from the bays. Do you know where Percy comes from?"

"No," Neil had replied, wishing his father would get on

with it so that he could work on changing his mind about neutrality. He certainly didn't want to talk about Clapp.

"Nobody does," Ernest had nodded. "And Percy won't say. Fifty places have claimed him for this reason or that. Perhaps that's why he won't say. He brought me home with him, Neil, when I had no one in the world to turn to. He finally got a lawyer friend to take me on as an articled clerk. I was advised to make better sounds when I opened my mouth, and in five years I would be a lawyer myself.

"It was there that I first met your Grandfather Priddle. He was the client of another law firm – your good friend, Albert Toope's, in fact. My law firm was on the other side of a transaction with your grandfather, and I was brought in on it for experience. It was a long, drawn-out affair, and your grandfather had to make frequent visits from Spirity Cove to St. John's. He often had your mother with him. She, and the surplus profits from his fish exporting business which he would invest under the administration of Toope's firm, appeared to be his life's chief delights. Old Eric Priddle took an instant liking to me as I did to his daughter. 'Eck,' he pronounced his name." Ernest pondered. "There seems to be an inability among the people on that shore to pronounce the letter 'r' between vowels."

It was, Neil thought, a sometimes distressing inability. He remembered the time when he was twelve or thirteen and there were four other Boy Scouts in his house waiting for his father to drive them to Swift Current to try for their canoeing badges. A half a dozen times, his mother, as she bustled about making sure the boys had everything they needed, referred to the river as Swift Cu'nt, oblivious of the boys' sniggers and her son's increasing mortification. All day on the river the boys had yelled back and forth about how much they loved to be on the Swift Cu'nt, to get their paddles into the Swift Cu'nt, and so on in that vein, and Neil had tried to laugh along with them.

"Anyway," Ernest had continued, "throughout the negotiations your grandfather was forever turning to me, even though I was on the other side. He'd say, 'The young fellow knows what I mean. He's one of us. First person I ever met in a

St. John's law office I could have a sensible talk to.' Eck Priddle, your mother, and I became close friends.

"The upshot was that I wrote your mother a letter of proposal. She wrote back, answering yes, and invited me to visit them in Spirity Cove. There, old Eck showed me around his magnificent business premises down near the beach by the Folkly Rooms, and expressed his pleasure at having me for a son-in-law – a son, really, he said, because he only had two daughters.

"Your mother and I got married and moved into an apartment in St. John's. Your grandfather transferred his legal and financial affairs from Toope's firm to the one I was with. He made me his St. John's agent and set in train the arrangements for me to become his full partner when I was admitted to the Bar as a lawyer two years hence. He placed a substantial portion of his investments in a trust fund for your mother and me and our children to come. I loved my beautiful young wife beside me, and she loved me. Oh, the flights of self-congratulation I had those nights, Neil! A life of quality lay ahead for all of us.

"A few months later, when the bottom dropped out of the international fish market again, I thought nothing of it. Eck Priddle had been through that kind of thing before and had survived intact. I was surprised, therefore, when Toope called in at our law office, got us all in the library, and flung a telegram down on the table for us to read. It was addressed to his law firm: 'Priddle undone stop Hold for us all assets wherever situate stop.'

"Toope said: 'A terrible waste. They used eleven words when they could have got the special lower rate for ten. Is it any wonder, Godwin, that there is such dreadful shrinkage in assets once the trustee in bankruptcy takes over!' I was too stunned to reply. Toope grinned and said: 'This is the beauty of being a lawyer in our whipsaw economy, Godwin. We lawyers are the midwives, witchdoctors, and undertakers of legal entities, assisting at their births when the economy is up, muttering mumbo-jumbo over their efforts to survive when the economy is stable, and burying their carcases when the economy is down – each time for a fat fee.' He had reverted to the mocking tone he had always used with me before I had stolen his best client. 'Unless, of course,' he said, 'a lawyer, or a would-be lawyer, is so closely connected with a client that he gets buried, too. I assume you'll accept service of this petition for Priddle's bankruptcy I've filed in Supreme Court, Godwin. You'll note in the partial list of assets to be held for creditors that trust fund he vainly tried to set up for you and your bride and the issue of your bodies.'

"I fired the file at Toope's smirking face, ignored the demands from the members of my own firm that I come back and apologize to their brother at the Bar, went home, got your mother, and left for Spirity Cove."

"Sorry, father," Neil had broken in, "but that's my driver blowing his horn out there. I've got to leave for a meeting. You've often mentioned Grandfather Priddle's bankruptcy to me and I'm certainly interested in picking up all the details a little later on. Right now, before I go, I was wondering if you could give some thought to how you might help – "

"Didn't you ask me why I supported the separation referendum?" Ernest had shot out. "That's what I'm trying to tell you. Did you know that it was Newfoundland's Confederation with Canada that caused your grandfather to go under?"

"Ah, no, I didn't. That's intriguing. Er, father, on this leadership thing – "

"Yes," Ernest had continued, "that was the root cause. I talked to Eck's bank manager afterwards, and he told me that following the referendum to join Canada, Priddle had studied the treaty arrangements between Canada and the market countries for his fish, and he found that the Canadian treaties were much more restrictive, and allowed fish into the markets on less favourable terms and with greater tariffs, than the treaties we ourselves had with those countries. In his usual, perspicacious way, Eck prepared for Confederation. He decided to increase his volume of business substantially for a short period, bought more fish, hired ships and trucks to carry it, made commitments, drew on an enormous line of credit to finance the increase, all to make sufficient money to tide his company over the rough period of readjustment which would follow Confederation with Canada. He was protected by take-or-pay contracts with buyers and middle-men in the market countries. It was a reasonable scheme and he was encouraged to do it by the bankers who put up the money. The only problem was that at precisely the same time, an unforeseeable glut of fish, unprecedented in size, developed in several other supplying countries. Eck was caught unable to unload his fish. Buyers in the market countries with whom he had take-or-pay contracts refused to take and refused to pay. 'Sue me,' they all said. Even then, he would have been able to weather the crisis; but his financiers got worried over the possible implications of the operation of the upcoming disadvantageous Canadian treaties which Eck himself had told them about, and pulled the plug when he was at his most vulnerable. Sad, sad, sad. If it were not for Confederation with Canada, you and your sister would have been worth between you today – conservatively, and in the normal course of events – half of ten million dollars. Independent. Doing what you want. Sucking up to no one. Not having to rely on anyone for anything. Go your own proper way. Sad, sad, sad. You wonder why my heart and mouth, at least, were with Percy on the separation referendum. An irrational pursuit of what might have been, that's all."

"Yes, father, I realize there's a strong bond between you and Percy based on the past, but in the future I need your –"

"Your mother and I arrived in Spirity Cove two days later by train and taxi, and went to Eck's house. Your mother's sister cheered us with: 'It's finished. He's finished. We're finished.' I asked where he was. 'Down by the Rooms with the fish,' she said. My heart leaped with hope as I ran down. When I rounded the corner to run along the Lower Path, the stench nearly knocked me down. There, on the beach, was a small mountain of fish, heaving and tissing with maggots. And on top of the heap, crawling around on his hands and knees, was Eric Priddle, J.P. I put my sleeves over my nose and mouth and went as close as I could to the pile. I could hear Eck counting to himself. Twice, he plunged his hands and forearms deep into the loosening guts and raised his arms high over his head, spilling handfuls of maggots like nuggets of gold onto his head and shoulders, and gurgling low in his throat, unable to hide some self-satisfied inner gloat. He took no notice of my calls.

"Eck's handyman came out of one of the sheds on the wharf and said: 'He's gone cracked, boy. The carriers had their reefer trucks dump the fish as soon as they got word what had happened three days ago. Nice time to do it, too; right in the middle of the hottest August we've had for years. This morning Mr. Priddle climbed up there, and he won't come down.'

"I told a boy to run up and get Eck's daughters. Then, the handyman and I put on long rubbers and waded across the rot. Coaxing proved futile, and we had to lay rough hands on the filthy, squirming body of the king of the Spirity Cove shore and pluck him off the lively slime. He finally kept still when his two daughters took him by the hands and gently led him home. I hung back by the mountain of fish and watched them walk along the deserted pathway, the daughters softly tugging their father forward by the hands, but waiting patiently whenever he would squat down to pick up something that sparkled or gleamed in the dust. They disappeared; and then reappeared in the distance on the Upper Path. I was struck by the shrunk size of the old man, a youngster between the two women, possessing now none of the nimbus of authority, wealth, drive, intelligence .... It was this sight that made me draw, right there and then, a radical distinction between Eck Priddle and myself: I would never, I vowed, never, never, never – come what heaven or hell might send – be defeated like that. Never!"

Neil had left his father to muse on what appeared to be a more aching than jubilant remembrance; and now, on his natural chair of stone near the cliffs of Folkly Rooms, Neil turned his eyes in the direction of Ecky's Fish and sat and thought. The moon came out and stayed, illuminating the sea and the land and the scattered clouds with a beauteous, depthless sheen. By its light, Neil got up and walked straight down over the Rooms. Near the bottom he saw Muck Barrows clambering up, slipping and stumbling. Neil called out, then waited as Muck ran up to him.

"Jesus, Neil, are you all right?" Muck was breathless.

"Where did you come from, Muck?"

"When Gillian told me you were headed for your district, I knew you were bullshitting her. There was no way you were going to listen to howling constituents right now. I knew that. So I took off after you right away. I drove along the highway looking for your car and turned off down here. I sort of knew you'd end up in this place." He eyed Neil anxiously. "How'd you like the bum fucks?"

"How'd I like *what*?" asked Neil, wondering if he'd yet emerged from the unreality of the last few hours.

"The islands off the cliff. Was there enough light to see them?"

"Oh, the Bons Phoques!" Neil grinned. "For a moment there I thought you were asking me how I liked what they did to me at the convention."

They laughed. "The Bum Fucks is what they call them around here," Muck informed him, looking much relieved by Neil's lightness of mood. Neil was thankful that his mother had never felt the urge to describe the geographical features of the area of her birth to his Boy Scout troop.

"Neil ... " Muck was surveying him up and down. "You've got mud and twigs all over you. My God, you must be absolutely exhausted by all this. Do you need any help?"

Neil's answer was to stride vigorously forward.

"Neil, for Christ's sake, watch those rocks! If you killed yourself, it would take me a good eight hours to plug that gap in my organization, so be careful, hey."

Neil turned to display his appreciation of Muck's humour, and walked on energetically. Muck trotted to catch up. "Listen, Neil, you haven't decided on anything yet, have you? I wanted to talk to you before you made up your mind too firmly. I tell you what. I'll give my car to one of the boys here to bring along later. I'll drive your car back and we can have a talk and you can sleep in the back seat. That suit you, Neil?"

Neil nodded as he strode. He loved Muck.

Several miles out of Spirity Cove, Muck turned to Neil who was sitting beside him. "That speech of yours at the end of the convention ... You know, there was a favourable reaction to that everywhere. I talked to people on the phone last night and this morning. No one thought you were a lousy loser. Everyone thought it took real guts to do that. Even a couple of ardent Clappers on the open line show this morning had to admit you had nothing to gain by doing it, and that you were therefore sincere. No one is saying a word against you. The paper *praised* you."

"That's nice, Muck." Neil switched on the radio and listened to music for half an hour. A news spot came on: "Premier Clapp predicts that Clyde Ferritt will be our next premier after he steps down." Then Clapp's voice: "Anyone who could do so well at the leadership convention as Mr. Ferritt did – with no campaigning and no money-spending at all but simply because of his established reputation for brilliance, hard work, and dedication – *must* rise to the very top of our political structure. This is the young man, remember, who so badly beat the other two and who came second in the leadership. Second to me alone. Oh yes, it must be obvious to everyone now that Clyde Ferritt will be our next prime minister. I see no one on the political horizon who can remotely approach Mr. Ferritt. It is very clear to me that he is the one."

Muck and Neil drove in silence for a while, and then they looked at each other and laughed like two schoolboys. "What are you planning to do now?" Muck asked.

"Oh, I don't know, Muck." In fact, Neil did know; but he didn't want to say anything about it yet, in case everything looked different again in the morning. "I'll have a little snooze in the back seat and then think it over." He climbed over the seat and stretched out.

Lying on his back and waiting for sleep, Neil visualized himself as top dog …. He is in his conference room surrounded by trusted advisers, each of whom is throwing advice at him. He has been agonizing for days on some decision which has to be made for the greater good of something or other. It is a true dilemma. But he knows what he has to do. The person or group trying to thwart his good ends has to be destroyed. He gives the order and turns his back to gaze out the window as Muck and the others leave to see to the execution of his edict. He feels the swelling surge of exquisite agony and pleasure in exercising such power over the evil of others to attain his own good ends ....

So energized was Neil by this new and joyous sensation that he could not wait. He sat up on the back seat and said, "Muck, aside from the prospect of unloved work, what is the greatest evil facing the two of us now?"

"Percy Clapp. At least on the local scene. We can deal with the Russians and the Yanks a little later on."

"Right. But if we stay out of politics, Clapp'll probably leave us alone. After that total defeat of mine, he wouldn't consider me much of a threat."

"I suppose, Neil, but –"

"On the other hand, if we challenge him again, there's no telling what the megalomaniac might do in his efforts to atomize me, us, politically – and probably physically."

"You think he's that hard a case, Neil?"

"I do. Just look at what he did to poor old Randolph Rute." Neil nearly added, "and Wolfe Tone McGrath," but stopped himself.

"Let me tell you something, Neil. That's a two-way street. I've done a lot of reading on that stuff. My son, just give me the word."

"I'm not talking about extreme measures, now, Muck. But the idea of us crushing Clapp is certainly more pleasant to contemplate than its converse. Don't you agree?"

"I agree."

"Stop at the next half-decent hotel, Muck. We'll spend the night there. We've got to make plans."

Muck nodded. "Great, Neil, great!" Then he stepped on the gas and whispered, "Oh, the lordy fuck, great!"

They turned off at a motel that, several months before, Neil had left in the middle of the night because the band in the basement bar beneath his room kept vibrating the two pillows off his head. Tonight, he and Muck paid little heed to the tumult below. They talked till long after the banging and wailing had stopped at two-thirty. Then, their plan of action formulated, they put out the lights. Aloud in the dark, each of them freely associated a dozen addenda to the plan – and went to sleep grinning.

Four days after the leadership convention, Jerome Finn, the television reporter, knocked on Neil's door. He had a cameraman with him, and wanted Neil to answer a few questions about his future. Muck had arranged it. While they were setting up, Neil avoided thinking about what he was going to say. Then the camera was switched on, and Jerome turned to him. "Mr. Godwin, it is widely speculated that Prime Minister Clapp will now call an immediate election on the heels of his leadership victory. When asked, Mr. Clapp said there certainly is a future for you in his party. Will you run under Mr. Clapp's banner if an election is called?"

Neil said, "There is no future for anyone in Mr. Clapp's party. There is no future for the country with Mr. Clapp as the leader of the government. I am leaving Mr. Clapp's party and I am joining the Opposition party." As he said it, mingled feelings of salvation and doom passed over him and he had to struggle to hear the next question.

"Will you be running for the leadership of the G.Q. and P. Party?" Jerome was jumping up and down in his scoop.

"I am not interested in leadership for the sake of leadership. I am interested in removing Mr. Clapp from office and replacing him with good government. I shall be running for election as a candidate of the ... ah, other party, when the election is called." Neil had not been sure he'd say the initials of the other party in the right order. He and his former colleagues had always referred to it as The People Last Party.

When he saw Jerome to the door, Neil walked about outside for a moment. He had an uncanny sensation of being in physical control of all the space and time he was moving through, of being able to reach out and mould them to his own requirements. He was certain.

After the story of Neil's defection was aired on the news that night, Clyde Ferritt was interviewed. He said: "Neil Godwin is just a little sooky baby, that's all, who doesn't have the guts to take a bad defeat, and is now picking up his marbles and going home because his political career is in tatters." Neil only laughed.

Between calls from newsmen, his close political associates phoned to say he was crazy. In another few years the leadership was his; there was no rush, he was still very young, and this rat-like ship-jumping would ruin him altogether. The courageous thing to do was to work for a cure of the evils from within; everyone despised a turncoat, especially one who was a lousy loser. His supporters were ready to follow him anywhere within the party – but not right out of a party of which they had been long-time members, into one that was on the point of being wiped out.

Neil merely answered, "The men and women out there will rally behind me no matter what party I'm in. Before this, they had no way to take on Percy. Now they have a way. Not years from now, but right now. Tonight." He seemed to be right. Within the next two days he received hundreds of phone calls and telegrams wishing him well. And this time most of them were not anonymous.

Neil's next step was to go to the lone Opposition member and his party executive. He was welcomed into their party on one condition: that he not seek the party leadership at their own planned convention, if, in fact, they were given a chance to hold it before Clapp called the election. It would be humiliating for them, they said. And it would look too ludicrous altogether if, after losing one leadership race, he ran for theirs almost immediately – especially if he won this one. Neil could see that the party president, who was the main spokesman on the matter, had plans of his own in that direction.

"There will be no election soon," said Neil. "Don't worry about that. Percy knows what I have tapped out there. And as for the leadership of your party, I've already said publicly that I am not interested in leadership. I'm only interested in getting rid of Clapp."

Neil's new party called their leadership convention for several months in the future. In answer to questions about his possible candidacy, Neil stated that he would not seek the leadership. He started his speaking tours once more, but scrupulously absented himself from the meetings to elect

294

delegates. Muck made certain that delegates who would follow Neil's instructions were elected. Most of the Godwin workers from the earlier convention had, in fact, followed him, and were now actively organizing under Muck's direction. People came to help him in droves. His meetings were even larger and more enthusiastic than before. There were numerous draft movements to get him to declare his candidacy, but always he said no. Only at the last hour before the deadline did he reluctantly sign the nomination papers which were attached to a list – prepared by Muck's men and rolled onto the floor of the hall in a wheel barrow – containing eighty thousand names.

Neil won this leadership convention with 97 per cent of the votes cast by delegates.

The next day, Neil went to see his father. It was the first time they'd been together for weeks. Ernest Godwin looked as if he had not seen the sun for a year.

Neil spoke to the point right away: "Father, I need your help. I am under no illusions regarding the strength of my adversary. He's quiet now, but he will be formidable before this is all over. I know he has been your friend for a long time, and that you may think it's terrible of me to put you in this position of having to come down on the side of your son against your friend. But that's the ugly side of politics, I'm afraid. The politics you always encouraged me to get involved in. Anyhow! I know I can count on you to spread the word quietly among your friends." He nearly added "this time," but caught himself, realizing that it would sound sarcastic.

"Neil," said Ernest, after a long silence, "did I ever tell you exactly how I got into religion and became Chief Elder?"

"Well, of course, father, I have a good general idea of how ... about your support, father ... "

"After we hauled your Grandfather Priddle off the fish guts in Spirity Cove and brought him home, your mother and I left for St. John's. When I went back to the law office, the senior partner handed me a small severance cheque with great regret. I had to be let go, he said, because of my assault on Toope, a fellow lawyer.

"I started to look for a job. In vain. I could not get around the fact that I had been fired. I could see the eyes glazing over when I tried to explain the circumstances. Eck Priddle's debts to business houses did not help. Apparently Toope spent days on the phone, badmouthing me to prospective employees. Have you noticed the contempt with which Percy Clapp always treats Toope? That's on account of what Toope did to me. Percy himself couldn't help at the time. He was at one of the occasional low points in his own career and on a book-writing kick. Your mother and I had been more or less feeding him after our marriage."

Neil broke in. "That's something I can't understand, father. Toope has been Clapp's right hand man for years. How were you able to support –"

"Within a month, our little bit of money was gone – spent or sent over to Eck. Payments unmet, your mother bloating with you, me unemployed, we faced the immediate prospect of shelterless hunger. You cannot imagine what it is to be possessed of a sense of dignity, and to hear your eighteen-year-old wife – unperturbed and smiling bravely during the day – bleating in her sleep during the night because of the onset of malnutrition and the near-violent ultimatums of the landlord and fear of the next sunrise …. She said years later that the worst thing for her about those days was listening to *me* lowing in my sleep ….

"Remember when I told you, Neil, that as I watched your grandfather being led home, I vowed that I would never be defeated like that? Well, two months later, when I again visualized that scene – Eck Priddle creeping into the evening gloom, crushed and undone and gnome-like between his daughters, and myself, upright, unyielding, and indomitable, my fist wrung up against the chasm, thinking baleful challenges – I could find little to choose between the two pathetic postures."

"Ecky's Fish is still there," said Neil. "It's a grassy hillock, now." He had been so unsettled by the look on his father's face that he had felt obliged to say something. He was glad to see Ernest's responsive smile, weak though it was.

"Yes," replied Ernest. "They say half the first-born of future

Spirity Cove families got their vital spark behind old Ecky's Fish ....

"Having failed to find an office position, I now put in applications for menial labour jobs, but there was no hope. At the best of times there was a 20 per cent unemployment rate in those sectors, which rose sharply as winter approached. I started going to church in my cornucopia of leisure time, both to the established ones, and to those where theological anarchy held sway. I would sit in the pew, nursing my misery, and allowing my heart to open to a comforting abstraction. It was not a sudden thing, like Saul: but gradually, every day for a month, my vocation grew within me. The children in one church ultimately convinced me there must be something to it. They were nearly all gaunt, sluggish, and pasty-faced, staring dully ahead while their parents clunked into the overflowing collection plate what would have been the milk and meat money if they had been better off.

"It was the elegant simplicity of The Gazers on the Godlike Glory of God's Full Fair and Fearful Face that won my allegiance. I found its sole tenet of faith attractive: God had chosen the members of this sect as the one medium on earth for the expression of truth. I went to see the Chief Elder at the Temple of Truth on Water Street and told him I had been called to be a preacher. He was openly sceptical when he learned my background, but I insisted, so he said he would put my vocation to the test. He supplied your mother and me with a coastal boat ticket to Maggotty Cove. One way.

"A week after our arrival in this place, a freakish change in the direction of the wind blew the fog out to sea for a few minutes. What I then saw made me sincerely repent having earlier cursed in my prayers the most providential mists which draped everything from view most of the time: black bogs; glacier-dropped boulders; twisted, windblown bushes two feet high called trees. The only wildlife consisted of the swarms of blackflies that ascended from the bogs and drove all living things indoors whenever the exterior temperature got warm enough for anyone to comfortably go out. The nearest arable plot and the nearest tree the height of a man were forty miles down the coast in Twillick. Everything was cast in dismal shades of dark greys and dark greens and dark browns. And black.

"In every single year of the remembered history of the place – as I soon found out – the fishery had been pronounced a disastrous failure. But not for lack of effort on the part of the fishermen. Every year they worked, strove, and sought; and every year it was to no avail. There was never any fish. Everyone had to live on the dole. I tried to learn why people had come to live there in the first place, or why, having made that blunder, they stayed. No one seemed to know. But whatever the reason, they were firmly tied by bonds of love and loyalty to those rocks and bogs and that empty, dark grey sea. Perhaps they loved the cove itself, the always safe, still body of water that lay inside the bar of rock and sand. The water joined the ocean through a narrow gut, the Motion. Men talked fondly about what a safe, snug, mooring ground it was inside the bar, and women planned their tasks around the ebb or flow of the tide out or in through the Motion – knowing their men would try to come home when the Motion was coming up and go out to sea when the Motion was going down.

"That's when you were born, Neil; down there in our little shack on the Maggotty Cove Motion, the day after we joined Canada, and nearly a month after we thought you were due. Your mother used to say she didn't blame you for putting it off as long as you could. And that's where you spent the first four years of your life.

"With your birth, I took up my ministerial duties with more energy, preaching in the kitchens of adherents. The same seven faces gazing at me night after night started to unhinge me, so I began to preach in the open air. I had no idea what kind of an impact I was making on my listeners. My sole experience in front of a church congregation before this had been as a flower in a Sunday school concert in Pickeyes in honour of a visit by the Bishop, when, in response to the Sunday school teacher's question, 'Why hup ye little flower, why hup?' I had to answer, 'I'm hup to greet His Grace the Lard Bish-hup!' That was also my introduction to the rhyming couplet." Neil was relieved to see his father grin again. Up to this point, his prevailing expression had been pained.

"Nor did I know how many people were listening to me outside. Sometimes I could see bodies shimmering in the mist. Sometimes I could hear my voice on a quiet evening resounding through the vapours for miles around. Sometimes all sights and sounds would be drowned out by gusts of wind and driving fog.

"One night, out of the fog, a voice asked a question I dreaded to hear. 'Elder Godwin,' it whined, 'I want to ask you by way of no harm, how we *know* we are God's chosen ones in the first place, that's all. Especially seeing as how I finds it the devil's own job to get anyone else to believe it.' I felt like telling the one *hefty* zealot I had in my small flock to flick that blasphemer into the sea – outside the Motion. I was about to utter the usual banality about believing on faith, when the mist lifted a little for a moment and I saw here a wretched shape, there a malformed hulk, a sunken chest, a glintless eye, a shrunken frame, a vacant face, a shivering pelt. The runty, scrawny, skinny lambs on earth! It was the only thought which came into my mind and I was compelled to tell them the truth. And why, if at all, the runty, scrawny lamb would be spared the savage butcher's knife.

"I had hit a credible cord. The next prayer meeting we held in someone's kitchen, about eighty people tried to join in. You've heard me preach the parable of the runty lamb, Neil? Years ago, when you used to come to my church, remember?"

"Yes, father," answered Neil, feeling uncomfortable with the line of questioning, "I remember it very well. It's not that long ago, really. It was a powerful graphic image. It's no wonder they elected you Head G – Chief Elder after you came back to St. John's. Umm, father, do you think you could spread the word among your people this time? I don't mean to mix religion with politics. But, you know, behind the scenes, just as my father, so that they'll know you're with me?"

"By the end of my third year in Maggotty Cove," said Ernest, "everyone there was with me, as well as hundreds up and down the coast. What? What did you just say, Neil? Spread the word around for you? Oh no, my son, wait till I'm finished this. You'll see then why I can't –" His father stopped suddenly, and turned his back.

Neil walked over to try to catch some last whispered words, and saw that Ernest had pushed the four fingers of his left hand deep into his midriff. "What's wrong, father?"

"Nothing's wrong. Go on. Go to that press conference you've called. I've got work to do." Up close, Neil was shocked at how yellow were the whites of his father's eyes.

What is *wrong with him?* Neil wondered as he went. *Does he have an ulcer? I'm the one who should have the ulcer, trying to talk him into getting behind me for a change!*

In fact, Neil was not deeply bothered by his father's continuing failure to help his political cause. Everything was going well. The press was good; editorial comment was excellent. Money was flowing to Neil's party in large quantities (the generosity of contributors having been stimulated by the published results of independent polls which showed that Neil was favoured by over half of the decided voters surveyed). And nothing, Neil felt as he campaigned, could diminish his vigour, or deflect him from his purpose, or affect his certitude now.

18

"My son, Neil," laughed dying Ernest Godwin. "My son, the great one. The great man to be. E. Neil Godwin, 'E' for what? Emperor? Emperor Neil. Could be. Why, look how he sits there across the room, aloof from us and eminent. Not a bad pretence to dignity for one who was ditch-delivered into this, the cess-pit of the empire."

Hunched around the deathbed, Ernest Godwin's elders shifted uneasily in their chairs and emitted dry chuckling sounds. Their eyes drifted in Neil's direction, but showed no mirth.

"This land, this country," continued Ernest. "The sport of historic misfortune, she's been called for pathos. The Cinderella of the empire, she's been called, for hope. A splotch of gullshit on the imperial crown, I call her, for truth. And for the sake of my famous son, here, who is bubbling and heaving to the top of this standing pool, intent on setting himself above all the other squirming excremental maggots herein spawned by the grace of God."

By now, the retinue had unfolded from their cluster. One or two were half-standing. They seemed not to like their Chief Elder's dying words: the metaphors of place, foul and laboured; the misplaced belittling of Neil's political efforts, without a word on his theological straying; the calculated blasphemy from the Almighty's top man on earth. They all looked to Neil to deal with this. He put on an indulgent face and gently waved them back into their huddle around his father.

The nurse's entry ended the short silence. "Time for your shot now, sir," she said softly. The elders used this opportunity to bid hurried *adieus* and to scuttle towards the door where they jostled to get out. On an afterthought, one of them made an about-face, shook hands with Neil, and whispered a formula of encouragement. The others did the same, and left.

"There they go, the genetic degenerates," declared Ernest, while most of them were still within earshot, "taking off like scalded cats. Don't you go yet, Neil. No, miss, no shot now. A little later on."

"You've got to, sir," said the nurse, directing her words to Neil. "It's already past the regular time. It'll stop the pain again."

"I said, no. No shot yet. Don't go, Neil."

The nurse kept her pleading eyes on Neil. "In a few minutes," he said.

She smiled grimly and went out.

Neil sat down again and waited for his father to speak. When he didn't start, Neil cast around for something to say. "I enjoyed your little talk to the elders just then, father," he lied.

"Did you really? Good, good. I may make some headway with you after all. Did I sound too much like Percy Clapp to suit you, by the way? I had the feeling I did. So long his friend, I guess."

Neil had to turn away from the torment expressed, not in his father's face, which looked beatific, or in his words, which sounded strong, but in the involuntary contracting and expanding of parts of his body beneath the sheet, like the movements of an independent thing unconnected with his head. Neil wondered if the sickness had reached his brain. Certainly, Ernest's apparent disdain for country and elders was a perplexing reversal of past attitudes. Neil hoped there would be no moments of derangement before church colleagues that might destroy the memory of a lifetime of good works and piety.

"Ah ... father ... " said Neil. "The elders seemed to be a little shocked by your choice of language, however. Is your illness affecting your, say, mental outlook? Do you –"

"I'm nearly dead, Neil. I'll never arise alive from this bed. I

302

don't have to be good anymore. I can be truthful again at last."

Oh, gentle God, thought Neil in profound sorrow. *Don't tell me he's losing his faith at the end, when it should give him comfort and support.* He said: "I'll get the nurse now, father. I must go and let you rest."

"I can help you, Neil, you who need no help. I can show you the way."

Neil kept his eyes on the bright face and away from the spasmodic jerks and twitches under the sheet. "I'm going to get the nurse *now*, father," he announced, and walked quickly to the door. "We can talk later. I can't stand to see you in such ... There's no need for you to suffer."

"Percy Clapp, whom you are about to defeat and de-throne," went on Ernest. "I've given you no help or support since you began to take him on. Percy was a great friend, my saviour in the early days."

Neil put his hand on the doorknob to steady himself. *Stop! Please stop. That's nothing now, nothing!* he shouted inside his head. But aloud he said, "Sure, that's all right, father. It'll probably make no difference in the long run. You don't have to explain or apologize for that in any way. My goodness, I had to stand on my own two feet, sure."

"That's not why I didn't help you, though. You're very busy campaigning these days but a few hours with me before I go will give you insight for life. I know what you are, where you come from, where you should go. I know all that, Neil."

From the door, Neil's full perspective of the frail wreck on the bed and the sound of the imploring words totally over-whelmed him with pity. He returned and touched the back of his father's hand. It felt like a rose petal to his fingertips. He closed his eyes to keep back the tears. He would stay in spite of the pain, if that was what was wanted. He gave his father's hand a gentle squeeze, and held it.

Ernest opened his mouth and a lugubrious howl came out of the round, dark hole. It ceased only when he had suc-ceeded in jerking his hand away from Neil's grasp. The sudden horrid awareness that his father's anguished wail had been caused by his own gesture of love made Neil grope towards the door in startled confusion. But the nurse was already rushing into the room with the hypodermic needle.

Neil waited to say goodbye while the balm went in. He took deep breaths and wondered why the bloody needle didn't hurt. "Sorry about that," whispered Ernest. "It seems to be hammering at every nerve in my body. When will I see you again?"

"Within a week, father. I'll come back within the week. Goodbye for now." He followed the nurse out.

Neil decided to walk the mile to his own house in an attempt to alleviate the misery he felt at the sight of his father. Ernest was home from the hospital, now; and the deterioration in his condition from just ten days before, when Neil had first seen him after the operation, was appalling. He was being devoured from the inside.

Neil asked himself, as he walked, why he had not realized earlier that his father was seriously sick. He felt great remorse for the cold and often surly manner in which he'd treated Ernest during past months because of his lack of political support. *If only I'd known*, thought Neil. *Goddamned politics! It blinds you to everything else but itself, hurts every good relationship in your life.*

He recalled his sudden knowledge that Ernest was finished. It had occurred during another campaign tour, after he had returned to his hotel one evening and had seen that the top message in a waiting stack was an urgent request to call his sister Jane. He had dialled, worried that something had happened to Roland.

Jane herself had answered the phone. "Neil! I've been trying to get you for two days!"

"Sorry, Jane. I wasn't at the hotel last night. We had a meeting eighty miles away and decided to stay at –"

"Neil, they'll be sending dad home from the hospital in a week or so."

"Oh, good!" Neil replied. He had a vague memory of Gillian telling him at home that his father was about to undergo some medical tests.

"Good?" echoed Jane. "Haven't you talked to Gillian yet?"

"No." Neil fanned the telephone messages. Two were from Gillian.

"They opened dad up yesterday morning – I *tried* to get you beforehand – to see what was causing those abdominal and back pains – goddamned doctors!" Neil caught a most unusual choke in Jane's voice. "He's been in bed with the pains for two or three days at a time for months. You've seen the agony he's been in sometimes, his face the colour of a lemon?"

"Yes, yes, I know," Neil had said to these revelations. (Only once had he thought his father might not be well: the fingers in the midriff, the yellow eyeballs.)

"Well, anyway," Jane went on, the firmness back in her voice, "it started in the pancreas. Metastasis had already taken place long ago. They've never seen it spread so fast, they said. It's everywhere. They darned his gut back up and gave him his choice: die in the hospital or die at home."

Neil still remembered how the shock had imploded into his brain and passed through his body. "How long has he got, Jane?" he had asked, stunned. "God, he's only fifty!"

"They don't know. A matter of months at most. Probably weeks. A vital organ could go on him at any time."

"Is he in much pain?"

"They've got him on dope. The doctor said, quote, only the worst pain will be outside the control of modern analgesics, and then only marginally so, unquote. When will I tell dad you'll be back?"

"I'll fix up around here and get back there as soon as humanly possible," promised Neil.

"Tomorrow?"

"Oh, let's see. I've got a half dozen rallies laid on." In his half-daze, Neil had been talking in his politician's knee-jerk way, avoiding being pinned down to a definite commitment which he might not want, or be able to keep, later. "People are counting on me to be there. I'll have to see what meetings I can get out –"

"Neil, in the name of Jesus!"

The line went dead. Neil had sat for a stunned minute, thinking they had been disconnected, vaguely wondering who should call whom back. Then, suddenly realizing what he had said to her, he redialled the number to tell her he would be back in the city on the first flight tomorrow to see their father. But this time there had been no answer.

He had to explain to Jane why he had seemed so callous that night on the phone, Neil thought now, as he walked home. He should have done it earlier. It had been months since he'd talked to Jane at length; yet he met with Roland on fund-raising nearly every week. His relationship with his sister, once so close, had become another casualty of the demands of politics. He *had* to get close to her again. Soon. But then, remembering what had happened to her during the past months, Neil wondered if that was even possible any more ....

The peace that had been established between Jane and Roland after their first violent fight had been precarious from the start. For several weeks, Roland had reported that Jane's behaviour had been marked with emotional outbursts. Gillian, noticing how gaunt Jane looked, despite her pregnancy, had urged her more than once to tell her gynecologist about the vague and undefined symptoms of illness she was experiencing. The doctor's only response (Gillian had informed Neil with some irritation), had been to say, "Well, Jane, you *are* having a baby, you know. You can't expect to carry on like a swinging single, on the town every night."

A week after that particular visit, Jane had had a miscarriage. There had been days of severe pain and bleeding, followed by a long period of depression. Although the depression had finally lifted, Jane had continued to have attacks of anxiety over trifles, attacks which increased in frequency and duration as time went on. For weeks after Jane's miscarriage, Roland had spent most of his spare time with her. But then his own work and Neil's campaign began to keep him away from home twelve or fourteen hours every day. Eventually, he began to take advantage of many opportunities to stay away from the apartment unnecessarily, and Neil, when he noticed, could hardly blame him. Jane's behaviour *was* tiresome and irritating. It was often also extremely embarrassing.

Neil had happened to be home on the night Gillian had finally discovered what was wrong. He had been in his study, while the two women sat talking in the living room. Jane was summarizing the series of useless visits she had been making to physicians, when, in one breathless spiel, she mimicked the doctors' questions:

"How does your husband treat you? Is your sex life with him satisfactory? What is your husband doing to make you so unhappy? How often do you have sex with him? Have you ever cheated on your husband? Don't you think you should try and have another baby? Wouldn't that build up your ego a little and make you feel less unfulfilled? Does your husband dominate you too much or too little? Have you been taking your little green pills regularly? Don't you think your voracious eating habits, your anxiety, and your jumpiness are a sign that you need more affection? Have you ever considered an affair?"

Neil had heard Jane take a deep breath before she continued. "Not *one* of the bastards thinks there's anything physically wrong with me! They hardly even examine me. No. That's not true. One of the younger ones, just out of med school, studied my crotch minutely and pinched my boobs at great length!" With unnerving suddenness, Jane had burst into tears and then, just as suddenly, stopped. Neil, coming to the door of the study, had seen her look up at Gillian with her hands on her face. "I'm always drenched with sweat, I can't stop shaking, I can't sleep, I can't stop eating, I'm nervous all the time," she said in rapid staccato. "Oh, Gillian, Gillian, I think I am going –"

"My God, Jane!" Gillian had interrupted. "Your eyes!"

"What is it?" Neil had come anxiously into the room.

"Look at her eyes. When her face was still for a moment I noticed.... They're popping out of her head. A friend of mine in London was like that." Gillian had turned firmly back towards Jane. "I think you've got an over-active thyroid."

And that was what it had been. Jane had had herself referred to an internist for specific tests. They showed that she had hyperthyroidism – and that she had probably had it for the past year or more. Treatments were prescribed and the condition was under control within a month.

Neil had had no chance of finding out if the curing of her physical illness would change Jane's attitude towards him and his political activity. When, shortly after her successful diagnosis, Roland himself began to feel unwell, the contrast between the treatment given her and her husband renewed all her fierce bitterness. Roland's symptoms were as undefined as hers had been, and Jane had warned him about the kind of questions he could expect from his doctor. Roland told Neil that she had joked with him when he left for his appointment. "When he asks about your sex life," she had laughed, "you'd better say I'm good in bed. If I could lie like a trooper about you, you should be able to tell the truth about me!" But the doctor had shown no interest in Roland's sex life. Instead, he immediately subjected him to a battery of physical tests. Within forty-eight hours, he reported that Roland was suffering from hypertension, gave its physical cause, and prescribed a cure. By the end of that week, Roland's blood pressure had been perfectly under control.

This disparity in medical approach, which depended, as Jane saw it, on the sex of the patient, made her permanently angry. By this time, Neil had become involved in consolidating himself with the Opposition, and one night he was at Roland's apartment, going over the budget, when Jane came home from one of her evenings on the town. She treated them both coldly; and when Neil tried to open a friendly conversation, she had turned on him.

"Don't try to sweet talk me, you bastard!" she said, speaking in soft and even tones. "You're all alike – except *you're* worse than the rest. You didn't give one sweet goddamn when I was sick. You avoided me like the plague. You thought I was acting just like a woman, didn't you? A whining, female hypochondriac. You're as bad as Roland, there."

"I didn't think that," objected Roland, trying to be authoritative, his guilty face showing clearly that he *had* thought that.

"Don't hand me that shit again, Roland!" Jane said, speaking as softly as before. "You didn't lift a finger. Face it! You just didn't care. You were more concerned with Neil's grab for power than you were about your sick wife. And brother Neil over there never gave me a thought from start to finish. Did you, dear brother?"

"Jane, that's not –"

"You are two, self-centred pricks," continued Jane with eerie quietness and control. "Like all the rest of the glorious males of the species: nothing on your minds except how to get ahead of the next man – when you're not thinking about how to stick it into the next woman.

"What a piece of work is man! Look at the two of us Neil. You and me. I'm as intelligent as you are: my marks at university here were *better* than yours. But who was pulling strings to get *me* into Oxford University? I can talk circles around you; I know as much as you do; I've certainly got as much guts and integrity as you! But was anyone pushing me into a famous career at the Bar, or calling on me, as a natural leader, to assume the mantle of greatness? No. No one! And why not? Because I've got these tits. See? Nice squishy tits. And I've got nothing hanging between my legs. Look! Not a sign of doodad or dangles, anywhere. *That's* why not. 'They look like identical twins, Ern,' says Percy Clapp. 'The male and female counterparts of the one person. Plato should be here.' Ho, ho, ho. I'm fed up with the whole bloody lot of you! You can all go pack yourselves. And I'm finished with you two altogether." She walked, calm and poised, out of the room.

After that, Jane did and said whatever she liked whenever she liked. She frequented the drinking holes in the city, though not, apparently, for the companionship of the men there. Any male who approached was driven off with an insult as she kept, exclusively, to the company of women. She used her apartment like a hotel, sometimes staying away for days at a time, coming home only for a bath or a quick change of clothes or a morning's sleep. And then she would be gone again.

Once, Neil had suggested to Roland that, for the peace of mind of all three of them, he and Jane should quietly separate. But Roland wouldn't hear of it. He felt largely to blame for the problem he said; and he continued to love Jane dearly. He was sure that she would change ....

Perhaps, thought Neil, as he strolled home from his father's house, Jane would see from Ernest's experience that male doctors did not restrict their blundering diagnoses to their female victims. Perhaps *that* would change her attitude. Without great hope, he began to think of ways of rebuilding a close relationship with Jane. But a picture of Ernest on the bed kept recurring in his mind. He speeded up his stride and blanked out all thoughts, concentrating, instead, on his surroundings. He became aware of the looks of recognition he was getting from people in passing cars. He saw his name mouthed as heads swivelled, and cars slowed to allow a better gape. Many people made the sign of the V. When Neil began to acknowledge their waves, some opened their car windows and shouted variations on "Give it to old Percy, Neil!" or "Keep 'er going, Neil, you'll do it!" The driver of one car showed Neil his middle finger, while the passenger stuck his head out the window and bellowed, "Go fuck yourself, Godwin, you're not worth the sweat off Percy's bag!" Academically, Neil judged the informal poll favourable – despite the fervour of the last sentiment expressed.

When Neil came near his house, he glimpsed Gillian's face in an upstairs window. By the time he reached the gate, she and Elizabeth were out to greet him. Little Elizabeth used his limbs and head as a jungle-gym for a few minutes, and then ran back to the television. Gillian put her clasped hands on his shoulder as they walked into the house, discussing his father.

Inside, she passed him a glass of wine and he hugged her with his free arm. "Read this editorial," she said. "It might take your mind off your father for a while." She handed him the afternoon paper.

The piece was headed up, "The New and the Bright in the Nick of Time." It stated that E. Neil Godwin was presenting a formidable and, it was believed and devoutly hoped, an unbeatable challenge to the kakistocracy of Percy Clapp. There was no comparison, after all, between the lives and parts of these two public figures. For while Godwin had been a brilliant scholar at that acme of institutionalized intellectual attainment, Oxford University in England, Clapp was such that any area of high-minded human thought was sullied by his bare entry. Godwin was no mere politician like Clapp, either, but a professional man of great ability and integrity – something dramatically shown during his short but revealing career as an activist lawyer before going into full-time politics.

Godwin's physical and moral bravery was unassailable: as evidenced, at home, by his very opposition to Percy Clapp's might, and abroad by his fact-finding visit to Vietnam, then, as now, in the throes of the Communist takeover – surely a risk-fraught odyssey for one unaccustomed to concealing his vision of the truth.

Was incorruptibility a desirable trait in a leader? Godwin's attributes in that regard had been amply demonstrated, both when he had been a member of Clapp's own government, and when he had later repudiated that government the moment he had seen the skulduggery going on within it (during a period, incidentally, in which the abandonment of Clapp had been by no means a popular or safe course to pursue).

There was a reference to his charming and attractive wife, Julian – "You've even got the gay vote wrapped up now," laughed Gillian – a bulwark of support in all his political travails.

The peroration of the editorial was: "Out with the old and the tainted, Percy Clapp, aged sixty-eight and in with the new and the bright, E. Neil Godwin, aged twenty-eight, into whose hands we can entrust our billions of dollars of forthcoming wealth from offshore oil resources. It is in this light that we say, 'Yes! And just in the nick of time.'"

Neil marvelled that small kernels of mundane half-truths could be enveloped so thickly with mythic grandeur. The irony was that he himself had never done anything active to perpetrate these myths. Nor, admittedly, had he ever done anything to dispel them. Passive dishonesty was the quintessence of political success, he thought. Jesus! Two weeks ago that fulsome editorial would have had him jumping up and down in joy at the triumph of truth. Here it was now, making him create cynical aphorisms with a Lear-like clarity of vision.

When Gillian had refilled his glass with wine, he gently pulled her onto his lap and kissed her tenderly. This was what was important and real in life, he thought: their love for one another. After one of their kisses had lasted a good half minute, Neil said, "Let's nip upstairs for a nap."

311

"I'm certainly in the mood for one if you are," grinned Gillian, tugging him to his feet. "We do have two weeks of sinful celibacy to atone for. I'll make sure the girls are all right in the playroom for a while. I will permit of no disturbance while you regale my receptive body with your creative, masculine variety of kinks, straights, and quirks."

That was the way she usually talked when she was writing for a women's magazine, thought Neil. She must be working on another article. But he didn't even know that for sure, he realized. He'd paid too little attention. He took her by the hand when she came back, and she led him up the stairs. How lovely she was. How finely tuned they were to each other. What good fortune it was for them to have one another!

After a long, leisurely time, they lay deliciously tangled together on the bed, having done most of the things to each other that were their secret little delights.

"Let's go out to dinner tonight, Gillian," Neil suggested. "Just you and I."

"Sounds nice. What about your finance committee meeting?"

"Shag the finance committee. I'll call Roland and tell him I can't make it."

Gillian was up and bubbling like a girl who had just unexpectedly been invited on the date of her dreams. "I'll call mother. She'll take the kids. She always loves to have them overnight. We can drop them off on the way." Neil grabbed her hand as she passed the bed and hugged her.

When Neil and Gillian walked to their table in the restaurant, all conversation stopped. Everyone looked at them. Some people waved. After they were seated, many diners stole frequent glances at them; and for a few minutes, Neil's whispered name threatened to drown out the muzak.

They ate and drank and talked quietly. Occasionally, a couple would stop at their table on the way out, introduce themselves if neither Neil nor Gillian already knew them, and wish Neil well. Neil was relaxed and content and he drank wine and liqueurs freely without giving the matter a thought. Gillian, enjoying herself, was happily imbibing as well.

At the same time that Neil realized he was drunk, he

became aware of remarks directed at him by a groggy-looking man sitting with a woman at a nearby table. It was the usual spiteful stuff spewed out by partisans of Percy Clapp. But because of the mood that had come on him today, and because of his present, blurred state, it all struck Neil as being incredibly stupid. His usual methods of dealing with such diatribes was to ignore them or treat them jocularly. Tonight he did neither. Instead, he flung some insulting names at the man in language that started spicy and became ever more foul as the exchange proceeded and the man joined issue with him on each intake of breath. The scene was loud and unpleasant. Several times, Neil was conscious of gasps from patrons around him, and of Gillian's hand tight on his arm. Finally, he acceded to her request that he leave with her.

Gillian drove the car home. "Great dinner," she commented acidly. "Just you and I! There's no such thing as just you and I in this bloody politics racket. Do you ever ask yourself if it's worth it?" Neil remained silent.

At home, he said, "Sorry I made a complete arse of myself there at the end, Gillian."

Gillian grunted and went into the bathroom; but when she came out, she put her arms around him. "You've had a hard couple of weeks," she murmured. "Beating around the country. Your father getting so sick. It's no wonder you over-reacted a little tonight. Don't worry about it, Neil. It only made you look more human, less perfect. I'd watch that booze, though. You're not used to it."

The next morning, as he set out for another seven days of campaigning, Neil realized that the vague feeling of indefinite foreboding and unfocussed regret aroused during the past week had now become centred in his mind: encapsulated, lumpish, immovably heavy. Thoughts of the essential point-lessness, the ultimate vanity of what he had dedicated himself to had penetrated his trance-like certainty.

The certainty of the sleepwalker was how he privately described the single-minded sureness he had possessed from the beginning of this campaign. But now a large element of doubt had slid into its place. Ten days ago he had been confident. And today, as he again left St. John's, he was sure of

313

nothing. It was strange how such a reversal in outlook could take place in him as a result of a happening unrelated to the subject of his certainty or doubt. It was depressing, too, how his entire attitude had changed with the turn-around in outlook. When he had been certain, the ingredients of politicking – the repetitive speech-making, the constant hand-shaking, the receipt of abuse, the ass-licking, the litanies of identical complaints, the insoluable heart-rending problems, the endless travelling, the exhaustion – had not bothered him in the least. At worst, he had felt neutral about them; and often, indeed, he had taken a martyr's satisfaction from the process itself. With the uncertainty that was now lodged in his mind, however, the prospect of another week of it and then another week, stretching into the future towards a doubtful end, presented itself to him as an unabideable ordeal.

He consoled himself with the thought that these doubts would pass. They were caused by the shocking evidence of the pathetic vulnerability of his father, and augmented this morning by last night's unaccustomed intake of booze. They would be replaced again soon by the certitude that made him soar. He fervently hoped so. He could think of no worse torment than to be plagued by doubts over whether he could sustain the effort to attain an end which seemed to hold no further joy for him.

En route to the evening's destination, Neil dropped in on a number of organizers. They were as sanguine as ever, and perked up his own spirits. Late in the afternoon, he stopped off at the Gander airport to pick up the day's newspaper from St. John's.

Early that evening, Muck came into Neil's room at his hotel. He was clearly agitated. He held a newspaper in each hand and stood in the centre of the room.

"What the hell is going on, Neil?" he demanded. "Yesterday we have an editorial taking the hide off Clapp and saying that Godwin's piss is maple syrup and his farts are vaporized *eau de cologne*." He held out the paper in his left hand. "Then, today, one lousy day later, we have madman Mahoney in his column in the same goddamned newspaper saying that the

314

public spectacle Neil Godwin made of himself last night has revealed serious weaknesses in the man!" He held out the paper in his right hand.

"Yes, I read it, Muck," said Neil, affecting nonchalance.

"I thought you went back to see your father. I thought you had a meeting with Maidment and the finance committee last night. What's all this about a vicious big racket in the middle of a restaurant?"

"Muck, I took Gillian out to dinner, okay? A drunk, fanatical Clapper was there and started an argument, all right?"

"Doesn't say a word about that here. I thought you said you didn't drink at all these days. Christ, if *I* can go on the wagon... 'Mr. Godwin, displaying a hitherto well-concealed fondness for a familiar mind-altering drug, i.e. booze, and behaving in a fashion consistent with his exceedingly generous intake –'"

"I told you, Muck, I've already read it."

"'Mr. Godwin, whose cherubic smile and honeyed tongue give the impression that he would not say spit if his mouth was full of it, scorched the air with a display of practised skill in the use of garbage-mouthed expletives – undeleted and undiluted – such as would provoke the admiration of R. Nixon.'"

"I read it I said, Muck."

"'The four letter words came so fast and furious at one point, that one of my informants thought that our would-be statesman had invented a new thirty-two letter swear word. *In vino veritas*, it is said. Well, if it was the true Mr. Godwin that the *vino* brought out last night, then I can only warn the people –'"

"I said I read the fucking thing, Muck!" Neil was out of his chair and had seized Muck near the base of his neck before he actually realized what he was doing. Muck was able to apply enough pressure to the wrists to keep Neil's hands from encircling his throat. Their eyes were inches apart and staring.

"Jesus, I'm sorry, Muck." Neil felt like embracing Muck and kissing him. His lunge at his friend had been the closest thing to violence that he had ever done in his adult life.

"I'm the one who's sorry, Neil. I didn't realize it was needling you so much."

"It was an out-and-out hatchet job," said Neil.

"We've got to expect that, I suppose, now that we've moved ahead of Clapp. It's just too bad they did it arse-foremost. It wouldn't have made the same impression if the shitty article had come out first and the favourable editorial afterwards. Anyway, let's forget it. I was only worried because we're all out here working our little holes off, we've got an ideal candidate, we've got Percy on the ropes, and the thought that we might shag up a sure thing at this point .... I know it's hard going, Neil. I'm amazed you're able to keep at it like this – especially with the news about your father. But listen, Neil, we've got to *keep* it going. If Percy got the idea for one minute that your father's illness was taking the good out of you, that's just the thing that would make him call an election. You know what he's like." Muck stopped and then grinned. "Neil, when this is all over, though, and you're elected premier, *then* here's what you can do. Go on television with a province-wide broadcast to the people, fifteen seconds long: 'My beloved fellow Newfoundlanders. I had to kiss your asses for five months. Now you can all eat my shit for five years. Thank you!'"

Neil and Muck laughed longer and harder at this than either would have considered warranted in other circumstances. Then they left, shoulder to shoulder, for that night's giant rally.

19

That week, Percy Clapp called a snap election for twenty-one days hence, the bare legal minimum. Neil and Muck heard about it on the car radio on the midday news.

Muck stopped the car. Neither of them could believe that Clapp had actually done it. There had been no forewarning whatever, either through media speculation or underground rumours. Objectively, there appeared to be no sense to Clapp's election call now. The polls, at least the last one conducted, showed that Neil was ahead. But that survey had been done nearly a month ago. Perhaps, thought Neil, Clapp had evidence that things had changed since then. In spite of his months of active campaigning, Neil suddenly felt ill-prepared now for the short three weeks before election day. And he knew that Percy Clapp, whatever his reasons for calling an election at any time, would be good and ready with campaign material, money, and a garbage bag full of ruses.

Muck, exuding a confident energy, whipped the car around and headed for St. John's. He kept saying, "At last, this is it, finally, what we've been waiting for!" But Neil noticed that he was mostly sober-faced as he drove.

Neil held his own press conference late that afternoon. He was pleased with the results until he saw the clips shown on television that night, juxtaposed with some from Clapp's conference. Clapp looked energetic, and fit – and fit for anything.

"Little Neily Godwin," he said in one segment, "has had it pretty soft going so far. There's no word in the English lan-

317

guage for smacking up against something hard as you're blithely going through something soft. But the concept exists, because, as he'll find out soon enough, here's something hard." He thrust his sharp and brazen snout in the direction of the camera. Clapp's eyes showed a determination that Neil felt had been wholly absent from his own.

Also on the news that night, a speculative story was carried that a former, vocal, political enemy of Prime Minister Clapp, the Right Reverend Rodney Wadman, had indicated to his closest associates that for the good of the country he was going to support Mr. Clapp during this election as he had done during the leadership battle between Clapp and Godwin. It was not so much that he favoured the premier (reliable inside sources were reported as saying), as that, based on private knowledge concerning the background of Mr. Clapp's major opponent, he could not in good conscience accept the thought of Mr. Godwin becoming the leader of the country.

"What a strange way for Wadman to practise his priestcraft," Gillian declared. "Can a person, even a Christian, be *that* vindictive?"

Neil replied that he was going to find out right now. He looked up the number and dialled. When he said who was calling, the holy man came on the line immediately. Neil started by saying that if the reports were true, he was astonished that a leading clergyman would not remain neutral in this political battle between two parties. He thought he deserved an explanation.

"You are right," allowed Wadman, "I most certainly should have nothing whatever to do with either ungracious crew. Both are so ambisinister that I fear I am putting my immortal soul in direct jeopardy by association with either. I have nevertheless irrevocably decided to influence whomsoever I can to support Mr. Clapp."

"Will you be good enough to tell me why?"

"No."

"I *know* why," said Neil, his voice rising. "It's because my father had the faith and energy to attract so many of your poor and neglected parishioners away from that turgid, elitist club you call your church. That's why, isn't it? Good God, man, my father is *dying!*"

"It's the way of all flesh," replied Wadman. "Goodbye, Mr. Godwin."

"People will be disgusted with Wadman," said Muck; and then, after Gillian had left the room, shaking her head, he whispered, "But listen, Neil, it would do no harm to have your father's word going around in our favour, not out front or anything, just word of mouth. Why don't you talk to him about it again when you drop in on him tonight?"

At his father's house, the nurse told him his sister, Mrs. Maidment, was in with the Chief Elder. When Neil entered, Ernest's eyes rested on him with pleasure. Jane only nodded and smiled briefly. As Neil sat, Jane mentioned and dismissed the election call in one short sentence. Then she joked about the temperamental differences between Roland Maidment, the chartered accountant, and Jane Godwin Maidment, the free spirit, apparently in answer to an earlier question from Ernest. Ignoring Neil, she went on to describe to her father the courses she had decided to take at the university.

Neil wished Jane would leave so that he could ask his father directly for his support during the next three weeks. But she showed no sign of doing so, and Ernest would soon need his painkiller. Finally Neil said, a chortle in his voice: "Father, you've probably heard that Archbishop Wadman has come out *solidly* against me this election. Heh, heh, sins of the father is how he sees it, I guess. Heh, heh. Now, I don't know how much effect it will have, if any, but it would certainly look better to *your* colleagues if you –"

"Wadman," said Ernest. Neil could not tell if his face expressed a grin or a grimace. "Rodney Wadman. What importance does he have in this? Can you imagine putting yourself into a position where you're concerned about the Rodney Wadmans of this world? Forget Rodney Wadman."

"I wish I could, father. But I have to live with his opposition for the next three weeks and I'd be very grateful if you could spread the word among your supporters that you're behind me this election. I need your help."

"Yes, my son, you need my help."

"You'll do it, then?"

"No, Neil, I will not help put you in Percy Clapp's place. You shouldn't be there. Neil, send the nurse in, please."

"Father, on this election," pressed Neil, hearing Jane moving to get up, "I'd like your advice about – "

"How contrary *are* you at all in the name of the Lord Jesus Christ! I've never seen the like of you. You're as bad as your mother up there. One minute you're arguing that I should have a shot and the next minute, when I want it, you won't let me have it. Now listen! One of you get out *there* and tell that nurse to get in *here!*"

Jane gave Neil a look of incredulity, muttered something which included the word "insensitivity," and went out for the nurse.

Neil drove home, swallowing away the tightness in his throat and trying to attribute his father's responses to what the doctor had warned the family about: an increasing irritability and crankiness on the part of the patient. Muck was waiting for him with several other advisers. He asked him if he'd had any luck, as if Neil had just returned from a trouting trip. Neil shook his head and, early in the evening though it was, excused himself and went up to his room. There he lay on his bed and asked himself what this game was he was playing – a game which could make him badger his dying father over the possibility of squeezing out a few more votes.

In the morning, Neil, Muck, and two advisers set out on the day's campaign activities. They discussed Wadman's support for Clapp as they drove and concluded that it would not deliver votes; in fact, it would cause a backlash of feeling against him for intermeddling. Neil, privately, did not feel so certain about that. Wadman's position was clever. He had given the impression of being against his old enemy's enemy – of choosing the much lesser of two evils – on the grounds of morality or character deficiency. He had nothing to gain. His motive seemed to be the public welfare.

"Look at it this way," offered one of the backseat strategists, continuing his positive analysis. "Wadman's position is more than offset by the mention Neil made at the press conference of his father's tragic illness. There should be an awful lot of votes in that news." Again, the others agreed. No one was struck by the callousness of the opinion, Neil noted, including himself. Had he set that tone of approach to politics for his followers? he wondered. Or was it the very nature of political competition to make such a remark seem absolutely natural?

Neil thought his speech that night was well-received. There seemed to be the normal rhetoric and roars. Afterwards, though, his advisers said that once or twice he may have lost his audience. But only very briefly. Nothing to worry about. The rest was great! Perhaps, they said, he should make sure that he got enough sleep during the rest of the campaign to keep himself from rambling into complicated thoughts. They didn't know how he could stand the pace he had set, as it was.

Before he fell asleep that night, a thought occurred to Neil for the third or fourth time since his visit to his father the evening before: he wished he cared whether he won this goddamned election or not.

During the second week of the campaign, Muck suggested that they dream up some contempt-inspiring guffers to spread around about Percy Clapp: the same sort of thing that had been received so well by the general population in the leadership campaign. He and Neil worked at it for two hours one night, but were able to create nothing good. Neil felt that his earlier teeming fertility in the area had dried up.

"Aw, this is only a waste of time, anyway," said Muck, when they decided to go to bed. "Sure the stories you spread around about Clapp during the leadership didn't change the vote of one delegate."

But in the following days, it was clear that the creativity section of Percy Clapp's organization held a more positive view of slander. And certainly, they did not suffer from Neil's guffer-teller's block. An orchestrated campaign of smear and innuendo had been set in motion against him.

Why wouldn't a father, especially a dying father, support his only son? was a frequently asked question. What did Ernest know that was bad enough to turn him so much against the thought of Neil becoming premier? And what about that sister of his? She wouldn't have anything to do with his campaign, either. "Must be pretty bad if *she* won't go near it" (was the bar-stool talk in the city, Muck reported) "judging by how she carries on herself in the clubs!"

"A godless man – young Godwin," was what Percy Clapp was saying at meetings where no press were present, people told Neil. "A great disappointment to his pious father. He left his father's own church when he was still a mere boy. He would never have gone into my Cabinet in the first place if I'd known that at the time .... A man of no faith or beliefs, and, therefore, no morals .... That's what finally led to our split. I couldn't tolerate a Minister of the Crown in my government whose actions were not controlled by a healthy fear of God."

A unique line of reasoning was becoming widespread among Catholics: Godwin had married Gillian Touchings, the daughter of Newfoundland's leading Catholic layman, on the express condition that he would have his children brought up in the Catholic faith. And there he was with two little daughters and neither of them had ever been seen by anyone in church. In fact, no credible evidence could be adduced that they had even been baptized! And his wife, Gillian – how come time was going by and she wasn't pregnant again? That was easy to answer. Wasn't she seen buying birth control pills at the drugstore? Yes, and not only that. Right after her last delivery, she had the doctor tie off her tubes. A nurse at the hospital saw the medical record, sure, and there was no mention of any medical need to perform the operation to safeguard life or health. Jeez, why hadn't Alec Touchings taken out a court order to stop that? He'd really fallen down on the job. Just wait till the next time he was up for an award, or for re-election somewhere! Poor little Gillian. She used to be such a religious girl. Nearly became a nun before she came too handy to Godwin and he sunk his ungodly meathook into her. Now he's got her made as bad as himself, next thing to an atheist.

"Neil," warned his father-in-law in a surly voice, when he had recounted this over the phone after a Knights of Columbus meeting, "you've got some urgent fence-mending to do

322

among the micks. Though I doubt that it'll do any good." Neil put spark in his voice and said he would get right at it.

"Okay," said Muck. "That's the Gawkers, the Anglicans, and the Catholics wrapped up. Now what can we do to turn the Buddhists against us. There's four or five of them at the university."

The next night, a story was carried on the news that a formal complaint had been received by the executive of the Law Society accusing Neil Godwin of professional misconduct in the handling of the asbestosis-lung cancer case a few years previously. The complaint, an unidentified but reliable source on the executive had indicated, was that Godwin had used his public office of Minister of Health to cause a change in the law of the land in order to gain public money for the benefit of his client. The logs of the government aircraft at the time showed that Godwin had made a special trip to his client's town shortly after he had had the law changed. This breach of public trust and professional misconduct, the complaint concluded, both of the lowest order, warranted immediate proceedings by the Law Society Disciplinary Committee to disbar Godwin as unfit to practise law and to proclaim him unfit to hold public office.

The recently re-elected President of the Law Society, Mr. T. Alexander Touchings, was questioned on the story, the reporter said, but would give no information on the substance of the complaints. The president did confirm, however, that an anonymous complaint had been received, and that, like the scores of other anonymous, unsubstantiated complaints received every year, this one would be investigated, and if, as appeared on the face of it, the complaint was totally without foundation, it would be dismissed. "Mr. Touchings, QC," the reporter finished, with a smirk, "is the father-in-law of Mr. Godwin."

Another theme (with many variations), that was making the rounds, had Neil receiving a huge bribe after the purchase by the government of the fishplant – a purchase made for an exorbitant figure which Godwin himself had personally fabricated for presentation to the Cabinet. He was now using this bribe to finance his campaign against Clapp in the hope that if he won he could continue with a plan to extort twenty-five million dollars from Plopnicoff's government project. Godwin had tried to pull that caper earlier, when he was a Cabinet minister, and he would, in fact, have done so, had not Clyde Ferritt come roaring back from vacation to save the day.

Yet another tale going around stated that Neil had not gone to Vietnam to keep alive a spark of freedom and truth at all, as he had tried to make out. He had gone solely because he had close connections with the murderous Communist regimes in South East Asia. Godwin's closest friend at Oxford University (that spy-recruiting ground of crypto-Communist queers), was a Maoist agent, who had sent the film back from Vietnam in the hope of boosting the political fortunes of his underground associate in Newfoundland.

A political commentator concluded, from the mud-slinging, that the campaign was getting rough. He interviewed Clyde Ferritt on a public affairs program and asked about all the rumour-mongering that was going on. Neil and Muck watched the program in Muck's apartment, where the two of them had gone for an hour alone together.

"Well, we certainly wouldn't stoop to spreading rumours and scurrilous stories around about our opponent," announced Clyde. "That's Mr. Godwin's speciality. Therefore, I have no comment whatsoever to make on all these widespread reports regarding Neil Godwin. Except to say this. Ordinarily, such reports can be examined by the electorate and rejected as unfounded (if, in fact, they are). When, however, you have the leading, most senior clergyman in the country expressing grave doubts about the background of our opponent and siding with a man whom he has fought against for years, then the general public would be well advised to take a darn good hard look at the situation. But, no, I have no comment to make on rumours. I'll just say this. And this is not rumour. It is my own first-hand knowledge. When I was in Vietnam with Mr. Godwin, at his invitation, I could not help but notice how friendly and well-connected with the Communists Mr. Godwin's friend was. He was the gentleman of Eastern origins who got us into the country to begin with – and was the same person with whom Mr. Godwin spent a whole summer in Communist Russia a few years ago. But we are fighting this election squarely on issues, not personalities. Of course, one of the most important issues for people to make up their minds on is the character and background of their leaders. Oh, that reminds me: one other important issue is the fact that it was Mr. Godwin who first proposed to Cabinet the nationalization of the fishplant in Pinchgut. The fact that anti-religion, Communist countries always nationalize industries, too, is only just a coincidence – but voters can never be too care –"

"That goddamned Ferritt is spreading all those stories around!" exclaimed Muck, switching off the set. "Everyone can see that, and no one will believe a word of it."

Neil nodded mutely.

"But Neil, I have to say this. We – you – need to be a little more forceful in our attacks on Clapp, now. We can't slack up at this stage. We wouldn't want to lose the head of steam we've built up over the past year."

Again, Neil nodded mutely. He knew he should deal with the smear-campaign against him, but he could not seem to galvanize himself into doing anything about it.

Muck eyed him for a moment, then went on. "I'm worried about money, Neil. I've had a couple of chats with Roland about it, but he's not putting as much time into it as he needs to. An escalation in his chronic domestic crisis, he tells me. But he's *got* to put on a big push all next week. Everything is cash on the barrelhead during an election. While we're here in St. John's for a few hours, how about you talking to him?"

Neil stopped himself from giving another silent nod. He smiled wanly, instead, and Muck stirred restlessly.

"Well? Will you call him now and get him to come down to headquarters? Here, I'll get him on the phone for you." Muck sighed as he went to the telephone, dialled, and passed the receiver to Neil.

"Roland!" said Neil, cheerily. "Muck tells me the figures in the bag book are not looking too healthy. How about coming down to headquarters and we'll go over a strategy for the last week."

"Gosh, I'd love to Neil, but I've got a prior commitment

tonight." When Neil remained silent, Roland burst out unhappily, "It's Jane, Neil. She's been giving me a hard time – worse than usual. It's playing on my mind. She says she's going to see that mawmouth" (he named a lawyer much loathed and respected in divorce court circles) "about her options, and –"

"Jesus, Roland. This is your own personal business, I know, but can't you get her to lay off for a few days till the election is over?"

"I tried that on her already, Neil. Told her she was distracting me from your campaign. 'What do I care,' she says, 'about the brother's Machiavellian machinations?' *You'd* better speak to her, Neil."

Neil put down the phone. "Muck," he said. "Roland Maidment may be a brilliant accountant. And he may be good at the tedious job of collecting money. But where Jane is concerned he's a goddamned rabbit!"

"Yes, I know," nodded Muck. "And why would a rabbit marry a lynx?"

"Or vice versa," said Neil. "What's wrong with everyone?"

"I must say," Muck admitted, "that your family has been a great help to you so far in the campaign." He grinned. "Well, as long as we can count on your mother and your wife not issuing a joint *communiqué* denouncing you, we're all right, I suppose."

Neil smiled grimly, and jerked his head up once to suggest that nothing was impossible.

"Neil, what *about* Gillian? Maybe we should get her to accompany you for the rest of the campaign. They're starting to spread the yarn around now that not even your own wife supports you."

"She's been after me recently to let her come," said Neil truthfully, "but you know she's not very interested in politics and she'd only be doing it out of a sense of duty. I'm not going to use her hypocritically like that." In fact he didn't want Gillian to see first-hand the indignities he was forced to put up with as he campaigned – or to hear the nonsense he had to say.

"Getting back to the money for a minute," said Muck. "We

need it bad. Listen, Neil, one of Plopnicoff's men called me again, yesterday. He asked me if there was anything they could help us with. Just say the word, he said. They have a healthy amount already put aside for supporting the democratic process."

"I told you, Muck." Neil stirred to life for the first time that evening. "Not one nickel from Plopnicoff or his no-necks. If ... when I get elected, the first thing I have to do is turf him out of that disaster that Clapp got him to build and cancel the whole deal. Not one red bloody cent from him, Muck!"

Muck put his palms on his forehead for a minute and then stood up. "Let's go, Neil," he sighed.

On the first day of the last week of the campaign, Neil passed an agonizing hour in his father's room before setting out on what was supposed to be the final great surge of effort. He wanted to do the job right; but within three more days he had to admit to himself that he could not regain his earlier flair.

The byword now among most of his top campaign organizers was that "the piss and vinegar has gone out of Neil completely." Neil himself could hear the lack of animation in his voice and see the lack of verve in his face when he watched his own television ads, in spite of the fact that most of them had been done and redone a dozen times to get the best possible presentation. He looked like a talking head. His supporters at rallies sensed the diminishing momentum of the campaign. Their applause and cheers were so forced on occasion that they occurred at inappropriate times in his speeches. And then Gorman, the former university president and Minister of Education, put out an unsolicited statement of support for Neil Godwin – as if to confirm that Neil's campaign was in desperate trouble.

"Oh, fuck!" groaned Muck. "We must really be looking like the *Titanic* now, if that idiot has hopped on board!"

Two days before polling day, Muck took Neil to a secret hotel room to discuss their problems in private. All the questions, innuendoes, and mud-slinging about Neil, not to mention his own diminishing punch, were having an impact on voters – not by increasing their support for Clapp, but by weakening their support for Godwin. The latest poll conducted for Neil's party measured voter opinion as of the day before, and according to the figures, Clapp had not gained one per cent of support over what he started with the day he had called the election. "But, Neil," said Muck, "but, but, *but*! The number of people who say they will probably not bother to vote is going up all the time. At our expense! That gives Clapp a larger percentage of the committed voters. The gap we started out with has narrowed steadily in recent days until now it looks like Clapp might have gone ahead of us. The difference is too small, the research boys say, to be measured with reliable accuracy. That's been Clapp's strategy all along. Forget about winning any new support. Instead, attack Godwin's soft support; make them stay at home on election day.

"It's working, Neil. And to add to the problem – because of Roland Maidment's cop-out, we have brought in less money than expected at a time when we need *more* money than expected to make sure enough organization is in place on election day to get the Godwin voters out – all those potential supporters who have lost some of their enthusiasm and might therefore stay at home. Jesus."

They sat silently for a while. "The sickening thing," Muck began again, "is that a majority of the people want Clapp out and a majority want you in, Neil. In spite of all that's happened in the past two weeks, we're still neck and neck. Christ, they *want* you, Neil, but we've got to give them something to bring them out, something that will make a hungry fisherman leave his boat and go to the polling booth instead of straight home to glom into his meal of fish and brewis. What? What? *What*?" When Neil remained silent, Muck finished with a tinge of irritation. "Neil, listen! The arse is after dropping out of our campaign."

Neil did not argue the point. He said, quietly: "Rute."

"I know it's a root," replied Muck. "One goddamned awful root. Right in the hole."

"Randolph Rute," said Neil.

"Oh, Randolph Rute, the labour guy." Muck looked thoughtful. "What's happened to him, anyway? Every second fisherman I run into asks me what's become of poor old Randy Rute, what he's doing these days. I didn't know; I haven't heard of him for a while."

"He's in a wheelchair. I believe the Federation of Labour is more or less looking after him."

"Why isn't he organizing or something? Lots of guys in wheelchairs are working."

"Percy knocked the shitbag out of him. The good went out of him. The Cowardly Wave."

"What?"

"Nothing. Fishermen are always asking me what he's doing, too. I've often thought about going to see him. Never got around to it." In fact, Neil had been half-ashamed to do so, after having joined with Clapp in capitalizing on the Fishermen's Union's destruction in the last election.

"Let's track him down and try to get him to come out for us," suggested Muck. "It can't do any harm at this stage. Nothing to lose."

"If we can get him to make a statement of support, he'll have to do it no later than tonight," Neil pointed out. "The electronic media are not allowed to broadcast anything on the election for twenty-four hours before polling day." The idea of Rute's support seemed so obvious and simple now that Neil felt like kicking himself for having overlooked it until it was probably too late.

The street where Rute lived was narrow and short. It consisted of row housing that had been tacked together right after the fire which destroyed the city in 1892. The wooden frames and clapboards were disfigured by rot, and paint was wholly absent.

"The Heritage Conservation people don't seem to have reached this street yet," frowned Neil, as Muck parked the car.

"Or they passed it by," replied Muck, "as too quaint to change."

They found Randolph Rute in the last house. There was a

ramp, which looked like an old, remodelled coal chute, leading from a side alley to his room in the basement. He seemed delighted to have visitors.

"You probably don't remember it now, Mr. Godwin," he said, after they had shaken hands, "but I met you first at the university here years ago, when you were a student. I thought of the time we met when I saw your picture on the news, after you first got elected."

"Do you live here alone, Mr. Rute?" asked Neil quickly.

"Yes. My wife and I separated when I was organizing the Fishermen's Union. Politics is awful hard on the women, boy."

They talked politics for a while and then Muck leaned forward. "Mr. Rute, we need your help. Clapp may win this election with his gutter tactics against Neil and –"

"I don't think I ever met you before this, did I? What'd you say your name was? I never forget a name or a face. I could call three quarters of my union members by name."

"Barrows. Neil and I have been friends for years, but he keeps me under wraps."

"*David* Barrows? Yes, I remember the name." Rute looked at Neil. "I remember. I remember. So you need my help, hey?

"I figured you were looking for something. It's not often I have renowned politicians making a special visit to see me in this hole. I didn't think you were here just to pass the time of day. No. I'm out of all that now, Mr. Godwin. I don't have the fight I used to have. I appreciate the invitation, even if it is at the eleventh hour, but, no, I don't think so. It wouldn't do you any good, anyway."

"Fishermen are still asking me about you all the time," said Neil. "It'd do a lot of good."

"Let them ask, my friend, let them ask. Ask, ask, ask. But what did they *do* when Clapp sent in his blackshirts? What did they *do* when he broke my back?"

"They had no leadership when you went, Mr. Rute," responded Neil. He went on to describe the low turnout of fishermen in the subsequent election. He recalled his own position and actions behind the scenes during his days in Clapp's government: the asbestosis case, the fights in Cabinet over the fishermen's strike, his efforts to buy the fishplant and turn it over to a co-operative of fishermen. "The terrible mistake I made, Mr. Rute, being young and silly at the time, was to think I could make things better in cahoots with the likes of Clapp. When I realized my blunder, I got out and took him on. But he's a wily one, and vicious, as you more than most would know."

Rute was slumped in his wheelchair. "I don't know," he said finally. "I'll think it over. I don't think so."

They talked for a while longer on unrelated matters and got up to leave. Neil reminded Rute that if he said anything publicly it would have to be done today. Rute remained sunk in thought.

As Neil and Muck were going out the door, Rute called "Oh, Mr. Godwin!" Neil turned hopefully. "Mr. Godwin, I'm getting a small disability pension from the government. Do you happen to know if Clapp has the power to cut that off?"

Neil heard Muck groan outside as he explained to Rute that it was a government program of general application for those who qualified.

"Knowing Clapp," snorted Rute, "he'd still find a way to cut it off."

Neil and Muck drove off. "I wouldn't count on much from that source," said Muck. They sat for a while in silence. "Neil, on the money we need for election day. I got another call last night from –"

"No, Muck. I told you before. No."

The deadline for election statements on television and radio came and went and Rute said nothing. Then, the next morning, Muck telephoned Neil in great excitement. "Rute wants to hold a press conference at noon," he announced happily. "He telephoned to say he hopes it's not too late. 'You've got a good man there in Godwin,' he said. 'And, Barrows,' he said, 'he's the best friend you'll ever have, my son.' Something worked, Neil!"

"But it *is* too late, isn't it, Muck? We might get a bit of coverage in the paper tomorrow, but the election will be over before the fishermen and their families even hear about it."

"I talked to Jerome Finn at the television station, Neil. He's going to carry it."

"But that's illegal, Muck! The Election Act says clearly – "

"Wait till the election is over before you start practising law again, Neil. Who knows? Maybe you won't have to. Jerome says, screw the Election Act. Let the station worry about that after it's done, he says. Neil, you don't know anything at all about this. I wouldn't have even called you about it, except that I had to let you know that I promised Jerome the job as your press secretary and PR man if you're elected premier, okay?"

"Jesus, Muck! I order you not to have anything to do with that. And tell Jerome Finn no – he will not be my press secretary on the basis of anything he does with Rute today. Is that clear? That is a direct order!"

"Of course, sir," said Muck. "I'm sorry I brought it up. It was irresponsible of me."

That night, Neil and Muck sat together in a hotel room to watch Rute's statement on the television news. Rute's face, half-hidden in the gloom yesterday, looked slack and pallid now in the television lights. It had none of the lean alertness Neil remembered from the strike.

"Christ, he's a pitiful looking spec," murmured Neil. "Is this any good?"

"I don't know," answered Muck with a grin. "I couldn't locate Jerome Finn after I was talking to you."

Rute spoke: "There's stories going around that Neil Godwin is a secret Communist and a crooked lawyer. It's easy to believe anything you hear about a politician."

"Lovely," said Muck. "Just lovely. We shouldn't have gone near the stupid bastard. And Jerome Finn! Job as PR man? Like fuck!"

"Percy Clapp and his manure-spreaders are fuelling those yarns," continued Rute, "by saying that when Godwin was in Clapp's government he wanted the government to take over that great bastion of free enterprise, the fishing industry. I've done a little checking of my own and I have found that that is true. It *was* Neil Godwin who first proposed to the government that the fishplant in Pinchgut be nationalized. And then what? Be run as an example of state capitalism like in the Communist countries? No. He wanted the plant turned over

332

to a co-op of fishermen and plant workers. He wanted it run for their sole benefit, with all the proceeds going to the producers and workers themselves, and with taxes on the profits going into the treasury for the benefit of the people at large. In other words, a fishing industry for the benefit of all instead of for a few. He wanted to do that as a pilot project, as an experiment to see if that was the direction the industry as a whole should take. And he wanted to do this for no other gain to himself than that he knew it was the right thing to do.

"The start was made on Godwin's urging. But, of course, Clapp took the first chance he could to turn the plant over to another robber-baron – so that he could keep his political pockets and other pockets full with large donations from the moneyed friends whom he had allowed to grow wealthy off the backs of the ordinary people.

"It's the same story with compensation for industrial lung disease. They're saying Godwin did it because he's a crooked lawyer. I know he did it for the workers of our country. No wonder Godwin got out of Clapp's government. And no wonder Clapp hates Godwin so much that he is willing to stoop to the lowest levels of the sewer to stop him."

Rute gazed at the camera for a moment. His eyes were shining and his face had become strong and set. "I've stayed silent too long," he said. "Percy Clapp is an evil man, and he's got to go. I say to the thousands of men and women around our shores who loved me once, and who loved what we were trying to do together: if you have even a spark of that love left in your hearts, you will support Neil Godwin tomorrow."

"Great!" said Muck gleefully. "Great stuff! At last! A shot of truth, Neil, to offset all those unfounded rumours going around about you."

Neil was already on his feet, pacing the room energetically and throwing out ideas on getting the maximum number of supporters to the ballot boxes: fleets of cars to be hired; bonuses to drivers based on the number of Godwin votes per poll; financial competitions among his polling teams for most votes. To hell with the cost! They'd worry about that after-wards.

For the first time since the election had begun, Neil wanted to win. And he *knew* he was going to win.

20

"Resign?" bawled Percy Clapp to news director Jerome Finn on television the day after the election.

"I resign? You only resign when you have been defeated. I will resign if, as, and when I lose an election. I will pass the government over to Godwin if, as, and when he wins an election."

"Mr. Godwin did win the election," said Jerome. "He won by two seats. He got twenty-six members and you, sir, got twenty-four."

"The official returns are not in yet," countered Clapp. "*Un*officially, Mr. Godwin won one of those seats by twelve votes and the other by nineteen votes. First we shall see what the official returns say a week from now. If the vote remains the same, then we are entitled to a judicial recount in the seats Mr. Godwin won by a handful of votes. If only one of those seats comes to my party as a result of the judicial recount, then we have a tie election on our hands. All constitutional precedent is clear: in the event of a tie election, the incumbent government does not resign, but is entitled to meet the legislature and put forward a motion of confidence. In fact, I would be violating constitutional principle *by* resigning. And I have no intention, *none*, of violating the sacred British parliamentary constitution. I have striven my whole life long to uphold it in this land against all the haters of British freedom, stability, and fair play."

"But, Mr. Clapp," said Jerome Finn, "Neil Godwin's party won a clear majority of the votes cast, just over 51 per cent, as against your less than 49 per cent. My goodness, sir, talking about fair play, doesn't the fact that you have been rejected by a clear majority of the voters, voters who have indicated their preference for someone else, mean anything to you?"

"Look here, my friend!" roared Clapp. "We are governed by a parliamentary democracy, not by the rules of the Miss America pageant! It is the number of seats that counts, not the number of votes. And I have the sacred, inviolable constitutional duty to do nothing until we know how many seats we have."

"Then, if the judicial recount confirms the election of Mr. Godwin's candidates in those close seats, you will resign?"

"What?" said Clapp. "Of course not. Don't you know anything at all about the constitution of your own country? It's obvious that you do not, or your station would not have flagrantly broken the Election Act the day before the election. No. This is not quite so simple as you would like it to be.

"In the unlikely event that the judicial recount confirms the election of Godwin's candidates in those two seats, then my candidates will immediately launch an action in Supreme Court to have the elections in those two districts declared null and void on grounds of irregularities in voting. Already we have unearthed enough evidence of improper voting by more voters than the seats were won by, to have the election there legally controverted. That would bring us back to the tie situation once more. Twenty-four to twenty-four. And that doesn't even take into account your violation of the law by having Randolph Rute make his paid political telecast when it was illegal to do so. We may have the whole election declared a nullity because of that!

"Do you realize what a terrible disservice you and Mr. Godwin did to our people there? Two days before the election the polls showed that I had a majority of the voters behind me. As a result of your use of television to inflame emotions the day before the election – the very thing the ban in the Election Act was designed to prevent – people who had no intention of voting (because they were content with the way things were), came out in droves to vote for Godwin as Rute's puppet. That's what you did. You and Godwin caused this constitutional crisis, this agony of instability for our people. My God, man, the people of Italy *hung* Mussolini for less heinous crimes than that!"

Neil and Gillian and Muck watched a minute of the following commercial on underarm deodorants before Gillian broke the silence. "Jesus, what is he like at all?" she said. "This thing is interminable. I see no end to it. Neil, when will this finish?"

"Well, whatever the final outcome of all of Percy's tactics may be," Neil sighed, "he can be expected to try to cling onto power for months, perhaps a full year, until the current budget runs out and he is forced to call the House of Assembly together. Unless, of course, something drastic were to happen in the meantime .... "

"Like what?" questioned Gillian, regarding Neil and Muck, especially Muck, with narrowed eyes.

"Percy could die," suggested Neil. "Or there could be civil unrest; or enough of his members could defect to our side so that the issue would then be clear-cut enough for the governor to use his residual powers to dismiss Clapp and call on me. Those are some possibilities. Right now, however, Percy is technically correct."

"Well, Neil," said Gillian, looking at Muck, "if you're going to stick with this, I hope you do it right. Don't get involved in anything underhanded. No short term gain is worth any skulduggery. You weren't involved with that Jerome Finn in breaking the law to put Rute on, by the way, were you? As Clapp just said?"

"Heavens above, no, Gillian!" exclaimed Muck. Neil had never seen such a look of injured innocence on anyone's face before. "To the contrary. As a matter of fact, Neil specifically ordered me on the phone *not* to allow Rute to go on that day. Didn't you, Neil? I've got his order on tape."

"Do you usually go around taping your leader's telephone conversations?"

"Yes, of course, Gillian, all the time. I've got a million things on my mind every day, and I don't want to forget or confuse any of it."

Gillian frowned. "Then in that case, Neil, you'll have to sue

Clapp for slander. You can't have him on the public airways accusing you falsely of criminal activity."

"That's a good idea, Gillian," agreed Neil. "Make a note of that, Muck."

Before there could be any more conversation, Neil excused himself. He hadn't seen his father for over a week, he said, and should go to see him now. On his way there, he contrasted his feelings with those of last night when, during his supporters' euphoria at the victory celebration, the words, *Thank God, it's finally over! I can start, I can start!* had kept running through his mind. Now he could only think of the wait; the long, perhaps unavailing wait. A wait during which he would have to cope with a thousand pieces of chicanery from Clapp, during which he would have to display vigorous leadership daily, during which one false step could finish him. He would make a good leader of the government if he ever got there, he thought. It was the getting there that turned his guts. No wonder so many politicians seemed to become enemies of the electorate after they finally gained power. It was pure and simple revenge!

When he arrived at the house, the nurse told him that his father was asleep. Neil opened the bedroom door and went in to spend an hour in the quiet darkness.

During the following week, Muck reported that Clapp's minions had already started working on Neil's weaker members, trying to cajole them into joining Clapp's party. "I honestly don't know how long a couple of them will resist Percy's temptations," he said. "Some of them are such arseholes! The ones we had to dredge up quick when Clapp called the election."

Still, Neil showed no enthusiasm for the variety of machinations, most of them illegal, that Muck was forever suggesting to him for wresting control from Clapp. Muck's latest idea was that – since death or total disability was the only way to get rid of Clapp – they should bring in an untraceable professional hit man from the west coast of the United States. It made Neil laugh. Until he saw the earnest look on Muck's face.

"Come on, Muck!" he exclaimed. "Get off that crap!"

"Look, Neil," Muck replied. "Do you realize what Clapp is

saying everywhere about you. He's saying, the longer he hangs on, the greater is the certainty of total collapse by Godwin. He's saying little Neily Godwin caved in during the election and has no stomach left for these new skirmishes. 'And we haven't even begun the battle yet.' That's what he's saying. Now, Neil, it's all well and good for you to be saying publicly: 'The majority of our people have spoken and the majority shall prevail. The representatives of that majority will form the government, yes, but only by legitimate means.' That's all right for television. But our members need more than that. They need real evidence of real leadership."

"Muck, come here." Neil knew that Clapp's assessment was probably right but, putting an arm across Muck's shoulders, he lied. "I know exactly what I'm doing," he said. And then, assuming a ruthlessness he did not feel, he whispered sternly, "I'm surprised I have to say this to someone who has read so much about Nazi Germany. Don't you remember that Hitler's colleagues urged a coup only months before he became chancellor, and thereafter dictator, by legal means! Now, I'm counting on you to keep the boys in line until I make my move. I know precisely what I'm doing."

"Hey, that's *right*," Muck agreed, with renewed respect. "And when you're ready, just give me the word." But even as Muck spoke, Neil was thinking: *I cannot stand this. I'm not made for this.*

That night in bed, he scarcely responded to Gillian's attempts at conversation. He lapsed into deep cogitation on what he was involved in, what he was up against. He wondered what was wrong with him. Anyone else in his position would be fighting Clapp to a him-or-me finish like a cornered, wounded tiger. Forgetting that Gillian was lying beside him, he groaned: "What am I *doing*? Is anything worth this ... this...?" He realized that he'd spoken aloud only when he felt Gillian stir and heard her sigh. And he experienced the humiliation of total emotional exposure during the ensuing silence before sleep.

The next evening, after a day of meetings and phone calls (to keep morale in the troops), and media interviews (during which he tried to portray leadership and strength, but not a grasping attitude towards power), Neil retired to his bedroom to watch the national news, away from the phone and the knocks on the door. Gillian came in from the bathroom, her body wrapped in one towel and her hair in another. She went directly to Neil.

"Do you know how much I love you?" she whispered, kneeling and kissing him on the mouth. She drew him to his feet, ignoring the lower towel as it dropped to the floor. Her body glowed. Neil turned the television down and negotiated her towards the bed, she expressing complete surprise at this turn of events and he saying they should have a little lie-down before dinner. They played and dallied.

"Another, apparently massive, oil discovery off our east coast was announced today," murmured the television set. "A step-out well from the Hibernia oil field, nearly two hundred miles off Noofnlnd, has evidently tapped into another distinct reservoir of oil. This *latest* find brings to three the number of large submarine pools of oil discovered in that area. The stocks of oil corporations involved in the offshore explorations have jumped following reports of this new oil find, which is described by some market analysts as having the potential to make Noofnlnd the Kuwait of North America. Other analysts are urging investor caution, however, owing to current political uncertainty in that province, where the incumbent separatist government is reported on good authority to have successfully beaten off an initially strong takeover bid by an opposition party .... Plans to reform the Senate ... "

Neil, who had been straining to listen to this through the thighs tight around his ears, wrenched his head free and vaulted naked from the bed, roaring, "What the fuck do you know about who's beating who the fuck off who for fuck's sake?" He shook his fist at the television set and offered to kick it. Then he looked back at Gillian, wild-eyed and rubbing his ears vigorously with both hands.

Forced by her pillow-elevated hips to crane her neck in order to see him through her open knees, Gillian looked first at Neil, and then at the television screen, where a man was dividing up the nation on a map. Finally, she stared at her husband in wonderment. "My gentle Jesus, Neil, boy, you need help, bad."

"Yes, and you! Goddamn it!" bellowed Neil, now tenderly massaging his scarlet ears with his fingertips. "You just hurt my goddamned ears with your goddamned legs. That's what you goddamned well did!"

He dressed while Gillian, her back to the headboard, watched his moves carefully. Then he went down to his den, ripped the telephone cord out of the jack, and slouched in his chair.

Had he, he wondered, gone off his head completely? Maybe he had actually picked up a quick-acting Asian syphilis or something that time in Saigon, and even now the spirochaetes were raging unchecked through his bloodstream, turning his brain into a yellow, porridgy pulp. And this was the first serious onslaught. Oh, Lord Jesus! What had he read about venereal disease among American veterans in Vietnam? No, if there was some horrible brain-ravaging disease that acted this quickly, he would have heard about it somewhere .... Why didn't he face the facts squarely? He'd got himself into a situation that he hated and feared and he didn't know what to do – and if he knew what to do he'd be too stupid and feeble to do it!

He was taken by an urge to drive across the island, all alone, all night long, to his mother's home near Folkly Rooms; to walk across the barrens; to sit in the safety of his chair of stone; to look over the side of the steep tor at the unimpeded view of the perpendicular drop to the sea. He walked out to his car and drove to the intersection. But instead of turning right to head out of town, he turned left and went to his father's house.

His father, said the nurse, would be asleep for a little while yet; and so Neil went upstairs to see his mother. She was in the sitting room off her bedroom, gazing out the window, a *National Geographic* open on her lap. She turned on his knock and entry, and her features assumed that look of love, pity, and anxiety that Neil felt on his own face whenever he looked at the perfect small-girl form of his older daughter asleep in her bed at night – her tousled head; her little foot, ankle, and calf stuck out over the side of the bed; her little hand and wrist on the pillow. He would die a thousand agonizing deaths if he believed it would keep her safe one minute longer, he always thought on those occasions.

He went to his mother and kissed her cheek. "Neil," she said gently, lifting her arm too soon from his neck. "You've got a lot to do. Don't waste time here with me now."

"I just came up from seeing father. I'm staying with him for a while after he wakes up."

"I don't mean Ernest." His mother shook her head. "Say hello to him and go. Don't spend needless time with him, now, either. You have got to make your moves, Neil. You can't delay any longer."

Neil drew back and looked at her. She had let her hair down. It hung straight and shiny-black, without a trace of grey, and the ends of one side rested on her lap. His own eyes were levelled at him from her older, woman's face.

"Ernest will only take the good out of you, Neil," she said. "There's nothing he can help you with. You have to do it yourself. Anything he will say to you will only suck away your strength. Do what has to be done."

Neil smiled faintly. "You mean politically, mother? There's not much that can be done at the moment. There's a hopeless stalemate."

"Hopeless, my son? Go and do what you have to do. Now."

He wanted to say, *I don't know what to do, Mom.* He wanted to kneel down and hug her. Instead, he fixed his gaze on the floor.

"Neil." His mother's soft voice tugged at him again. "I said go and do whatever has to be done. You are the one who must do it."

"Am I, mother?" he asked. "Does anyone who wants it so little have the right to take it from someone who wants it so much?" He wondered why he had said that to her. What did she know about politics?

"That's when the right is greatest, my son. And it's got nothing to do with what you want. Get rid of Percy Clapp, now."

"I've got plenty of time for that .... "

341

"Have you, Neil? What time have you got? What time did your Grandfather Priddle have? Dead at fifty-nine after a lifetime of victories, killed by one defeat. What time did your Grandfather Arthur Godwin have? Dead in his forties after a few years of ranting, leaving nothing of his alleged brilliance behind him. What time did your father have? Dying at fifty after only just coming to terms with thirty years of self-deception. What time will you have? Do it now. Not because you want to. Not because of a strong, beloved mother whose expectations, they say, a leader is always impossibly trying to fulfil. God knows I haven't been that. Do it because you *can* do it. Because it's right for you to do it – for yourself and for the others who can't, and who are *looking* to you to do it."

Neil said goodbye and backed out of his mother's room. What the hell had she been reading? he thought. When did she make up that speech? He went downstairs feeling, not like the selfish classical hero who performed gigantic feats without a thought to the worry he was causing a gentle mother (as he had sometimes felt before), but like a craven cur pup, forced out of the den and skulking around the underbrush, fearful of the shadows in the sun. He stood in the hall, puzzled by his mother's unwonted exhortations about some kind of undefined action. But were they unwonted, after all? Or did they only appear so because he had never taken much notice of her contributions before, hearing them as a kind of essential but unnoticed background noise in his universe? Ah well, he thought, exhortation was easy in your armchair. He went into his father's room and took the chair nearest to his father's head.

Ernest Godwin stirred and his eyes floated into focus on Neil's face. "Good," he muttered. "Neil. Are you ready to listen now?"

"Hello, father. I'm here to talk. If you want to."

"Oh, Neil, I have such remorse, such remorse, oh, such remorse," Ernest groaned immediately. Tears were flowing from his eyes, shockingly copious tears for the shrivelled face.

Christ, was that it? thought Neil. He made his thoughts harsh to keep his own tears back. Was that what his father had been trying to tell him, that his life had been a self-deception, as his mother had said; that he felt guilt over having lost his faith at the end? What exactly was Neil supposed to do now?

He leaned over his father's bed. "But, father," he murmured, "there's no need for you to feel remorse. You have every reason to be proud of your life's work. Pain and suffering do strange things to people's minds. You've had thirty years of faith and belief and good works. Think of the beautiful picture you've put in thousands of people's minds. Think of the comfort to thousands of bodies. The religious denomination you built up is respected and flourishing. Father, few people on earth have more to be proud of."

"Neil." Ernest, controlled now, looked steadily into his son's eyes. "From the moment I preached my first sermon in Maggotty Cove Motion, thirty years ago, till I preached my last words in the Temple of Truth here this year, I have despised every minute of it, every separate, isolated second of it. For thirty years I have never believed a word of it, not one word of what I said or heard, except for one little flash of insight in Maggotty Cove Motion. My life has been nothing – for thirty years a lifelong lie. Nothing, nothing, nothing, except for that parable of the runty, scrawny lamb I invented down by the Motion. This is my remorse at the end, that my whole life was not *filled* with moments like that one vision. And this is my salvation as I approach oblivion, that my life is saved from being utterly worthless and meaningless by that small vision of the runty, scrawny lambs on earth."

Neil regarded his father with the ineffable sadness reserved for someone whose mind, filled to the exclusion of all else with something totally inconsequential, has been overturned. "I understand the bitter mental anguish this has caused you father, but I think –"

"Do you, Neil? Do you understand? You, too, are going the wrong way, my son – and that is also part of my remorse. I pushed you the wrong way. But I can remedy that now. I've watched you, Neil, and I know what you are. You believe nothing, and that is good. You know that no proposition has any ultimate validity, and that is good. You know there are no truths – only one truth: the exposing of falsehoods and idiocies. I listened to your twelve-year-old gropings. I sneaked a look at your teenage scribblings in the desk in your room. I watched your discontent in your brief practise of law. I observed you in politics, especially after you left Percy. I've seen your perseverance, your compulsion, your brilliance, your delight, when pulling down, exploding, annihilating, the cause, the proposal, the person in your sights. I've seen what you are and what you should be, compared with what you are trying to be, because I've had the benefit of the example of my own life. I never once heard you say what you'd do with your power if you got it. I never once heard you express delight over actually taking over power ....

"You are not a proposer of truths, Neil, because you know there are none. You are a disrupter, a destroyer of lies, an uprooter of all received truths. Your creations should be destructions. You are Adder Godwin. Don't be me. Don't do with your life what, aside from one moment's vision, I did with mine, because it was the soft and easy way to go, because it appeared to be the right way to go in the circumstances.

"Your Grandfather Arthur Godwin was right. Men of politics and men of religion are the same. Their basis is in superstition and ignorance and blind faith, and they are maintained by artificial disputes, fostered misunderstandings, and faithly butcheries. Politicians and preachers arguing whether the bubonic plague was caused by a god or a devil. Government and church maintained by superstitious guesswork; emotional appeals to selfish interests; power shored up by fear; theories, cast in terms of progress, based on foundationless faith – all of it made appealing from time to time to the dubious, yearning masses by the inspired madness of the occasional great man." Neil could not credit the strength and power of his father's voice. They were growing instead of diminishing.

"What do you want with that nonsense, Neil? That is not you. You have no more to do with that than I should have had to do with my little sect of medieval religion. You are a howler of execration, a bringer down of exalted truths. That is your way. As prime minister, you would make the cerebral effort, go through the motions, mouth the words, strive to contrive and provide more and better nosegays to cover up

344

the stench, knowing as you do – as I knew for thirty years, less one moment – that the efforts, the motions, the words, are false, vain, and hateful, and the cause of the stench remains. And Neil, you'll go to *your* ultimate bed of *peine forte et dure* without even the consolation I have of one small moment of honour and truth …. Get the nurse, Neil. I can't stand the pain."

Neil walked to the door, unlocked it, and went into the hall like an automaton. He stood in a bemused trance for a moment, overwhelmed by the conflicting parental advice. His father's moans brought him out of it. He called out to the nurse and heard her answer from the living room down the hall. He went back to his father's bedside.

"The nurse is coming, father," he said. "Can I get you anything? A fresh pillow? Your head is kind of sunk down in that one."

But Ernest's eyes were focussed on the door behind him. The nurse was entering with the needle and his father had forgotten Neil was there. His eyes followed the woman's every action. He was whimpering. She emptied the contents of the hypodermic into him somewhere. Neil didn't look to see where she had found enough flesh. Ernest's eyes closed and all movement and sound ceased. The nurse waited at the door for Neil to leave, but he said he was going to stay with his father for a while. She smiled, and closed the door.

Neil sat in the far corner of the room and thought about what Ernest had just told him. A couple of months ago, he realized, perhaps even a week ago, he would have dismissed his father's analysis as, perhaps not totally wrong, but much too extreme: the bitterness of a disillusioned man dying in pain. But now Ernest's analysis and advice seemed timely. They provided Neil with a rationale for doing what he had wanted to do for several days; they were an intellectually satisfying way out. His father was right, he thought. Under his political disguise that was his own nature. His mistake had been in thinking he should use his destruction of falsehoods to advance himself into the empty place. He would get out of politics without any further delay – and seek the means to follow his proper path …. At the decision, every *cliché* about scales dropping off eyes and burdens falling from backs, rolled through his mind.

To shore up the decision, he added a few more confirming facts to what Ernest had said about his nature. He suffered from – not a moral cowardice, exactly – but certainly a strong desire not to be bothered by any inconvenient consequences that might result from his own actions. He was too accommodating and amenable face to face; too treacherous behind backs. He loved to attack, yes, but at a distance – a squirt of venom from the underbrush. It wasn't because of a wish for anonymity in his actions. It was more of a desire to hit and run – no, not even that – a desire to do or say whatever he wanted without having to worry about whether a counterattack against him could hurt himself or those for whom he was supposed to be responsible. He was a lone and sinister creature of the woods, content only when creeping under cover of shadows and half-lights, impatient for a chance to exercise his negative talents. Well, not as melodramatic as that, but akin to it. Mediocre? Yes, but only in the doing of what was not in his proper nature to do. In his true sphere, brilliant. Negatively, destructively (in the best sense of the word, of course) brilliant. What a pleasure it would be finally to be like Adder Godwin. Or like Jane! To say and do what he liked. Of course in his own case he would concentrate his time and his efforts on his family – but to hell with the rest!

Neil breathed his thanks in the direction of his father. It was a beautiful realization to have come to. For two hours in the dark with the quiet, motionless form of Ernest, Neil firmed it up in his mind. Once or twice, the nurse quietly opened the door and looked in. Each time, in the beam of light from the outside, Neil gestured to her that all was well.

But at home, Muck was waiting for him.

"Your father's illness has been really affecting you, Neil," he said, following Neil about the living room. "I apologize for being so insensitive about it during the election."

"Thanks, Muck," Neil replied. "I'm okay, now. I know what I have to do. I'll give you a call tomorrow morning and we'll get together on it."

"Neil, are you all right? I mean, are you really feeling okay?

You haven't lost interest in this, have you, Neil? You're not going to cave in on us at this stage like Percy is saying, are you?"

"We'll talk about it in the morning, Muck. I know what I have to do." Neil laughed gently. Muck was a guileless child.

Muck looked at Neil's hair, forehead, eyes, cheekbones, nose, mouth, and chin, in turn. He slapped him on the arm, said, "See you in the morning, Neil," and walked out to his car.

Neil wandered around the house planning how he would make his escape tomorrow. After Gillian had kissed him goodnight and gone to bed, he went to his study, grabbed the day's accumulation of political mail in two hands, and carried it out to the adjoining garage. There he undid the tie on a green garbage bag and thrust the letters deep into the greasy contents. He tied up the bag again, and washed his hands in the kitchen. After this first act of divestiture, he had a fore-taste of the deliverance to come.

Upstairs, he went to the spare room to sleep in the lumpy, guest-repelling guest bed. He did not sleep well and woke up often. He blamed the bed. Although he knew that his decision to get out of politics and thus avoid, *escape* from, a lifetime of going the wrong way was correct, a number of points occurred to him every time he woke up .... Clapp and Clyde would stay on in power, and have the billions of dollars of offshore oil revenue in their own hands .... Now and histori-cally, he would be perceived as having been defeated by Clapp, unable, at the crucial time, to muster the strength for the final victorious jab .... He would never be able to put his and Wolfe Tone McGrath's idea into general effect: to turn the isle into a Renaissance jewel with the vast wealth that would be at his disposal .... Muck, and the thousands of other supporters who had sincerely and genuinely cast their lot with him, would now be abysmally forsaken. He saw their dismayed and angry faces, and stirred restlessly in his doubt. There were always second thoughts over a radical turn-around in direction, he told himself. Even if the new direc-tion was right. He hoped, however, that whatever mechanism it was in his body that clung onto residual misgivings or hopes would soon accommodate itself to the reality of his situation.

Finally, Neil fell into a solid sleep; and this time, it was a dream that disturbed him. He saw the gnarled face of old Toope, the oleaginous features of Plopnicoff, and the vulpine visage of Clapp lighting up in malicious glee as the logical solution to the Godwin problem occurred to them. From a delirium of descending fish prongs and gutting knives, Neil awoke in the grey dawn, instinctively turning over on his side, and drawing up his knees in a gesture of self-protection.

And then he knew! Percy Clapp would gladly see him dead. He sat up in bed. Clapp would have him killed! Just as he had tried to destroy McGrath in that airplane crash; just as he had finally succeeded in having McGrath killed through some mysterious means at the hospital; just as he had engineered the injury of Rute during the fishermen's strike. Neil's certainty about this terrified him.

He strained to hear a human element in the creaking and groaning of the old house. The rising sun broke through the mist and glinted off the window of the attic in the house opposite: a perfect place for an assassin to draw a bead on him as he lay helpless in bed! He rolled off onto the floor and crept down to the kitchen, where he sat with his back to the wall away from the windows. For two minutes he had been absolutely sure that Clapp would have him killed at any second. His certainty had stemmed largely from the irony of his predicament: now that he had made a decision which rendered him harmless to Clapp, this was just the time that Clapp would have him done in.

On other occasions in his life he'd had visions of dying gloriously or tragically or even obscurely, as once on the cliffs of the Folkly Rooms. But this was the first time he had ever thought it possible that he would die ludicrously. And even now, upright in the full light of morning, he was by no means convinced that it would not happen yet, before he got a chance to remove himself publicly as a threat to Clapp.

When he had felt certain and purposeful, Neil reflected sardonically, when he believed that he had a valuable end to live for, he would have laughed in the teeth of any suggestion that Clapp might kill him. Now, when there was no certainty or purpose to his life, and no specific end in view, and he really could not care less if he survived or perished, the notion from a nightmare – the idea that Clapp would have him killed – had frightened him witless! He got up to make himself a coffee. "Sensible or what?" he said aloud; and immediately regretted making an attention-attracting noise. He wanted the time to go by more quickly so that he could get the preliminaries leading up to resignation over with that morning – before something stupid happened.

When Gillian came down, he gave her a coffee and started to tell her his decision; but when she got diverted by Anne's crying before he reached the point, he was just as happy. He had had a little trouble articulating his preamble. He'd tell her after Muck arrived.

Muck came around midmorning and sat with him in the study. At every movement of Neil's head or body, Muck would look at him expectantly. Neil wished he wouldn't do that. What the hell did he expect, anyway? He must tell Muck his decision. What words to use? Neil knew what he felt. Freedom. The words Sartre gave to Oreste tripped through his head: *"La liberté a fondu sur moi comme la foudre."* That was it exactly! Translate it. Then would Muck understand how he felt? (Muck, listen here! "Freedom has melted on me like lightning....") No. Mightn't quite make Muck apprehend the situation totally. Perhaps a helpful analogy would occur to Neil later, to make the explanation easier. He'd wait a little while longer. Meanwhile, the phone rang incessantly. Gillian would come in each time and tell him who it was.

"Jerome Finn. Wants an update on your next moves for the one o'clock news."

"Tell him I'll get back." Neil jotted down the message on a scrap of paper and jammed it into his pocket.

"Fellow from CBC National. Wants statement of intention re: political crisis."

"Get his number. I'll call back."

"Honourable Member for the historic district of Dildo-The Tickles."

"I'll talk to Az." Neil took this call as well as the calls from six more of his elected members, mostly to avoid the looks of alarm he would have received from Muck if he had not spoken to them. Each member considered it imperative that a caucus be held without fail by tomorrow noon to allow the members to hear a full statement of Neil's definite plan of future action. Neil assured them of a meeting tomorrow. Buggers! he thought. They were obviously getting together to gab and conspire in his absence.

"Daddy!" Little Elizabeth ran into the study, and pointed at the television set. "On TV! That fuckinprick!" She ran out again.

"I wonder which one of the thousands it is," laughed Muck. "Cute kid."

"Oh, lovely!" commented Gillian from the hall. "Isn't it marvellous how much meaningful parental example a father can provide – even though he's been home only four days a month for the past year?"

Neil switched on the television set and flipped channels. "... and you feel you can say that, even though he was educated at Oxford just as you were?" The hostess of a talk show was inquiring.

"Oh, yes, of course." The camera switched to Clyde Ferritt. "How *well* did Mr. Godwin do at Oxford is the real question. And how did he get to Oxford to begin with? Oh, I'm very familiar, unfortunately, with the type. You know, the self-confident ignorance exhibited by those who have been educated beyond their intelligence, which is especially dangerous when combined with a rat-like cunning."

"Thank you, Mr. Ferritt. The Honourable Clyde Ferritt, Minister of Industry and, many would say, heir apparent to Prime Minister Percy Clapp. Till tomorrow, good morning."

"That fuckinprick!" breathed Gillian. Then she laughed softly with a shake of her head at Neil, and went out to answer the phone.

Neil had felt his stomach rolling as he had watched Clyde's arrogant and self-satisfied face, the knowledge that he and Clapp had succeeded in beating back Godwin's attack written all over it. But Neil's reaction was not jealousy or chagrin that Clyde was gaining the ascendancy over him. The days of that worry were over. His feeling now was directly related to the new way he had chosen for himself, to his knowledge that

Clyde was a grasping fraud, an enemy of the people, and that one day Neil would expose and destroy him.

"Neil," said Muck. "There are two ways of looking at this thing. One, that we are letting Clapp get away with murder. Two, that by doing nothing when Clapp expects action from you, we are knocking Clapp off-balance, driving him around the bend. Is number two your strategy?"

Neil shrugged.

"Well," said Muck, "if it is, it might just be working. I hear that Clapp is gone right off the head trying to figure out what you're up to. I even have one report that he asked someone if an accident could be arranged to put Godwin out of the picture completely."

Neil swallowed. "When was that, Muck?"

"Oh, two or three days ago. I had half a mind to go to the RCMP with it, just out of spite. But I figured that it was too foolish to talk about, and if it ever got out, it'd make you look like an idiot."

"You did the right thing, Muck. It would look as if we were a bunch of nervous nellies, or as if we were manufacturing death threats to try to curry sympathy." Jesus, Neil thought, an accident! He'd better move quicker.

Gillian came in with more messages. One from the head of the Federation of Labour who wanted to discuss a new Labour code they had drafted and the feasibility of calling a general strike to protest Clapp's failure to resign.

Another from the president of the Teachers' Association: several branches wished to pass resolutions calling for civil disobedience to Clapp's government for clinging to power without the people's sanction; but they were wondering whether Neil was being aggressive enough. If they passed such resolutions, they would not want to be left in the lurch afterwards.

A call from the bank: large overdraft on party chequeing account; contrary to Bank Act; must be dealt with immediately.

Neil began to explain his decision to his friend. "Muck, I have a feeling of freedom. A freedom to go the right way with my life … " Muck regarded him quizzically. "A freedom to

351

escape the wrong path … Escape may be the wrong word, Muck … A freedom to *do* rather than a freedom to escape." Muck seemed to be picking about as much sense out of these words as Neil felt he was making. "Yes, a freedom to do," he faltered on. "To make a choice."

Neil inhaled and exhaled deeply. He fingered the dozen crumpled messages in his pocket: people depending on him to do, to speak, to act. Feeling Muck's expectant eyes on him, he concentrated on the sky outside the window. He saw his mother in her chair, his own eyes watching him from her face. He saw his father's ruined features, eyes bright at having expanded a pathetic moment into a lifetime of meaning. He visualized an amalgam of Clapp's, Toope's, and Ferritt's sneers and smirks as they put the boots to his own prostrate form.

"To make a choice," he repeated. "Muck, let me see your list of all the members who just got elected." Muck drew the folded sheet out of his jacket pocket with practised speed, as Neil closed the door.

After studying the list, Neil wrote digits next to some of the names. "Muck," he said, "starting with the weakest and most mercenary, I've numbered eight of Percy's members. Memorize the names." Without looking at the sheet, Muck spieled off the names in nearly the same order as Neil had numbered them. Only the seventh and eighth were interchanged. He looked at the list, and they both laughed. Neil set the paper afire in the grate and sat back for a moment. "Muck, I'm spending tonight with father. All night. And I'll be telling Jerome at the television station that, too."

"Good, good, excellent," nodded Muck.

"Get two, Muck. One is no good. Do you hear what I'm saying to you, Muck? Get two of them."

Muck bounded towards the door. "And Muck, listen." Muck turned around. He was trying, self-consciously, to keep the grin off his face, like a little boy, observed with envy by his friends, sitting behind the wheel of his father's new car. "I am not one bit fussy how you do it, Muck. Use any source of – Just do it!" Muck left the house so quickly he barely had time to say goodbye to Gillian.

Alone in the study, Neil called up Jerome Finn, the television news director, and apologized for not having been available during recent days. "My father has been dying, Jerome, as you know. Well, he is just about to go, now, anytime. I was with him last night, and I'll be there *all* night, tonight."

"Jesus Christ, Neil, man," pleaded Jerome, "can we use that stuff? A lot of people are wondering if you're playing your cards right. I've been telling them your father is sick. You spending all your time with him at the end would explain everything."

"Well, it's all very personal and private, Jerome. I don't think so. Who'd want to hear about my private family burdens? People have enough troubles of their own."

"Who'd want to *hear* about it? It's a good thing you went into politics instead of television news, Neil! That stuff is better than 'As the Guts Turn' as the boys here call it, and we've got a 70 per cent daytime viewing audience for that crap. Sorry, Neil, I don't mean to be offensive, but we're in the middle of ratings, and I'm a bit up. If we could run that story all night and tomorrow, hyped and dramatized up a bit – human element, away from the pure political puke – it would knock the shit out of the CBC so bad in the news ratings you'd be able to stuff the whole bloody lot of them into one shoe box. How about it, Neil?"

"I don't know, Jerome. I'd love to help you. You know that."

"Look, Neil. You're a public fucking figure. People have a right to know these things: why you've been so quiet; how well you're bearing up under these terrific strains. We should have you on film, too."

"Okay, Jerome, I'll trust your judgement on this. If you think it's newsworthy, go ahead and use it. I'll be available tomorrow for film."

"Neil, you won't regret this. I really appreciate it. Neil, boy, I've got to say something. You're the best I've ever seen in politics around here. Most of the mealy-mouthed bastards would have put out a goddamned press release on something like this, trying to scab a bit of sympathy. Thanks, Neil .... You been talking to Muck, yet, by the way?"

"I talk to him all the time, Jerome."

"Nuff said. See you tomorrow. Sir."

Neil sat in his study all afternoon, jotting down thoughts on the future. Between brainstorms he leafed through three months' back issues of *Saturday Night* and the *New Yorker*, reading only the theatre, movie, and book reviews. When the phone rang, he answered it himself and chatted amiably with everyone who called. He made a note of each name and the time of the conversation.

Eventually, Gillian came in. She knelt down and put her arms around his legs, and when he took her face between his hands, she closed her eyes and hugged.

"Yesterday evening," she said, smiling, "when you had the row in your bare buff with the television set ... that was like the bursting of the boil. You're so relaxed and content, today. And that's the only way to be about this, Neil. If you win you've done it cleanly. If you lose, there was no greater effort you could have made without doing something that would bring you lasting regrets."

Greater effort, thought Neil. What little relationship there was, finally, between effort and headway! Kill yourself day and night for months and months – and reach a deadlock. Heave off in your chair for an afternoon – and wait for success to drop in your lap. He had no doubt that Muck Barrows would achieve that success for him today.

Before leaving for his father's house that evening, Neil watched the evening news. "Mr. Godwin," Jerome said to the camera, "already afflicted, as an only son, by the very grave illness of his father, has been required as well, as a political leader, to bear the weight of an unprecedented constitutional tangle caused by the outcome of the election. Anyone wondering at Neil Godwin's comparative silence on political matters in recent days will fully understand why when they realize that tonight Mr. Godwin will be spending *yet another* all-night vigil at the bedside of his father, so as to lend him a devoted son's comfort at the end. Tomorrow we shall have Mr. Godwin on camera, and you, the viewer, can then judge for yourself, as we have done, the strength and character of this young leader who ... "

Neil noticed Gillian standing quietly in the doorway, watching. He got up and kissed her on the cheek. She made no movement at all but looked at him hard. He averted his eyes. "I'm spending the night at father's," he said, as he put on his coat. "He doesn't have much time left now, Gillian." She said nothing and did not come to the door with him.

When he was again on the sofa in Ernest's room, Neil found himself directing his thoughts towards the unconscious body on the bed. *You may have been right, but I can't pass up this chance, any more than you could, twenty-five years ago when the chance to become Chief Elder presented itself. Besides, even if you were right about my* nature, *there's no reason why I cannot use this* way *to follow my role as an uprooter of lies, a howler of execration against falseness, just as you briefly did, I suppose .... So much is dependent on chance: what happens outside, what there is inside. Pure chance.*

Chance. Luck. There was no doubt, he thought, that he was lucky. Percy Clapp had been right. But luck was always in the past. One could not rely on lucky breaks occurring in the future. Pompey had made that mistake, he considered. Caesar, too. And Napoleon. And Hitler. They all had: each of them having come at last to the point where he had acted in his egotism as if his past luck as an individual had been as reliable a principle on which to base his future actions as the law of probability was in predicting, on past behaviour, the overall future activity of billions of particles. They should have remembered they were each only a particle, Neil thought. He wouldn't make that mistake. *Particula sum.* That would be a good, secret motto for him to bear in mind .... Perhaps he was one of the more interesting particles, though. The gene pool on the little rock was small, yes, but who knew what was in oneself. The number of possible combinations of human germ cells was greater than the number of protons in the known universe, after all! With what he had (whatever that was), he would do what he could (whatever that might be), and he'd stretch both to the outer elastic limit!

Neil revelled in his feeling of clear-eyed realism. He told himself that he was thinking big thoughts for someone who might still be Leader of the Loyal Opposition five years from now, for all he knew – unless, of course, Clapp had them all executed as traitors, in the meantime. He would assume, however, that Muck could accomplish something tonight. (Neil *knew* Muck would, but he wanted to convey to any malignant intelligence in the universe listening for thoughts of hubris, his lack thereof.) *I need to decide, in that event, what kind of a dominant male I'm going to be: a bloody baboon or a goddamned chimpanzee. Wait, now. I've got to start being a little more intellectual: agonistic or hedonistic – that is the question. Christ. Let's stick with baboon or chimp?*

Sitting in the dark, Neil considered these two modes of leadership. Both had their merits. As a baboon-like leader, he would concentrate on shoring up his power. He would aim for absolute control, using the offshore oil wealth to maintain and exercise power and dominance without restriction. He would eliminate all rivals. Certainly, he would do away with all those who had been, or who might be, hurtful or trouble-some: Clyde Ferritt, Percy Clapp, Toope, Wadman ... He was surprised at the shortness of the list of people whose liquidation would be sweet. It was, however, a start. There would doubtless be others from time to time. Lord Jonathan Cantingsworth! Why not? And Victoria Montagu. Neil experienced a soaring thrill at the thought. *You determined a terrible doom for yourself when you first chose to toy and dally with me, Victoria, my little lovely!* He squelched the sensation: first things first. He would continue Clapp's drive towards separation from Canada. That would be necessary for the agonistic mode, precluding outside interference with his exercise of power. Moreover, what was the point of staying in Canada, agonistically speaking? Even if he rose to the head of the nation, where would it put him, as a baboon, in the international scene? Nowhere. Much better to use the oil wealth, if there was enough of it (and it looked as if there might be), to gain control and dominance in poor, third world countries, welding together an empire of the poor and underprivileged. Good baboonish possibilities there. Or, perhaps better still, join up with the United States as a state. Become President. Why not? He had everything it would take to get elected to the post – not even considering the appeal of his unscary, boondockish origins. Tremendous potential for the role of the destroyer of false positions in *that* office. Yes, he thought, the way of the baboon had its attractions.

Possibility number two: the chimp-like leader. Following this route, he saw himself taking it easy. He would stay as leader as long as enough voters enjoyed the sight of him there. He would remain in Canada as a prosperous and happy part of a prosperous and happy nation. No fuss, no bother, no power-struggles, no straining for control over other countries.

He would follow the way he and Wolfe Tone McGrath had plotted so long ago. Encourage artistic development of all kinds. Make that the main emphasis of government programs. Turn the place into a veritable Athens. He saw himself exercising benign, loose, hedonistic stewardship over the gentle, lovely people of the rugged little island for as long as they wanted him; loved and revered by them for his goodness and his fostering of freedom and dignity and quality in their lives; admired and respected abroad for his farsighted achievements. A tremendous flowering of indigenous arts and culture. Beautiful. A pleasing picture: chimp of chimps.

It was going to be a hard decision to make, Neil thought. For example, baboons in power never seemed to get assassinated – Alexander, Attila, Napoleon, Hitler, Stalin – no matter how evil they might have been. (Caesar? Not baboonish enough. He straddled the two modes.) Chimps, on the other hand, often seemed to get themselves murdered – Lincoln, the Kennedys, Martin Luther King, Jesus Christ – no matter how good their actions. Not all prominent chimps got killed. No, of course not. But *enough* did to make a fellow chimp nervous. There was something to consider there in deciding what to do. That goddamned Percy Clapp! He could strike at any time. He had to be got rid of – Clapp, Ferritt, Toope, all three of them – and it would be much easier to realize that laudable end under the baboon mode. Still, if the chimp mode was better on objective grounds, it would be a sin to spoil it for the sake of making away with a trio of psychopaths, even for self-protection. But in spite of himself, a vivid sequence of images rolled through Neil's mind: Clapp, Ferritt, and Toope roped together, their backs to Ecky's Fish ... or

357

to the edge of the cliff on the Folkly Rooms ... or against the Gawker's Temple of Truth in Maggotty Cove Motion. Clapp, Ferritt, and Toope ... standing beside a statue of Rute (to be erected in Pinchgut) ... or within the old abandoned store in Pickeyes where Adder had told his guffers ... or on the spot where Wolfe Tone McGrath's plane had crashed – while the four brutal notes from Gluck's *Iphigénie en Aulide* boomed out, and Muck Barrows and some faceless minions fired their rifles into the bodies until ....

Neil checked his thoughts. *All incidental stuff, that. Where to go myself?* Premier Neil Godwin. Prime Minister Godwin. President E. Neil Godwin. E. Neil Godwin. *E. for what, says Ernie Godwin. E. for Emperor? Emperor Nil. Nihil?* There was a mixed and varied jumble of implications there, suscep-tible of a good wide range of contradictory interpretations – copy for the self-abuse of the brains of the psycho-historians. No rush to use that name yet, though. Wait till the timing was right. Twenty-eight now. Even Napoleon waited till he was thirty-five. Christ, he wouldn't dignify the baboons by com-peting with them. No hurry, anyway. Forty or fifty years still left to fill up with creative destructions for the world ....

Oh, dying Ernie Godwin. Right way, wrong way. What odds? What odds? Where was his father's moment of vision now? Where would his pain be in a week? Or anybody's pain throughout time? What dusty corner of the universe was it all piled up in? If the end of all was nothing, could one's passage there be something? The answer might not be no. Perhaps the *knowledge* of no-hope-for-any-of-us could meld with the *faith* of I-am-the-one. *Ah! Pretty little religious mystery there, Head Gawker, old man. Better than your paradox of the runty lamb, if you ask me.* He drifted into sleep.

At eight o'clock in the morning the phone rang, and the nurse told Neil it was his wife. To take the call, he left his father's room for the first time since he'd arrived.

"Neil, Muck was just here at the house," said Gillian. "'Tell Neil three,' he said. 'Three what?' I said. 'He'll know,' he said. 'David, tell him yourself,' I said. Frigging Barrows! Slinking around with that slimy grin on him all the time, hatching his sly plots. 'I can't,' he said. 'You have to call him. You're his wife,' he said …. Three what, Neil?"

Three! thought Neil. He had to hand it to old Muck.

"Three what, Neil? What three?"

"Muck is getting cryptic on me, Gillian," said Neil. "Three days? Three members? Three petitions to court? Is that all he said: tell him three?"

Gillian was silent for a moment. "Neil, I don't like the look of this one bit. When are you coming home?"

"After I get some breakfast and listen to the news."

Saying goodbye, Neil smothered a pang over his first disingenuousness with Gillian. As soon as he put down the receiver he switched on the radio.

During the next hour he listened to four newscasts: nothing, not even speculation. He began to hope that whatever deal Muck had made had fallen apart. He formulated in his mind denials of the rumours that would be circulating of his failed attempt to suborn members of the legislature. Gillian's hurt, disbelieving face was often before him.

At twenty past nine, the open line program was interrupted by a breathless special bulletin: three newly elected members of the legislature had just announced they were leaving Percy Clapp's party to join Neil Godwin's party. This would give Godwin a clear, undoubted majority of support in the House – and therefore the government.

The voice of the spokesman of the three came on. "We were elected to represent the best interests of the people regardless of party stripe," he droned, rattling his prepared text. "We cannot stand idly by and watch Mr. Clapp violate democratic principles and attempt to thwart the clearly expressed wishes of the majority of the voters. We have decided to join Mr. Godwin's party, effective immediately, in order to give him the support necessary to form a government with a good working majority in the House of Assembly. We take this difficult step without expectation of favour or reward from Mr. Godwin. We have not even spoken to Mr. Godwin about our move, and we make it freely and independently, as a matter of principle and conscience."

Sitting with a confused sensation of excitement and sadness burning in him, Neil answered the phone next to him when it rang. "Oh *that* three," said Gillian. "Now I know why Muck wanted *me* to tell you, Neil. In case the phone was tapped, a wife's conversation with her husband can't be used as evidence in court. Is that it?"

"My God, Gillian, what a thing to say! Didn't you hear them on the radio? They did it of their own free will. You make it sound as if I bought them or something."

"I *know* you didn't buy them, Neil, because buying something implies having it for as long as you want it. But how much were you able to temporarily *rent* those three for?"

"Come *on*, Gillian. I've never had anything to do with any of them. And I was here all night with poor father, sure." There was a sigh at the other end of the line which Neil took to be a sign of susceptibility to persuasion. "Gillian my love, listen to me. It's over now. All the foolish nonsense is over. Now I can start, at last, I can start. Look, the newsmen will be here in a little while. Why don't you hop in your car and come here. Then we can go out and meet them together. Bring the kids if you want to."

"Neil. That man Plopnicoff called just before I phoned you. When I told him you weren't here, he said, 'Just tell Prime Minister Godwin that we were happy to help.'"

Indiscreet bastard! thought Neil. No. Not indiscreet. Just confirming the existence of his IOU. "Plopnicoff!" he said, with anger in his voice. "What the hell is he talking about? I haven't seen him or any of his crowd! I prohibited any of my organizers from having anything to do with –"

"Oh, Neil, Neil, Neil. I'm so disappointed . . . I'm so *sorry* for you. What did you say was the difference between you and Percy Clapp again?"

"There's a *big* difference, Gillian. Now I have a chance to –"

"No, Neil. And I'm not coming there. I could take it if you were just the Goofy Newfy banging on your empty tin can to the glee of a mob of vicious children. I could even stomach being the poor old Hump marching at your side. But I'm having no part of–" Gillian exhaled as if further talk was futile. "Goodbye, Neil."

Neil listened to the dead line a moment. Then he went upstairs to see his mother. The nurse was sitting with her and as he told his mother the political news both women smiled and said they'd heard.

"I'm some delighted, Mr. Godwin," the nurse went on. "Myself and my daughter at the university were worried sick it would never happen. Mr. Clapp and them seem to be such hard cases. My daughter is always saying, 'Neil' (Neil, she calls you–she sees you on television all the time) 'Neil is almost too good to be in that politics racket,' she says." His mother nodded her agreement at the nurse and turned to Neil with a grin.

"Your father had his needle this morning before we heard the news," added the nurse. "He'll be asleep for a while yet. You want to tell him yourself, of course. If you let me know when you're coming back, I won't give him a needle till after you tell him, so he'll be wide awake and'll understand everything."

Neil smiled and shook his head. "Thank you. But I'm not sure when I'll be back, today. Keeping father free from pain is the most important thing of all, so give him whatever needles are needed for that. I'll see you later."

As he went down to shave and shower, he heard the nurse's voice behind him. "That boy is a saint, Mrs. Godwin! What everyone says about him is true."

Oh Gillian, Gillian, Neil thought, *defeating evil by a little ruthlessness does not preclude the doing of right things thereafter. You've never been naive about power struggles before this ....*

At quarter to eleven in the morning, Neil stepped out of the front door of Ernest Godwin's house into an array of newspeople, live microphones, and whirring television cameras. He moved slowly, deliberately, and erectly, "... his face and eyes showing mingled tragedy, strength, and concern above the navy blue of his high-necked sweater and blazer," he could hear Jerome Finn reporting to the people. He was asked how he felt about now having a majority in the House, with the certainty of forming the government.

"My wife and children, who haven't seen me since this news broke, are waiting for me at home," answered Neil. "I must see them first and then hold a press conference this afternoon. For now, I'll just say this:

"The essence of true leadership is in being ever ready and willing to lead *whenever* the people demand it, no matter what personal sadness or tragedy may surround the leader at that time of need. I am therefore prepared and eager to do my duty. I know my friends throughout this land – and that includes all our people, for everyone is equal in my eyes now – I know my friends will forgive me, however, if today my heart is with my father who is suffering his final illness, and will soon have his final peace after a lifetime of goodness, piety, and faith."

Neil walked towards his car in silence. The newspeople seemed to consider it sacrilege to ask anything else after that. Then he heard the pipe-organ voice of Jerome Finn, murmuring into his mike: "Prime Minister-elect, the Honourable E. Neil Godwin, moves to his small family car now, scarcely showing the fatigue of a devoted son who has watched throughout the night at the bedside of an ebbing father (in this very house), or the strain of a leader in an unprecedented constitutional crisis – but displaying, in spite of it all, the dedication of a husband and of a father, and (most importantly for us, the citizens of this land), demonstrating the strength, the proof of inner resources, of a man able to shoulder such burdens after months of wearying campaigning, a man capable of assuming the mantle of leadership with the true humanity of a real human being who ... "

Neil started the car and drove slowly away, undecided on whether to go to headquarters, home, or Muck's apartment. He switched on the radio and listened to the wrap-up of an open line program, *The Voice of the People*. "... Like I just told that last caller," blared the host, "Percy Clapp can bawl about foul play and skulduggery and whatnot all he wants. So what else is new? Not going to put up with it, he says. Listen here, Mr. Clapp, the people want you out, look. Out! You might as well say you're not going to put up with the law of gravity or something. Oh, listen to yours truly will ya. I'm after becoming a philosopher on top of everything else. Wasting my perfume or whatever on the barren air or whatever, as they say, insofar as Mr. Clapp is concerned, though. My-oh-my, the board is still lit up like nothing short of the proverbial Christmas tree, what with everyone and his dog phoning in to talk about this fantastic story on Percy Clapp and young Godwin. But time has a way of passing, as many of you out there may be already well aware, and that's something we're after running completely out of on the show, I'm very, very much afraid. I'd like to stay on the air a little tiny small bit longer – I say that from the heart – and hear some more of your views (all within the realm of good taste of course). My God, my God, I'm shagged, I'm frigged, I'm finished – I haven't talked to Mother Welfare this morning – she's on the line there, now, more than likely, fuming at me something wicked. You'd have to clean up the studio floor with a super-duper-pooper-scooper when she gets on again. Tell you what. I'll get Mr. Godwin on the show tomorrow morning and you can all have a go at him then in person. Hear that Mother Welfare? So don't be mad at me, now, look. Save it for Neil Godwin, tomorrow. Listen, my lovelies, I got to go. I missed my supper last night – I know the wife wasn't poisoned at me, either! But what happened was the news stories have been coming in so fast and furious for the past couple of days, they've been working me like you might as well say a dog here at the station. Something else! What with new oil discoveries, political turmoil, premiers getting the flick and whatnot. It's something wicked, I can tell ya, when the station has to work the King of the Open Liners that long and hard, here I am now going home to have my supper in the morning. This is *The Voice of the People*."

As he switched off the radio, Neil wished Gillian were there with him. He would have liked to share a little sarcastic fun with her, to show he was still a realist about all this. He would say, "Did you hear that, Gillian? It's the beginning of the new golden age I promised you I'd be ushering in. 'Supper in the morning,' quoth the King of the Open Liners. I'm in power only a few minutes and already we have a budding latter-day King Lear on our hands, there."

About to turn the car in the direction of home, Neil smiled to himself as he thought of how Gillian always laughed whenever he drew incongruous literary allusions out of zany situations like that – and of how she unfailingly responded in kind. But he felt his smile die as he heard, in his head, her unlaughing reply this time: "Then, according to the script, young Godwin must answer, 'And I'll go to bed at noon.' The last words of Lear's Fool."